"Tone"
Palmer "Echo"s
Bergen
for "The Bussy

IN THE AMERICAN TREE

 NATIONAL
POETRY
FOUNDATION, INC.
UNIVERSITY OF MAINE AT ORONO

In the American Tree

Edited by

Ron Silliman

Published by The National Poetry Foundation
University of Maine at Orono, Orono, Maine 04469

Printed by The University of Maine at Orono Printing Office

Library of Congress Catalog Card Number: 85-61157
ISBN: 0-915032-33-3 (cloth)
ISBN: 0-915032-34-1 (paper)

Cover by Francie Shaw

ACKNOWLEDGEMENTS

This page represents a continuation of copyright information from the verso.

"From *Sonnets (Memento Mori)*," This Press, © 1980. "Misrepresentation" from *L=A=N=G=U=A=G=E 12*, © 1980. "Funnels In" and "Letters" from *Wobbling*, Roof Books, © 1981. "From *R + B*," Segue, © 1981. "From *I Guess Work the Time Up*" and "From *Confidence Trick*" from *Give Em Enough Rope*, Sun & Moon, © 1985. All works reprinted by permission of the author.

"Anti-Short Story," "Tone," "Xenophobia," and "View" from *Extremities*, The Figures, © 1978. "'Why Don't Women Do Language-Oriented Writing?'" from *L=A=N=G=U=A=G=E 1*, © 1978. "You Float" from *The Invention of Hunger*, Tuumba Press, © 1979. "Single Most" from *Ironwood 20*, © 1982. All works reprinted by permission of the author.

"The Picture Window" from manuscript, © 1985 by Tom Beckett, used by permission of the author.

"Echo" and "Narcissus" from *Blindspots*, Whale Cloth Press, © 1981. "From *The Busses*," Tuumba, © 1981. "Blue Book 42" from *Tottel's 18*, © 1981. "On Realism" was published as "Realism" in *Ironwood 20*, © 1982. All works reprinted by permission of the author.

"Inside Cheese," "Amarillo," and "Spinal Guard" from *Cafe Isotope*, The Figures, © 1980. "Wave Train" from *State Lounge*, Tuumba, © 1981. All works reprinted by permission of the author.

"St. McC." from *Shade*, Sun & Moon, 1978. "To Which I Never Wanted" from *Senses of Responsibility*, Tuumba, © 1979. "The Blue Divide" and "For Love Has Such a Spirit That if It is Portrayed It Dies" from *Controlling Interests*, Roof, © 1980. "Part Quake" and "The Klupzy Girl" from *Islets/Irritations*, Jordan Davies, © 1983. "Writing and Method" from *Poetics Journal 3*, © 1983. All works reprinted by permission of the author.

"My Poetry" and "By Visible Truth We Mean the Apprehension of the Absolute Condition of Present Things" from *My Poetry*, The Figures, © 1980. All works reprinted by permission of the author.

"A/per/ginning/verted" from *Space*, Harper & Row, © 1970. "From *The Maintains*," This Press, © 1974. "From *Polaroid*," Adventures in Poetry/Big Sky, © 1975. "From *Quartz Hearts*," This, © 1978. "From *Weathers*," from *United Artists 5*, © 1978. "From *Arrangement*," from *Talking Poetics from Naropa Institute*, Shambhala, © 1978. "From 'A Letter to Paul Metcalf'," from *Stations 5* (Clark Coolidge Issue), © 1978. All works reprinted by permission of the author.

"Howe" from *L=A=N=G=U=A=G=E Vol. 4/Open Letter, Fifth Series, No. 1*, © 1982. "Raymond Chandler's Sentence" from *Pessimistic Labor 1*, © 1984. Reprinted by permission of the author.

"Brahms" and "Summer Letters" from *The Prose of Fact*, The Figures, © 1981. "If To Witness," "The Article on Geneva" and "Scales" from *The Landing of Rochambeau*, Burning Deck, © 1985. All works reprinted by permission of the author.

"' 101 '" and "Shared Sentences" from *ACTIVE 24 HOURS*, Roof, © 1982. All works reprinted by permission of the author.

"Paradise and Lunch" from *Vanishing Cab 4*, © 1981. "Heavy Clouds Passing Before the Sun," "Gas" and "O" (from "Trencher Letters") from *Linear C*, Tuumba, © 1983. "D," "F" and "Q" (from "Trencher Letters") from manuscript, © 1985 by Jean Day. All works reprinted by permission of the author.

for Larry Eigner

IN THE AMERICAN TREE

A bitter wind taxes the will
causing dry syllables
to rise from the throat.

Flipping out wd be one alternative
simply rip the cards to pieces
amid a dense growth of raised eyebrows.

But such tempest (storm) doors
once opened, resistance fades away
and having fired all the guns you find you are left
     with a ton of butter,

Which, if it isn't eaten by some lurking rat
hiding out under the gate, may well be picked
up by the wind and spread all over

The face you're by now too chicken to admit is yours.
Wheat grows between bare toes
of a cripple barely able to hold his or her breath

And at the crack of dawn
we howl for more
beer. One of us produces

A penny from his pocket
and flips it at the startled thief
who has been spying on her from behind the flames

That crackle up from the wreck.
The freeway is empty now, moonlight
reflecting brightly off the belly of a blimp,

And as you wipe the red from your eyes
and suck on the lemon someone has given you,
you notice a curious warp in the sequence

Kit Robinson   xiii

Of events suggesting a time loop
in which bitter details repeat
themselves like the hands of a clock

Repeat their circular travels in a dream-
like medium you find impossible to pierce:
it simply spreads out before you, a field.

Now you are able to see a face
in the slope of a hill,
tall green trees

Are its hard features,
a feather floats down
not quite within grasp

And it is Spring.
The goddess herself
is really

Feeling great.
Space assumes the form of a bubble
whose limits are entirely plastic.

                                        Kit Robinson

LANGUAGE, REALISM, POETRY

"I HATE SPEECH." Thus capitalized, these words in an essay entitled "On Speech," the second of five short critical pieces by Robert Grenier in the first issue of *This*, the magazine he cofounded with Barrett Watten in winter, 1971, announced a breach—and a new moment in American writing.

As his essay was careful to make clear, Grenier's declaration was not to be taken at face value. Indeed, *This 1* was obsessed with speech. Several of its contributors, such as Robert Creeley, Larry Eigner and Kenneth Irby, were associated in the minds of many readers in 1971 with the project known as Projective Verse, Charles Olson's unification of free verse techniques with the rhythms and breath patterns of the speaking voice. Olson himself, who had died of cancer a year earlier, was represented in three photographs and a memoir by Elsa Dorfman. Other contributors, like Tom Clark, Robert Kelly, Anne Waldman and Anselm Hollo, were equally identified with other tendencies within the broader movement of "New American" poetry, the self-consciously anti-academic tradition of the 50s and 60s, a wide range of writings whose only points of agreement were an insistence on the centrality of the influence of William Carlos Williams and a preference for poetry that, read aloud, sounded spoken. "Wintry," one of Grenier's own poems in that issue, is in part built upon the dialect variations in prosody and pronunciation of his native Minnesota (a distinction whose value is explicitly discounted in "On Speech"). Finally, two of his five critical texts focused on the work of Robert Creeley, one of them stating by way of judgment, and all in caps, that "'PROJECTIVE VERSE' IS *PIECES* ON."

This complex call for a projective verse that could, in the same moment, "proclaim an abhorrence of 'speech'"—a break within a tradition in the name of its own higher values—proved only one axis of the shift within writing which became manifest with the publication of *This*. The other, specifically Watten's contribution, lay in the title, a pronoun of presence which foregrounds the referential dimension of language. That this aspect of Watten and Grenier's critical position was no less difficult or

Ron Silliman xv

central is evident from their choice in a first poem, an untitled piece by Robert Kelly, which starts:

If this were the place to begin
is not

Watten and Grenier were by no means the only young poets in 1971 who sensed the claustrophobic constraints of a poetics with which they nonetheless largely identified, and who thus sought other avenues, new methods that might lead to a more open and useful investigation, hopefully to renew verse itself, so that it might offer readers the same opacity, density, otherness, challenge and relevance persons find in the "real" world. Nor were they the first: some of the "word salad" compositions in Clark Coolidge's *Space* date from 1965; Aram Saroyan's Lines Editions press and *0 to 9*, a mimeographed magazine edited by Bernadette Mayer and Vito Acconci, both 60s publications, reflect similar impulses to break free from a poetry grown narrow and categorical. However, it was the particular contribution of *This*, in rejecting a speech-based poetics and consciously raising the issue of reference, to suggest that any new direction would require poets to look (in some ways for the first time) at what a poem is actually made of— not images, not voice, not characters or plot, all of which appear on paper, or in one's mouth, only through the invocation of a specific medium, language itself.

This anthology documents what became of that suggestion.

As is manifestly clear in the pages that follow, neither speech nor reference were ever, in any real sense, "the enemy." But, because the implicit "naturalness" of each, the simple, seemingly obvious concept that words should derive from speech and refer to things, was inscribed within all of the assumptions behind normative writing, the challenge posed by *This* was to open a broad territory of possibility where very different kinds of poets might explore and execute a wide range of projects. If nothing in the poem could be taken for granted, then anything might be possible. In turn, the poet must be responsible for everything. A parallel demand is made of each reader.

The resources available to this moment in writing were remarkably abundant. A latent tradition of a poetics not centered on speech already existed in the work of Gertrude Stein, Louis Zukofsky and Jackson Mac Low. The poetry and prose of both Robert Creeley (who had himself called reference into question as early as 1953) and Larry Eigner, two early "projectivists" whose writing had transcended the problematic constraints of that tendency, offered important models of rigorous and honest practice. The xenophobic limitations of the Anglo-European literary paradigm were being revealed by the anthologies of Jerome Rothenberg, demonstrating the possibility of a much broader and richer poetics. Alternative uses of method were visible in Mac Low's work, in John Ashbery's *The Tennis Court Oath* and Ted Berrigan's *Sonnets*. In other media, people as diverse as Simone Forti, Anthony Braxton, Lucy Lippard, Steve Reich, Meredith Monk, Robert Smithson and Joseph Beuys were challenging basic assumptions. Magazines in the early 70s, such as Barbara Baracks' *Big Deal* or the issue of *Toothpick, Lisbon & the Orcas Islands* co-edited by Bruce Andrews and Michael Wiater, functioned precisely by putting all of these elements into play, while also serving as a means for young writers to come into contact with each other's work.

Such contact had impact. In 1974 Kit Robinson published a one-shot magazine, *Streets and Roads*, in San Francisco, bringing together for the first time writing by himself, Watten (who had also settled in the city and was now entirely in charge of *This*), Provincetown poet Alan Bernheimer, Bob Perelman of Boston, and two Los Angeles residents, Steve Benson and Carla Harryman. Within three years, all would be living in San Francisco. Watten would begin a reading series at the Grand Piano. Perelman, who began *Hills* before he came west, would host talks on poetics by writers at his Folsom Street loft. This concentration was further deepened with the arrival of Lyn Hejinian, Tom Mandel and others. A mirror image on a smaller scale saw Charles Bernstein, Bruce Andrews, Alan Davies, James Sherry and Ray DiPalma converge on New York City during this same period. Like Perelman's talks series, *L=A=N=G=U=A=G=E*, the first American journal of poetics by and for poets, was at least partly a consequence of the number of writers in one place with related concerns having reached a critical mass.

Ron Silliman   xvii

While this dual pattern of migration to urban centers on different coasts greatly enhanced the possibilities of face-to-face interaction and sharing, another transformation of poetry was taking place—into prose. Of the 38 poets whose work is included in the first two sections of this anthology, 29 are at least partly represented by prose writing. Others, like Ted Greenwald, might have been. And in certain pieces, such as Grenier's "Sticky Fingers" or the works by Alan Davies and Stephen Rodefer, the distinction seems trivial and arbitrary at best. In contrast, neither Donald Allen's *New American Poetry* nor Hayden Carruth's *The Voice That Is Great Within Us* contain any creative prose. Yet, in the sense familiar to us from French modernism, there are no prose poems here. And, beyond organization into paragraphs, these works share little with the dramatic monologues and surreal short stories that characterize other recent prose writing by American poets.

The simple visibility of poetry composed in paragraph form combined with its appearance in the work of so many authors who read, and talk to, one another has helped to set up the often-controversial response which this writing has received. Some critics have sought to name this new prose, precisely to differentiate it from the normative prose poem, metafiction or other non-narrative prose creations. But even a phrase as neutral as "poet's prose" or name as thoroughly qualified as "non- or inter-generic prose forms," by sheer virtue of the nominative function, insinuates that what is being done under this rubric is essentially homogenous, one thing. In fact, this seems to be exactly not the case. The discrete paragraphs in Michael Palmer's "Echo" differ radically from the irruptive journal of Hannah Weiner, a work whose subverted continuities are very dissimilar from those found in Lyn Hejinian's *My Life*. A virtually parallel sequence of oppositions could be drawn between Perelman, Bernstein and Watten, or between almost any three of the contributors here. That each sometimes works in prose is worth noting, as is the absence of plot in their writing or a willingness (not universally held) to discuss poetics, but this evades the more important question: what, within this territory, is the individual doing?

Extended from the form of prose to the collective existence of these poets, this impulse to name confuses a moment with a movement. In a sense, this has always been true for alleged schools of writing in America. The projectivist section of the Allen anthology lumped Olson and Creeley in with Denise Levertov and Paul Carroll. Here, beyond the recognition that the failure to write and speak seriously about the work cedes the authority to define critical terms to others while cancelling the possibility of any articulate self-discipline within the community, a combination which had disastrous results for portions of that previous generation, the felt need on the part of many of the poets gathered in this volume for a public discourse on poetics reflects a lack of consensus. This anthology is a record of the debate. What is shared, at best, is a perception as to what the issues might be.

These are not to be underestimated. The nature of reality. The nature of the individual. The function of language in the constitution of either realm. The nature of meaning. The substantiality of language. The shape and value of literature itself. The function of method. The relation between writer and reader. Much, perhaps too much, has been made of the critique of reference and normative syntax inherent in the work of many of the writers here, without acknowledging the degree to which this critique is itself situated within the larger question of what, in the last part of the twentieth century, it means to be human. Invariably, however, attacks which have been made on this writing (and no other current poetic tendency in America has been subjected to anything like the constant flow of dismissals and exposes, many of them composed in the threatened rhetoric of fury, as have the poets here), make an appeal, explicit or otherwise, to a simple ego psychology in which the poetic text represents not a person, but a persona, the human as unified object. And the reader likewise. This, in turn, is usually called "communication" or "emotion."

It is intriguing that an art form be perceived as a threat, a curious verification that poetry remains important business, and a testament to the power of the writing involved. Yet, if the collective thrust of these poets to a possible or normative reader is that you must change your life, this anthology offers no single prescription as to how this can best be accomplished. In editing it, I have tried to keep the distinctness of each person's work uppermost in my mind. I have tried also to give a sense of the great range of writing which has been carried out within this debate, as well as to point to concentrations of concerns wherever they might occur. These objectives determined much of the shape of this book.

In general, I have selected only those poets whose writing provided a larger focus for a number of singularly different forums, such as the magazines *This, Hills, Roof, L=A=N=G=U=A=G=E, Tottel's, Miam, The Difficulties, A Hundred Posters* and *QU*, the Tuumba Press chapbook series, publishers such as The Figures, This Press, Roof, Asylum's and Segue, the San Francisco talk series now part of the residency program at New Langton Arts, five previous magazine collections, two of which I edited for *Alcheringa* and *Ironwood*, the Andrews/Wiater issue of *Toothpick*, one edited by Charles Bernstein for the *Paris Review*, and one published in translation in "l'espace Amerique" issue of the French journal *Change*, plus a similar critical feature edited for the Canadian *Open Letter* by Steve McCaffery. For reasons of space and clarity, I have excluded poets working in other nations, such as McCaffery, Tom Raworth, Christopher Dewdney or Allen Fisher, those whose primary medium is something other than poetry, such as the filmmakers Abigail Child and Henry Hills, playwrights Eileen Corder and Nick Robinson, or novelist Kathy Acker, as well as authors, like Larry Eigner, Bill Berkson or Kenneth Irby, whose mature style and public identity was largely formed prior to this moment in writing. These individuals and many others participated in the greater discourse of which this poetry is but a particular axis. Finally, there are literally dozens of other poets and writers whose work has both influenced and been influenced by the debate reflected in these pages. A volume of absolutely comparable worth could be constructed from the writing of Tom Ahern, Robert Gluck, Bruce Boone, Beverly Dahlen, Rosemarie Waldrop, Karl Young, Alice Notely, Dick Higgins, Curtis Faville, Laura Moriarty, Barbara Einzig, Jim Rosenberg, Laura Chester, Lydia Davis, Johanna Drucker, Kathleen Fraser, Gloria Frym,

Peter Ganick, Merrill Gilfillan, Ed Friedman, Gerald Burns, Gerritt Lansing, Chris Mason, Doug Messerli, John Godfrey, Michael Amnasan, Loris Essary, Keith Waldrop, Geoff Young, Marshall Reese, Craig Watson, Marina LaPalma, Steve Roberts, Bernard Welt, Gil Ott, Ted Pearson, Jerry Estrin, Marc Lecard, Kirby Malone, Norman Fischer, John Yau, John Taggart, Gail Sher, Joseph Simas, Cris Cheek, Joan Rettalack, Rafael Lorenzo, David Gitin, Jed Rasula, Keith Shein, Charles Stein, Leslie Scalapino, Michael Lally, Dennis Cooper, David Benedetti, Bill Mohr, Leland Hickman, Charles Amirkhanian, Steve Katz, Doug Lang, Bill Corbett, Rachel Blau DuPlessis, Maureen Owen, Mei-mei Berssenbrugge, Aaron Shurin, David Levi-Strauss, Sandra Meyer, DeLys Mullis, Carole Korzeniowsky, Frances Jaffer, Donald Byrd, Charles North, Jim Brodey, Madeleine Burnside, Barbara Barg, Lorenzo Thomas, Tim Dlugos, Steve Hamilton, Gary Lenhart, and others. As I noted above, the resources available to this moment in writing have been remarkably abundant.

I should note also, if only in passing, that this larger debate has not been the only transformation of and in American poetry during the past 15 years. Of particular importance has been the full articulation of a literature by, and consciously for, women. Parallel occurrences on a smaller scale have taken place within the gay community and those of some ethnic minorities. The pluralization of American writing has permanently altered the face of literature, and for the better. While the old dichotomy of "academic" (i.e., the follower of received European forms) and "non-academic" (everybody else) has not disappeared, it now sits within a very different context. This makes it possible to see that each audience is a distinct social grouping, a community whether latent or manifest. It is now plain that any debate over who is, or is not, a better writer, or what is, or is not, a more legitimate writing is, for the most part, a surrogate social struggle. The more pertinent questions are what is the community being addressed in the writing, how does the writing participate in the constitution of this audience, and is it effective in doing so.

I have geographically divided the poetry in this volume into two sections in order to more clearly foreground the particular distinctions that occur within this writing, this debate. No doubt some of these differences can be attributed simply to who lives where and the important, but informal, influence of face-to-face interaction. Poetry, however, is a much more highly visible art form in San Francisco than in New York with its active (and capital intense) visual and performing arts scenes. New York had, and still has, a highly defined literary topography, whereas the context in San Francisco was much more diffuse in the early 70s. Eight of the twelve women in this anthology live in the east. The majority of its publishing, and other institutional, resources are in the west. With only two exceptions, the poets in the west live in the San Francisco bay area, while the poets in the east are spread out from Ohio to Massachusetts to Virginia. In practice, I believe one can find very different orientations toward such issues as form and prose style (especially with regard to syntax) that relate closely to this geographic division.

Each of the two sections begins with a writer who can, with some confidence, be seen as a point of origin for this moment in writing. From there, I have edited according to an intuitive principle I can only describe as complimentary difference. The arrangement of critical materials (some of which are also "works") in "Second Front" is more thematic, and is intended to show how the concurrent discourse on poetics which has been so much a part of this debate relates to, and illuminates, the writing. Because of this I have tended to stay away from pieces which were more generally about aesthetics than writing per se. In one instance, the collective introduction to the feature "For *Change*," the essay has never been published in English. It in itself might stand as an alternate introduction to this volume. Two articles were written by persons who do not appear in the first two sections of the book, Jackson Mac Low and Nick Piombino. Mac Low's presence violates the above-mentioned principle of not including persons whose mature style and public identity were firmly established prior to the publication of "On Speech." Nonetheless, like Eigner, he has been a constant source of information, inspiration and support, and his critique of the misnomer "language-centered" is essential to an understanding as to why this debate has so consistently resisted the destructive "convenience" of a shorthand name. Piombino, to my knowledge, has published only critical prose since 1978. Trained as a Freudian analyst, his contribution to the specificity of the discourse on poetics in $L=A=N=G=U=A=G=E$ was one of that journal's most important attributes. I regret, however, not being able to excerpt from a long essay by Alan Davies, whose linguistic idealism demonstrates emphatically just how diverse the positions within this debate have been.

There is of course a story behind each contribution in a project such as this. I have no doubt that every single contributor here would have done it differently, and that each such volume would differ from one another. Anthologies are not facts, but individual viewpoints over complex fields of information. My perspective is obviously partisan, for which I make no apologies. But I have been fortunate also in having valuable advice given to me generously by virtually every poet included here, and by others as well. In particular, the students in my graduate seminar at San Francisco State experienced as their reading list a very rough draft of what turned out to be the core of this book. Their commentary is reflected throughout this volume.

In 1973, during the process of my editing a feature for *Alcheringa* magazine on this same subject, Jerome Rothenberg first suggested the possibility of a booklength anthology. It would have been premature then, but the door, once opened, never shut. Jerry, in his capacity as editor of a "new poetics" series for the ill-fated Ross-Erickson Books, asked me if I was still interested in 1981. He has of course always been an advocate of any work which could- actively and usefully extend the potentialities of poetics. I have no idea if he knew that the *Alcheringa* feature was itself the direct result of his having given Bruce Andrews my address two years earlier, but it is perfectly evident that this anthology could not have existed without him. I owe him the greatest debt of thanks.

Ron Silliman
San Francisco
March 25, 1984

IN THE AMERICAN TREE

EAST

SECOND FRONT

Cover by Francie Shaw

IN THE AMERICAN TREE
IN THE AMERICAN TREE
IN THE AMERICAN TREE

I: West

WEST

Instead of ant wort I saw brat guts

ROBERT GRENIER

. . .

a long walk
a long
walk a long
walk a long
walk along

WINTRY

German
Magnus massive
Dagny Dagny calling
call me call me

lazy prairie icy
streams, nicely
nicely nicely nicely Norwegians

vell I, well I
vell I, vell I
snowy vell I
vell I don't know

oh vell I, oh well, I
well I don't know
oh, vell, I don't know

Ah yah
ah, yah
ja
a sod hut

. . .

snow
blue
eyes

ice
blue
rocks

rocks
rocks of
getting dark

WARM

bones in the child
child in the womb
womb in her
body in
bed in the room

room in the house
house in the
plain
moon
drifts

blackness
because we have
drawn
curtains

CROSSING ONTARIO

joking and somber
and joking and sober

.

all the stores closed
afternoon Wednesdays

very dark
snow clouds in
July
in
the first days
of August

west southwest to
east northeast
it flows

cafe brightness
light blue walls
mirrors lake scenes as if
reflected off snow

hard to order
a vanilla sundae easy
one small cold ball
round in stainless steel

see the model station over the road
spur line here
to Hudson's Bay

where the railroad must stop
Esquimaux

.

they want you to work

they don't want you to sleep

.

what
I move so
thickly through into
very furry

.

not so much
the forest

with its
gleams of silver

meadow fucking
meadow meadow

.

blue birds
mountain rings

the toe
of the body

STICKY FINGERS

E
it almost twelve

oh it is twelve

all the creatures are comin' out

(le)
jazz
simple

actually it's the drummer

E
Charlie?

how else would they
know where they were

he's
bettern a
metronome

but
then
they're
the

Robert Grenier   9

songs
without
anything but
instrumentation

that sounds like Dylan
under some funny ('funky'?)
echoing cover

this one is actually
really good

we got
ta get a
machine
Emily though

Emily
said Bob
Dylan said
to Mick Jagger

'I
could've written
Satisfaction but you
could *never* have written
Tambourine Man'

it said
in *Rolling Stone*
so
Sister Morphine

E
I should've
married
Keith Richard

instead of Mick?

Keith Richard
is starting to
overshadow Mick

do you think they
do it with each other

E
I hope so they're
a group

I didn't know Keith Richard
could sing

Oh

I didn't know Mick could sing

Charlie
Watts

that's a
little
bit
faster

just a
little
bit

you see the drummer controls it etc.

it produces a
different dream in
everybody it
touches

can you hear the words in this

did it say *Daniel Boone*

E
No
I don't
think

'click click'

is it over

or *play it again*

E
shd think of the
people next door what if
they came in and
smelled it

there's
part of this
record can't be played
on this machine

I'd
really like
to hear that
somewhere

sometime

'poor'
rhymes with
'low'?

gee I like it

don't you
(despite)

E
I like it *best*

should send it to
Rolling Stone

probably too square
too 'straight'

E
send it to
Erma Bombeck

are you really tired of this

huh?

'buttoned
yr lip?'

Barbie Boobie
Barbie Boobie
Barbie Boobie
Barbie Boobie

'how come ya dance so good'

E
don't you feel
cozy toward
Keith

I feel cozy
toward the whole group

that's *too much* / just the same old *Stones*

let's go to bed Emily

E
not yet

E
I'm a
finish
my green

that *guitar* is just
so
so good

it's
disgustingly good

like Keith Richard

somebody
should give them

some reward

this is the
flip side

that's like some sort of
athletic
marathon for
the
drummer

odda
bum

odda
bum

odda
bum

odda
bum

stealin' the
trumpets from

James Brown

what a *bruiser*

E
I adore her

E
when we're over to Janet's
Janet's mother
reads it aloud to us

E
I was
young once

you were?

E
in the end
she disappears into the weeds
or he does

it's
two o'clock

we got to go to bed Emily

people are going to
be here tomorrow at twelve

E
remember when you used to

actually
it didn't
get really good until
around *Revolver*

around 1965

cuca
cucaracha

Desi Arnaz

E
Ozzie
Nelson

trash

to *dance* to

come &
get in Emily

E
bring it in

STRIPED CANVAS

the clouds
of the summer
before

by extension to
the clouds
of the following

summer

and who for
the chair

who for
the beer

the doghouse
of the summer
before

the doghouse
of the following
summer

don't
give it a
second

thought like

where's
the dog

A SEQUENCE / 28 SEPARATE POEMS FROM *SENTENCES*

of life days like

.

dream
y belly

.

a port to a green

.

AUTUMN

frogs for the first time since autumn

.

the snow with snow

.

corroborative mountainous panorama

20   Robert Grenier

POPLARS

facing away

•

repetitive bird and black

•

yah gee
yah gee
yah gee
yah gee
yah gee
yah gee
yah gee
yah gee

•

- rain drops the first of many

•

branches are then moved by negligible quantity the

Robert Grenier 21

·

saids

·

TWELVE VOWELS

breakfast

the sky flurries

·

stepping through the water to the rocks

·

SNOW

snow covers the slopes covers the slopes
snow covers the slopes covers the slopes
snow covers the slopes covers the slopes
snow covers the slopes covers the slopes

·

tomato

struck by hail

.

hungry on toward suppertime

.

previously leaves were red

.

heard jet up by opening window

.

roams

.

BIRD

I wonder if I do

.

in the morning after work

.

or the starlight on the porch since when

.

SPRING

at four it would still be dark

and raining

.

JOE

JOE

.

yawns at solid

.

someoldguyswithscythes

.

having
swum

BARRETT WATTEN

PLASMA

A paradox is eaten by the space around it.

I'll repeat what I said.

To make a city into a season is to wear sunglasses inside a volcano.

He never forgets his dreams.

The effect of the lack of effect.

The hand tells the eye what to see.

I repress other useless attachments. Chances of survival are one out of ten.

I see a tortoise drag a severed head to the radiator.

They lost their sense of proportion. Nothing is the right size.

He walks in the door and sits down.

The road turns into a beautiful country drive. The voice isn't saying something, but turning into things.

Irregular movements spread out the matter at hand.

My work then is done.

His earliest dreams were prerecorded. Pointing a finger at a child in the act of play.

Light grows from the corners of the state map.

The universe is shaped like a hat. I lose interest and fall off the bed.

Tips of the fingers direct the uncontrollable surface.

The dim-witted inhabitants fuse with the open areas. All rainbows end in the street.

Subtitles falling in show water rolling underneath.

The question would lead to disaster.

A person is set in motion by a group of words.

Running water and filthy glass lose the ability to reflect. Blindness is always surrounded by a variable.

They blew the whole thing up and were presented with a fragment. An obvious mistake.

The tennis courts are of different pastel colors.

Civil servants guard the unclaimed packages.

Horses coming out of the sea keep the eye jumping. Background lighting is for this reason always varied.

The sun sets through all weather.

Otherwise the damage already shows.

The telephone rests on the range of inattention. The telephone book is complete.

Grey alphabets light everything else in grey. Black designs make a simple logical twist.

Power of taxation is supported by a well-paid armed force.

He never arrives in his work, because he is already there.

The flag bends on its hinges. A woman walks through the window glass. A rock argues with the door.

The voice spreads out, fighting with circles. The object in descriptive writing is to disappear.

The roadbed tilts upward, devouring detail.

We eat the most agreeable mountain, the words themselves.

To suddenly turn on the crowd would be suicide. The map retains its sanity, almost past the use of anything.

My ideas will change in time. Now that you know what the words mean, you can leave.

I must force myself to breathe. We must be prepared to abolish this way of life.

There's no traffic. The traffic has stopped.

Dreams are an accident of birth.

I was normal. The music suggested the leg of a chair.

The grey scale makes painting vertical. Evidently we are dead.

The burden of classes is the twentieth-century career. He can be incredibly cruel. Events are advancing at a terrifying rate.

He thought they were a family unit. There were seven men and four women, and thirteen children in the house. Which voice was he going to record?

That's why we talk language. Back in Sofala I'm writing this down wallowing in a soft leather armchair. A dead dog lies in the gutter, his feet in the air.

For the artist the moment of seeing can also be one of revelation.

When you've perfect, people can't wait to pick you apart.

You and I are always going in opposite directions.

I remember the eerie devastation of an explosion that never happened. The embarrassed percipient is changed into a field.

It fades and has an edge. My public works extend over years and cost me much thought and anxiety. Inside my mother I make a fist, and then I figure it out.

Thereupon he sailed for home. The rock is the ideal in the world of objects. The mind must merge with the universe, or succumb to it.

Anything specific he says is by way of an example. Two hours later he comes back to his point.

A zigzag line is notably the graph of an enraged neurosis. Constant attention makes every square inch of the wall a horrible fact. When columns rise out of the ground, his emotions are engaged.

Chaos has been variously interpreted. It may mean "a yawning gap." Thank you very much, the source of all life is hunger.

How to understand things you have names for? After the demon of fear was released in 1789 . . . . now it's 1923. Now it's 1975.

I had over-anticipated the event. I don't understand this idea of construction.

But there is another level of complexity to ready-mades. Which gets us home if you talk poetry. You can say what happens and have it be a part of that.

If you want to say yes, say yes.

The experience of the cemetery is inexorable. Looking at the landscape's variable browns and greens.

The mountain is such that it makes its own weather. Meanwhile it is being spoonfed with a wheelbarrow. That makes it more like a vacuum. The rock itself is awful looking, an egg which petrified before someone forgot to throw it out.

Poets have something wrong with their eyes. Later we come to be comfortable with them.

Art instead of being an object made by one person is a process set in motion by a group of people. Anything one says comes back eventually as a mistake. There's no use in keeping accounts or records. If it's a good idea, it results in a permanent change.

Everywhere there are spontaneous literary discussions. Something structurally new is always being referred to. These topics may be my very own dreams, which everyone takes a friendly interest in. The library extends for miles, under the ground.

My demons are gone. I haven't thought about it yet, but I intend to pull down the pyramid, one step at a time.

So I'm inside a Jackson Pollock painting which is a house of ordinary structure but increased affect. The floors are copper and blue, there is gold twill in the green rug hanging from the wall. A displacing effect, like oil over glass, pushes every object outward. So the edges of things stand out like drip lines of paint.

A telephone pole is an edited tree.

The natural gas towers extend down into the ground. His speech is clipped, a short pause before each phrase. The frog is about to jump into a bowl of cherries. New Mayor: "No conflicts!"

The waves beat against the shore.

The lighting is important—night outside, a high contrast interior. An egg within the unknown. Conflict will take place among three unrelated individuals. The curtains are drawn, wind like boiling water.

The mind is not concerned with persons.

Exlamation point, question mark, three dots.

The argument is elastic. It ends with a physical description of going up stairs. "I cerainly wouldn't try this carrying anything." He pulls himself out of this world, a moment of relief and panic.

The whole man is a concept, waking to sound.

Into a falsely centered chain of command, she's leaving permanently. Obviously the brain will make the best story it can out of the available details. I have only to pick up my bags at the station, and they sure are there.

Such is night in the mountains.

POSITION

The monument speaks correctly.
    To get results
that all might disappear. As
extreme. The words themselves
    reversed, "going
forward." The apex settles on

Tones in surrounding heads.
    A test case, or
exile. No wires account for
failure of specific response.
    A triangle gives,
circles branch out. Forced

Exposure to limit distorts.
    Accumulation of
artifacts in identical tombs.
Any view appears as a hole.
    Each is a unit,
and all else. Corrosive air,

Hit by something. Spot-lit
    on center stage.
Correction, a large boulder.
The parts avoid being seen.
    Portraits of
witnesses other than oneself,

Pasted, stacked. White clouds
    and blank tape.
Architects bury their careers,
survived by their mistakes.
    Mirrors tension
of surfaces at work. Lies,

Extension of screen. Grammar
        signifies refusal
to correspond. Multiple cracks
spread out. A sequence of
        obstacles blocks
the memory of facts. Voice of

The word it approximates.
        The foundation
floats without opposing tides.
Into the center of potential
        stop. The road
decaying into frame. This

Impression turns inside out.
        In perspective,
feeding on industrial waste.
The endless text manipulates
        by fatigue. Street
where no one lives. Pressing,

Yielding to the arguments of
        mass. The hawk
tears the sparrow to pieces.
Coded sparks, holding patterns.
        The privilege
of vanishing speech. All size

Diminished to expanding scale.
        Shifted in
the order by which it occurs.
Identity is the cause of war.
        The point both
pans and zooms. "Our father

Would be bored to sickness."
　　　The shadow of
difference predicting retreats.
Water follows in its steps.
　　　Ironic index
of what seen. Further claims

Of shape built into line.
　　　The spectator
hiding his uncertain springs.
The story holding the man in.
　　　A series of
reductions. Suppressed end

Where nothing is explained.
　　　The town dissolves,
its factories work at night.
Signals in neutral terrain.
　　　Fog explodes into
perfect control. A spasm of

Zig-zags of mannered sweeps.
　　　The type of prose
departs in ascending steps.
The perfectly natural figure's
　　　tight orange face.
Exits take down signs. Obvious

Fragment. Wandering through
　　　the static list.
A fluorescent toy depicting a
miniature solar system. Inert
　　　metaphysic of
effect. At the same time

Everyone is aware of distance.
    The irritant spins,
without any help from them.
A method to invent disbelief.
    No one decides
not to notice. He would die

Resisting total thus achieved.
    A record of
all that remains. Museum tour
conducted by mutes. Language
    palpable as
continuum over shape. "Substitute"

Not equal to stand for itself.
    Progress into
retreating barriers makes sense.
Return to the beginning and note.
    Ends in a heap,
exhausted. Branches touch cloud

At the bottom of the well.
    Print monitors
illusion of depth. Counter to
river stones, mineral samples.
    The moment of
mixed lots. The skeleton at

The border instructs. Spread
    of the fingers
between keys. Telephone poles
standing on disputed ground.
    The fountain gels.
Blinks in the sun, intuitive

Technique. Rocks fill the eye
        at the corners.
Sleeping man walks into house,
turns on the light. Rolling
        over hills to
concretize plains. "Because,

It can say that." Threat of
        motion from stills.
A statue surrounded by priests,
lying face down on the ground.
        A puffy rope,
gathered manfully. Wish for

Invulnerable sentence, walking
        in air. Thought
mechanics of emphasis places in
reach. Decapitated mannequin
        takes a few steps.
Inherent strain. Unlocatable

Entrance at odds with address.
        Window glass
obscures the intended effect.
Ventilation furnished with keys.
        Thereafter fused,
heated to an improbable degree.

REAL ESTATE

I

The drillground endures to revise the worst effects of former studies' monstrous parade. Its position a guarantee: they ride on your backs "of severely formed masks." Like a map rolled up (exposed and condensed) in tightly stretched wires. The abandoned warehouse surrenders itself to discourse: in the deliberate advance of repetitive texts. Because anyone can make a typographical error to wear down the pyramid by identity with word. The essence of poison is the power to soothe: the citizens spit flames of a rationalism they don't understand. The impression is a point of departure: a tower of ashes (a coat full of holes) floating in air. Water flows from the tap as time reaches zero: unforeseen floods rise exactly to the level of the words. Everything offers itself: a shoe polish learns to speak (avoiding subordinate clauses) from a crumpled umbrella. Propellors inhabit air where thought originates to whir in place of the word. The brainworker has no basis: to adjust the birth rate all abstraction leads to a shorter route to the ocean. The intended confusion assumes all wishes to encounter anything interpreted as itself. Balancing all prefigurations to be caught in the throes of "that is how I am."

II

The blueprint doesn't work, vanishes into intervals: only the buildings are left behind. Others have written on this safety valve to support the catastrophe of theory. The walls of the reaction chamber closing in: "I speak of a proliferation of windows." Therefore prose is restored to the assimilated fact: a microballoon rising inside the original movie. Discordant frames approach and slip from their feet: the plotline succumbs to a general inertia. Documents packed up in crates buckle under the weight of: "to study the laws of gravity, I fell." Here sentences translate the other side of the code: to fill in holes and cracks in the pavement. Restrictive screens stand out in relief: concrete networks bypass perspective.

Barrett Watten 37

"The unyielding constructions speak as though nothing has happened" in the language of various devices. A lease has been drawn up (the motif): walking backwards across the entire length of the system. Plaster casts are struck from the voice: standing figures betray a cartoon potential. The perfect psychologist becomes tired of himself. Traffic is extended to the organs of speech: the retina arrives at an arrangement of solids.

III

The invulnerable sentences verge on prophetic fatigue: "What are you thinking about? Nothing!" Hollow blocks pile up in windowless rooms: the train ceaselessly reinvents the station. Chains float through discord in the taxonomy of the dead: the argument is suspended. The weather writhes in its tracks, impeded by the least particle of detail. The clouds are wounds: the deliberately lit arena turns clockwise around a vertical axis. Time stops to penetrate mass: nuts and bolts opt for statistics. The linkage gives way to a package of matches: built-in entry points write these things down. Invisible glass (circles in the water) (glare) (a white curve on a black background): the involuntary barrier supports the private vacation. Anything is a vehicle designed primarily to obstruct the view: the foreground is the tomb of intention. Materials cut into strata emerge at right angles: the exponential city includes us to forget. Friction between buildings evokes celestial play: "a man cut in half by a window." The lens disappears in an opaque solution: everything out there pushes ahead. "To be someone else at exactly the same time": the surface gives way to test patterns and static.

IV

Doubt compares with everything: in pure air the constant ringing of a distant alarm. The magnetic needle links up to remembered North in a bipolar manner. The exercise yard refuses to yield: a mid-Oakland freeway stack marks a drop in potential. The battle of fixtures stabilizes at a determinate point: vertigo is aware of inscriptions (territory melts down in time). Neutral fillers make a hole in one's life: the lights go on, the suction pump prepares a seduction. Furnished apartments decorate the cube of the state: the slag heap is backed up by polished metal engines. Parallel avenues converge on a syntax having no center of its own: a motionless drill restores the site to crash landings. The increments multiply in the absence of scale: the landscape retreats to vague promise of suspension. A tour of Mt. Erebus is conveyed to the equitorial plane: the camera releases energy into the world it dismantles. A vaporized world built of airtight containers (the size of the prison) and cryptic flux (the time spent therein). But the job of the driver is to muffle the sound of the new car turning into parts. To perfect the extraction of data from what's not event: the "sign-off" radiates from the end of the broadcast. All this gets us nowhere: the cloud arrives at ground zero, ready to stop at once.

COMPLETE THOUGHT

I

The world is complete.

Books demand limits.

II

Things fall down to create drama.

The materials are proof.

III

Daylight accumulates in photos.

Bright hands substitute for sun.

IV

Crumbling supports undermine houses.

Connoisseurs locate stress.

V

Work breaks down to devices.

All features present.

VI

Necessary commonplaces form a word.

The elements of art are fixed.

VII

A mountain cannot be a picture.

Rapture stands in for style.

VIII

Worn-out words are invented.

We read daylight in books.

IX

Construction turns back in on itself.

Dogs have to be whipped.

X

Eyes open wide to see spots.

Explanations are given on demand.

XI

Brick buildings shut down in winter.

A monument works to change scale.

XII

False notes work on a staircase.

The hammer is as large as the sun.

XIII

Connected pieces break into name.

Petrified trees are similar.

XIV

Everyday life retards potential.

Calculation governs speech.

XV

Rules stand out as illustrations.

People climb over piles of rock.

XVI

I am speaking in an abridged form.

Ordinary voices speak in rooms.

XVII

An act is comprehensible.

An explanation effaces words.

XVIII

Language ceases to be the future.

Thinking becomes a religious device.

XIX

Nothing touches the surface.

The arbitrary is meant to be sensed.

XX

False songs restore information.

Everyday elements are mixed.

XXI

Death is an accident.

A measure is given by use.

XXII

The air witnesses an abduction.

Motion isolates this effect.

XXIII

A single step makes a resolution.

A pile driver is not a device.

XXIV

Thought remains in the animal.

Each island steals teeth.

XXV

A true sensation buries its dead.

Thought is embedded.

XXVI

The issue is not divided.

An identical sequence follows this.

XXVII

Tongues expand into choirs.

Wishes break down to facts.

XXVIII

The foot senses an explanation.

Mass returns in the curse.

XXIX

A white line leads to thinking.

The slave is carried off alive.

XXX

Decoration orders the task at hand.

Coincidence is cut into squares.

XXXI

Three kings build a false motif.

They arrive by the longest route.

XXXII

The materials motivate storms.

Play is felt to be constructed.

XXXIII

A boot steps into an example.

Conviction is selected from space.

XXXIV

Two unequal figures complete an act.

The wife turns out to be sane.

XXXV

Night opens up with eating.

Later the words are filled in.

XXXVI

Thought identifies missing links.

Errors are in constant use.

XXXVII

Art is admonished on this basis.

The author speaks to the known.

XXXVIII

A straight road is unconvincing.

Not to kill the hero is a crime.

XXXIX

Rules stick to the unexpected.

Sound is locked in by a chain.

XL

A man torments the sun.

Cows are disturbed by their calves.

XLI

Players make the appropriate moves.

Absence is given as a way in.

XLII

Time strikes between abutments.

Art transposes thought.

XLIII

One picture ceases to vanish.

A doctor makes words out of glass.

XLIV

Candles stand up to icons.

Science gives features to the world.

XLV

Another indifference is invented.

They speak it like another word.

XLVI

Howls fit in to a perspective.

Photos of relics cover the earth.

XLVII

There are no literal examples.

A narrative is not a report.

XLVIII

Sensations are lost on the market.

A fact can kill a book.

XLIX

Familiar processes are arbitrary.

The arbitrary is broken down.

L

Use vanishes.

The violinist arrives at a spot.

LYN HEJINIAN

The inanimate are rocks, desks, bubble,
    mineral, ramps. It is the concrete being
that reasons. The baseboard weighing
its wall span. The clouds never form regiments
    and don't march. The gap in my education
needn't be filled. Stubbornness is provocative.

The pessimist suppresses a generous anger. A trace
    linked to a fence of forgetting. Lying awake
may serve the purpose that dreams do. In the dark
opaque disposal of the missing past. Canned laughter
    is white noise. Comparable repositories freight dust
into the shadows. Anger the animate of stubbornness.

Such displacements
alter illusions,
which is
all-to-the-good

Those birds are saying, over and over, this tree, my branch, my field of seeds, my herd of worms. Thus was it told to me. I made signs to them to be as quiet as possible. It was at this time, I think, that I became interested in science. Yet that was only a coincidence. The penny disk, the rarer dollar disk. Her hair is the color of a brass bedstead. We were proud of our expertise, distinguishing the ripe ears of corn from the green, speaking knowledgeably of tassles and the breeds of corn: Butter & Sugar, Country Gentleman, Honey & Cream, Silver Queen. The old dirt road, broken into clods and gullies, or clods and ruts, over which I was walking under some noisy trees, had been reversed in the dark. And so I was returning. For such words present residences on a brown ground. A pause, a rose, something on paper. When I was a child, the mailman, Tommy, let us walk his route with him until we reached the busy streets, and then he sent us home, dragging the dog. The sky was studied with stars, he said, white, low, as heavy as stones. It was utterly sincere, though not completely sincere. That troubled my reply. On such a hot day, a "scorcher," the wind helps. An airplane passes over the baseball game and one hears it in the air and over the air, amplified by the transistor radios belonging to the fans. Stay, after the others go. It convinced a few and attracted many. Live birds are heavier than air. She showed the left profile, the good one, with the light behind her casting a shadow on the near side of her face. Any photographer will tell you the same. I am looking for the little hand mirror. The summer evenings saw window shoppers in a reflecting system, man with merchandise agog. It is hard to turn away from moving water. He made me nervous as soon as he began offering a special discount. The work is probably a good deal wiser than the horny old doctor he was. I wrote my name in every one of his books. A name trimmed with colored ribbons. They used to be the leaders of the avant garde, but now they just want to be understood, and so farewell to them. If I was left unmarried after college, I would be single all my life and lonely in old age. In such a situation it is necessary to make a choice between contempt and an attempt at understanding, and yet it is difficult to know which is the form of retreat. We will only understand what we have already understood. The turkey is a stupid bird. And it is scanty praise to be so-called well-meaning. The washlines run with garments hung.

The coffee drinkers answered ecstatically

The traffic drones, where drones is a noun. Whereas the cheerful pessimist suits himself in a bad world, which is however the inevitable world, impossible of improvement. I close one eye, always the left, when looking out onto the glare of the street. What education finally serves us, if at all. There is a pause, a rose, something on paper. The small green shadows make the red jump out. Such displacements alter illusions, which is all-to-the-good. Now cars not cows on the brown hills, and a stasis of mobile homes have taken their names from what grew in the valleys near Santa Clara. We have all grown up with it. If it is personal, it is most likely fickle. The university was the cultural market but on Sundays she tried out different churches. In the museum, attention shifted from painting to painting, the eye forced around, so that it was impossible to focus on any single work. The nightmare was of a giant bluebottle fly which buzzed, "I'm all there is." Where cars don't go are shortcuts. My grandfather was forced to recognize his age when another, younger, man offered his seat on the bus. When one travels, one might "hit" a storm. The shoe must be tied to the ankle. As for we who "love to be astonished," McDonalds is the world's largest purchaser of beef eyeballs. They went out with bows and armbands to shoot at the hay. It's as easy as waves, slopping water. He had the hands of an artist. Europeans shake hands more often than we do, here in America, yet I don't think that constitutes a "daring to touch." I'll just keep myself from picking up the telephone, in order to get some work done. What memory is not a "gripping" thought. Only fragments are accurate. Break it up into single words, charge them to combination. Thinking about time in the book, it is really the time of your life. I was experiencing love, immensely relieved. It was, I know, an unparticular spirit of romance. Giving the back-up o.k. to the loaded semi. It was a long, 3-story apartment building with the apartments set like drawers into slots, and windows only at the front and back. I wouldn't mind if we were actually paying for something with our tax dollars. She threw off her coat, took off her dress. It was not difficult to interpret her mother's clatter at the sink, sometimes the voice of comfort, sometimes the voice of reprimand. You must water the ivy that is creeping up to the bird bell. The morning is past and the sun remains but the sunlight is brighter. Could the prairie be this sea—for love.

We are not forgetting the patience of the mad, their love of detail

The summer countryside, with the round hills patchy and dry, reminding one of a yellow mongrel dog, was what one could call a dirty landscape, the hills colored by the dusty bare ground rather than by grass, and yet this is what seemed like real country to me. I had idealized the pioneer's life, sinking roots. Known for its fleas. One could touch the flesh of their secrets, the roses of their behaviour. One didn't know what to give a young woman. Watermen are such as row in boats. They don't hear a word of all this, floating like plump birds along the shore. In extending, then entangling their concerns, they are given a thousand new names. The lace curtain Irish hate neighborhood Blacks. The coffee drinkers answered ecstatically. We looked at the apartment and took it. Space has small neighborhoods. As for we who "love to be astonished," each new bit of knowledge is merely indicative of a wider ignorance. One might cultivate a charming defect, say a romantic limp or a little squint. I made curtains out of colored burlap from Sears, hung them at the four windows of the green apartment. Down manholes, through pipes, to the mysterious sea. Though the pantry smelled more strongly of spices than of herbs and was dominated by nutmeg, the kitchen itself tended to smell of everything that had ever been cooked, but only because it was dark. If you cut your fingernails they will grow back thick, blunt, like a man's. In a little while, he said, we should be thumbing home. There were five little kittens under the car. They had put curves in the highway to keep drivers awake. The obvious analogy is with music, which extends beyond the space the figure occupies. She was pumping her violin over the piano. Each evening before dinner my parents sat for awhile in the "study," to talk, while my mother knit decoratively designed French sweaters called Jacquard. The house sparrow is a weaver finch. The front door key is hidden under the aloe. How did the artist think to put that on the outside. Such displacements alter illusions, which is all-to-the-good. Now I too could find a perfect cantaloupe, not by poking at the flesh around the stem of the melon but by sniffing at it. At some point hunger becomes sensuous, then lascivious. Not a fuck but a hug. My mother threw away all those little objects of sentiment, billed foolishness. The reference is a distraction, a name trimmed with colored ribbons. It was Father's Day, a holiday that no one could take seriously, yet someone admitted that he was planning to telephone his parents that evening and another said she might do the same. What can those birds be saying. That day there was wind but no air, because we were inland. Is pink pretty.

from WRITING IS AN AID TO MEMORY

6.

you must show yourself to catch
to be amused, to equate the man, to
shoot his autobiographical work

7.

ideas move and move the thinker
more parted, pasted dog up
in return far of the information
the schoolboy is decent to retort
unfashionable and compassionate whose
tones
dive order
the rate of forgetting is greatest
storing that and these processes
the principal source is his own and
desperately
life is quantity through a language
substitute inventing music of a series
of changes very little understood
binding men for driving through a new internal logic fire
to fish
of despair of failure for knowledge
by way of despair for the road
something edible to his nose like an ape
great heat to melt on emotional sympathy
his eyes were closed by a student and close friend

28.

                    we are parting with description
                  termed blue may be perfectly blue
            goats do have damp noses
                        that test and now I dine drinking with
              others
adult blue butterfly for a swim with cheerful birds
          I suppose we hear a muddle of rhythms in water
    bond vegetables binder thereof for thread
and no crisp fogs
                          spice quilt mix
            know shipping pivot
                      sprinkle with a little melody
                  nor blot past this dot mix
                  now for a bit and fog of bath rain
      do dot goats
                      swift whipper of rice
a type as cream
          into a froth
                          ranking a time when rain looms
          I part the swim and width whereas
        hob for swing yard note
              product in the woody weeds
                      trees in the foreshortening
a source "draws" shortening
    by an inkspot over the four rivers
      darkness ficing no flaw pink
                      the stain whose at him stuff suggested
        is visible as follows (cone in space)
            old waters
                      this morning over fringed crop involving
          quantity
      it lasts into the empty sky shopping and glittering
      I can picture the marked page
          poke beauty
                      sunset like a pack of dogs
                  swaying with daylight

                                        Lyn Hejinian 55

it is late afternoon and I hurry
    my fault of comfort
        the streets of traffic are a great success

THE GREEN

I am nearsighted and therefore cannot tell, though I would, whether the shapes in a field across the road are rocks, or shrubs, or cows. There are many figures in this scene which might form separate scenes. At the head of what is known as endlessly receptive the river crosses an occasional rain. The symmetry is broken by the wind. My attention trails off to the nether side of the clay mustard jar in which a collection of pencils is kept. So far I am disposed to think, yet I mean to be especially honest. For a moment, just as the stars spread out, drifting apart and diffusing their light, the early morning holds less promise. Dim materials. We used a little mirror to compare one part of the sky with another. The walls interpose strict shadows. The night would draw the daylight back. I wouldn't swear to all the details, were this the time or place for them, since one may reasonably question only that which can give an answer. Nothing appeases the accessory facts. Watched fathoms are rarely matched. In a portrait at this hour Ginevra is shown against a juniper bush which seems to refer to her name as well as her virtue. A distant nod, and solemn waves are launched over the firelight. Water governed by the sky is bound to come out again. Waiting for more sleep itself waiting for more days. The punctual are doomed to wait. A spray of small pink flowers grows on, or off, the rosy cliff surface of a rock above the creek. A lasting compromise. Vertical geology. A very little water, filled with the roar of the waterfall. Its poetry is too hard for romance. Garishness fills the air, island pictures painted by a hyperactive imagination. Lighting the way with flaming paper bags, daylight is tinged with a marine blue. The visual corollary is luckily rocky. Offweight tautologies are fused, assumed. The explorer's notebook strikes confusion, secret quiet, seldom allowing out-spoken enthusiasm to pass by without some hostility. Warm gestures, very closely jointed, appease only briefly the irritation born of doubt. Not the creative but the created await more, with all the pleasures of the last days gained. Irritation underlies idealism, craving a zone to mime. A glass face relays four eyes. A strong wind gritty with dust under a blue sky blows over this adjacency. Ideas remain fundamentally the same but the

Lyn Hejinian 57

details change radically. I stagger to the fore in my disguise. Knowledge is behavior directed into a mirror. My afterimage strikes the general dryness of the rocks. An attempt at duration. One tries to give the reader the benefit of what one knows. The page is an artistic case, accessory to light, a zone under construction. I cannot tell the nature of the fence and may be going into a gravel pit. Gallant descendant, quoting the lines, "Listen to the sweet sound Of life death bound." This war poem includes a battle described by one who has never witnessed war. The power of the work lies in its sentences, the dependent clause mulling over the fact. The bulk of distances, the mounds of home. Water and air are the media for light. Basalt flooded valleys and cooling formed dams which caused the streams to pond forming lakes. A strong wind lay back on a low hillside covered with rosemary. Its weight above the water is the middle of the day. At the beach my father and I built intricate sand castles, a shell courtyard within walls cut vertically on the interior and banked from a moat without, with a small sand stairway leading to the corner tower built of sand drips from which flew the gullfeather flag, situated near the water in the path of the incoming tide, where we worked intent on our project while awaiting its destruction, the return to peace, the literal proof of ebb and flow, of something yet more vast and continuous. The local side of a shape snakes along. The road to the High Lakes went out. The defined, its limits, a distinction between romanticism and scepticism, the engine designed so that any broken part might be easily accessible. The sunset was not art. The trail traversed the slopes to and fro over rocks between heavy spruce trees and clear meadows on which the melting snow had left lush grass growing over rivulets and mud, so the sun shone hot first on my left arm and then on my right. I have difficulty with matchless information, descriptions of vivid things, compelled by what I may want to admit. The humanist loves cities. Two sides contain the windows, one a door. We frame our world for inspection. The transition is natural: all solid objects are thin. In huge doses of paradox, things felt as unformed are juxtaposed with things felt as volumes. Accuracy gives one illusions. Lamont Cranston, Hyacinth Robinson, Earl Warren, Herbert Pocket, Margo Lane. The family rabble makes its own demands. They have the manners of persons in a tableau vivant. I peek over the edge and listen, eating raw peas singly from a blue and green coffee cup. Las Casas sits in a corner forlornly shuffling a sticky pack of cards, to make them run smoothly for Napolean. This ingenious pictorial has the unusual feature of two reserves. Three time explorers have entered the bee-hive city, where the air previously had lain heavily. I capture the scene in words. Slowly it grows late, and the yellow afternoon light casts a somnolent glow over the room. The nested mass of light stretches out in the vast apartment. The millenial pulse is slow. In spite of an occasional rain I had the run of granites, niches that underlie the purple flowers, receptive to accessory facts. Paradise is green and brown and gray, of which the first two are indistinguishable in this light but disconcertingly clear as black and white detail. So we don't stumble. The day gets wider there in the middle. The only sense of motion is static, a vibration. The mirror is big enough for the largest family. Shadows of slanting mesh are flush with the surface. Outdoors a motor mumbles, a car door slams, the gears pull in two tones. Following a probable and ordinary course of experience, it is someone, and someone has a history, which soothes him or her into a darker mood. The preceding note is deeper, there is a pause, then in second the sound disappears. From the air uphill bleary shadows settle early, over the foreground coulisse, the middle-ground pool, the distant mountains. The household beyond this feeling lists the echoes, pragmatically, at points of contact. Cupped. I sat on the beige couch and drew a serpentine abstraction on a blank page in pencil behind my grandmother's shopping list. Why this should be so is social. Once I've formed an opinion it's unlikely that I'll keep it to myself. I speculate about the corner, useful in a room—an allusion to a parallel world. A mathematical formula translated into perfect form. At the top a dome and an oil injector. I in the room, still under the spell of the family, am laboriously working on my big cartoon. A resting line tilts into active space. At Fall Creek we built dams which were self-defeating across the small branching streams, since the pool forming behind the dam had inevitably to overflow it, making our barrier of rocks and pebbled mud a mere line constructed in water. The spy develops a code based on the rules of English prosody, composing poems in which his messages are embedded. Space is crowded with perceptions in the curious shades of private life. A glare. The gloss, riddled with philosophy. They change their sky. Here I am, crossing the Baltic Sea, on an energetic ferry, just having sampled the smorgasbord. Grand green and abundant crystal beads, plinking, draw my attention to the furthest points on the horizon line. It shows us how things look, or how we may want to look. A straggler among snippets. Some years before in the cold of an inner city park beside a muddy pond without my glasses I had fed bread crumbs to a beer can mistaking it for a duck. The prisoner in the book passes his time by taming a spider. The bird retires to its hybernaculum before the early snow. Human forms contribute subject to a scene cut from the absolutely natural. Bars of sunlight slant through the redwood trees neither as tall nor as wide as they might be. Watching moths bob at the shanty, dabbling in what's left of a fog. They are playing musical boats, in a season of light incredulity. I compare this phenomenon to my afterimages, which I have grown used to. It is not the unknown but the absence of the known that is mysterious, poetic, producing a state of heightened syntax. One watches for the repetition of certain ideas, then sprinkles them with numbers. When I was nine or ten, my father began to paint from nature, declaring his intention to become, in time, to a degree, intimate with her infinity. I have broken with fidelity to big things. I had misunderstood "hallowed" for "hello" in the prayer. In the foreground, our human figures are dwarfed by the great rock formations yet seem at peace with the setting. One examines the tableau clinique. The neighborhood children, my brother, my sister, and I built a miniature city of mud bricks, accessible only by dirt roads the width of three fingers, lined with pastures in which metal farm animals stood fenced with white cotton thread and feeding on yellow grass from the vacant lot. Out of the hills to the blocks, via orchards planted in rows whose lines interplay as I pass, form distracting patterns that encourage me to return, to alter purpose, wander back and forth, delaying my arrival elsewhere. I do not experience single-minded devotion. I do not see the wind in the trees. Errors simply dissolve, leaving nothing. Several times as a child I had ridden horseback with my grandfather to the old ghost town, whose attractions to me were neither historical nor ghastly, and it was only later that I was curious to know whose ghosts they were, or what was so persuasively haunting. The past is the erotic element in this stirring story. Event vibrato. A palm reader once pointed to evidence in my hand that proved the existence of a double life, the "second" of which was probably furtive. One feels remote, remorse settles over aspects of the familiar. Perhaps the ghost town was unreal—weathered siding on kitchenettes, the pulp of pure poetry. A spray of greenery in light silence. My visual memory selects a view. Light shines through a glass chunk, the rock in a clear stream remains magnified. Lessons which are good in poetry can't be bad in prose. The law predicts a potent force but not the exact form. Beside the shadows of erratic boulders, the sunset illuminates our picnic. The counterspy, reprimanded for failing to intercept messages sent to the enemy, replies: "I didn't know it was a message because it was a poem." There is wind on the trees. Small fish contained in an occasional rain populate a new lake. Dozens of small faces alight on a sad head. The misanthropist prefers an isolated spot where he or she may seesaw through the beauties of the countryside. Great bruin. Guernsey lovelorn.

The erosion of rocks blooms. The world
  that's for you thanks (you) in actuality actuality.
Large broad marks without interruption.
    Things as they fall in the hotel reduce
    the view. This is in the world you
    all add up, re miniature terms of detail.

Sugar, less coffee, a clean towel, the archive.
      All add up to from the minute after after all.
    The theater is less exciting. The shore worn
potable. The erosion of rocks less salt.
      A carnival for posterity is a machine
in its early stages. A clean towel
    pulled out. The theater suggests a house
      a machine. I am irritated by this
contradictious optimism. The world pretends
    to get a fair distance on unshod horses.
The theater shares the optimism of the carnival.

    A conservative year is a suggestion. The mechanical
use of photos yours. Using nails
      reduces the view. Things fall some of the way
      out into the street a new scene. A grid
worn by water from one place to another. The erosion
of rocks, two away. The theater of holes dug for trees.

pandemonium hews
no clouds

wakefulness
is active

one is a statistic
an ideal of exhaustiveness

it meets this
precise redundant limbo

stars of keyholes
laud the rain cloud

shapes sloshing
off an awkward clay

a sea that only scatters
in a halfbox

the gloss of observation
in the dark

the sounds are in the ears
a prima ragged brio

mute water crashes rise
in a cloud

Rain on the macadam quaver ticks.
The lay of the land is armed
with its pattern of occupancy.
Landscape depends on sequel, is romantic ground
in a context of necessity. Polish tinfoil
with pennies and make silver.

Windows upon close inspection swing, medaled
with the setting. Highlights work
back and forth, relocate to swap greenery.
The finished man is horizontal, a cliche.
The watch hand is a pointer
through thick lenses on a setting.
Statues have status in the park.
All one can do is go around them, directed
by the curve. Return to lengthwise.

The tidal throughway from a distance
dispersing everything sloppy, anything
resembling an excessive spell. All that's left
is lambent, like lakes. One misses
the remarkable detail of continuity.
Light devours the visible world.
A slack windsock, sole identified sequence.

The garrulous landscape is stoked
and synoptic; the synonym list
is doggedly on plot, gleaming
in the sunlight, husbanded with enchantment.
The glass on the way down flowers. I did
or am doing in common speech fully informed,
unafraid of repetition in the same person.

BOB PERELMAN

AN AUTOBIOGRAPHY

Everyone keeps shouting in my ears. But rest assured, dear papa, that these are my very own sentiments and have not been borrowed from anyone.

Has the reader ever been madly in love? One does not load up on odds & ends on the chance of their proving useful. The utmost reduction compatible with efficiency is the first & last thing to aim at.

But I am putting off for too long a necessary statement. My mother was a charming woman and I was in love with her. One night, when by chance I had been put to sleep on the floor of her room on a mattress, this woman, agile as a deer, bounded over my mattress to reach her bed more quickly.

In loving her at the age of six (a charming place with handsome horses) I had exactly the same character as now, crusts & air spaces in layers. Bitterly cold wind & low drift. The surface terribly soft. My way of starting on the quest for happiness has not changed at all, with this sole exception: that in what constitutes the physical side of love (it froze hard within a very short time) I was what Caesar would be, if he came back to earth, with regard to cannon & small arms. I would soon have learned, and it would have changed nothing essential in my tactics. I wanted to cover my mother with kisses, and for her to have no clothes on. It was quite usual to feel one side of the face getting sunburned while the other was being frozen. A journey of this kind is no joke.

I abhorred my father. He brought with him memories of how it feels to be intensely, fiercely hungry. He came and interrupted our kisses. Be so good as to remember that I lost her, in childbed, when I was barely seven. You will easily conceive what I have had to bear—what courage and fortitude I have needed to endure calmly as things grew steadily worse between the depots. He came and interrupted our kisses. During the period from November fifteen to February twentythree, he had but one full meal, and that on Christmas day. Even then he did not keep the sense of repletion for long; within an hour he was as hungry as ever.

I always wanted to give them to her on her bosom. Be so good as to remember that I lost her, in childbed, when I was barely seven. She was plump and looked forward to each meal with keen anticipation and an exquisite freshness, but the food seemed to disappear without making her any the less ravenous. The evening meal was pretty, only it froze hard in a very short time.

My father became rather primitive when he was hungry—weakened, hopeless, spiritless; but my mother had an expression of perfect serenity, and, to conclude, she often used to read the *Divine Comedy* of Dante through in the original. Long afterwards, I found five or six different editions in her room which had remained shut up.

We could not joke about food. My aunt dared reproach me with not weeping enough! You can imagine my suffering, and what I felt! Besides, she took no part in love. She thought about it most of the time, and she used to talk about it, but always in the most serious manner possible. As for me, it was with strange feelings that I was 'as criminal as possible.'

I did not experience really severe hunger until I was much too preoccupied with the heavy and dangerous to be able to talk much. Those were silent days. I had been the first to be horrified by the sounds which I had produced. I would get up at 5 A.M. in order to make a start at 7 A.M., and would eat my scanty breakfast that only seemed to accentuate hunger. Then I would describe things in the good days to come.

The 'Wild Roll' was to be the high water mark of luxury. My hand refuses to write. I have been pacing around for a quarter of an hour. If I reduced myself to reasonable limits, I would be unjust to the frenzy of happiness, the excess of happiness. . . The only civilized experience that is akin to it is when one steps unknowingly on the pavement.

Her room remained closed for ten years after her death. No servants entered it. I alone had the key. My father was severely reprimanded. The moisture on his clothes froze hard. He sold them to build his new street and other follies. This ruined him.

"Now we are on board ship," he would say. "We wake up in a bunk, and the first thing we do is to stretch out our hands and get some chocolate, some Garibaldi biscuits, and some apples. We eat those in the bunk, and then we get up for breakfast. Breakfast will be at eight o'clock, and we will have porridge, fish, bacon and eggs. . ." His eyes were sparkling with rage. ". . . cold ham, plum pudding, sweets, fresh roll and butter, marmalade and coffee. At eleven o'clock we will have hot cocoa, open jam tarts, fried cods' roe, and slices of heavy plum cake. That will be all until one o'clock. Nothing can prevent madness."

Here I interrupted him. I said I was never in such a good humor when I was quite unknown. I complained to him of being appallingly hungry, of tragic dreams of getting food to eat, but of never having the satisfaction of dreaming that I was actually eating. Last night I did taste bread and butter. He laughed. "I assumed," he said, "that you would be guided by your common sense and that you would have had more confidence in your father's judgment which you know is so sound, than in your own futile wishes. For lunch we will have Wild Roll, shepherd's pie, fresh baked sodabread, hot milk treacle, pudding, nuts, raisins, and cake. After that we will turn in for a sleep, and we will be called at 3:45, when we will reach out again from the bunks and have doughnuts and sweets. We will get up then and have big cups of tea, and fresh cakes and chocolate creams. Dinner will be at six, and we will have thick soup, roast beef and Yorkshire pudding, cauliflower, peas, asparagus, plum pudding, fruit, apple pie with thick cream, scones and butter, port wine, nuts, and almonds and raisins."

He raised his forefinger. "These seemingly trivial matters may often bring success, honor, and wealth, or, on the other hand, disgrace. At midnight we will have a really big meal, just before we go to bed. There will be melon, grilled trout and butter sauce, roast chicken with plenty of livers, and a proper salad with eggs and very thick dressing, green peas and new potatos, a saddle of mutton, fried suet pudding, peaches a la Melba, egg curry, plum pudding and sauce, celery, fruit, nuts, port wine, milk, and cocoa. Then we will go to bed and sleep until breakfast. We will have chocolate and biscuits under our pillows, and if we want anything to eat during the night we will just have to get it. Trust no one! Keep your medicines! Go to bed early! Do not catch cold! Perspire a little every morning! Be careful in your diet! Good night!"

I spent my life with my grandfather. The dangers I did know were preferable to those I did not know.

By the painful process of forcing my eyelids apart with my fingers I was able to see a little, but the pain was severe. I endured six hours of agony, ending in a good long sleep, from which I awoke much refreshed. By midnight I was walking to the rookery, where I had great fun with the birds.

Bob Perelman 69

MY ONE VOICE

At the sound of my voice
I spoke and, egged on
By the discrepancy, wrote
The rest out as poetry.

Read the books, duets
From nowhere say they speak;
Why not let them. Habitual stares
Leave trees in rearview mirrors.

I came from a neutral point
In space, far from the inside
Of any one head. O say can I
Still see the tabula rasa outshining

That rosy dawn on the near side
Of the genetic code. Doubt,
Thy name is certainty. Generations
Of recordings of the sunrise

Picture the light until the page
Is white and I predict
The present, hearing a future
In the syllables' erasing fade.

GOD

Ay chinga!
Bright sun shines.
God appears.
Down in front!

I want to put
This word here.
The mind at
Its shuffle.

I want to
Hear this word.
Dull person,
Fish fish, water.

HISTORY

The sun shines center stage,
Lights up a material sentence which,
Though visibly complex, is obviously
Not complete. The damage is literal,
One thing no one can argue with.

An endless chain of bodies
Wants to call it home, walking
Along the bases of the buildings.
Having survived the history of ideas
For x number of days does not

Make us ideal readers. Nor
Are we mentioned in the text.
The dead should have known better.
Shrines cry out for affection,
The wounds of Freud competing

With Newton's perfect corpse.
Their thought makes total sense
Until we open our mouths.
Private tongues multiply barely
Audible pleasures. On the books

The sun stands still, a thing
Of beauty. The stopped shadows
Develop moral overtones and these
Are what gets put into circulation.
Gargoyles and church music are one

Of many false doors. Words
Blame objects for lack of effect.
Dreams echo food and housing. The air
Turns dark to bright and back,
Sped up in the brain.

PASTORAL

One person each, out
Into one world, back into many.
The collection, the alphabet. He imitates
Its power, sentiments, antiquity. Scenery
In the form of a dramatic monolog.

She trails out of the present
Both ways, but is sitting
At the table with him. Sprays
Of bay, laurel, and their natural
Interpretations are tacked above them.
Hearts beating. A storm at sea.

Gossip at length, hours
Yoked together, sun shines,
Air presses on their capillaries,
Actions. Desire pronounced and
Punctuated, their minds end
In their senses. Pleasures
Lag across solid bridges.

Time to eat. Light is suffused, revised
Among the letters. Their ears fill
With sounds of the visible world.
Minutes surround them, trees
In the foreground by voice vote.
Their eyes close. It is night.

OCEANOGRAPHY

A small mechanical
device, composed
of the desire

to be a single
substance, sees
the simplified white

bird under
even grey
cloud (lazy

brown dog).
Be quick
(slow) (aloud)

with what I
say. Nobody
can pronounce

all the words
at once (show
stopper). Pull

the plug.
The sea
is all under

the water.
Nothing remains
but the sound,

a public
memorial
to comprehensibility

Looking out
the screen,
segmented light

and dark walks
the space
and speaks.

Calling the
thing to
mind invokes noise.

Small talk
dominates
the seconds

but falls
into step.
The clock ticks

and I impersonate
that motion,
or read word

to word,
marching
straight sideways

out of time,
as if no one
says it,

said it.
Ideas end,
industrial

overflow areas
wither, flowers
dot aimless

square feet.
A pretend king
brings disaster

onto an unlikely
nation, each
day's

continuation
farther
fetched.

Talking jelly
thinks in parsecs
(parsnips)

and feels
proud, humble.
The weather fails

to respond.
Crickets
take up the slack.

To open the mind
too wide
is a discourtesy.

Manners are
no joke.
Laughter is forced

through the sieve
used
to speak

said mind.
The letters
are not

the characters
of perception.
The ancient device

yields an open
book. Repetition
teaches the numbers

one at a time.
I've already forgotten
how to divide.

Cells slip
out of action,
spill, fucking

for attention,
lost in thought.
Night has fallen

(experience) throughout
the area, a big job
effortlessly done

by the matter
at hand.
A plane

sounds, saws
its way through
the windless

air mass,
paroling
the langue.

You've (you) (I've)
got (get) it (me) (you)
bad (all wrong).

Does one find
his or her way
home century

after century,
making the same
sounds mean

the same well
loved, hated (heated)
rooms (thoughts)

that vanish
by definition?
Not to mention

carpet bombing.
Glazed
intelligences defend

the playpen
to extinction.
There will always

be more of them
than us
(Present arms).

But we ourselves,
in random samples
of one or less,

are vastly
unequal and stare
apotropaically

when we pass
in the street.
Punctuation

lights a thicket
from the outside,
but people just

talk, eyes
light up.
Cross purposed

distance must advertise,
travel, raise
expectations, and extend.

Deferred hours bend,
bombed, smashed
at Land's End.

The desire for
analysis invades
the rotting empire.

The hourglass
provokes
the Bert Parks

grin (time
capsule). The mind
goes naturally

to seed,
word of mouth,
gravity feed,

wind twanging
miles of country
phonewire.

A soft core
of destruction breeds
rock solid attitudes

fencing off
the range
civilization

intends to
master at
a glance.

You just can't
tell by looking
or intuition

or experience.
The train
is on

the track.
No more
than a single life.

Is this Earth?
Starship Earth?
Do you read me?

We have to
stay here
this time,

stretch agily
over the
gaps. Great blue

blocks of salt
water. I take
up space, unable,

finally,
not to.
Remote refusals,

meant to avoid
debris, end
stuck, in a room,

somewhere, somewhere
else, or just
outside. Minds

plug holes
in unknowable systems.
Poignant impressions

issue thoughtful
blurs. The survivors
get old quotes,

high prices. Access
to myth is
automatic, layers

peel in the sun.
A named species
of moth

shadowed against
the wall.
A man goes

underground,
boards a train.
That says

anything, seasonal
noise generalized
for effect.

Enhanced sensation
builds, piles cities up
in waves.

Events (the gods)
crash forward as headlines
meter anxiety.

Very close
to shore,
it's over

one's head.
The facts make
an unclosable suitcase.

Each time I
speak, I feel so
incomplete,

whoever you are,
my own
true love,

reciprocal wash
of pronoun
back and forth

faces across.
I, for
example, breathe

water in the air
and a view, colors
blocking the exits.

JEAN DAY

HEAVY CLOUDS PASSING BEFORE THE SUN

Walk this way mudra. A glance. Separation of events:
pads: breeze. Distend or refract in the act of holding back.
After the first mile there is no other. Take it away,
take it away bob. It tears up to see. Once.
Oh yes, Russia. They made say that. Swan
Lake. Inchoate curtain. Just that as a lonely kid.
What to do to make fog light. Don't understand
passing in this unreadable fashion. Mounting another production
of Orphêe. Though harder, the second more interesting than the
    first.
Always subtract. That's not sound, that's not woody guthrie.
Run limbs straight, sic transit arc. To prove this finite and
    unstoppable
fever, find a place to sit, sit. Little sister put your blue dress on,
that everyone should leave. First one direction,
then opposite. Fold cups. Watch out joe. A patch
of censorship. The heart of park central. It is dark of day.
This way before, now slit, slitting. Must with, with must.
To go straight. Learn what it means to receive syllables.

GAS

After this conversation have another
hill, high meadow, stream there. Then
squat in a chair, this V a vector to that smoke
across from the Chevron station.

Where there is pause, rush in.
If a taxi gives kosher jelly, schmaltz.
Your friend is a member of the US Labor Party. Even so,
without sticking your head out the window

sound is. It is possible to go from A to B
and not get trapped. Try being a moorhen or Jane Austen.
Think how it will look when you are really more.
When traffic resumes, it's not night anywhere.

Okay a moment. I have a meadow.
The unit is a comet of meaning as is gas, a glass of milk.
Slow as this instrument is, the labor of parts
makes matter apart from us and money.

The number 13. Swallow a ball of wax
to see how important you are. For the first
few hours the air seems perfumed. Then utterance
throws in, where the modern lake should have been.

PARADISE AND LUNCH

You do that because I will. In the yard parts of us resemble
early sculpture, but only partly. About to go to prison
in fur, extend to rest like no other. I think it was alone the head
backed up for a refill. A little less tender than will. A little
butt. Look but sharp and if it seems dumb, wonder, don't drink.
Smoke two. Plus could make anyone happy. Just keep permuting...
I miss X, the flayings and paychecks we once were. Is that
leather, or is this the knockout supreme? That's funny, I thought
I was the one doing quality control. Certainly there is the motive
sea around us; one look and the lip is fresher for hours.
Though later it turns out merely to be a resort.
The flimsy palms sometimes make it easier to blow it all away;
"in irons" means no wind but perhaps also wholly fossil.
Going and coming we are getting stupider, as matter
expands becomes water; however, this is unacceptable shit
on my glasses. When I started living with you I stopped thinking
about you. What binary stardom: when the old guy wanted the girl
or his sister, he took a cottage and talked about it.
Why *can't* we be rock forever. No end but I'm going nuts
thinking what can't is last. Luster, was it for you last night?
Fueling the ruins of seduction, there's an insistent
objectivity to will or won't, make it or not, live or die.

from TRENCHER LETTERS

D

What I want from truck-driving is friction. After the preface we have the penal code. You understand I'm just passing through. Shut the light to say a story, and you have power. I feel so isolated I could have a baby. What do you remember, his double lunches or the way he pushed? Sweet, meaning wonderful, not tasting of sugar. Getting in bed for his art and out again hitting the clock.

This passion conceived in a dream on the night of the parade. Think of attachment on a high platform with a view of the distant city. As a matter of fact he did want to come in for a drink. Two plateaus. On the way to deities every bathroom has its lipstick. Until she's through with me, exogamy. It's a mistake not to see the converse coming and go with it, but I'm sympathetic; dealing with a man breaks him up like a set of cards, gray and pink. You can read Jeep, Mack, Emanuel Ax (pianist).

A problem is neither good nor bad. I went down to city hall but they were selling 9 hotels. The lobby effect is the rage for flattened affect; back to bed on successive levels now that the yelling has stopped. Not to mention all that high-class stuff—contractual artwork, burdensome consideration cancelling out action. Simultaneous bliss and destruction with cold sprouts.

Our parthenon, an overland route.

F

The print, pronoia. Not immaculate conception, not *our* church service. Susan bought half a dozen things and Sharon brought quite a few things. I think we can go ahead and make Christmas plans; it's what she would have wanted. If she lasts long enough. She looked so nice. Has hysterics again.

I went up to the altar this morning and prayed that this ordeal should soon end, not to be selfish for my sake, but for Gloria's. I hate that freeway anyway. She certainly looks immaculate though. But that's Wednesday night ain't it? No, 80 years earlier. Anyone that wants to can go. You kind of wonder about her husband.

O

We hit the pit to clean up in, the slam shack. I ask if there is anything but your greedy eyes to help the police make marks on us, but soon we are safe again in fake rags heading west of that. Oh Popeye, I can't wait any longer for my pay. That is what *you* say with a tree standing through you.

Stand back, the elan is about to become a nail. We beg for the restrictions of the past to sit on since the new ones are so hard; it's a question of guessing how to act in the middle. I think you can think at the same time you're hauling ass, so demand compensation!

A pun makes time. You missed some of that grayish stuff over there but so did I. If you will drop dead I'll know you mean it; then we will be alive and dead together. You're coming in very clearly now.

I work. My apple. Nuts.

Q

I came all this way for a single glass of water.

If you are dissatisfied with this product you have no alternative but to boil it up and smack it. Tails beat house, grunts outside screen. I see a name and it is everything. A rebus is a disturbed place. I hiss. Thirty sails, running from a life in Kansas. Vertical construction stacks up. Pileated woodpeckers go out for cartoons, out of scale. The dip on top of the ridge. Dotty deserves it. His dog does. Watch your elders consult their compacts. Arthur Rimbaud was like that. No, *you* are Raymond.

I want the world to cough like me.

Wash hands, hair, underpants. Hot up fire. All are mothers, trying to be better. At the image of the runcible spoon sky, knowledgeables flip through their magazines to say what *that* is. Empty on one side, revelation on the other. That wasp describing your space is your companion. I think we have a chance for great happiness or do you want to be made low? The air is churning and below me. Identify *me*, dead birds. Iambic construction. Back home, Providence.

DAVID MELNICK

from PCOET

1.

thoeisu

thoiea

akcorn woi cirtus locqvump

icgja

cvmwoflux

epaosieusl

~~cirtus locqvump~~

a nex macheisoa

33.

seta

colecc

puilse, i

canoe

it spear heieo

as Rea, cinct pp

pools we sly drosp

Geianto

    (o sordea, o weedsea!)

73.

meom-a

74.

meom-b

from MEN IN AIDA, BOOK ONE

Men in Aïda, they appeal, eh? A day, O Achilles!
Allow men in, emery Achaians. All gay ethic, eh?
Paul asked if tea mousse suck, as Aida, pro, yaps in.
Here on a Tuesday. 'Hello,' Rhea to cake Eunice in.
'Hojo' noisy tap as hideous debt to lay at a bully.
Ex you, day. Tap wrote a 'D,' a stay. Tenor is Sunday.
Atreides stain axe and Ron and ideas 'll kill you.

     The stars' foe at eon are radix unique make his thigh
Leto's and Zeus's son. O garb a silly coal o' they is
Noose on a nast rat-honor's sake, a can, a lick, on toe delay.
A neck, a ton, crews in a time, & ceteretera.
Atreides oh girl tit, oh aspen-y as Achaians.
Loosen 'em us, tea, toga, trap her on tap (heresy a boy now).
Stem Attic on anchors, in neck cable. Oh Apollo on us.
Crews say oh Anna skip trochee, less set to pant as Achaians.
A tray id, a them, a list, a duo, 'cause met to rely on.
"A tray id I take. I alloy a uke, nay me day's Achaians.
Human men theoi doyen Olympia dome attic on teas.
Ech! Pursey Priam's pollen, eh? You'd eke a Dick his thigh.
Pay Dad, am I loose! Ate a pill. Lent Ada a pen to deck his thigh
As oh men idiots who unneck a bowl on Apollo on her."

     Nth alloy men panties up you fame as an Achaian.
Aïda is thigh the aerie a gay eagle a deck thigh a boy now.
Alec Atreides Agamemnon and Danny the mo'
All a'cackle, sappy, eh? Cracked her on dippy mouth. On a telly.
"Me say, gay Ron, coil lay sin. Ago pair ran you sick, a hue
In undy. The noun tea hystero naught is you to.
Me now toy. 'Oh,' cries me, skipt Ron & stem math theoio.
Tend to go loose. Opera ink eager as he pays in.
He met a Ron, a Yoko, in our gay Tell, loathe the pat trays.
Is tone a boy? Go men in gay. A moan, lick, oh sandy ocean.
All if I'm me, merit. Is Esau Terah's husk in a Yea?"

     Horse fat. Eddie send ogre. Ron keep it at a moo, though.
Bay dock yond pair a thin, a pole, a flow is boy oh the lass is.
Pole odd a pate, a Pa, new the key on Hera though gay rye is.
Ah, baloney! (A knack, Teton-y.) You come most to call Leto.

94 David Melnick

"Clue the mew are goo, rot ox. Hose creasin' am fib a bake
        Cass.
Kill, Auntie's a Thane! Ten idiot if he Anna says.
Some in the Huey. Poe tit, toy car, a yente, a pin. Knee on your
        rep, sir!
A yea day: potty, toy cat, a pee on a Mary Achaia.
Tower roan aide, aye gaunt ode. Ah! My Creon on nailed door.
'Tis saying Dan I am a dog, rue as aye Sibyl lessen."
        Hose fat you commie nose toad, igloo, Phoibos Apollo.
Bay deck at Olympus, carry none. Come on us, Oscar.
Took some more sin, eh? Horn 'em fair, a fay at afar, a train.
Ache lanks, and are oh a stirrup, oh moan, come on all you.
Ought toke in net & toes. Oh day & nuke tea, oh egos.
Is it a pity pan? Newton neon met. Add ye on ache-y.
Dane aide day clang, again he'd argue Rae. Oh boy-oh!
Oh Rae as men pee wrote on. A poke at o.k. keen as our goose.
Out are épée et out toys. Sibyl loss, a cup you Cass if yes.
Ballet and a purée, neck you on Guy on totem, may I?
In name mar men. A nest rat on o.k. Tokay La Theoio.
Tea deck a tea dagger and deck a less a toll lay on Achilles.
Toga rip if Rae sit, take a thee, 'll you call on us Hera?
Kay debt. 'Oh guard!' A noun note tear at knees, cunt as Erato.
Heed épée Honegger, then oh may gay Rae stay again on toe.
Toys see Dan is Tom and Osmet, if he Poe dares accuse Achilles.
"A tray a day, noon am maypole in plank. Then dazzle you.
Apse upon a stay scene, eh Ken? Then atone gay fug. Oy men!
Aide day oh mope pole lay most a damn Mac high low i' most
        Achaians.
All a gay day Tina man tin a ray, oh men he hear ya.
Ache I on a rope alone, guy guard on a wreck, day oh say sting.
Hose cape pee, oh tit, toes on echo sat. O Phoibos Apollo.
Eat tar O you coal lace. Happy men fate: I ate hecatombs.
Hi Ken, 'pose our known knee says 'I gon' tit to lay on.'
Bowl o' tea, Auntie? Ah sauce! Hey me nap, a log on a moon,
        aye."
        Ate I a goose, a punk? A tar is a tot toy, Sid a nasty.
Calchas Thestorides, soy on a pole. Lo, no ochre his toes.
Hose Eddie tight. Tea on the tatters, summon a pro. Tea on tac—

Ky nay, yes, say gay. Sat a quai on Ilion is so.
Ain't he a man to sin in! Ten high, pour a Phoibos Apollo.
Whose pin, you pro? Neo nag, a race, a toe? Guy met taping.
"O Achilles, kill, lay, I Amy, Dee feel lame. 'Myth,' he says, 'thigh.'
Men in Apollo, a nosy cat, table ate our ('Enact!') toes.
Tiger agone areo. So decent they o.k. my emotion.
Hey men, my prof Ron, a pacin' guy, cares in a rake's seine.
Egg are oh yummy. Andrews call o' semen hose Meg a pant on.
Argue on, critic. All high pay, then tie Achaioi.
Gray song Arbus ill use Hot Tea Co. Set I and Rick Harry.
Apse ergo art echo long gay guy ought to mark, ate a Pepsi.
All at a quai met a piss then a cake, a ton, a prat, a less see.
In stay the sin, nay, oy Sis you dip. Ross sigh, Amy 'sow' says."
    Toned a Pa, may Beau men, as prose a fib, odes, as 'Oh cuss
        Achilles.'
"Tar says a small ape ate the oh pro pee on hot tea oyster.
Ooh ma' Gar! Apollo on a deep hill, oh no Tess Sue, Calchas.
You come on us, Danaans, sit thee up, rope your son, a fine ace
        ass.
Ooh 'tis same you zone toes, sky a peak: Tony, Dirk, all men.
        Oh, you?
Sea coil lace spar Annie you see bar Rae as a care as a boy say.
Some pant on Donna all nude and Agamemnon nigh pace.
Hose noon pollen are his toes a guy own uke a tyin' eye."
    Guy to Teddy thar' says a guy you'd a mantis a moo moan.
"Oh tar a gay you coal lace, a pea, ma'am fit tie you the heca-
        tombs.
Allen neck a rhetor rose. Oh net a mess, Agamemnon.
Ode apple, you say, the got Reggae uke up a deck sat a boy now.
Two neck are all gay: Ed, Ken. Neck Kay ball us aid at id (oh say).
You'd oh gay preen Danaan nigh key alloy gonna pose he.
Preen gap up at rip a load o' men, ay a lick up it accu-rain.
Opry a Tina nap and a boy no nag ain't here in hecatomb bane.
Is cruisin' to take Ken mini-lassy many peppy toy men?"
    A toy, a goose, a punk cat, a raise. It a toy said a nasty.
Hey Rose Atreides, you rue crayon Agamemnon?
Ach! Noumenous men. News deem a gay friend of some female
        lie nigh.

'Pimple land toes,' said Day. 'High puerile a lamp at town take
        ten.'
Cal can top pro 'tis cock oh so men nose prose say pay.
"Man, tick cock. Cone new pope Poe tame me toke Rae you on
        a pass.
A yea toy, take cock, is too full of fresh men Tuesday.
Is the lone doubt a tip o' ape? A set oh suit at a laser's.
Cane un-end a now, sith Theo protein nag gore, you ace.
Hose day étude in a cusp in necky bowl, us all gay, a tea o.k.?
Hoo neck, ego coo race, crusade does. Oh clap peña.
Ook Ethel on decks as thigh, up pay Polly boo loam my out ta'en.
Eek, he a can! Guy Garrick Clytemnestra's probable 'ah.'
Coo rid yeas all loco, he pay you the nest, he carry on.
Oh dame as oh deaf, you in out, tarp prayin' as oh titty air ya.
All a guy hose i' the load o' men, I pal in eight toga men on.
Pool loam ago lawn sowin' he men night, eh? A pole his thigh.
Out are Emmy, gay Roz, out ticket toy mass at opera may Hojo's.
Are gay? Own a gay Roz? Toss you a pay, you day. O.k.!
Loosened a garter gay panties oh my gay Roz her cattail lay."

MICHAEL PALMER

ECHO
(texte antiparallèle pour Pascal Quignard)

which resounds. Re-sounds. Where first would
follow. The letter he had lost reappeared in
his palm. Identity was the cause. Not that the
word spoken had been heard. Not that a word
spoken can be seen, even partially, traced
against the screen. Language copies him in its
listening, tracing his imperfect copy. Which
re-sounds. Echoes briefly. The rustling a
wall transmits by interference. For example:
raised both arms above his head. And said:
a letter a letter can be reckoned with. Rustling
as of an article of clothing such as a dress or
green dress. An even greyness as of a page,
recording events. The subject is this, rustling
at the moment of enunciation, to be reckoned
with. Not that the words thus raised above the
head and turned into hills. Could possibly. Be
recognised in his own misunderstanding. After
the talking is done a kind of attention to each
mark, an injured identity traced against the
screen. Soweto-Miami. Cremated beside the river.

which sounds (sounded) different at night. Not
that the words reassembled among hills, exactly,
where there were none. A rustling seized him,
the history of cloth and wind, hedgerows. Or
windows above rivers, cornflowers and forget-
me-nots, an even blueness as of a page, a failure
at translation. The distant past visited and we
whispered her well. Heard prior to itself and

dressed as a shadow. Not that the words re-
sembled hills exactly, hidden among them. Soweto-
Miami as of a particular light, a quality. Hills
where there were none, only sounds. Body of per-
haps a dog, afloat, the first ten notes, major
then the minor mode. Echoes an attention.

as if preceding, preceded by, itself, depth of
the forest. The subject is this, disregarded,
story of cloth and wind or the space between
events.

misunderstood as a measure of distance. It
takes no time in that sense, repeats nothing,
figures the shape of the flames. Gesticulate.

a failure of translation. In sleep the language
he spoke was one he didn't know. Waking it
sounded the same. Waiting there it seemed a
succession of names, a level field of things in
constant motion, exchanging identities.

neither followed nor following. Two are there as
she counts to one, to one and one then three five
eight defining the spiral, to double sevens to
begin, to instauredness. Left arm and right and
the figures like the fire. There must be a
different metric, a gesture and that's all, this
this and so on, concomitance, like writing but
it's not a writing, the pieces actually are.

across water. Soweto-Miami with no distance, the
figures the fragments of a picture. She refused

Michael Palmer 99

the explanation before it was made. Who (pre-
vious to speaking) woke against a door. Right
arm detached these past weeks, greyness modi-
fied at each stage.

This I saw and said at once.

Case where he has visions of his dead friend.

in gesturing there. The letter he had lost was
the cause, an imperfect copy spoken among hills
or reassembled there.

The letter he had lost was the cause, a dead
friend traced against the screen. They are
listening to songs while waiting for morning.

Forgetting the name as it sounds, an unknown
city, the journey never begun. Letter (book)
deafened by echoes, figure (form), an even grey-
ness indicating the river.

What we call depth then, of forest, mirror,
conviction etc, voiced as fake history. As
morning is said to offer new hope or no hope
in what must be or may have been a court-
yard where photographs substitute for trees,
benches and walls, each detail perfectly re-
produced from the story he was told about how
it all would eventually appear. Thus the severed
head is an object of polite discussion and
necessary to the tableau like the polychrome
statuary and exotic flora we admire more than
words can say.

She claims they are trying to fuck their way
into history and so to change it, and for a
moment we both do and do not agree. The river
in the background is muddy, the lamenting
figures the same shape as the flames. The
subject, disregarded, is the frequency of
the oscillation, the coincidence of cloth and
wind, hedgerows. She discovered the pen be-
neath her bed.

of interest because unspoken: to the eye over
water; softly repeated; erasure in the naming;
'many-tongued'.

She discovered the pen and returned it to him.

disappeared then, leaving a voice behind un-
like her own.

They do both agree and disagree, the numbers
and voices projecting above the ostinato figure,
violinist the father's son, lawns crisp and
green, indifferent, the visible world, auricle
of the ear cool, fresh, rough, succulent to
the touch.

She claims they want to agree but disappear
while speaking, brief redness of history softly
repeated, the severed head a substitute for
trees intended as an aid to memory.

She claims they want to eliminate history, legs
turned to smoke, carriage passing a row of
columns said to be endless because it does end.

A very narrow but not very tall glass-domed
house with two entrances. Nodded as if she be-
lieved what I'd said, carriage rocking on its
worn springs, a constant trembling.

So it is equivocal and precedes its beginning.

I over there, he-she here, table and lamp.

is brought forward from, toward the eye. Water's
moment as of blocks, uninvited, a one-hinged
sound that sleep recited, what he was of, half-
yellowed now by leaves, as of blocks carved
clumsily and set afloat, stairs cast in dark-
ness, curtain held tightly shut then drawn a
little apart, a redness to history reflected
wherever words might turn to talk and tell of
a mirrored door.

which to be so must remain closed?

and so and so. He told her what she'd once
told him.

Dear Janet, When I want to get away from it all
I pick up one of your novels and—presto—
mission accomplished!

Whether dreaming is thinking about something.
Whether the eyelids moving are seeing.

which to be so must remain closed?

naked to waist with back turned, arms enfolding
head, world large by lamplight rolling us even
in sleep, a redness to the story they'd been
told.

He painted her beside herself as a likeness,
and each face seemed identical with the one they
had known.

She claims they are trying to erase the story by
repeating it exactly as it was told. Thus clema-
tis, tea, rhubarb, Indian fig, water and its
cognates, of worlds twice seven, wheat and corn.
Thus table and lamp (or desk and light), sheets
(or leaves), wordless talk, gestural dreams
empty of meaning, palms in paramuthetic wind.
This with my own words she told him.

And told him again.

ECHO
(alternate text)

The two poles. We didn't disagree
that meetings should be begun

upon our foreheads—slender
memories had been put to death

in the proper style, encounters
with forests, mountains

and fields, creatures returning
from islanded sleep

said nothing
nervous and unattended

as we wept. This habit of yellow paper
is recent and without effect

upon our foreheads—slender
runners outstripped them

and said nothing
as we wept. What

time of day now
might say differently

'this weapon is invisible,' or
this name so pronounced

with lips inconceivably apart
has been lost

within its sound,
might then among the *llaneros*

recite tales of night rides
that take no time

or nothing if not time
to tell. Visitors gathered there to hear

it said—backward
it's true—that

he and she were
this and this, not

any one shade exactly
not any one thing

outlined by its clarity
against the milky glass.

At a given moment lovers pass
in complicated hats

the wind will later take back.
The bedstead is iron, with-

out ornament and not mine. Its
fading is what recalls it

to them, an imaging of the rings
of fractured ice

coating volute and column
overhead. Yet some of those

paths were like maps, green
for no reason, pale

orange where no one had been.
Knowledge is empty claimed the swaying bridge.

She recognised the voice as her own
resounding in the damp hall

though the rest,
what the words now said

again and again,
seemed entirely different.

ECHO
(a commentary)

which in a dry season might
begin or might precede its
beginning with a list
of truths self-evident: these
clouds (these crowds) you
now see are permanent
and fixed; the arboreal splendor, the
meadows and chalk cliffs
are artificial, devised
of wired concrete and paint
by a developer in the forties
and therefore beautiful; he took
three breaths for every one of hers;
the sun's chariot hurried backward
in its path to a point
exactly overhead and two months before;
the child had trouble speaking;
war was once again in the air;
the space program was to blame for the
snow; nervous
brides waved
weapons in the air; passions
and sensations succeed each other; I
stumbled; I recognised Bugs Bunny;
the darker one had not yet
closed her eyes; weight of a mass
of fair hair; below
a certain temperature the pen
would not write; below
them lay a square
filled with soldiers and statues;
the road north from the city
parallels the river; some
laughed and turned their backs;
enclosed were seven songs;

Michael Palmer   107

the letters grew bolder;
heat, cold, light shade;
the key broke off in his hand;
they lived beneath the streets
to evade certain death; the name
began with a *L* or possibly an *R*;
he scored the loaf at each day's portion;
the distribution of brightness oscillates;
bells mark points in space;
an odor of sulphur penetrated the room
though the windows had been carefully sealed;
one could see the outline of a movement
there; was I the source of such dreams
without meaning; actual
dancers traced against the ceiling;
a bluish violet; echoes
as of such voices
which once had claimed to be real;
a city then they would later imagine
pendant to the west like a jet bead
except empty; the rose she called *cette*
apparition sanglante, cette image;
the apple falls straight down
injuring thousands; we mounted the scaffold
at his unspoken invitation;
a liquid darkness there;
figures lost among the bands of light
came slowly forward; a duplicate
of herself encountered in passing
nodded and disappeared; it remains
visible above the narrow shore;
they are visible against the shore;
the forgotten word for waves; hazelnut
and monkey-flower; the key first
spoken of; wide azure borders.

LARRY PRICE

LOCAL MOTIONS

Simple weight, as in "declarative bank buries words."

Present generates "apparatus drops car."

Uphill may be "content is credit."

Inflated but miniature head of bed reflects distance as "compression softens footsteps."

Decide (elbow on table) agree (silence without gall).

Original background "repaired" by information finds rhythm in words "grid, aboriginal."

Apes comes inside for relics.

Formed from without is "clothing."

Past generates "that picture" must be "coded body at rest."

Inserts arrow in trunk complies with "quotes just multiply."

Start with numbers up to "doesn't blur, shrinks."

Door generates "can't say" or "found so fall."

Body generates "denotes with but commerce whom."

Remote shoe nailed to chair, or as is said: more future.

An ordinary empty room.

The name is true in ordinary language by being the curve of an emptied room.

"I" generates "cords mesh" equals "suitcase, sequential sound."

Raises ears to irritate traveling companion.

Stillness sequence.

Paper crumples, sips of water, glass ringing against pitcher.

Passive generates "tangle means speaker" changes to "embeds margin."

Epidemic says "praising stage claims closet."

Plural generates "but not meant."

There is speech as prominently "that word again."

What can be said proves "forgotten in frame."

There is reason simpler than "author takes stand."

Mental barrel collects risk of rain.

To satisfy the functions of "prime" knee-deep in the bog.

Observation about name natures.

Immobile of "speech steals, mind strays."

Habit becomes the weapon of a party.

Singular generates "equal but contrary."

One is not one generates "property toward combines example."

One couldn't catch the words, so backstage rivalries continue.

Giving the clock to support one's musical equal.

No room is to "thrown in the river" as "storage teaches something twice."

More landscape says nothing.

Figurative hand, boot, cup.

Self-contradiction is enzyme.

Active generates "rebel, epoch, house in which the family, borrows breach."

Argues "think screen."

Passive generates "limit" equals "just a mess."

Mechanisms of "fixed" and "legend."

Lighted rooms seen through coded uniforms.

John is John.

Would be "this movie" as if "apply thumb for answer."

Critical mass turns to physical love.

Term suggests door.

Appetite causes work.

Folding the map end to end for a view of the ideal city.

"Unattached, the only alternative is to accept the movement."

"Random pomp" from archives motoring by, meaning "think round, think thing."

A hand takes hold.

A bolt is a straightened factory.

Exactly recognizable would be telescopes fold into perfect cubes.

Building blocks partition is "beam, basic side of foot."

Tar trembles.

Stop generates "coincide."

Size fits ground.

"Don't answer" generates "think in noise."

The sentence "solid object" or "holds no opposite."

Odd generates "would be node" means ex- can't fly.

Unidentified fingerprints veer through discarded laboratory objects.

North generates "trope spins on blind grade."

People to a parable.

Each piece is impact.

Turn finds transform matter into mood "gang up."

Up generates "fat terms parking fantasy."

Reconciles code for package in store.

Head shrugs.

Tones gain skin.

Television is minutia quick as water into 1950, sex-starved facts sponging up panic.

Mouth paints map on hand means "one's figment is the hint to leave."

Appetite under "fundamental leaves no room" happens to lost cities: irregular forms empty without being possible.

A room empties standing still.

Table generates pretext separates "somebody is talking."

Surge of press generates "not" generates "and what" so wipe hands on disguise.

Breathe yields "fall on the referee" and "millions call species theory."

Past connects fatigue.

Authority impersonates program notes.

Opposite generates seamless categories roll back colonies.

Annul links "arguing exercise self deludes" to "nature gets hollow."

Insatiable technique braves work.

The verb is language breaking in pieces.

Its truly fuse calls this "cutting room out of the machine."

Telephone rings with centrist "pick up the garbage."

In generates ruthless strum.

Space jumps into "pull uses, solves core."

Get the book comes up ardent term, freight term.

Conversation much as things but institutions fill "with."

Present generates "change organs."

Calls it "pick up paste, palace, throne."

Polis is "peel in writing."

Engines mark table sound, table word.

Rags lay on sermons.

Curve generates "brawl comes home."

Self-styled reads lakeside mileage of right beam.

Carboniferous declares intercept "am I" of builds building.

Through generates all this realist ought.

It generates use generates "mix farm" generates "element, street, anticritic."

Storage gauge of "then they sleep" seems "button foot to born rudder, last stop."

So pillar storm means "breed lawyers."

Neural classic ring, crowbar assures hand, foot thought almost anyone, him.

Most generates "model in commonsense" is "come back, cubist neighborhood."

Short stride avoids up.

Camouflage appropriate squashed semaphore than single descriptive tool.

Automatic thermometer means too old as in "see sleep make traffic."

Daily frames "daily hardly moves."

Window with "de-fuse" confirms "own property."

Body opens empire meaning "cryptic surface in our said."

That secret adage of design expands "behind nothing must wedge."

Think nothing says nothing into proxy making definitive "crossed out."

Bone generates "new science" reads "don't budge" on purely sentimental or parasentimental "eclipse club."

Only a tiny proportion are crooks.

KIT ROBINSON

ON THE CORNER

I want things.
You hear birds.
The heat is on.
Someone driving.

They have theories
to place facts
in an order.
They prove useful.

You all come back now.
He is the third person
to come in here
to answer the question.

Or she is
wary of his
possessive assertion
of theoretical fact.

Pages turn.
Why does the sound of them
credit such attention.
What listens to one is.

Steps on the floor.
He is absorbed in
his activity, apparently
typing something.

Imagine travelling
to different parts
of the world.
Jumps off boat.

Light blue map water.
Would money be available
on trees. Imagine work
or criminal exploit.

The prison house
of Latin. Pig latin
's granma. Hear tap
water drawn upstairs.

Present technology
porcelain punctuation
associative principle
pinholes via Joe Spence...

Writing writes itself.
I am not an animal.
I remember movies.
This is not an example.

Who needs obscure poetry.
What is the price
of cola product.
Why is reading such.

Now can anyone tell me
what question
I am asking you
said the teacher.

The sun goes down
into the town's
back pocket
like a figure of speech.

She calls her mother.
The other draws signs
at a table.
These persons are rhymable.

I is the other.
Having said that
is an ancient construction.
He split.

We live in a house.
I live in a room.
You stepped out of a dream.
You could have fooled me.

They made all kinds of money.
The long green. Great!
if you are reading this
in an airport.

Reader, writer, how
does the poem go.
Inner ear and eye
take a vacation.

I want to work.
He plays out the line.
You've seen this before.
So we meet again.

TRIBUTE TO NERVOUS

bottle-neck
oh I'd
humor my
behemoth!
tales
take
powder
pills
set sea
ordinarily
arbitrary
time of arrival
estimated as
The Channel
"The World's Greatest Assortment!"
ORANGE RICE
ATLANTIC OCEAN
The Novel
part of a trilogy
after an episode
based on fact
of Dante's Inferno
in London
in 1920
& so
snow falls
deep snow
further off
the train passes
behind a red temple
in the interval
is a correspondence
like across an arc
triumphant tranquil
mechanical take
all round
on the roofs

Kit Robinson 119

SEVERANCE

how it goes
is out. A really
hand hampered
negative in the
yes, I would say
narrow margin
and comes up again.
If you, the way
affects me. That's
say. What's really
weird is no big
surprise. I
think that much
for something to do.
Talk and I
too. The connection
generic or commercial
Central Square like
bounce sounds outside
building upside
corner of the painting.
put it out. But I
interrupt. Precise
measure of the rut,
constricted apperture.
predicate to right
Dust bowl pipe & jacket
effort music total
at the top of
besides the horse.
colonials. The days
tangent off to
unit gardens. A
rhythm clinches the
ace. Near pen art
I didn't. The river

nice hear. Otherwise
quiet or pumped gas
station tower there
bird level. A
rain on the back
town where all the
signs. By this
sound a rear wall
tuned to seven
ten cents in part
car strap. See
you there. I
gotten a thing,
all right here.

THE SEPARATENESS OF THE FINGERS IN TRANCE

O how righteous, X, are all your days!
Earth blue jag scrapes heaping love glove,
Harsh descent drubbing puffball in
Wind blowing a scrap of paper against hot green.
The subject, meanwhile, of some interest at eye level

Vibration's masses door away, trembling
Thick with garbage and the dust of stars.
Flag steady. Heart of the minute.
O it is an interesting afternoon
Amid general hubbub ("Mambo!"), touch of cold gringo scrotum

Like a truck through tiny lapses.
I am remote. Sky been to dusk aflutter. I drank.
Consolidate the Harvest of Exact Calculations!
With nothing to do for three months
Loudspeaker jabber over white-clad Louie Louie

Smooth morning troops hasten vertical.
We asleep, Jesus up. Sky the stuff open safely.
Stand back five paces and blow white side wall,
As light flickers from a point with abandoned machinery.
("I want to talk to you about that second Louie. . ."

She makes my heart work. Silence.
Dazzling puffs in station undertone,
Black rubber riddled & strewn. Sun. Drink.
The powers of speech are returning the ticket.
"Since when?" "Since right now.") is walking in.

Word thought all words white: back here and back back in.
And across the border, through the bad areas of the city
Sexual Copper. "Get off of my property."
Finance, strict back fast. My skin is dark
At a moment's ungainly notice. Sprinkled with water.

Back eye gets game born. Noodle grove at 28 km.
And you do not like this very much. So Far. The car

There's water on the parade grounds.
My head large and my clothes are nowhere.
Here is my corpse and there sits my patient mastiff,

The road itself looks like something that could talk
Stops at a house. Car bird finish is hand.
I, though out played daily, by stars simply outrun alone,
I'm pre-habit. My nails are plectra
Andante. Loathesome magma of my pre-

And tell you which way to go, through green fields
Empty, it still carries the message. How many
Have learned at states' noise to field our machine head.
Along flightless birds of rain and moan habitude
Supposed and double sanctum stands to reason a day.

And trees, like a stray dog, to the canyon floor
Times have you heard an officer question a dog?
I prime freely what today consigned is here accorded surface,
Scuttled in favor of pinions surmounting eyesight
One and the same day in many places at the same time

And still not separate from itself, sky the limit.
Hang then above house tops. Place then lacks up.
As some drift off when lights are low mine does
You might as well spread a sail over a number of people.
I see what's that you say, recall in cold up tops,

Still emit faint glow over glass near empty and head
Enter above on pressure, place one foot up.
Have long heart, bald air, the sky has a tree in it.
Golden apples of our summer's work fumbling in the backseat
The green canoe-like beef tasted salty for days after.

Strong hat waves, waves motorcycles have anti-ravaged,
The western basins of the great continental chain.
"Into pitch darkness the stairs twisted and. . ."
Top back all 100 lights, red filters,
Bobbing high above what I suppose (light fog) to be

VERDIGRIS

The sign is a raw shape. People river. Space lights up the porch. Dust clouds the window. Ashes break down into sky. A bird flies parallel to slope of roof. Wires hang at a like angle. Comings and goings are frozen in the new room. Wind rooms in the street. Business gets complete thoughts down on tape.

Writing breaks off at mid-letter. Sound resumes. Shirttail. Waves heap themselves at your stone feet. The life of facts is undone in a day. That it organizes itself to work will identify the formality of the office. Three girls unite against a midsection. Paste-on stars glow in the dark. Bare legs, asleep on the floor.

Whatever became of thinking in a downpour meant a light on the stairs. Alternation. Big pattern. A shot full of holes. See-thru. Broken, weak, servile, sentimental, clawing at air. I'm seeing to you. Saying the number two to make it round. Grey white dock. Electron city.

The art of falling. There's more of a line there than you could let out. Trading fours. Candlestick and empty frame in the mirror Jack jumped. Squeeze yr knees into these. She listened for the sun to wake the birds. Things came to her indirectly by way of an echo from a canyon wall or the side of a ship. The telephone woke her thru the wall. Political characters are held up by signs. Exposure is an enclosure.

Journalism is the tip. An iceberg depicted on postage stamps is set adrift. Edges, x's, zig-zag lightning, rips, wakes, cracks, canyons open on fact plains. Cool damp day fills in between Oakland and a chest of drawers, so I'm left to my own photos for a series of correspondences, cooking and picking out curtains. Clean lines. My vision is ok. Sound affects thinking.

124 Kit Robinson

TRIAL DE NOVO

The writer is a mirror, the writing is a crack. Copy shop. Air surrounds the armed forces. Birds pierce the stillness. Notes scale down into rhyme. A song goes straight to the heart. Words said do later too. Off and on a feeling is stopped by a new tune. Words tone down the street. History repeats itself onto a master.

Change now tomorrow is another different day. Senses assume. Supports. Rave reviews crash against the steps. Lifted from water the infant knows less than it did. Workers organize the workplace by and for themselves. Jars light up from bugs on a state map. The light from the stars is a mine. Cloth flat on a shoulder.

People don't know what they're thinking about for a half a minute. Polarity. Grillwork. A blue flame. Audible. Quick, thin, digital, hot, seizing right to acute. I'll be expecting you. Repeating the tune to a song on the window. Red drayage. Levee town park.

The bird impressionist. There's more to that line than meets the ear. Rhyming notes. Empty earth and full sky in the water follies proscenium. Accommodate yourself to this slum. She pays attention to the motors. What arrives comes little by little or all at once. A hole in the room holds the room in place. There may not be a car, but the mediator is laid bare. Place rhyme here.

Relief is supple. Politics is business in a taxi. The analyst is a fellow traveler. Cues, carpets, horns, hides, sounds at the bottom of the basement stairs. Holding my breath I air out the curtains which separate me from my neighborhood counting the current. Deal the climbs. When I see the glory. Sounds of a dime are hits.

Kit Robinson   125

One story leads directly to next. The deluded Don is a perfect cipher. Any reeds I office they start with greater care. The machine missed a stitch on this page. Corn dogs of ancient Britain. Lonesome whisper blow. Still laughs from a wake across the street. Sentences break. Down to material.

Plane noise more than it lets on. "Then how about our position?" Changes are infinitesimal or imagine a bird. Around the point rocks back growing light. The news's continuous, broken to bits. Keep active mind on long trips. The slogan is a model for how to write. You are engaged in the half of it.

A chill came over the freight. A brick wall registers to race. Spokes twirl in foreground. Angles are cut in the sky when I live and work. What music shows thru double numbers. Wheels make showers that draw nowhere. Player piano roll scored by flight, birds above a west end theater.

Downstairs for a move. Animal spaces when staring into light we think. Complications are swept away by the foreground police. I reached for another, thinner slice of pie. Knit sweat.

Belly over arse sidewise. Time between bubbles. The fourth makes these lines in a song. Noon habits clay bank hours in a collection. Red cleavers made this table. Square holes form its ironclad surface. Wood laughs at facts because it's grooving. The light! end of side.

Clam falling, punk falling. Flame blackens brick. Ash breaks down into sky. It's wet out. Corrogated cardboard baffles. He pulled himself up by word of hand. Going thru the door he found himself

One gunshot leads immediately to two or three or four. The casual bystander is a shoe-in for a witness. A book of photographs called evidence from different files. Agreement as to number can be problems. La Moore says Johnny Alexander popped her in the snoot. Heart in sweet surrender. Slipped the gun into a brief case and walked back into the Tishman Building. A well-dressed woman. Up to no good.

Will will out another day being equal. Say something's made in Japan. Runover. I can only be responsive up to a point. A man becomes an infant again. Language organizes the world by and for itself. Alcohol consumes the space between California and Florida. In the light of my stars the stars. Pullover on soft shoulder.

A fever melts the tracks. A wing stays on air as a retainer. Gears mesh in background. Often I wake at peace with the earth in my gloves. That fingers push keys is a must. Darts tumble to moving target. Pictorials displace time and a half, go unnoticed until after an audience.

Up in back. Great to be borne on lives vicariously hospitable. Simplicity can hardly wait to take the floor. I checked the agenda for crabs. Eyes ring.

Pants zip up from ankle. Train time to stand stationary. The third is urge. Day parts stack up in an adverb. Warm bodies built this bed. Wide wheels roll it down the hill. Sound backs up light up to a point. The end of the line side.

Scorpio Lucifer rising rising. Rats on fire. Patch a story together. Air is a different color. Science and memory in a box. She wrote every note of it. She opened the door to the office, went in, and

Kit Robinson   127

in another room, itself with a door in the far wall. Don't listen to this music the music seemed to be telling him. The world is made. It's a made thing.

Elements of style show thru successive layers. Memory conditions rhyme. Interrogation aces line the precinct with scripts. If I were an oval no noise would come from the other side of the yard. A light bulb screws in slowly, lights up all at once. General electric patterns in a landscape. Stave the remaining heat off forks of lightning while I'm out. Range sequins. I inaugurate sleep.

Diagonal cross-hatch yields a diamond field. Numbers identify which parachute is falling from which balloon. Our first snow had to push wet light across the page. Cobalt to magenta, pea green to pink against space. Spear Street Towers. Be collected. To work push all of this out of the way.

If you can describe it why do it. Cross-bred strains dot the map with an I. If these lines were longer I'd write them. What reason could I give to you. Singing: I've been far away. Pine cuts sky in three. Diagonal.

Of x of. Shoelaces, table, wood, the metaphors are all mixed up. Walnuts, paper, leather, talks sound back of a wall. The phenomenal field is history. A gear box is to shift speeds. I ran upstairs to write this then back down to pour coffee. Dreams perforate a waking state. People grow larger, take on more dimension.

Home from the war, the war at home. Revolving door gives onto electric eye, stableboy statuette. Way back in a cave shadows move on a wall. Shoulders take shape with greater care. Let's talk about Silver. I dig the trio sides. Gold light from bulb rounds the corner.

chapter eight tells the rest. Light coming from behind the venetian blinds made them impossible to see. "Thing" is a fine thing. The world that was already is not.

Water rushes downhill to tell a story. Memory conditions fact. Police expert says damage is consistent with case in point. Maybe the anonymous caller was himself the hit and run driver. Information arrives in bits, gels in an instant. Particles collect on a file. Unhand the steps. I'd be delighted in sequence. I boy clams.

History states that politics rewrites space. Names combine in a series of red trees. The rain is fine, air all wet. Pounds to guilders, guilders to Belgian francs. Terminous. Tell us how it is you make of yourself a wall against the sun. Clear the decks.

What's needed's present definition. I had a sense of how to be in those towns. The last of the second, am I a moment ago? Fast actions are my greatest month of the year. Sizing: in bricks you hear. Language is a sand bar. Not music.

Make copy. Repeat, vary, derive, strike down, do what you canonical well please. The birth of capital, the rise of Venus, the heart of the artichoke, sounds back up over a yard. You're asking me some hard ones. To downshift, double-clutch. I wrote this in the mint. Metaphors are a dime a dozen. In the future we will not be around to discuss it.

Words in sleep made better sense. Bright day gives onto no such number, memory mere as a trace. Where these materials come from is immaterial. Reeds form the middle ground. Elvin cardboard sky. I love the wheel. Legs are modes, parting the reeds of

Kit Robinson 129

Ink blurts out well. These pages aren't stitched in. The subject is liable to fly apart. Striking parallels broadside.

Up to move. A car. The height subtracted space from a can. On all sides there were waste spaces with only stoves and chimney stacks still standing, and here and there the blackened walls of some brick houses. A soldier on leave, a shirt outside pants. Barn doors open here on air.

Times square, space circles round. Past the boundary of self. A colored rectangle, longer in its vertical dimension, its surface void of detail, hangs suspended. Its edges, as if slightly raised, can't be seen past, form the periphery of the visual field. Motion a point near the telephone. Wall or side in a sea. Letters fell from tablets translated by tan. Words in the sky in the middle of the month. Diagonal slashes.

Pencil the attic. Bells chime in with the scissors. Light glances off chrome plated cutlery from joy in Germany. Thus, an essay, trace, tale, nexus, gossip, plan. Any thing might do to flesh out space. Every metaphor is a fable in brief. Stripping foam off tops, blue pieces stuck to the wood. Put a bunch of names in front of them and they were. Air was invented somewhere above the street.

Walking between these sleeping people. An aroma, a texture, a tonality, a rap on the screen door. Stop something, it repeats. Lyrics. Spontaneous pile of rags. Screen door. Pierre stepped over broken ground to the right, far away over the fields on which these men were floundering about, and there stopped, stood, sat or lay.

form. Bells could eat a click. This page is taking days to write. The form of the instrument makes the song madrone, stronger than oak. Suffering suffix dash.

Up to heat up. A model. A revolving midsection glows in the dark office. No night of terror is as dark as this durable lacquer night. I saw a box with a picture of a seated woman selling cigarettes. What time tomorrow.

Voices print, emotional registers vote. Self is tacit. The prisoners, supplied with rifles, pace about the yard, one crouching to fire into rock so the bullet ricochets back killing him instantly. Another shoots his adversary, using the other man's weapon, and prying open a basement window makes good his escape. The subject a point on a screen, alive. Not waiting to move hand and eye. Government lies, covers the globe with a false map. Words in the head betray the active willing subject. Sun script.

Everything staccato of optimism. When workers seize the means of production. Men and women rugged not seduced. New revolutionary perspectives dismantle the machinery of oppression. Workers see these words. Eyes open the world. My word—ground in a box! The wages of death is work. I demolished 530 Bush.

Working amid these talking people. An angle, an edge, a chill, a flame in a dark street. Start something, it repeats. Laws. Specific pile of tires. Dark street. Now you have to see the enemy and draw a bead on him and not grieve that the battle has been reduced to many minor engagements.

Aerial wages piece about the sky. Over in a dream. Awake, a walk with the stars. Out, up, there, in, the sky. Rain on green slate and baby fir makes lines above the house. They brought play daily into the rope. There is strength in the overlap of many fibers. Letters fell from the word envelope. He took her legs on his back. She put his arms on his shoulders. The sun obscured them.

Far channels come in the night. Wired beyond belief. *I* am a great nation of dreamers. In, down, here, out, the earth. Plane noise going about the houses makes for scale. Can you see this perfume? Everything that we call destruction lies in the separation of elements. Thought is surrounded by a hall. Sit down and take your feet off. You're training periods to dance. In light of the words to this song, yes.

RON SILLIMAN

from TJANTING

Not this.

What then?

I started over & over. Not this.

Last week I wrote "the muscles in my palm so sore from halving the rump roast I cld barely grip the pen." What then? This morning my lip is blisterd.

Of about to within which. Again & again I began. The gray light of day fills the yellow room in a way wch is somber. Not this. Hot grease had spilld on the stove top.

Nor that either. Last week I wrote "the muscle at thumb's root so taut from carving that beef I thought it wld cramp." Not so. What then? Wld I begin? This morning my lip is tender, disfigurd. I sat in an old chair out behind the anise. I cld have gone about this some other way.

Wld it be different with a different pen? Of about to within which what. Poppies grew out of the pile of old broken-up cement. I began again & again. These clouds are not apt to burn off. The yellow room has a sober hue. Each sentence accounts for its place. Not this. Old chairs in the back yard rotting from winter. Grease on the stove top sizzled & spat. It's the same, only different. Ammonia's odor hangs in the air. Not not this.

Analogies to quicksand. Nor that either. Burglar's book. Last week I wrote "I can barely grip this pen." White butterfly atop the grey concrete. Not so. Exactly. What then? What it means to "fiddle with" a guitar. I found I'd begun. One orange, one white, two gray. This morning my lip is swollen, in pain. Nothing's discrete. I straddled an old chair out behind the anise. A bit a part a like. I cld have done it some other way. Pilots & meteorologists disagree about the sky. The figure five figures in. The way new shoots stretch out. Each finger has a separate function. Like choosing the form of one's execution.

Forcing oneself to it. It wld've been new with a blue pen. Giving oneself to it. Of about to within which what without.

Hands writing. Out of the rockpile grew poppies. Sip mineral water, smoke cigar. Again I began. One sees seams. These clouds breaking up in late afternoon, blue patches. I began again but it was not beginning. Somber hue of a gray day sky filld the yellow room. Ridges & bridges. Each sentence accounts for all the rest. I was I discoverd on the road. Not this. Counting my fingers to get different answers. Four wooden chairs in the yard, rain-warpd, wind-blown. Cat on the bear rug naps. Grease sizzles & spits on the stove top. In paradise plane wrecks are distributed evenly throughout the desert. All the same, no difference, no blame. Moon's rise at noon. In the air hung odor of ammonia. I felt a disease. Not not not-this. Reddest red contains trace of blue. That to the this then. What words tear out. All elements fit into nine crystal structures. Waiting for the cheese to go blue. Thirty-two. Measure meters pause. Applause.

A plausibility. Analogy to "quick" sand. Mute pleonasm. Nor that either. Planarians, trematodes. Bookd burglar. What water was, wld be. Last week I cld barely write "I grip this pen." The names of dust. Blue butterfly atop the green concrete. Categories of silence. Not so. Articles pervert. Exactly. Ploughs the page, plunders. What then? Panda bear sits up. Fiddle with a guitar & mean it. Goin' to a dojo. Found start here. Metal urges war. One white, two gray, one orange, two longhair, two not. Mole's way. This morning the swelling's gone down. Paddle. No thingdis crete. Politry. Out behind the anise I straddled an old chair. O'Hare airport. About a bit in part a like. Three friends with stiff necks. I did it different. Call this long hand. Weathermen & pilots compete for the sky. Four got. Five figures figure five. Make it naked. The way new stretches shoot out. Shadow is light's writing. Each finger functions. The fine hairs of a nostril. Executing one's choice. What then? Forms crab forth. Pen's tip snaps. Beetles about the bush. Wood bee. Braille is the world in six dots. A man, his wife, their daughter, her sons. Times of the sign. The very idea. This cancels this. Wreak havoc, write home. We were well within. As is.

Wait, watchers. Forcing to it one self. Read in. It wld be blue with a new pen. Than what? Giving to one itself. The roads around the town we found. Of about under to within which what without. Elbows' flesh tells age. Hands writing. Blender on the end-table next to the fridge. Out of rock piled groupies. Hyphenate. Smoke cigar, sip water. Mineral. This was again beginning. Begging questions. Seams one sees. Monopoly, polopony. Blue patches breaking clouds up in the late afternoon. Non senses. It was not beginning I began again. In Spain the rain falls mainly on the brain. The gray sky came into the yellow room. Detestimony. Bridges affix ridges. On the road I discoverd I was. I always wake. Not this. The bear's trappings. Counting my fingers between nine & eleven. Factory filld at sunrise. Three rain-warpd wood chairs in the back yard. Minds in the mines look out. Cat naps on the bear rug. Bathetic. On the stove top grease sizzles & spits. Lunch pales. In paradise plain rocks are distributed evenly throughout the desert. Electricity mediates the voice. All difference, no same, all blame. Lampshade throws the light. Noon's moonrise. Burn sienna. Feel the disease. Denotes detonation. Not not not-not-this. The sun began to set in the north. Reddest trace contains red blue. Metazoans, unite. Of that to the this of then. Break or lure. Out what words tear. One ginger oyster between chopsticks rose to the lips. All elemental crystal structures are nine. Helicopters hover down into the dust. The blue cheese waits. No one agrees to the days of the week. Thirty-two times two. We left the forest with many regrets. Meters pace measure. New moons began to rise. Applause drops the curtain. The elf in lederhosen returns to the stomach of the clock. Chiropractice. Furnace fumes. Crayola sticks. Each word invents words. One door demands another. Bowels lower onto bowls. Come hug. Sunset strip. Holograms have yet to resolve the problem of color. Thermal. This is where lines cross. Hyperspace, so calld. Mastodons trip in the tar pits. These gestures generate letters. Industrial accident orphan. Driving is much like tennis. Orgasmic, like the slam dunk. We saw it in slomo. Cells in head flicker & go out. Zoo caw of the sky.

Sarcadia. A plausibility. Gum bichromate. Quick analogy to sand. Not this. Moot pleonasm. Cat sits with all legs tuckd under. Nor that either. Table lamp hangs from the ceiling, mock chandelier. Trematodes, planarians. Featherd troops. Books burgled. Blood lava. What wld be was water. Bone flute. I cld barely write "last week I gripped this pen." Allusions illude. Dust names. Not easy. Green butterfly atop the blue concrete. Pyrotechnics demand night. Kinds of silence. Each is a chargd radical. Not so. Photon. Pervert articles. Extend. Exactly. Descend. Plunders & ploughs the page. Read reed as red. What then? With in. Panda bear claps. The far side of the green door is brown. Fiddle with a mean guitar. "I don't like all those penises staring at me." Go into a dojo. Mojo dobro. Here found start. Dime store sun visor. Metal urges worn. Only snuggle refines us. Two long-hairs, two gray, one white, one not, one orange. Spring forward, fall back. Mole's way in. Build an onion. This morning the blister gave way to pus & half-formd flesh. Hoarfrost. Paddleball. Tether. No thindgis creep. Tiny plastic dinosaur. Politry teaches just what each is. Cameroon tobacco wrapper. Out behind anise I stood on an old chair. Southpaw slant to the line. O'Hare airport bar. Sounds the house makes. About a bit in part of a like. Shutters rattle, stairs "groan." Three stiff friends with necks. Your own voice at a distance. Done differently. Monoclinic. This long hand call. 'Her skirt rustled like cow thieves.' Sky divides jets & weather. Far sigh wren. Got for. Bumble. Figure five figures five. Dear Bruce, dear Charles. Make naked it. Negative. Out the way new stretches shoot. A thin black strap to keep his glasses from falling. Light's writing is shadow. Rainbow in the lawn hose's shower. Each finger's function. Beneath the willow, ferns & nasturtiums. Nostril fine hairs. Stan writes from Kyoto of deep peace in the calligraphic. Executed one choice. Pall bearers will not glance into one another's eyes. What then? A storm on Mount Sutro. Forms crab forth from tide pool's edge. Refusal of personal death is not uncommon amid cannery workers. Snaps pen tip. An ant on the writing alters letters. About the bush beetles. This municipal bus lurches forward. Be wood. Several small storms cld be seen across the valley. The world in six braille dots. Gray blur of detail indicates rain. A woman, her husband, their daughter, her sons. A pile of old clothes discarded in the weeds of a vacant lot. Time of the signs. Some are storms. The idea very. Borate bombers swoopd low over the rooftops. This cancels not this. The doe stood still just beyond the rim of the clearing. Writing home wrought havoc. In each town there's a bar calld the It Club. We were within the well. Many several. Is as is. Affective effects. Humidity of the restroom. Half-heard humor. Old rusted hammer head sits in the dust. Clothespins at angles on a nylon line. Our generation had school desks which still had ink-wells, but gone were the bottles of ink. Green glass broken in the grass. Every dog on the block began to bark. Hark. Words work as wedges or as hedges to a bet. Debt drives the nation. These houses shall not survive another quake. A wooden fence that leans in all directions. Each siren marks the tragic. Dandelions & ivy. A desert by the sea is a sight to see. A missile rose quickly from the ocean's surface. A parabola spelld his mind. He set down, he said, his Harley at sixty. It is not easy to be a narcissist. Afterwords weigh as an anchor. Cement booties. Not everyone can cause the sun to come up. On the telly, all heads are equal. In Mexico, the federales eat you up. The production of fresh needs is the strangest of all. I swim below the surface. Room lit by moonlight. Words at either edge of the page differ from those in between. An old grey church enclosd in bright green scaffolding. Left lane must turn left. A dog in his arms like an infant. Each sentence bends toward the sun. Years later, I recognized her walk a block away.

Downward motion means out. Watchers wait. In motel rooms the beds are disproportionately large. Self forcing one to it. Croatians were restless. Read into. Between hills, a slice of fog. With a blue pen it wld be new. Not wanted is not wanted. Than what? This not. Self giving one to it. Time lapse photography captures the sky. Around the town we found roads. A roil of deep gray cirrus. Of about under to within which of what without into by. A taut bend to the palm tree to indicate wind. Flesh at the elbow goes slack as one grows older, gathers in folds. Fireworks replay the war. By the fridge on an endtable a blender. A fly's path maps the air of the room, banging at the windows. Hand writings. Recent words have been struck. Groupies pile out of rock. An accidental order is not chance. Hyphenateria. On the wall hung abalone. Sip cigar, smoke water. Who holds what truths to be self-evident? Mineral water bubbles in a glass. Each mark is a new place. Again this was beginning, being begun. Stick cloves in an orange for incense. Questioning beggars. Under golden arches we gorged to heart's delight. One's seams seen. Not ink but point scrapes the page. Polopony, monopoly. At sea side a city of rust. Late afternoon clouds breaking up into blue patches. Pigeons gather round the writing. None senses. In the back of the Buick were sleeping bags, pillows. Is this not beginning I again begin? Orange Opel's dented fender. In the rain Spain falls mainly on the brain. Gold-leaf sign on the glass reads X-ray. Gray sky comes into the yellow room. Peeling leather off the tatterd jacket. Detestimonial. Predictable people wear Frye boots. Ridges attached by bridges. Waiting for that bus to come back this way. Pine koans. Uganda liquors. Each sentence stakes out. Knot this. Can cups fill a cupboard? Tamal is the name of a place in the place of a name. I was on the discoverd road. Caterpillar is a tractor. I am in each instant waking. To him her tone was at once tender and gruff from long years of rough intimacy. Not this. I saw my blood, a deep red, filling the vial at the far end of the needle. Ing the trappd bears. I wanted to catch a glimpse of her face, but she never turnd this way. Between nine & eleven counted my fingers. Each cloud has a specific shape. At sunrise the factory filld. Cut to montage of forklifts & timeclock. Back in the yard three wooden rain-warpd chairs. Scratch that. In the mines minds gape. Try to imagine words. Bare cat naps on the rug. Haze hued those hills on the far, gray side of the bay. Bathetic. Underground, the mock coolness of the conditiond air. Grease sizzles, spits on the stove top. Sand sharks swam past. Pale lunch. A city of four tunnels. In paradise desert rocks are distributed evenly throughout the plain. We saw the sails at sea. Electricity translates the voice. But what comes thru depends on you. Blame all difference, know same. Thru the window I see the apparatus of the modern dentist. Shade throws the lamp light. Light green lines between wch to write. Noon's rising moon. This one squints at a thick printout in his lap on the bus home from work. Sienna burns. Suddenly, in the hospital corridor, the familiar smell of balsa wood & model airplane glue. Feel a disease. Or, thru a window just after sunset, the faces of watchers turnd blue by the light of an unseen television. Detonates denotation. For an instant I was unable to remember how to get the change back into my pocket & pick the bag up off the counter. Not-not not-not not-not this. Crystals hung in the window to refract the sun. It began to set in the north. Ploughshares turnd into gongs may be playd without actually being touchd. Trace of red blue contain within the reddest. Each day's first cigarette tastes stale. Metazoans united. The true length depends on the size

Ron Silliman 139

of the type. Of by that to the this into of then. Morning, mourning. Brick or leer. The buzz of flies fills the room. Out words what tear. Chinese coins with holes in the center. To the lips, thick & poisd open, rose a ginger oyster between chopsticks. A blue glass ashtray filld with wooden match sticks. All 9 elemental structures are crystal. Each statement is a mask. Down into the dust hover helicopters. This script a scrawl. Wait for the blue cheese. A motorboat for the salt seas calld Twenty Languages. No days agree as to the one of the week. We make our deposit in the cloud bank. Thirty-two times two-squared. Black smoke of a structural fire belched up out over the docks. Regretfully we are leaving the forest. In a string net, a bundle of groceries. Meters face measure. Charging for lapis but giving you sodalite. Moons begin to rise anew. Cool coffee kindld thought. Applause curtains the drop. Me too in general yes. Back into the stomach of the clock went the elf in lederhosen. Certain sentences set aside, others set off. Chiropractical. Dr Heckel & Mr Jive. Furnish fumes. The red hook-&-ladder snakes around to back into the station. Crayola sticks streak a page. Like radios talking of radios to radios. Each word once the invention of another. These dark glasses serve as a veil. One door is the demand of another. Gulls fly, strung from hidden wires. Over bowls lower bowels. For "wires" read "wives." Hug come. Time flows, pouring forward from the past. Strip set sun. Vast vats of waste water aerate in the flatlands by the bay. Holograms have yet to tackle the problem calld color. Walking as tho one had to think abt it. Thermal, Tamal. Fresh odor of new dung. This is where the cross lines. Too late to catch the bus, they slap its side as it pulls away. So calld hyperspace. An old Chinese lady wearing a light-purple tam. Mastodons in the tar pits trip. An ashtray in the shape of a heart. These letters generate gestures. The shadow of buildings upon buildings. Accidental industrial orphan. The lines abt swimming meant sex. Tennis is much like driving. Fire escape forms a spine. Slam, like the orgasmic dunk. Drunk. In slomo we saw it move, try to. Against that cream stucco the gray flagpole has no depth. Heads in the cell flicker & go out. In that sandal I saw countless toes. Zoo sky of caw. A transmitter, like radar, atop each tall building. Transbay transit. The word is more & less. The history of the foot. The fogbank heavy on the beach like a slug. Stopping the car to make a quick phone call. You will never stop learning how to read. Hyper/formance. What really happened to the C. Turner Joy. Up & down scales on reeds. Not this. The words were in the page already. Summer without sun. I like white space. Truck towed tons of tractors, all yellow. Plotting the way ahead. Instrument landing. The flutter of clarinets. Boar bristle hair brush. Toilet's handle says "press." These letters more angular than I used to write. Congas in the urban night. Cans of beer & fear. Sunrise behind fog means light changes on the green steep slopes of the hillside. A small pen-like instrument used to apply wax designs. Cut. He staggerd about in the intersection, whooping & making wild gestures, then sipping from a can of beer, oblivious to the early morning traffic. Pain in the lower calves from hours of walking. Potato chips at war. With heavy hearts, we set out to follow the river to its conclusion. If he has no sideburns, then it's a hairpiece. When we got to where the clouds were, they were too thin to see. Industrial siren meaning lunch. Quips & players, or diamonds in the blood. There are clues nearby. In each major city, the ugliest mansion was the French Consulate. She & I strolld thru the rose garden. Nor that either. An architect's model of a rest stop. Tulis is not tulip. Shaking the brain awake. Each word is a wafer of meaning meant, minded. No fish imagines water. I surface at the center of the pool. A dress shirt halfway between pink & lavender. Tautness of the warp while on the loom. Each sentence is itself. Two fives & a nine. A nose that points slightly to the left. What I am writing is writing. Tics dig in. Wicker throne. Scratch that. Keep moving. Dressd to kill. Burgundy jumpsuit.

False start. Circadia. True start. Applause, ability. A run around a ring around of roses read. Gum bichromate. Jets swoop low over the destroyer amid bursts of anti-aircraft fire, dozens of bombs going off in the water, then rise up again & the audience cheers. Sandy analogy to the quick. The poem plots. Not this. Indented servant. Moot pleonast. Opposable thumb. All legs tuckd in, the cat sleeps. Mandibility. Nor that either. Cumulative tissue calld tonsil. Mock chandelier tablelamp hangs upside down from the ceiling. Pages of description. Planarians inch forward, trematodes retreat. Eat lady fingers. Trooping feathers. This

to me is tmesis. Books burgld bought back. Roller is not coaster.
Lava blood. Larva blood. What wld water be was. What you are
reading is the dance of my hand. Flute bone. Brothers & sisters
I've never met. Barely I cld write. Brown door, white door, green
door, all along one wall. Allusions elude. Grip this. Names dust.
That was last week or weak. Not easy. Pi. Mauve butterfly atop
the ochre concrete. Footsteps on the stairs. Pyro demands night
technics. Insert new modes of thought. Kind to silence. What
then? Each radical is charged. The sound of a telephone dial, turn-
ing, turning back. Not so. Air is zone. Photon. Milk of Indonesia.
Particles avert. Milk of amnesia. X tends. Warp is vertical, weft is
horizontal. X acts. Ten million without power. D sends. Once I
was a needle freak. Pages & ploughs the plunders. Any cloth or
fabric structure. Read red as read. Ronnie 2 Baad. What then?
This is another sentence. With inn. What gets seen thru a speculum.
Claps the panda. Tofu turkey. The near side of the brown door is
green. Indirect sunset. Mean with a fiddle guitar. I like the shapes
of thing. "Don't like all those staring penises." The tar-heater
stands in the street, breathing loudly. Into a dojo go. Holes in the
petals from unknown eaters. Mojo dobro. Rough tough cough.
Start found here. Roofers holler down. Sun visor from a dime
store. Words secrete letters. Meddle, urge, warn. Dog climbs up
onto the couch. Only ray struggle finds us. Half heard. One
white, one not, one orange, two longhair, too gray. Grinder
buffer sander. Fall back, spring forward. Out of the rooftops
grew types of pipes. Mole's way into. Brushing to rustproof. Build
a better onion. The man who invented spikes to go into the sides
of phone poles. This morning the blister was replaced by tight,
tender new flesh. Backstairs are a proposition. Hoarfrost. People
who don't understand cats. Ballpaddle. Muted trumpet. Tether.
What is the ocean's porpoise? No thid gnis crete. B complex.
Plastic tiny dinosaur. Gary Moore, Henry Morgan, Bill Cullen,
Betty White, Allen Ludden, Jack Narz, Gale Storm. Politry—each
is, just what teaches. Poultry—features creatures. Wrappd Came-
roon tobacco. Rough waves move quickly. Out behind fennel I
stood on an old chair. Cantalope halves in the bay "look like the
moon." Southpaws slant their lines. Chinese youth in the parks
of North Beach. O'Hare airport bartender. Strokes of the pen.

Sounds make the house. Pigeons fly past sleepers & sunbathers. About of a bit into part of a like. Bread crumbs in dry grass. Shutters groan, stairs rattle. Two bell-towers & 21 crosses go into the cathedral. Friends with three stiff necks. The war between grasses is ceaseless. Distancing your own voice. Trenchcoats in warm weather. Differently done. Down vest. Monoclinic. I see her walking in my direction. Long this hand call. Opcorn. His shirt rustld like cow thieves. Coming in by ladder. Jets divide sky & weather. Party conversation: familiar voices focus. Fart saw run. Kit grins to see me write. Get fur. At a reading, watch friends listen. Bumbles. Tweeze each letter. Five five figure figures. I hear footsteps come up the stairs but no one arrives. Bruce dear, Charles dear. Kleenex is a trade name. It naked make. Unpoppd kernels at the bottom of the cup. Negative. Listening, they concentrate, stare. Way out the new stretches shoot. Star. To keep glasses from slipping, a black elastic strap. If it's speech you got to listen. Writing light's shadow. Flougher. Lawn hose' shower makes rain bow. These lines stretch in all directions. Each function's finger. Amyl burns the brain. Beneath the ferns, willows & nasturtiums. This is how the Dutch thought to spell it. Hairs nostril fine. Later he said he saw me just sitting there, waving a pen in the air, & thought a smile wld give me permission. Stan writes from deep peace of Kyoto in the calligraphic. Using a stage whisper to call cats. Executed choice one. Jerusalem artichokes, Canadian potatoes. Pall bearers look away. Campd on the couch in a light blue nightie. What then? Embeddedness, in bed with us. Mt. Sutro rainstorm. I hear faucets off & on. Forth from tidepool's edge crabs form. Bufflehead is a duck. Cannery workers commonly refuse personal death. Hear change in pocket to pull jeans on. Naps spend tip. Whisky with an "e." Ant alters letters of the writing. An old friend finds me at the Savoy. The about bush beetles. Pens prick the page. Lurching forward, muni bus. Newsprint on elbow. Bee wood. A hum in boiling water. Across the valley several small storms were at once visible. Scribble. The world six in braille dots. Cats bat the wind chimes. Blur gray of rain indicates detail. Blank page is all promise. A man, a bald deaf man, his wife, their silent daughter, her sons. Crazy to do this. In the weeds of a vacant lot, a pile of old discarded clothes. Any verb trails noun. Sum our

Ron Silliman 143

storms. Only part of the table seen in the mirror. The signs of time. Inversions face affect. Idea vary the do eye. Tiny scars appear. Low over our rooftops swoop borate bombers. Porn jury giggles at throat. Not this cancels this. Wld you ouija? Just beyond the rim of the clearing a doe stands still. Soft contacts dissolve. Wrote home wrought havoc. Ought not to have. A bar calld the It Club in each town. Six separates this. Were we within? All words are some language. Several many. Jots. Is as is as is. Dry cereal chewing sounds. Effective affects. This drug enhances pleasure. Rest humidity of the room. Hair combd back to dry. Heard half-humor. Just who set George up. In the dust sits old rusty hammerhead. Write right into the binding. Clothespins angling from a nylon line. Weaver. Our schooldesks had inkwells, but no bottles of ink. Bacteria under foreskin infects friend. Green grass & broken glass. This is one example. Each dog on the block starts to bark. Counts consonants. Hark. Not this. Words work as hedges or as wedges to a bet. Cloth spin. Debt driven nation. Our epic is the draftboard meets acid. Another quake shall not survive these houses. Think of cat to feed. Wood fence leans in all directions. This brain has no rough edges. Tragic markd by siren. Ducks that fail to fly. Ivy & dandelions. Kibbles. Sea desert sight see. Elastic band about doorknob. Missile shoots from ocean surface. Articles are fibre. Parabola spells my mind. Cat's up. At 60 sets his Harley down. Not impossible to not think. Narcissism is not simple. Toes don't go straight. Afterwords weigh anchor. Spacey. Boot cement. Melissa is a missile. Everyone cld cause the sun to not come up. Food good. All heads are equal. Yolks slip from the shell. In Mexico, eat the federales. Love letters. Fresh production of strange needs is all. A woman dressd in nurse whites & a face just that pale. I swam beneath the surface, sun lighting the water. She, constituting the assemblage. Moon lit by room light. Beware the pook—ump no rubbish. Words in the middle differ. Wire rope. Enclosed in bright green scaffolding, a freshly painted white church. Watch & traffic passes. Left lane turn left. Writing standing is not simple. Infant in his arms like a dog. Spine straight, one walks. Each sentence bent toward the sun. Wind makes hat delicate proposition. I recognized her years later a block away. Remember—you're asleep. This sketches, drawing itself out. Some weathers arouse a longing for years ago. A pair of small, silver, military jets zip past. Eyes, you hoped, were not lies. Cargo containers atop flat-beds behind cyclone fence. To the west, fog spilld over the hilltops. One spot at the bay's center where the sun shines directly. Hand or tongue to the eye adds mind. Man sees hoss. Hear airplanes above these clouds. The London of the west. Fishsticks wrappd in wax paper. In an of into by. Not this. Holds his shoulders like umbrella over spine, neck bobbing. Mexican hot chocolate. Cork, where once door's latch was, protects children. Furnace lights up with a whoosh. Written down, sight ceases. Sky blue eyes. Shoes form a platform. Run against light to catch the bus. Riding, writing. Heads of hair dot the air. Not this calls flaws forth. Boppo, boffing. Hi drawl it. Any glyph of words crafted twists in the ear. Bare feet cross linoleum. Engines rev. Indirect light of late afternoon. For whom prose is not without context. Mantis, end stop, the power of the poor. White ash at cigar's tip. Kites from far places. Eyes whose hue depends on clothing's color. Shingle Shoppe. Beard knots. Sails down, anchord in the bay. A chopper slides between islands. Huskies chase birds into water. Cameras dangle against belly. Fat men, slender wives, children run ahead. Wax paper cup in which cola has gone flat. Lavender & green in pigeon's gray neck. Kids buying chilidogs, skateboards in hand. Neck pulls in when pigeon sits. Out on the breakwater, watching whitecaps. Charterboats bob. Lower clouds move quicker. Black smoke of a tugboat. Gull just opend its wings & let the current lift it up. All trite when you see it, she said. Fly's eyeball. Odor of urinal cakes. Reading aloud is not speech. People try to imagine how to sit in chairs. Water in glass never its own color. Where you put the lamp shapes the room. The adroit tigers. A fire, smouldering, in the cigarette. Beer washd over the chocolate & down the throat. Plants move indoors. Concentration stopped at the lens of his glasses. Apples meet the bowl's curves. Ether, either. The height of pepper shakers. Lacuna coat. All shoes on some feet. Mountains, gardens, harbors. Brown bottle under ice plant. Where the talk took him. Difficult to recall the former ease of thought. Leaves the bathroom like a rainforest. More letters are than we know to write down. Scratch, scratch. Graffiti's day is by. Which gin, which tonic? All faucets drip little. Light is to language as. I had one foot in the sailor's grave. Your eyes dilated with anticipation. Old soap slivers sat in the blue plastic dish. Gums recede. Fingers print always in the region of the knob. The slow lift of any launch. Several words too many. Cut.

RAE ARMANTROUT

ANTI-SHORT STORY

A girl is running. *Don't* tell me
"She's running for her bus."

All that aside!

TONE

1

Hoping my face shows the pleasure I felt, I'm
smiling languidly. Acting. To put your mind
at rest—how odd! At first we loved because
we startled one another

2

Not pleased to see the
rubberband, chapstick, tin-
foil, this pen, things
made for our use

But the bouquet you made of
doorknobs, long nails for
their stems   sometimes
brings happiness

3

Is it bourgeois to dwell on nuance? Or effeminate?
Or should we attend to it the way a careful animal
sniffs the wind?

4

Say the tone of an afternoon

Kindly but sad

"The ark of the ache of it"

12 doorsteps per block

5

In the suburbs butterflies
still spiral up the breeze
like a drawing of weightlessness.
To enter into this spirit!
But Mama's saying she's alright
"as far as breathing and all that"

6

When you're late I turn slavish, listen hard for
your footstep. Sound that represents the end of
lack

YOU FLOAT

You dazzle all eyes by increasing.

You wear a cross of gold, a bit of history,
regions, riot gear, polemics.

Every familiar piece
made of delectable candy.

You eat chocolate "lentils"
from France. Butterscotch barley.

You float above necessity, shooting.

*

You restore order with
a lead crystal gavel,

sleek periodicity.

You float on frosty-colored hiring freeze,

see no major damage,
danger to Niagara Falls
or evidence of spreading.

You seek only
to impersonate Queen Victoria.

You float above the state of nature
in a miniature Japanese cart.

*

You seek only to spangle
essentials
with rhinestones.

HYPNO-SEXISM

AUTOPSY
wink from theatre marquees.

You wear long strands
of sign language.

You float above refugees,

dazzle all eyes with searchlights

XENOPHOBIA

1

"must represent the governess
for, of course, the creature itself
could not inspire such terror."

staring at me fixedly, no
trace of recognition.

"when the window opened of its own accord.
In the big walnut tree
were six or seven wolves . . .

strained attention. They were white."

(The fear of cloudy skies.)

like strangers! After five years

Misgiving. Misdoubt.

2

(The fear that one is dreaming.)

The moon was shining, suddenly
everything around me appeared
(The fear of)
unfamiliar.

Wild vista
inside or near the home.

(Dread of bearing a monster.)

If I failed to overlook
the torn cushions,

three teapots side by side,
strewn towels, socks, papers—

both foreign and stale

3

when I saw the frame was rotten,
crumbling away from the glass
in spots, in other places still
attached with huge globs of putty.

The doctor forced me to repeat the word.

Chimera.   Cold feet.

scared and unreal looking at buildings.
The thin Victorians with scaly paint,
their flimsy backporches linked
by skeletal stairways.

4

After five years
(The fear that you are not at home.)

I was sitting in the alcove where I never sit
when I noticed a single eye,
crudely drawn in pencil,
in a corner near the floor.

The paint was blistering—
beneath it I saw white.

5

Sparrows settle on the sagging wires.

(Fear of sights not turned to words.)

Horrific. Grisly.
"Rumplestiltskin!"

Not *my* expression.

Not my net of veins
beneath thin skin.

(A morbid dread of throbbing.)

Of its own accord

SINGLE MOST

Leaves fritter.

Teased edges.

It's vacillation that pleases.

Who answers for
the 'whole being?'

This is
only the firing

     *

Daffy runs across
the synapses, hooting
in mock terror.

Then he's shown
on an embankment, watching
the noisy impulse pass.

     *

But there's always a steady hum
shaped like a room
whose door must lead to
what really

where 'really'
is a nervous
tic as regular

     *

as as   as as

the corner repeats itself

　　　*

Dull frond:
giant lizard tongue
stuck out
in the murky distance
sight slides off
as a tiny elf.

　　　*

Patients are asked to picture
health as an unobstructed
hall or tube

through which Goofy now tumbles:
Dumb Luck!

Unimagined
creature scans postcard.

　　　*

Conclusions can be drawn.

Shadows add depth
by falling

while deep secrets
are superseded—

quaint.

Exhaling
on second thought

VIEW

Not the city lights. We want

-the moon-

          The Moon
none of our own doing!

CARLA HARRYMAN

PROPERTY

for Barrett Watten

The rowboat was caught in the mudflats. A few gulls padded around it. The mud fizzled. A grey mist was broken by a narrow sky. In the distance a solitary cathedral interfered with the sensuality of endlessness. The earth was small and even cozy, until, looking up at the beaming monstrosity, one recognized the meagerness of its claim on space.

PROPERTY

"Come you are a mad revolutionary," said her uncle with a smile. He pointed at the wildflowers. "My vision of the aspects I more or less fortunately rendered *was*, exactly, my knowledge. Anything nature puts in the sea comes up. A fierce man's rainbow is in his head. If there is no Spain? If there is no Oakland? The original field, once cultivated, returns to high weeds where privacy is absolute. The shape of the story ought to be that of a spiral of doubt. The landscape demolishes the house in our heads. The conclusion is a point of departure for the speculator, but the spectacle is lacking in furniture. The pack of lies is insulted. The song is sung but where do we get the words compelling us to repeat it? My blood runs cold at the sight of death so I tell the story. If the wide obtuse inside is a yardstick in this sanctuary, perhaps the universe views the world like I see a two dollar bill abandoned in a cashbox. Kiss my ass." He stood up straight.

"Anything pleasurably tolerable but only endurable when it is remembered in the middle of the night, fields we walk on as carelessly as bamboo shoots creaking in the tropics flooded with gross species of rodents nibbling stains on trikes, dictate to any happy man what he can't live without." He held her up so she could be closer. The crystal ball glowed with murk. She cut her finger on the left front fender while trying to smash some limestone with a stick. Her uncle led her back over the property.

POSSESSION

Inside, the ear spins beautiful webs.

"With one clear picture of an individual collective abstraction is exposed. There is no smoke rising from over there.

"Let me tell you," he swallowed her and spit her out, "it is a bargain."

"Sing to me," she slipped.

"I don't intend," he said, "to imitate poetry but to be imitated by it.

"I live in a fabrication near something I have never said before. I can't see my doctor and when he . . . I do see him he pelts me syntactically. My assignation burns toward abstraction. Because imperatives never blow over, get on your feet! Stumbling through this padded interstice, my body has limits. Yours doesn't compare notes.

"But let me tell you a story. I am civilized:

"The high illusion constrains the pent-up trees. We float beneath them tortoises bathing in the night. It is primitive. We creak in the fog. The outboard motor racket mutes the wall like a powwow. A small echo fishes with a person's features. Me talking fuses to you. Puberty here, fantasy there." He paused, basing his headtrip on the profile of a sated barbarian. Then proceeded to deliver his child with unconscious mirth.

Surprised by his use of words, the moral presence swelled to veracity plunging the social salad into the contemporary fork. She looked deep into the merchandiser's past. "Yes," she said, "but you enjoy suffering."

Because there was nothing else, he waded across the pool, fading into a mental fog, which, to this day, fuels its maws with the purest minds.

A robot adjusted her sea in the ornate theater. If this were merely an eidetic image why did she want to be nursed? Nothing stuck out.

It was hot, beautiful. True and the same at the same time. The scooped-out center of the continent described the middle of life without describing a figure. Standing around in serialized plateaus was enough to make you cry. But fleeting mammals sucked up revolt.

Oversensitivity was wrong. She wrenched her mind from its wasteland of souvenirs. "Where is that bastard?" She couldn't get enough.

He was behind the door, hiding from the spirit of the new world.

PRIVACY

The insects hung in the air, frozen invisible pouches, contorted parodies of medieval fate. How right for such an afternoon! Do not pull down those varicose blinds. Motion and noise are one thing. The red dragonfly behind the dangling rope is alone forever but the grey has a hundred mates. Brushing aside the air with the power of propagation they yield, like boulders at a hydro-electric plant in Siberia, to the touch obscurity bestows on them via a cook displaying a mound of fried food for two thousand fund raisers, whose charitable ideas drool, green-eyed, onto the turnstile of insect life so often compared to the web of human saturation points in an adept squirming of an old, an approximately plowed field. A dog's obedience can't be more touching. Everything is allowed to pile up. And why not? Why is the shade thick? The house is lumpy with numbness, protruding from below. And so the quiet day is heavy from a body in a sink.

Expression concludes existence. Though though and though. A thousand red spiders living in brick and that's what refusing to talk is like. Below is below and in is in and this is in. People are surprised. They wake up to find the room, a tiny machine. This is not the time for subjectivity. But it survives. Because space is small. For example, love me but don't talk to me. A size crosses the street. The street asks, what's going on? Some facts are to be gotten around while others remain external to their shapes.

People in the kitchen picking at bones don't want to pay attention to the heavy air. We let them go on—they're not hurting anybody. This special mode of address is used to captivate inanimate objects, in our sanctuary. We look at our things because they have our respect.

THE MASTER MIND

"Eve will bruise his head."

The enigma froze behind the triangulated bellow.

"Let me take over."

On another wall, an allegory. Holding her curly head, Cupid touches tongues with Venus. One of her nipples is caught between his fingers which are stretched over her breast. Venus is both sitting up and swooning back, an apple in her left hand down at her side. Her right hand is raised and pointing back behind her, to the confusion back behind her, and away from Cupid's deliciously prominent ass. So in the background of this perfected lust a near-infant cupid is stepping over a dragon about to hurl flowers upon this passion. Some anonymous being is holding rocks. A young girl's head floats on the blue background which a winged god and goddess are holding up. But from behind appears a naked tortured hag. Cupid is nearly stepping on a dove.

"One thing I always recognize is panic. Such fragility can not go unnoticed to the devils with silks. Are the drain pipes of the bathroom supposed to 'suck' us into the work, and the mock bed to 'envelop' us in its embrace? I stand outside order and look in on its premises. Or take a background of precise historical settings. A romantic bleeds in the foreground while death carts the rest of the picture away. We look on helplessly like children eating candy. Then shove the loads off our backs and obtain permits. And all this in order to understand the external influences that pressed the theme into a particular mold!"

Doors in back streets burst sullenly open.

The guard turns on the underling at the end of the shift. "You are awwk-waard, you are awwk-waard."

The population dispersed when the thunderous voice snapped.

A strange thing, when you come to think of it, this love of Greek, she thought pilfering her uncle's rhetoric. For in the tropics there isn't even a ditch to huddle in. Nor a hole in the landing strip sizing up industrial designs.

Standing behind the door, listening in triumph, uncle noticed the sky. "One forgets to run it down it is so obvious. Day light without day. Meditate, mediate, what is the difference?" He looked at the same clouds, bent in revery. Concluding that what he heard was good enough but what he thought was even better. But in the back of his mind he was throwing out a rope, he was robbing museums and cracking into tiny parts. He could not blame the other countries.

ACTING

The earth is as narrow as the sky is full: a postulation, on a rudimentary level. Clouds protrude to the point of abandoning context. Ducks fly across teasing the edges of clouds with their wings. Reason tells us not to make anything out of these events. Birds fall into the sea. The sea swells, pushing the land under. A seeming eternity, by force. So all that's left is a narrative concealing an error. Contentment is sediment below this image. Passivity has been accomplished through the descriptive process, a mechanism which devours objects, subjecting them to the decay of inner life. Perfection is a disease. Each rock, each sentence suppresses an embryo, elevated as they are to the status of isolated objects to be regarded unto themselves.

There is nothing in the room to look at, unless there is an image to head. In other words, there is no sun in chaos. A vague enigma turns on a death bed, "Body, body." The privilege to confuse, the privilege to refuse (canny familiarity with detachable pieces in an unforeseen design: for example a pseudonym), privileged stupefaction, dazzling, to eat one's words. "You think when I said what I didn't mean I didn't mean it?" A face comes out of hiding the minute you look the other way, a landscape of inner jargon deprived of the distinction between abstract and concrete.

Derision is the investor in big moves. "When I was born, giants walked the earth." Moving forward, inside the picture, are pieces of a plan. Whether or not it is possible to equally objectify the minutia of bodily activity, and whether or not there is any kind of analogy to be made from personal observation of these discrete exposures, is beyond the realms of *that language* to know. To be well informed is a *matter* requiring a cruder sensibility, i.e., not self-scrutiny.

"I have destroyed my ammunition in order to make myself distinct." To look for an accomplished fact is a word on the other side of a bulldozed tunnel. "Later we'll have dinner, eggs." There is no order to the search. "And I know what I mean eating love." As equipment, something has failed. "This, the creature of habit, brings to the synthetic mind a dead space, or as they say, a moment of relief." She breathed into a glass tube, "The periods of parturition dissolve into moisture." But the frog wants to hold her, to rest his belly on her clavicle and wrap his arms around her neck, to feel the vibrations from her tongue dancing against the walls of his miscellaneous trophy.

The state is drenched in wind and heat.

"Looking up at the sky, I am startled and then eat dirt—opening scene. Anything is possible. In the meantime I have found a bug in the dirt which I devour. The shack crumbles and a few feathers float into the cloudless sky.

"Next scene I am on a cot in a teepee pretending to be a wizened old woman. But look up! Get out of the way. Nibble at a purification ritual and succumb! Shot of dead spiders dangling from webs with maniacal young toady stomping on a lariat while brandishing weapons. Not what you would expect to find at the dump where they're breaking up cars. So get off that rock—the mental picture of one's story and the taste for a particular life. All the juice is in a ditch.

"This is a flower." She cracks eggs into butter.

"Lush, yes. It may well be the grave which is the place for narration. My children are stunted and want the world to be a better place than it is now. There is nothing but perfection in their speech. Let us get to the point of the feminine imagination: 'Suffice it just here that I find the mental bearing I can project the latent historic clue toward—the beast still functions in my hand; again with easy recall I no longer want to marry anyone, but I still dream that I am marrying a very large cat to make a story about art'—Henry James and Colette. Unpaid-for pagans. When I get out of bed a pteradactyl blots out the rattle of my machine."

The path of destruction gouged out its eyes. They sprinkled it with nuts to absorb the pus and walked to town where they were to see a number of weddings. "Auntie, why won't I ever get married?"

"Ask your uncle."

"He's dead, but I'm no, I don't know, and don't even believe you have to die. So what am I talking about? Furthermore, why should I even open my mouth?"

"Your uncle is about to give a speech."

The uncle was standing in the middle of an amphitheater in his bathing suit. "I want everyone in the audience to hold up a . . ."

"Let's come back when he gets hot. I think we are missing something."

"What do you mean?"

"When one thing is entirely different from another, it cannot be in any respect capable of behaving like the other, can it?" Aunt Mildred inserted a powerful fingernail under the corner of the veneer.

"Auntie, auntie, this child is not formed yet."

A Cadillac escorting a bride and groom crossed the intersection. A woman emerged from the dime store with stocks inside a plastic egg. The lights in New York went out. Men came out of the sewers with clubs.

"Hold me, hold me."

All things are now true by inverse. The ocean is heavy below the suspended belly.

SCENE I

Some 'deep image' like a three-way collision which occurs beneath the exterior form and as a consequence has no effect on daily habits.

PAM

Sing to me. Let me tell, tell you about, about my education—some likenesses have changed to something else, quasi . . . bird . . . to the point. Am I capable of enjoying a stability of verbal forms? No! I am not capable of understanding because I am a mouth.

Mirror mirror on the wall
Who's the mouthpiece for us all?

MIRROR

Noise.

TIKES
(just emerged from a pit)
Gleeful   Needful

Carla Harryman   167

Gleeful   Needful

Gleeful   Needful

Hump!

Gleeful   Needful

Gleeful   Needful

Gleeful   Needful

Lump!

(They jump into a boat and row out to sea.)

SCENE II

Jungle gym working out with proffered structures. Time: about the time of the discovery of the meaning of their names.

MAY

So, breaking up ground.

HELEN

When one says lily pad but means grasshopper what trick is that? The lily pad sits placidly on stagnant water. We don't get off our asses because there are too many life forms but because the harshness of reality can be eliminated by comparing one thing to another.

PAM

Working for a living and living are the same thing.

MAY

Murder!

SCENE III

Devices of leisure arrive someplace.

MAY

The dregs of society eat me alive.

SCENE IV

Ideas fall into a pit because the sun is always shining on
their stomachs.

SCENE V

A collision creates a wrapping around of hostile forms.

MAY

What do you think of a psychology that equates boredom
with nothingness? Pretty dumb, huh?

PAM
(talking off stage)
No, I can't *see* they are polar opposites!

SCENE VI

Forced to wear clothes, consults an image.

MOTHER
(in a tree)
Horace Mann? Now who is Horace Mann? Go look it up.

MOTHER
Now I want you to bring me the pieta.

CHILD
All gone!

MAY
Sitting on a fence post watching all the feet go by.

HELEN
Easy come, easy go. *(Throws a big chili pepper at May.)*

SCENE VII

Holding the left in the right hand and the right hand in
the left, lavishing attention on others.

Carla Harryman   169

MAY

What are we going to do with this chili?

HELEN

Eat it alive.

SCENE VIII

The strain lingers at a sonorous dinner.

PAM
(on phone)

The spray torch at the machine shop will do. Yes, isolate him for a few days. That's what I thought. A pea in a pod? That's no concern of mine. No, I can only say don't eat.

SCENE IX

Jungle gym, lawn chairs.

The woman reclining on the sofa can almost see into the future. She holds up her hand as if searching for a landscape in the contours of domestic time. Her niece enters with fodder.

"In the days when parents gave up their children to powerful influences who could spot new blood a mile away, you could hear children screaming from great distances. Not from separation anxieties but obliviousness. The stoney image of weapons growing out of pods on overbearing trees irrigates the child of that old spa in the new age. I wish you had apprenticed to Goya."

True to form, the niece prostrated herself at her aunt's feet. But outside, her back was arched in grief. And the muscles of the hills were hidden in the hills.

The street they turned onto died immediately.

"Who is going to notice this error?" Uncle was usurping their experience again, speaking from his platforms to hundreds of acres as crowds gathered on the fringes of his discourse.

The child tumbled to her feet in time to bathe in the dying light of another admonition. . . .

EPILOGUE

*I was delighted when I managed to de-
prive those bewitched lines of meaning.*

Gorky sits in the dark with his mother. Clearing away the spots from a face, 'the last falling leaves of a dying day,' a person is an episode but the wilting subject strips the maneuver of its tight name, a lineup of masks, Damascus.

Seaweed poses wolfishly under the currents as water splats the neck with busy thumbs.

He turns off the light, gets into bed a stupefied hero. Motioning to the shadow who is scrambling dinghies in a mist, the statue of undelved-for memory undresses. In the garden, it busts up a song, the only song it knows. Wolves hide from the moon.

"Islands," it says, standing by the hitching post.

No cheers faded in the swelling tide. Man did not have misery in the future life: he no longer moved. Immortals were immobile, residing in an imperturbable calm. The position of divinities was static. People sat on nets strung over rocks ruminating in the fog. The child sat in the corner hammering forks and knives in front of some icons.

Grownups wandered around on the streets behaving themselves, seemingly, which was troublesome, seeing that the dark tiles and brick pillars had been there almost as long as the three surgeons in white robes dangling and jiggling cigarettes and glasses at the end of the empty hall. A captive jumped at a tray of food. The child climbed into a robe. The visual strain was too much. "We know what bothers them by the angle of the street or a room or by the surface on a table, or the shine from a bottle, or the proportions of the clouds."

The child fled into a jar and turned the dials.

" . . . supplying intensity and chronic confusion to imprints on the lacquered tiles. My report of experience is my appreciation of it: pinning down this equation to the ensemble of animals parading in a field of human activity, in an abyss of mutual ambiguities,

Carla Harryman 171

mutual accommodations where the victims of the exposed and entangled state remain, keeping up the complexity of the grounds."

Aunt Mildred grabbed the full implications of an identity whose sense of immediacy depends on a state of temporal abeyance.

PROPERTY

"The period between the hyphen of marriage is best forgotten," said her uncle, salivating at the gate of that boundless menagerie primed with a moral shape which is framed to break down on approach to vivid fact. The property was neglected. A label peeled away from a jar in a city under cloudless skies. Anybody in the center of the meadow where the cows stand still, where rivers spit and salt subdues the perspicacity of skin with humdrum metabolic flowering diminishing the general regard for this miscellaneous Hector while staring at one's own face through a deserving mirror, might hold to her bosom the happy halting view of this interesting case.

ALAN BERNHEIMER

INSIDE CHEESE

The aged gouda had grown complex, its acoustics swollen to visibility, and the sunny complexion inherited from a northern polder was laced with the whispers of photons cruising the waxy mantle of layered gloss left by each demented glance that had fallen from eyes on the brink of sleep. The brink was lurid and echoed the roar of termites from a nearby windmill. Time and again the prodigious sails swooped out of the sky like an amusement park on fire, and with each revolution the lattice lost molecules to robot bacteria whose cousins had long since polished milk to a half life in the low gear rotunda.

AMARILLO

I hear the sentimental music dying
that makes my helmet ring
—Blaise Cendrars

I was born alive
the sky was all you could see
eating and running
a part from a world

rendered obsolete by the violin
granular lubricity the equivalent
of gravity streaming past limbs
and torso

     watch my smoke
give me a perch   I'm not talking
while the flavor lasts   listen to
the sugar pour

       along the rim
       word of mouth
now this
and now this

       is what I call crisp
New York is a department of the sticks
chicken today feathers tomorrow
you can't see because it's radio

traffic draws away from you
on specular fire   eyes smart
not good at what not like
ill at ease in the offing

you are "it" as is
viscera means iceberg

Alan Bernheimer 175

that wasn't no buffalo
that was thunder

a raving beauty at the turn
of the century known for its
helium and silhouette of beef
hoofing the horizon

much feasting little fun
lunar gaffes of benzedrine proportions
wings cross in consequence of air
you are allowed to copy the weather

keys in one pocket change
in another say hello
to the phone who are
sure of dinner

at the back of the mind
when it rains it shines
landscape
            as nature intended

nothing is sweeter than figs
but it's nice to drink the water
words row across the surface of
oo la la or snorkle

what is known by heart
as the glass harmonica
absorbs loss like champagne
and the streets are music to police

I am descended from my ancestors
hare brained antics freeze
my tears in their tracks
where the anchovies spawn

a domino of light from the rear
view mirror across the eyes
falling as the dusk idly
disappears on the road ahead

circulation drops hardly stir
the odor of fragility
is the weight that it carries
talking through altitude

handwriting cures personality
some roles played by ideas
the language of mechanics
gives the hand a head

it is a sunny day and
no mountain stood a chance
of more neighborhood
emulsifying vitreous humor

early tensile flyleaves
at the edge of valence
faint from farsight
one routine is pulling teeth

off also rans
the last dinosaur turns back
for a blink at the ginkgo
with a weakness for feet

chiefly diehard furlongs
feeling vapors
                drop away
shy on geography

I started out younger
all over the place

merely sportive slippers
thought a sign of decadence

to dispel abandon they ate the experiment
on ladyfingers at the end
of thirst a close shave with an
afterthought

                business end overboard
no such animal
                    out on a spree
is a nuisance

like the feel of imminent wealth
drills through night
every favorite tree
occurs to a silkworm

those geographers know how to travel
long on luck
short on luxury
lucky in love's one track mind

underarms are circling overhead
outbreaks of innocence dot the map
with clouds of baby powder
childhood ends when the dog blurs

and the blush dies away
to vestigial foghorns
relieved of decisions
they make themselves

cautious to a fault
orphans to be
live on thousands a year
limber and chagrined

nearly posthumous certainty
forms the meniscus
big molecules draw flies
natives burnish the lapels

shall we stroll into focus
bereft of octane
populations eyes only
elevation byo

drogue chutes popped first
initials at large
envelop their own gyros
frantic in amber as

cigarets keep gloves apart
once any stint beckons
foreground to impudence
of each an equal amplifier

take the heat as casualty
semibreves minims crotchets quavers
there was age and space
crank the awning up

a rash of mileage
weekend p.m. lull
for want of cordials
there is more than one Carolina

Chickadee combing telephone
wires stranded in fugue
I was touched
you want to leave something

to hang the botanicals on
and evidence snaps up the extra

far back behind the groceries
a passion for optics

diamondback terrapin in its day
took care of the afternoon
tandem red brick diagonals
wound up on an arm of the sea

get results in person
gas is more hedgy
where the hero is arch
room approaching body

temperature instead of intelligence
architecture shadows this man's world
delicate in its feathered coinage
and ornamental hermits

close calls are their specialty
mustering hairline watermarks
whose incandescent dewpoint
furnishes the mirage

what is enough
practically displays elements
bordering on dismay
myself included

SPINAL GUARD

for Louis Postel

No snow falls from blue sky
with the effortless slide of the trombone

Besides, the blind drive slow
with the nonchalance of boys

and uncanny gentleness empties
the planetarium into the street
courtesy of Mozart
who detested the flute

eager, destitute, a/k/a Wolf
his secret slang the wind

Some spectacular fish for pets
and afterwards infinite novelty, clinging

Versus three meals a day, knockout drops,
frankly hopeless downtown fever

WAVE TRAIN

The subject matter sports points of definition deployed in its field. I see luggage, and people walking down a gangplank into the water, where what looks like a sunken ferryboat lies just below the surface. Therefore it must emerge and drive on the bay, a huge station wagon, the lights on its wheels spinning through the dusk like Ferris wheels. But for the luggage, I would buy the descent.

The subject stands at the near end, flexing in the shimmering optics. It is a distinction. The drinks at this club, which is such that, have one big piece of ice each, roughhewn, in them. That is how we know we are here, since the prices reflect a modesty that belies its name. But it is hard to remember where the car is parked. Some morning it will be impossible.

The idea is to get a really big picture with a short throw. Wake to find the boarded-up newsstand across the street is open on a large scale, flashing periodical numbers two feet high, each brush strokes that recall all its high recognition factors. Say Red Grooms without silly putty. The wrong gauge, O in an HO world. Or someone decided to start with the model instead of the parts. All along I thought that spot was a triangular lawn left by an old Southern Pacific cut, bordered on two sides by geraniums, roses, and fuschia, on the front by red pickets faded to redwood.

A point of focus. Having ridden the J Church streetcar too far, down to 66th Street, and on the ride back seen San Francisco's outlying legitimate theaters, white fire escapes on their sides zigzagging against the night without top or bottom connections.

The subject relieves the object of its knowledge. A jet appears in the sky, climbing from horizon to peak in its spherical track, to come screaming straight down, like a gannet diving, into the water. Seconds later, three dripping naval officers emerge from the harbor, a few scratches and cuts. I interview them on a scrap of paper. They say the plane ran out of gas.

Or, the object has the subject by the tail. Lugging giant peanuts through dry Panama Canal ditch so ship, by this time an elephant, will keep moving behind me. The captain sends me out for a long bomb.

Aerial shots of golf course with spares for the future as the holes wear out.

We commonly regard the subject as a thing with miscellaneous attributes, out of which the lists and full proportions are all made. The earliest known form of subject is the plain song, suitable for a definite site or effect.

"Most subject is the fattest soil to weed." Heading south along Gulf causeway in Florida, we spot tropical architecture, and distinctive colorful aircraft. Police on the narrow road issue "moving tickets" tacked on the back of vehicles and payable at the exits, because there is no room to pull anyone over.

Accidents may remain without their subjects. The story of a doctor in China who traveled on his own yacht with medicines— a dramatic staging with audience participation where roast turkey turkeys fly in on wires. Arriving is a maze of New York City green wooden elevated stairs and passages, yellow mustard oozing out of cracks, preceded by snack bar where franks on buns are dunked in Coke.

Number is the subject of arithmetic. Street scheme of offering $1000 to someone for a penny. Collect the pennies and get rich—$2 a day. Try it out next to the street vendor of tiny flashlights, springs, and junk.

The subject is inclined to pose, at least, or cry out as a figure or incident. The house is small and rustic on a hillside above the southern river, and the bird life is fantastic, with colors on them you've never seen before.

The limits taken are open to doubt. Some say swallows submerge in ponds.

Example is gratified by its spot. 1931 doll mechanical cat, run on rubber bands and small battery-powered motors. Store in its box in DC-wired closet, so that "field pressure" will charge batteries and keep its fuses clean.

Much of what is bordered by quotation marks will never be said. They are hooks for an extracurricular enthusiasm to lodge on, or tracks of some two-toed editor who left the page to turn a phrase and returned to find it burnt.

Optics are no particular clarification. The buyers arrive in small cars, fold up their maps, unfold compact, daub, hitch up jeans and take to the stairs. A piece of property.

Everything is made of something else: maisonette-mayonnaise. Inside are shelves, dusty with years, the most astonishing of which is some eight levels high, one dense track configuration with connecting ramps piled on the next, including a side ramp all the way from top to bottom, so as to form a closed circuit.

The transaction includes a debt of allegiance, speculators walking with palms scooped back, duck style, breeze under knuckles. They mean business in black.

Fundamentals peculiar to concentration. Let's have another cup of coffee. Let's have another piece of pie.

It fell out I thought on my feet. Vehicles are always changing places beneath me. Some so fast they don't need motors, rugs, boxes, anything that will go uphill fast, even monogrammed silver. A little slope-backed church being built in the green woods by a blue pond. The pieces arrive on a truck.

Material in question for many fields is self-evident. Transparency is nonetheless alluring. "The condition was characterized by ideas of reference."

Strengths: claro, colorado, maduro. Shapes: belvedere, corona, panatela, perfecto, cheroot, stogie.

Down behind the lines the characters walk streets with searing self-consciousness. They believe in the invisible, the bus without brakes, checkpoints, the spiral notebook.

STEVE BENSON

ECHO

The carrots tried to *be* mushrooms. Their songs cried *to* the sonnet.

Singularly, they flipped off into the tied tree.

Their insides waving in the dead light of a fantastic sunset.

Their skins tight against the lids of the withered intensity draining the scattered mass.

You are trying to *be* the sunset. You are trying to make a person out of me. A person you might know.

Know me but do not meet me. Hold me up to this tree and see the light I shed.

Like tentacles of ivy fed through the vines of

the previously unencumbered except for wings and gnats and views

space in between. Lying there on a high rock

with your biniki unlaced, man, you plant your eyes

against the naked whiteness between my thighs and stomach

we get to shining apples making time go by till 5:30

when I go home. Staring off my business suit at the sunset

fading cloud incessant dream

and unstrap the curtains from the walls. Hit me over the head with your shovel and demand I scoop more sand into the bucket.

Your eyes are watershot and you've got a pubescent erection.

Your nose is turned like a hawk's, you're afraid I won't play fair. Is this, like everything else I'm told, about love, hate, fear, funny?

I'm saying I'm in love, hearing it funny. The echo is blundered.

On the way to L.A., I meet a surrogate for you in a bar, give him room in the passenger seat and desultory conversation, a smoke, kisses, blowjob, encouragement, $5, concerned disturbed uptight look. How can I characterize you that way?

You're really gone. I confuse you with the reader. The love poem is always addressed to you.

I look at the walls, totally up in the air.

The meat had started to spoil. A blind lemur bit off his hand.

He was an artist. But he was no artist. He was a principle.

He was an inevitable recluse and he held words to be impossible bores, whom he impersonated compulsively in hopes of getting rid of them.

She convulsed before dinner in the shower, with softer lap hands.

She was all there. Let's look ahead. Someone says, don't talk to me like that, and drops the book. The big eye opens at the back of the head and blinks

to blow away the hair. A certain resemblance of technique, if you care to look at it that way, is merely hinted at, named by

association. This *is like* that. Black beads

sweat on the pillow. You unlight the fire and undrink the beers

186 *Steve Benson*

while the TV. When the blast

knocks the walls away you are standing, the night sky hugging
below your nails, the idiot advice I tried to give you blown away.

Released from inexplicable code.

NARCISSUS

Someone happening in, now back. Even the very mildness of the reliefs is jolting. He gazed into the pool blah blah blah— pool, blah. No, I don't mind. Don't put it out in my hand. It comes with you, lasts while you are there; it goes when you go, if go you can. A white fence imported by teenagers from Tangiers.

Some kind of change is expected & apprehended in the bud. A rock singer is expected to change. They didn't know how to *see*, they were so hung up on targets. We meet at the movies. The name, the words, the precision, the permission is a fantasy, a factory blazing edges into dead trunks, evil architecture beyond the ecstatic rock festival. The doctor knocks on the ribcage and it gives, or he does, till all that's left is peaceful mess.

Morse code of x's and spaces leaping back into branched-out disciplined memory untugged from the core of wall. He lunges from chest, the eyes blink, huge in the absence of neon and tombs. The news suspended in some out of the way place. In plastic case are both tape itself, to listen to, and negative or replica. This happens catches up fast, puts off listening to break into passage of time. He introduces his grandfather's work in the catalogue.

You feel people should *expect* you to be moody. Keeping the lid on is to insist on it. You obey the only law you *feel* any responsibility to, guilt. I hardly say anything, just sit there reading. They look out, wave their little hands from the drear red and green light emptying the sky from sun. The fear others will see what's different in me, hold me to it, eats my mind.

The road bends round about here and wanders to meadow. One of us may be nobody. I stand myself. Nobody the same as you remember them, yet you go on, as if good hands held you in mind till child-murderers pass.

Coming down here, shattering and beaming isolate flecks, the movie freezes. Stand for myself, carefully cutting and joining. I write everything out in my head on long walks.

A camel bashes the line of vision across a white shed. I adore you.

They went from one of them to another, acting, for them to mirror each other and you become reduced to a single person and it became clearer I would come closer or be alone. Excuse me I don't want to pounce but the pressure at this point is great.

Wings gnats and space views space thrown one-way like large rock over plain of water. Both ears blond silent paraphrase swimming.

We walk and stand in the middle of the cabbage garden. A random form fills the two of us. Shock-white-reflecting grey airplane blurs stop orbit. I lie racing disarranged and the hall clock says the sun's setting and it's still hot when you come up on me face in cells the trees waving as if simple penis held aloft the angle of eyes gasping after direct breath.

Air loves to blend behind, can't decide to escape or bend act around little bit.

Go home and stare violently into the undulating sunset—the pith cuts the attention to the object. You plunge a fork into the plate and think about everybody else. Observing facial characteristics, between songs. He's learned to play while he inhales.

Tune in white plaster icons. Eyes in night-worn spirals against skin and backdrop everything world skin. I can think of everything but not right now. Face green under gel betrays envy and indigestion. Sign over door obscured by plants from trough suspended there too. Same voice, trailing elements of disorder.

The tent white burlap stretched wet taut in hope it won't shrink something called *personal knowledge*. The way wishing dogs crawl among terrifying verdicts, and all his love hates the way vice works against a trend to reconsider an easy answer. Incessant clouds face back words.

Put more sand in my pocket, or die.

Yesterday I had to ask where you had been. If I wanted to know you like blood in the midst of water. He doesn't know what he sees, but is fired by the sight. What do you want to grab that sheer slipped image that fakes you out. What you see is just the shadow your reflection casts. It is nothing in itself. At any rate not what he wanted, though it appeared to be, all he wanted being what that appearance signed. His eyes made an end.

In the picture you put over your books he leans over the stream, red cloth draped like untucked sheet, his ribs show slightly, his ass angular, not sexy except the face barely seen staring dumb for the first time at the face upside down that looks back astonished. Echo watches. Little places torn in the sky, someone only I know, no secret, just no room anymore. Your never having seen him is again beside the point.

Isn't it not a disinclination to discipline but rather a sort of impatience that makes transitions sudden no matter whether ugly or elegant, makes the fought-for virtue of liveliness thick with gains and miffed, mixed intentions, and demands the whole grain specified by particular charges, so that a wave is less a meant than willful embarrassing thing threatening all one's effects.

The echo blundered— knocked off the runway. Driving down route 100 tell story about you to efface rock baseline. Step over the outline, lean into the fall, symbolic assurance anchoring, strange as it seems, an appeal for help.

Loses its meaning if you say it enough times. I wouldn't have burned down the highschool if it didn't. I look totally through my head in this.

It aches, I think I asked too much of it. I'm bent over here, leaning into my own smells and hearing— how I could separate myself from my body, without killing him off. I stare into your hurt look and wonder what made you fall in the car today. My passage window, stomach flat if I look in— a trick imagining I'm here, car isn't, I on my way, and parked it turns into a still stream. The size is immaterial.

190   Steve Benson

Receding horizon. Negative assertive undertow. Alain Delon and Brigitte Bardot unrecognizable in nude embrace. One chest preferable to another, without an expectation to its use. Sprays in the direction of consensual agreements, white towel in a fiat of reckless lace. We became elements, forsythia crowding the house. A brilliant enigma covered with lips. The taste was elastic, like strawberry, brought in on wheelchairs. No sound, no other people, no noise, no emotion. At their feet the crocus brake like fire.

White line down center of handheld camera. The curse of mere glibness embarrassed the brown chest. Okay, what you do to your eyes is your business. Slow-down along production line though is no-go. The forelock of hair was light but I hold this bored gentleman frighteningly against me, sucking him onto my chest with heaving throbs. But he finds everything hurts, seems insincere in terms of the moment sent before the others. His eyes over the figure a ground black pencil, thrown every which way by the individual blasts of the showerhead.

I can't scream in space. I come at myself in this threatening way. There's a secret code in language that doesn't distinguish it from my body or the way I use my eyes.

So I'm constantly making up this tense inner attraction before sense. He speaks from any corner that exists, confirming its middle, trying not to see what is invisible. There is a moment in any continuous quarrel when we encounter the psychological postulate of consciousness in others. Sometimes his retina, as moments pass, can compare some object with the form of its movement. The air is full of infinite lines, straight and radiating, intercrossing and intervening. He feels he has some visible desire to picture the insides' invisible whole which he has given some visible parts.

"We've been following you a long time." Slow burning air. At lunch we had nothing to say, it all came back to her body, the table, that voice in the head that made something think. I looked at myself across the table, seeing myself through his eyes, if you will.

Steve Benson 191

from THE BUSSES

First and foremost
formulated by cat hairs
all over the clothes
of the massive butcher
with a pained smile
breaking tradition over
the hull of a remodeled
tanker. He sought the words
he had heard so often
in recent days, in
advertising, the press
talk around him, video
speeches, community sings---
fried rice for dinner.
He'd had enough beer.
It'd be okay. His function
in modern defense had been
assured him, a role in the---
but did he--- his language--- he
was *not* the figment of a paltry
imagination, even if--- he was
really the only sense he'd---
          I'm soothed, anyway,
when I calm myself thinking
in terms of wish-fulfillment, that
     I can put anything together
A lot of varied impulses,
marginal paraphernalia
in my sleep, as it were,
compared in passing
merely with some others
but not looking dead at
          them.

The lesson learned,
extracted, as it
were, from the
baleful reactions we
gave my tipping
credo, wobbling
incentive arched over
restless, evasive
circumstance
like a boil over
peas, practice
grew shelter as
in effect defense
and solitude
against the
exhaustion of the
evidence in time.

I was trying to realize
an ideal form but I was
stopped at an intersection
presumably at any rate
the cop told me it was
having forced me to pull over
My head was bandaged with
thoughts of this ideal form
with which I wrestled unable
to get out the car door
he was leaning on, filling
the ticket out in duplicate
explaining this was just
routine and nothing to get
defensive about.

the cold shoulder, wrinkled
with time's stain, of ham
or a roast, nice for the
holidays, but I'm
softer now,--- that's
not ringing I look out
for me, is the fat hole
it, after all.

Dangling from
the skin of
the cooking
pudding were
globs of as yet
unestablished
went on to
describe, sensation
trickling that way
consideration
with which you
aren't obliged,
it must be admitted,
necessarily to agree

an opportunity
to dock my sinking
ship, to bail out
frantically at
some tourists,
amid the groans
of other ships
way off away...
so much space
I don't see.

The crisis passed
we all released from
our congested stained
chests a relieved groan
The sun figuratively
speaking emerged from
the attenuated and yet no less
riotous dumb clouds
God what kind of grotesque
judgment will bring this
to a close?
A square barge came floating
around, soft and cylindrical, like
fashion in the ice floes of couturiers.
I went to hear at the master's house
with his emaciated wife, whose brain
seemed helplessly engendered with indifference
of me. The brutal fallacy of facticity---
"It's so weird out. What do you think is
happening, with the air?" "I don't know. I
think it's getting overloaded, with something."
The spelling was
peculiar. Always two
or three pencilled-in
statutes compromising
the innocent head of
the sleeping justice.
They had turned the
interest off their names
in order to increase
fitted in to the value of derivation.

preconceived I can barely cross off
expectations--- my forces in the blur
of stretching back to
seal my arms
against the rubber
hoist relaying
tight calm messages
of triangles over
the parkway
system idling
at the docks.
He had said
enough. He
rampaged against
the walls of the house
as though they were the
headboards of his child's bed.

192   *Steve Benson*

BLUE BOOK 42

I can hear myself, my voice that is, in the
distance. Which of us is answering back?
Go inside, where it's warmer, not safer.
Painstakingly, then, not for other eyes, or
ideas; independent of the idea of what you
bring to it, don't be just nothing but
nonsense, I go out when my roommate comes
over to read a play by her friends, I'm
distracted by the sound of my own voice; my
reflections on it are an influence on me,
none of this is hard and fast, it's pleasant
to abuse clumsy beginnings because honestly
the form doesn't work for me as pre-established,
like a farmer I have to work it. I can hear
the past out the window: I'm in the yard, on
the lawn, it comes out the upstairs window —
colors. Silly shit — man, you really caked
up in that one. Aren't you embarrassed? I
want to find how it ends. The tone of
metaphor taking over, generalizing, not
advancing the argument in its own direction
but telling you to it, giving up as to a
sexual experience (no transcript), why is
this philosophical? You guys are growing a
lot of weeds in your patches of the garden —
I'm just talking to keep myself possibly on
the verge of alert, available to criticism.
What do you think; of course it's not. In a
certain way it could be very funny (if we
concentrated, hearing how it's listened to
by each other) — I'm not interested in
pursuing lines of thought. It's astounding
how they grow, larger, bolder, not more
advanced but more overall, as I pace through
a given — you can hear the shape and limits
of the room, my acquaintance with — my

Steve Benson   193

relationship with myself mirrored in my
relationship with Chris, or vice versa, as
in a dream, everybody represents me to someone
who only admits he's watching at the risk of
introducing art or the layer of self-consciousness,
like a resin more than a finish, as a, not
a figure so much as a controlling quality,
not stylizing the whole so much as
determining the reification of its forms
in its terms, the qualities of successful
alienation or disturbing but consistent
dislocation which I unfortunately, foolishly,
needlessly . . . attribute to those
qualities. Two people in a room, both of
them me, I'm outside, overhearing very
deliberately but as though I'm not there,
through a window: dumb. Not self-abnegating.
Ignorant, deliberately, actually — myth,
childhood fantasy of homosexual seduction
by itinerant mature man, invented since,
I think. What jogs is not my memory.
Peculiarly toned down. The full force.
You can *hear* the tentativity, the *sense*
of limits, no realization — how they
"deform" the process taken into account in
the implications of the product.

Neatly arranged on the tabletop, people,
instruments, places. Ink smears on my
hand. I plan to upgrade the modes of
production, I do so, talking to a so-called
friend. He *is* a friend, "is" in quotation
marks, I offer him some criticism, and he
accepts the offer but declines the position,
walks away into the toilet to unload a big
shit. I'm not mad at anybody when I say
this, I say, isolated, alone, to myself —
what madness is that, that doesn't express

itself in sadness, its true form — oh stuff
it, you sheik. Some moments I'm just not
so mature — I pretend to have an overview,
but really I'm just watching the connections
hammering the points home; not wandering,
not as sterile as it seems — the model of
sterility really is the condition of propogation
of individually discrete organisms, isn't it,
conventionally with a positive moral applied,
like "better luck next time" or your own
offspring won't hurt you — a branch of "you"
to which "self-knowledge" need not apply.
Does this time have your name on it? Do you
have a cold? I woke up with something funny
in my throat, presumably the residue of
reruns of all those old dreams decomposing
like reconstituted tape. Nothing looks
interesting, everything looks better dusty,
one can't tell the cultivated plants from
weeds without a guidebook. I tried to
watch my father do it but not knowing where
I was going to be living I couldn't remember,
I had no fantasy to apply it to except being
my father, which was clearly untenable by
that time in my life — so I'm stuck with
research in books, and the idiosyncratic
policies of friends who are somewhat like
me in their headstrong clipped improvisations
into the hastily deconstructed bombs that are
our life. The planet streaks through its
stratosphere. I go off alone to try to put
the particular end to end as though history
were a unity of science and the novel but am
constantly interrupted by all the books I
want to read. Like walking down the street
I lambast myself for not feeling more
emotional, thinking I'm reporting on this.
I intend to see the relevance of all these

fragmentations, oscillations, interruptions,
and dislocations — I intend to bear witness
to their inherent mutual compatibility and
discovery of structure within that deconstructive
self-consciousness within a flux based on a
lamentable primordial stick in the mud within
solid wind. The beep goes on. Rhythmic,
elastic — I sense it out, pressing my nose
against it, coloring it with my face, the part
I cannot see. Do you think he really wants
to be in it? Well if he doesn't he can always
drop out, he's proved himself good at it before,
he agonizes but he knows he's right. I was
asked for things to think about; it was
surprising but right and not disturbing but
steady and friendly but inwardly very disturbing
because I was losing something without admitting
it, my grip on what I thought. It was easy
enough to tell her but afterwards I thought of
other, qualifying, more general things that I
wanted to tell her but have forgotten them now.
Don't eat without chewing! "There's not
enough time left to do anything else but
continue this."

When now all that day dies monosyllables
down long, that memory ipso facto syllables
come like ride this dowdy lowlife clinging
bow-wing sequinned bracelet with calfskin
gloves. Like a character in Henry James,
she charms her charity first, wins rides
and claims monstrous gravitation among the
rides and soups the monster wears to work
and the horse shoe factory. Boll weevils
belts gloves glow into heavy seeds negating
weakness down low in the driver's seat where
James Dean crunches a piano into a cigarette
pack in advance of the tobacco industry.

Sentences start up like cars that aren't
going anywhere until they through that part
of the operation interrupted sentence on
till midnight jaggedy still thought croaks
in reedy fitness squabbles long time march
winners end losing streak to carousers' glow,
like wondering what will happen if you get
famous — haven't you been preparing for
this all your life? Not that the by-product
is essential, it only lasts for a short
while compared to the process of the whole
work, like this sentence meaning shifts into
low and high gear without needing to but
wanting some kind of reification, reintegration,
and a negative grace to counter the facile
purposeless (seemingly) quasi-grace to challenge
an active or maybe we say realizing what's the
watchword these days a grace that would hold
up not only to inspection, which is important,
but to the impact of waves and flying things,
diversions of attention from this ground we
need, being people, to stand on. Over all of
us a cosmic sort of sky, grey light hanging
with its hands up and its head full of
cigarettes, unsmoked so not so bad. The
washing machine towers over the scaffolding
raised to unwind its listening touches — a
burglar soars over the houses and gets lost in
the trees: the trees have sent extensions into
the air above and rerouted systems of learning
for the birds whose wings now tip into dully
squeegee wet brown precipitantly sedentary words,
car radio sounds coming out of their cars. It's
not the last thing I do to change the sentence
in the middle — my mind is so stubborn I couldn't
tell you I changed it. It resolutely refuses
to be challenged and I refuse to believe it.
So how are we going to start the revolution?

Steve Benson   197

I don't remember if I dreamed that I once learned,
meaning managed, to light a fire by rubbing 2
sticks — if I really did it I didn't believe
it. This by way of example, quoting myself last
night, I don't remember either way, the but
notion of that I . . . often appear as an
example, usually of an exception, but perhaps
less often than I'm aware. Having lived and
experienced a lot of history, ambivalent about
whether and how it shaped him and he carried it
around with him, wanting to shake it or let it
slide off his back, hence finding himself not
so out of joint with the time as so unavailable
to it for his personal freedom and its perception
of his historical necessity, once pitted, he
considered his option to approach those living
in time with the freshness of makers peeled
by consequences as a independent agent and a
cringe of history situation missed value in them;
not a follower but a inspector or procedure, he
was immune to advice or criticism, plunderer of
his own track, which would violate, if unresisted
them, and which talking back to was informing.
His disdain for the subject was eagerly mocked
by the quest to have something to do — he was
not one of those who would have liked to retire
into persona — he kept himself earnestly
figurative, neither begging nor in any way
demanding but certainly tending to keep the
doors of communication (a good way to conceive
them) open or at least ajar for the endlessness
that would leak out and that he could in any
way find relatively (to possible alternative)
free forms for. The doors of communication
were or possibly are of access, and now I'm
taking on his voice more consciously and so I
know and can tell nothing is happening anymore.
I remember a lot of opinionated poetry, some of

198   *Steve Benson*

it in letters to the editors and book reviews.
Not the words themselves but a sort of destruction
or why don't you like John Ashbery or the
roles of ill health hurling themselves up
through the brain — rolls of wadded time
and paste gabbling ironically against the
monkey — you can read the setting of the
ass in the chair in the insensitive tension,
deliberately prepared, of these words — not
mine, I'm talking of someone else's — Diane
Wakoski's, and the persons she argues with.
Is this "being" unsupportive? *Does* one have
an ax to grind, or *is* it obsolete? If I
like a friend, I like to help him, or her,
or it. It's impersonal, whether I like one
or not, it's not a value judgement, it's
valuing pure per se. If you can volley for
serve you can play the game. I can't make
it up to you; you can easily make it up to
me. Let go of your chest, hold your arms at
your sides, walk over to me.

3/23, 3/24, 3/26 / 80

Steve Benson   199

MICHAEL DAVIDSON

BRAHMS

All five of them
(including Mr. Rubenstein)
lost forever, their boat
made out of the same
lousy plastic.

IF TO WITNESS

If to witness is to persons unafraid or blank that is where a blue line meets a convinced corner. If to judge by violins or a lozenge the results be they of a mottled or variegated surface and distinguished by no less than three nor more than five contusions upon the skin a confidence may be restored, the guests issued into the cold night and you satisfactorily returned to your small rural home with dog. Which is to say if to declare by canopy or other brightly colored awning that a person of such-and-such a height wearing green or grey plaid could exert him or herself in a way so as to render amazement, as it were a foreign sentence dropped amidst the conversation and you off by train tomorrow for the north then passing references to your person incomprehensible during the evening and concerning the better part of one's capacity for writing in journals might attain that point or points wherein your intention to speak coincides with their intention to hear, the resulting uncomfortable silence being the only sign of such freedom that further conversation could only exacerbate an already tense moment and remind you of a technical device something like a microphone or perhaps a mushroom growing beside a fallen cedar somewhere else.

SUMMER LETTERS

The l's live in caves under the earth,
down here, it's summer
and hotter than anything else,

when it was winter
we did all the work
and nobody disturbed us,

the letters were written
in the cool mornings
and by the afternoon

they were received
and nobody cared
how;

the i's and e's ride together
on a motor scooter,
they know where they are going

(into the wind probably),
they love one another
with a tenderness quite unknown

in the real world,
these are not my words
but those that summer gives me

in order to create love
as my cat creates another, larger cat
to hiss at,

"hiss" is made out of an agreement
between wind and tongue
not to recognize their limitations,

the way memory and summer
reveal their terrible affinities
while speaking separate dialects,

I wish the poem of satisfaction
would write me a letter
as though I had written to E

in the full flush of their conjoining
as in neighbor and weigh
where friends share a sieve

where there is little to remember
but stormy days
I would have a house of my own

words, and they would comfort
as you do
living between us,

for now, great uncertainty strides
across the film of sea
erasing all distinctions

I need
you fill
we move.

THE ARTICLE ON GENEVA

for Steve Benson

*It is not that they disapprove of the
theatre in itself; but they fear, it is
said, the taste for adornment, dissipa-
tion, and libertinism which the actors'
troops disseminate among the youth*
—M. D'Alembert

Something passing over possible without a usual engine or landing
lights. Without introduction or otherwise commentary simply
one's self or rather where one stands so that the words. Wednesday
for example seventeen letters and seventy laps pursued by a grip-
ping drama of life in Wyoming ca. 1910. Rather then to stand
before you in underpants, as it were, floating ammunition across
treacherous waters. The bomb factory lay on the opposite bank;
only the peasants chose to remain behind which was hard on them.
Something unlike a helicopher or insignia to explain national
allegiance, something in other words foreign. That's the way they
think in Oregon. Then home to receive the piano assisted by the
fair one of translucent hands clutching Chopin's Preludes. As if in
her silence a passable meaning averted he was bound to dig out
and sent carbons to several witnesses.

The problem is whether the flame comes from within (soccer) or
whether the flame is imposed from without (baseball). Whether
in the nimbus of gaseous matter swirling above the central core
some residue or memory (Africa) resides in each atom or whether
through our so seeing and stating the case (Asia) such correspon-
dence is invented. The "exquisitely tempered ponderousness" of
his stating the case for something passing over possible without a
usual prolegomena or frame thus leaving him. Simply to do one's
work and get on with it as though a stone were brought in for fif-
teen minutes. He collected words about his work and made a
work she reminded him of something. The word she never had a
chance not to be an object. I refer to you.

Those "genteel baubles" you see at the corners of your eyes a part of the eyes and yet "self-excluded" from them, swimming around in their watery appropriate figure of speech. He tried to corner all of them; he didn't want to know of their crimes; he lined them up against the wall; they tried to speak; they had tried to use their eyes to see him with. Trying not to make the connection between them was his job but the intervention of a foreign imperial power wearing the insignia or a refining fire helped him somewhat. Once the continent (Alabama) is split in half they can begin to isolate (Oregon) the ones who talk funny (California) where they live. The old sagas and the quaint words they used: stone, ship, sea, wind, pine, island, shield, tape recorder, father, grey, he, she. Some geese flying south honking or perhaps a child next door crying in waves. They speak "slippery as glass" with a world to anticipate them but without an audience. I am only stones.

SCALES

I

One block two block again to sit and quoting numbers to help us
read into it red car brown car small truck waving palm red car as if
it moving moves its own accord by or not so rapidly three pause
four pause keeping some record men must be waving from the
deck a table glows in sun some blue area opens itself in the middle
of five table six epic wars nine blouses whereas because winter
weather she pauses to turn ten page eleven page a puddle then a
bus not to make a clarify but a cognate of speaking that breath
wished out of here he is twelve pencil thirteen radio scan war data
breathe after sleep we wake and talk drink fourteen ellipsis fifteen
ellipses then sixteen and twenty green car sign daily weekly
monthly makes this this open number box grid picture hill bleak
saturday degree register street pencil halfway man in blue jacket
walking I think dejected and straight ahead.

One block again having walked then encountered eyes a mouth
some jackets with sayings and a pier they cast and in white lines at
end of a block we walk two blocks a letter a second letter "B"
your two small puddles pushed into they also we have small things
or not protuding noses economy and then the phone it's john or
yellow warming up into at four blocks pause the wind fences and
of course red sky four letters then a fifth's being instant grey
giving way to bay in between a wind and an object a map is
needed with its boats its pianos and umbrellas the prophecy and
seven rocks before creation because of which music right angle and
straight ahead four yards dear figures a fifth.

Not alone but perhaps not alone and a way of walking around
corners one corner two corners three cornered four home not
alone having walked all the way a woman on a bicycle wearing
red that's noticed a woman in blue with a bible that's noticed two
men bouncing balls a child toddling over sand a dog chasing a
phrase without other person indistinguishable from you it passes
small storm the midst of night in which we lay thus traces of water

called puddles my two bells the carriage returns I start one corner then two perhaps nature is not alone there's I.

II

Two does not equal a double music. When two bands play then a third is possible you go away with. Which is not a trio. The name Flaubert is a useful marker, also the name Safeway where we bought the papaya. I am left with one, the one wearing the green shirt. Anything can happen at this point. There have been five articles recently in order to name part songs. Let us meditate on fucking. As the morning grows on towards afternoon the wind raises the newspapers in the trashcan by the hedge adjacent to the street upon which the cars roll towards their destinations.

Let us meditate upon the I necessary or adjacent to identity, the one the two could get along the better without. The map the plan the toy the can the fish the catch the dime the small native boy in shorts beside the large silver ship in midday heat beneath the many panama hats in the South Pacific. Many of us do not equal nor own a chorale but have voices we write down in the form of letters. Providing a comforting music for the widow for whom the service named the loss of one beloved by many. Two is comforting; two is not a scale.

III

Two as easy as one this one looks at herself in the mirror this one is him and we hear music. This one is on a hillside or a plain far from the ocean and there is the sea. This one receives a letter but he has no friends. A music plays two musics whereupon the intention breaks down. A fourth will be one too many will be not a clown will wear the latest in pastels she is two women I am two women he writes saying it's me that's cleverness for you.

The letter includes the Page of Cups his fish a copy of the card she uses to think of him with by which he thinks of her in that city the queen looks out of falling towers he raises his cup toward her priestess and hierophant she traces something old and something gold out of rock then sends and reads to him he writes from there being so little else to begin with and returns thus move and despite of arrange and reduce from now pausing looks up forgets fish striking out of that cup this cup this proferred hand in which nothing looks out of to see you it is you.

TOM MANDEL

ALL THESE EXAMPLES

       This the quick halibut's so rusty
so's a piece
       jab-jobs
knocks rue it, no header am spared it
Sir Witzio, e.g., crossed finder hairs &
one dead halibut
shoulder it, center upon the shoulder
ante trivial monday pringles
tu(taterpops)esday genuisti filium
teacup in   wednesday's rain
on donnerstag two dogs   halibut traces in fog

my friend with the long nose and strides
is an appreciative person resisting thought
'a work of 18 years fishing'
in these waters: no doubt many molecules the same
of fishers and farmers. Came out the house in Lans
the day we left, to find the elder Ravix on the path
asking had we seen his cow (famous for escaping).
The son had been to school in Lyons: there were
milking machines & in back the old stalls. The old man
appreciated that   he showed me his hands
                          warning me to
drink quickly on such stormy days—anyway their faces
pure slav like their name, yet the town cemetery revealed
stones back five centuries named Ravix
This is the Latin peasant stock straight back to Eastern Invasions.
Farmers and Fishers: for several years these spectra
will dwarf the two men, resisting thought, advancing in the bus
longer and longer these same bowls grow white
and in the forefront a phalanx of seven. 'Step
right this way, I'll make you a farmer of men.

SALLY

Wet wipe out rust dry over oily flame
Bend again to thing time type and oxide hall of
Chinks ending with a little music
A useful mind steeled toward decoration
Theatre circles stars
Red binding shelf of weeks
Whose maudlin engine stops the gypsy capitol
Foot in grave in mouth
Words press up inside the sheepish face
Lowered blue roofs approximation
Hidden holds of argument and the year
The hand I know yet you wears the tie
Ink lines in a pair of lips
Bays willed of action grease report
The sweet pace lower limit to see
Certain kind unintelligence answering
That terrain goes by called in
An absent stance of burden acts their echoed names
Mutters don't want disturbing the breast
Cool palm shakes neck of
Dawns stacked back in the projector
White up fender well blisters hysteric
The vapid anapests
Stands there shadow stones in water
Narrow gnostic turns
Lowers a tic into his will
Teeth turn on kiln hands that wheel the waste
Optical gripper stagnate in this guise
Distant appreciative continent of current novelists
So did were got flirt
Our walking places keys in their hills
Machine serrations disturb hems and thumbs
Year's sense of what performance
The bright pinhead warbles words and banks
Sense of butt in door or ordered hulking
Sane permission ink and image

A bay of pastel plasma forms
Willed actions in this ear
A tower disassembles for her hands
All do and would really rather can
Ineligible words letter the center the life led here
Demanding midyear mirror
The sky weighs on the dirty turf
Loss words mutter flatters upper stops
The hilly contusions & mates their cluttered table
Out there message in these
Slow afternoon levers exact gaseous stares
Diving gray arithmetic falters
In our country metal ducks fight back
As arrived in train to meet the plane
Hard muff bright inverted sky
Radioed equivocation disappears
Clouds prepared once in a lifetime spheres lie down
Mean she remains
Midnight that fled to the tables
Got on pads of meaning blitz lifts
Essay feathers cirrus
Memory back through war to birth
Ball bearing dream fragments the still pan of cones
Rattle static evening appetites
Marry to procedure those absent wills
Does western rhythm still exist
Reparations pages move through this
Left every night phrases contusions of youth
Assent stanzas
That does the pure white bag
Calls point lit left old vary
Her second may pronounces robber george
Documents of the Dacian rise
Or cluster class ending coeval
Tempt at of phase
Yearly stippled hits long notebook backs will go
But cannot push it away from face
As seems close I catch

None dare call it language
Hauling moon of grimmest stitches up
No spacious antique passage or feudalism
Want the mark again that without
Edges frayed onto the green bag
Sill sits a literal holder
Walking the words to their places
He combs his visible hair
Curious cold side of the phone
Specifically and that one sees it
Stops recorded them from the bottom
And knowing how to think becomes afraid to
Of what period travels this one
Visits flex a mosaic
After what he did he stayed in thought of it
Lamp sheds shade
She writes a thin strip of recipe ingredients in verse
Blooms burst on jacket
A left & right hand paging knuckles cigarette
Sit back on the back of this chair and collect you
Chords of motion rest and the rest
Dim then unfindable startling warrior glyphs
Magnetic charge to warded-off excess orbs
Vatic static rusts button sounds
Throbbing the crowd gaps enough to notice
Disguised gray dyes
A simple interior contented laboratory
Kicking bluntly engulfs construction
These venues gently mounded of their man
Sprightly still speech of a failed liveliness
High tide low wind caramba song
Vagary pockets displace
Stammering dream fragments of strike start
Aloha headache
Unsolicited usual sky or salient
Pleasant face distracted by tears in phone
The sending glasses double the light what's there
Motionless birds work the air

Long brown cuffs of the second hand
Trumpet what she really wants to do
Smart manning of his holes
Tires crush a.m. jewels
You just laughed about it there
What found added object
Mills climbed the forested gorge till day
Expert criminals throng the sign-out tables
Home with its halls
Mind strays to what's doing
Alter all the singing traces

REALISM?

This is the only thing as large as that. I regret I am not the physical giant to practice all I comprehend. Underground—bush, facade, horizon—burns with a *realism* you cannot go back on.

Recognition dissolves the object. We hum along. The symbol of home is a pale light bathing an object at a high horizon line. Beneath it materials, somewhat close to us, we stamp on them; they are resumed on our home ground. The more I think . . . well, I hear it. The flesh circles the sofa, is in favor with the consciousness seated there, then is ejected. Recovered sounds hear new songs, and each inaccessible in its own magic competence. Chaotic shapes nature merges in a style of play. The only space there is still surrounds me. Electrical charge sucked out of sockets by its active loss in light over objects. The time to read is now. It's neutral outside, it is use. Better to pare your nails, the better your nest to feather. While the idea does its work and returns happily to the head that thinks it. A dog barks at dogs in a film, then quietly waits for a cut. It is this absence of sound we perceive as the sign of silence. It is sufficient that it grow quiet for no one to speak. After abundant harvest, a field lays fallow. But through the sketch of a window, he looks onto the page itself. Now, cut the highway out of the heart of a map. The white wall, the blue architect, half in sun. The sky is these words above you. Rain is the converse story of seeds that remain. The transparent monolith opacified.

Have you seen the carpet, have you looked up from the carpet. The faces that pair off do so to remember. From minds gingerly emerge terms of fate, facts and sentences singly. The buildings are few and low, the temperature is high and low; snow tumbles from your heart directly onto the issues of popular survival. It has the habit to feel slighted and that it goes out of the way to incur it.

The limits of the world leak in from its edges, pervade. Thus did he take up the sentence and play it for all he was worth. But what was *it* worth? The context commands.

Reality authorizes my speech in speech. Each dimension iterates its two worlds. Sign here and the ink will fade in conditions of its own choosing, an icon overcome by just what made it so.

214 Tom Mandel

The text guards the door to the reading room. Try as you will you will hear it all. Sorry, try as you will you will hear it *fall*. Try as you will you will hear it all. Before an object, something modern—a building, a person—one falters, sorry, *one alters*, one falters, wondering whether to look up at it or straight out from the shoulders. Even the vaguest order is perfect, as everyone knows. If you change me, I begin to see without light.

DAVID BROMIGE

MY POETRY

for Bob Perelman

My poetry does seem to have a cumulative, haunting effect—one or two poems may not touch you, but a small bookful begins to etch a response, poems rising in blisters that itch for weeks, poems like ball-bearings turning on each other, over & over, digging down far enough to find substance, a hard core to fill up the hand. It's through this small square that my poems project themselves, flickering across the consciousness, finally polarizing in the pure plasma of life. The reader grows impatient, irritated with my distancing style, coming at him in the rare book format, written under not one but two different kinds of dirty money, & knowing me to be an english teacher.

"The Protestant Poem"[1] & the prose piece "He Was"[2] typify my tendency to write over-elaborated series of possibilities which become arid & abstract. It's possible for even the best current poetry to sink into oblivion without wholly justifying itself through such an absolute renunciation of mediocre success. "The Protestant Poem" & certainly, "He Was," are not arid, they're great (except maybe, "kaleidoscopic world"). My poetry is "curiouser & curiouser" as it makes a descent into the rabbit-hole where descent becomes the subject of the poem's concern: a dazzling dimwittedness that makes sense of its mackerel-textured absence. A respectful abstinence from knowing what I'm doing? Therefore, my style seems to have fallen apart, deteriorated in the three-year interim between books; some kind of decadence has set in; it has become problematical, not to say impossible, because if it limits itself to the traditional language & form of a literature it misses the basic truths about itself, while if it attempts to tell those truths it abolishes itself as literature. Chiastic sentence:

---

1. *Tight Corners & What's Around Them*, Black Sparrow, Santa Barbara, 1974.
2. Ibid.

not true, MAKE IT NEW, caps, has always been the case, it's what literature means, should mean.

At this point, then, we begin to glimpse what is the profound vocation of the work of art in a commodity society: not to be a commodity, not to be consumed, not to be a vacation. Isn't this the piece talking to itself, hoping to be overheard, & contradicted. Because, the interest evident in the construction, rhythm of the sentences, obviates the need for the content. (Not to deny the feelings, of course). And I, as you probably do *not* know, am a sucker for children in pain. If you allow Cézanne to represent a third dimension on his canvas, you must allow Landseer his gleam of loyalty in the spaniel's eye. I really don't think I'm demanding too much. The idea that poetry is good for a person & should be choked down like a horse pill is ridiculous.

> All night you've been stiffed
> upstairs across the bed as if
> composing, I plump up your
> pillows, & measure my tread in
> the hall. Off & on I hear you
> snoring & nearby. What else
> is there? Isn't this Saturday
> morning—isn't that Alice out
> side, in the snow? I stare her
> down however long it takes. You
> get up to relieve yourself & we
> encounter in the parlor & ask me
> whatever am I up for? This
> passes for communication.

This is a good example of Jay Gutz's work. Bill Bisset inhabits an entirely different poetic & spiritual universe, & so does Jay. Like Blake, Bisset is a visionary, mystic poet who makes his own rules of poetry as he goes along. Trying to mount a woman with half a hardon is infinitely more terrifying than anything you can trot out from Blake. More terrifying? I should read more Blake. Malcolm Le Grice, the film-maker, proposes a distinction in structural films between the "compositional" (work=composition) & "problem-atic" (=problem, e.g. people who want to write language & not poems, just as McClure wants to write his body). Bernstein

David Bromige 217

composes using a vocabulary which at all points (nearly) proposes itself as the other—this vulnerability, constantly expressed, is a sign of what (why does he insist on it?)—yet "what I want to call attention to is that there is no natural writing style" which of course is exactly what Barthes was saying in '53, *non*? These are the poles & what moves the piece is that there is no resolution, point of equilibrium. Here too, the problematic mode proposed as a strategy for composition, as such—this whole body of poems is a big jump forward for me, in that I'm no longer writing "just poems," each work is somehow myself.

Able to Describe the Verses

Able to describe the verses more sad each night.

In the night like the two of them between my arms.
They kissed like tarantulas beneath an infinite sky.

She quizzed me, I quizzed her back.
As if I had a friend with big fizzy eyes.

Able to exactly as I said before.
Thinking that I can't go on. Feeling lost.

Ear to immensity's night, immense with her.
On the other hand my soul turns rocks into paste.

What does it matter my love can't guard its shame.
The night is starry & she isn't with me still.

So much for death. For song with its laws. For laws.
My soul is not contented with having lost her someplace.

As if she were here, I admire her hair suit.
My heart her hair suit, & she isn't in it.

The mismatched night blanks out the mismatched trees.
Our sisters, those who entice, the same backwards as forwards.

I don't know why, that's certain, perhaps I should ask her.
My voice grows furry as it blows about her idea.

The other. Be the Other. Come kiss me like before.
Her voice, her clear form. Her infinite pupils.

Why I don't know for sure, maybe we'll discuss some ways.
The short tan of love, the large tan of oblivion.

Why is night like the two of them between my arms:
my discontented soul with the beauty it has lost.

Although this sea is the ultimate sadness she can cause me,
&, as I told Sean, this is the ultimate paper boat I shall make her.

I suspect people won't understand why I think this is language-oriented writing, but it certainly is. I'm a "mind" poet rather than a "body" poet, terribly involved with trying to understand my processes. There are too few memorable poems.

The stars
are insatiable holes, we argue, I hold them
Davy lamps. The stars
are. The night is
cold, I slurred the word, is
coal, I said, & she heard, the blonde kiss holding, Gold.

The "insatiable holes" are spaces created by desire; substitutions around a phonemic center create phrasings & cadences of great intensity as they seek to "fill" an erotically-charged context. It was a *cold* winter, we were out of *coal*, she was sitting on a *gold* mine. Engels writes poems on the disjunction between a consciousness doomed to ask ethical questions of a body & natural order incapable of giving certain replies; I, on the other hand, am more concerned to show the disjunctions inherent in the field of discourse itself. It's like I've moved from tight corners to perfect circles. Still so tight. It's all so every word utterly true, & at one & the same time, utterly flip. Shiny as glass . . . slippery as glass.

I don't like it, for hurting my head, & I mention it only to relate myself to a particularly productive current in American writing, one associated mostly with prose (e.g., W. S. Merwin's recent narratives, or those of Raymond Federman & Ronald Sukenick). The hipper among you will be able to identify what drugs went into each one of these sad works & god knows, there is hash, speed, coke, opium & alcohol in all of them. Quasimodo was right—Mozart was right: *Bald, oder nie, & Bob's your uncle*. I cannot say the word e, y, e anymore . . . there is no e, y, e—there is only a series of mouths—nothing strange about my powers of speech, so many typos that work, sort of.

My Typos

The long tea high of love
—the tranquil distances
from *m* to *o* in amor soldered
& *o* says *o*, don't stop:

you ask my why *o* insists on existence
& *a* means your life is complete?
Who can precisely explain
o's moment & *a*'s fragrance to Rosa

& persuade her to drop her
inhuman arrogance?
If not her pants?
O *n*, that intercepts what's past!

The world is *not* all that's lowercase. The environment I most readily take into myself as subject is the feminine, my intense interest in mummy being the inner space I most characteristically bring into the writing place. OPACITY—*si*, mysterious cohesion/cohesive mysteriousness, no—is the magnet, what brings anyone *into* the work of another, the announcement of the new *within a specific matrix*. The matrix of the mature artist is largely determined & governed by his own works:

this is the essence, where mine
& the general nightmare mesh.

I work in monochrome, & am *all* attention. What I choose to write "about" is another problem. I constantly delve into confession & what Frank O'Hara called "personism." That's one form of contemporary *hubris*. So, *Birds of the West* was a birdwatcher's book I was using. All of it seems to me individual & skillful. The constant erasure of signs for presence leaves the poem as an interstitial agent in the service of intentionality, & the uncertainties & doubts which Keats saw as the essential conditions for poetic creation become the characteristics of generation in any form. The non-instrumental, which gives instance of what stands for itself & so not a call to revolution or a representation of the struggle & how it is peopled, but an instance of it (product, the unalienated or re-integrated itself: while still putting off (& on) other myths of "presence" which turn on a misunderstanding of how language operates & how we operate in it, which is to say no e, y, e, s).

The blurb on the book says the usual blurb-things. "David Bromige writes carefully, with *pleasure*—which is the point." Well, which *is*? I am the author of previous books, which is the point. A stunning achievement. Good images ("as carefree as a coffin-nail commercial"), & often a good use of language. "Still there"[3] is a remarkably clear, unaffected, beautiful poem. The poem ceases to be a process of discovery. You go to step on the boardwalk & it's rotten. I try to transcend my petty anger & bring you into an area of engagement under the rule of Poetry. Notes are made along the way toward a remembered edifice. Even a divine physics cannot make categorical thought-determinations of realities intuitable in the plain, ordinary way; as little as divine omnipotence can bring it about that elliptic functions should be painted or played on the fiddle. The tone is objective, rendered ironic by contrast with the monstrous behavior portrayed. What does the "one who knew this" know? It's about some chick whose husband was at the war. The mind's always going west. It's really about the style & aplomb & frame of mind needed to bring it off:

> like in the long-ships, at the war to elude us
> he's waging over the dwellings where we might'v lived
> because from his birth, those grooves in the heavens
> had been manifest as soon as remarked on
> & the good bright glint off their wolfram wings
> Dum dum de dum dum.

Anyone for "Lili Marlene?" In my poetry the search shows, & so do the seams often, but my poetry gains authenticity from its deliberate ruggedness. Bull shit. Everywhere there is the tension of an incomplete sentence, an ambiguous antecedent, an unnatural act, an illogical causality.

3. Ibid.

A sentence, as the expression of a
complete thought, is not natural &
does not exist in nature. Is not
natural & does not exist in nature.

The prose pieces are of a deft, dead-pan order, hinting at more
than they state. It's difficult to say whether this prose makes too
much ordinary sense, for it is less zany & irritating than *Tender
Buttons*—as if that were some kind of discus mark set in 1911 for
extra-syntactic competitors. Yet is it teasingly nonsensical when it
is most clipped & aphoristic. One thinks of cummings at his most
tricksy in some instances: pixie, pig-stye, pistils, stilettos, & e, w,
e. The disclaimer at the end suddenly opens a double-bind; it HAD
happened before—the previous page, the previous time.

But what, then, to make of disclaimers: by what agency are they
rendered? The poem I like best is:

> The Sign[4]

A slight, simple poem is slight & simple, & for A. R. Ammons
there's no getting away from that. I've been thinking lately about
some sort of code of ethics for reviewers. Everywhere the cere-
monies of the Phallus are rehearsed, questioned & continued. It
is that agonizing lust to express with which I can personally
emphathize. My book *Threads* used a rhetoric which reminded
Diane Wakoski of Eshleman's work, & both of us together brought
to her mind the language of Michael McClure. Students can learn
to write better-made poems but those poems with their elegant
turns of phrase, their vivid imagery, even their conceptual excel-
lence often seem to add up to nothing. To a wisp of smoke, like
the poet Mark Strand, whose work is filled with beautiful lines,
ideas & images & yet seems to add up to a zero. When holes taste
good, we'll put 'em in our bread. She kept remembering how
easy it had been to read *Darker* (Mark Strand, Atheneum, 1970,
47 pp.), & how pissed off she'd been at the poems all the way
through, feeling they were hollow & empty & loving the beautiful
language & wondering why that beautiful language didn't seem
beautiful to her the way a Lorca poem would with its beautiful

---

4. *The Gathering*, Sumbooks, Buffalo, 1965.

language.* But she did not wish to waste any time detracting from one poet to praise others, feeling that too much of that is done in this nasty world. The poet A. W. Purdy was gleeful:

> I have a very low opinion of the Black
> Mountain "method" of writing poems
> (which is partly the exclusion of any
> other method), & have seen some of
> David Bromige's reviews of myself &
> others before.

Either poetry is real, real as, or, as Shelley for one believed, realler than, life; or it is nothing, a stupid & stupefying occupation for zombies. Freud's condensation & displacement are figured here in the poetic tasks:

> Not the cracking of the ashtray on my
> skull was the indicator but her
> repeated scream, What do I want with a
> husband—never once my name.

This syntax like algebra seems not unlike that which Hoffmansthal claims for his early lyrics. For me, also, everything disintegrated into parts, those parts again into parts; no longer would anything let itself be encompassed by one idea. Single words floated round me; they congealed in e,y,e,s, which stared at me & into which I was forced to stare back—whirlpools which gave me vertigo, &, reeling incessantly, led into the void. A few years ago there was a fad which entailed going to the laundromat, putting a dime in one of the large dryers, & jumping inside. This works in a short poem. But many of these poems aren't short. One is a very long nine pages:

> Whoever stood furthest up the trail was master
> of the trail.

---

*Possibly she had in mind these lines:

> We stopped for grits.
> Three carbine-carriers came.
> The dusk of her kneecaps
> & the gorillas in her heavens.

> And I entered cunt. Clayton, weeping buckets
> her adventure a gentle gazelle,
> in the teahouse of the pizza parlor
> came, furiously, gnawing on all within reach.

Pitiless duration—I suppose that's well here I am & it's the morning & I've got a day to get through & tomorrow there will be another. And there'll be a lot of dependent clauses & you have to go out & support them. There's a whole struggle in there that breeds murder. My own father was forced to go out & commit murder, not once but a number of times. All I ever did was unplug some tubes, doc. . . . But there *is* an insistence, almost purely sexual, which would apportion the poem as a longer event than is popularly conceived in 1973.

Psychoanalysis

Often people fuck merely in order
to keep from having to talk

but I don't remember everything
else I said.

I have a strong imagination which sometimes interferes with the poem & becomes distracting. Suddenly, "the sight of this creature/ turned them (the "two" "friends": twin children of adversity) & they fell to arguing." It's the trouble with all museums.

If it sounds as if I'm too loose or sloppy, that is not the case. Example: This burg isn't big enough for both of us. I just pulled the strings. I'm not the craftsman George Ellenbogen is, & in some of the poems I appear to display no craftsmanship whatsoever; nevertheless, at the personal surface I'm one of the most appallingly human of the west coast poets, perfectly willing to reconcile myself to whatever comes along on a given day, hence enjoy this moment, that moment, no questions asked, no answers needed. No theory today escapes the marketplace. All are put up for choice; all are swallowed. The writer is the widow of an insight. Slandering Croatia with a false esteem. It was the last class-meeting of *Eros & Civilization* & we were eating brownies. What can look at itself is not one. Many Europeans & Orientals speak English far more vividly than those of us for whom it is Mother Tongue. So, one evening, being driven on a winding road by our friend Stella, & narrowly escaping being struck by an oncoming truck, I screamed, she reprimanded me, an intense awkward silence ensued relieved only when 3 sentences appeared before me, a prompt sheet passing across the windshield:

> The truck had nearly struck their
> car. He had screamed. She had
> asked him not to.

I spoke them aloud & the mood in the car turned on a dime. It could also read "One's Poetry." For my poetry is informed by something inside that doesn't flinch & won't budge:

> Because a cold rage seizes one at whiles
>   To show the bitter old & wrinkled truth
> Stipped naked of all vesture that beguiles,
>
> Because it gives some sense of power & passion
> In helpless impotence to try to fashion
>   Our woe in living words, howe'er uncouth.

I like the way these poems scan; they are tight, rhythmical, colloquial, oblique lyrics. I find it exciting the way the terse English accent breaks through at times, asserting facts:

> The hornéd moon to shine by night
> Amongst her spangled sisters bright:
> *For his mercies ay endure,*
> *Ever faithful, ever sure.*

& more facts:

> The water o'er the pebbles scarce could run,
> And broad old cesspools glitter'd in the sun.

This is just to say I've gained the art & language in which I bring my readers deeper than any consideration of a personality to the awareness of a living man—hence in reading these recent books of mine one may find oneself in a solitude & a—"Tight Corner," I might call it—edge or risk of Being that seems even as it is most mine to be speaking for a depth of one's own inner being. Climb bean sort of is substitute destiny. Extremely useful & succinct on the problem of writing verses literature. Silence amounts to the same thing, recommended for university & large college libraries:

Sign on Librarian's Desk

REVENGE

David Bromige   225

I could never have done it alone. The self to write about the products of the self which the self tries to make as selfless as possible, in order that they may be seen to come from the true self, by involving it with & invoking it for contiguous other selves (readers). The constantly shifting perspectives of the sentences. Even a lower limit, speech, & an upper limit, song, leads instanter to song—

You make me dizzy Miss Lizzie

—& to a speech, where soon enough we get pygmy, tangled, spittle, spread, bobbles, bangles, broads & rich or poor. One does not inherit an audience: one builds one, a reader at a time. I join these words for four people, some others may overhear them. This air of seeming indifference toward the reader often succeeds. Join now.

STEPHEN RODEFER

Pretext

Then I stand up on my hassock and say sing that.
It is not the business of POETRY to be anything.
When one day at last they come to storm your deluxe cubicle,
Only your pumice stone will remain. The left trapezius for now
Is a little out of joint. Little did they know you came with it.
When nature has entirely disappeared, we will find ourselves in Stuttgart.
Till then we're on the way. The only way not to leave is to go.
The gods and scientists heap their shit on Buffalo and we're out there,
Scavenging plastic trees. When nature has entirely disappeared,
We'll find ourselves in the steam garden. Evening's metonym for another
Beady-eyed engineer with sexual ideas, who grew up eating animals.
Do you like the twelve tones of the western scale? I prefer ninety.
I may work in a factory but I slide to the music of the spheres.
My job is quality control in the language lab, explaining what went
Wrong in Northampton after the Great Awakening. So much was history.

My father is a sphinx and my mother's a nut. I reject the glass.
But I've been shown the sheets of sentences and what he was
Really like remains more of a riddle than in the case of most humans.
So again I say rejoice, the man we're looking for
Is gone. The past will continue, the surest way to advance,
But you still have to run to keep fear in the other side.
There is a little door at the back of the mouth fond of long names
Called the juvjula. And pidgeon means business. It carries
Messages. The faces on the character parts are excellent.
In fact I'm having lunch with her next week. Felix nupsit.
Why should it be so difficult to see the end if when it comes
It should be irrefutable. Cabin life is incomplete.
But the waterbugs' mittens SHADOW the bright rocks below.
He has a resemblance in the upper face to the man who robbed you.
I am pleased to be here. To my left is Philippa, who will be signing for me.

WORDS IN WORKS IN RUSSIAN

I was working in a factory. I'd seen BLOW UP and had a mini skirt,
AKA yack yack, ready for puking.
The yoghurt was really happening. Leaning against one of the pillars
with his axe in his hand, something different about the way he behave.
What *was* that little black thing you saw there in the white?
It sure was a lay that day. Propose to be a godfather and
carry it out. Send scarlet Brazilian orchids to the fired workers.
The two one-eyed bandits D and C, about as famous
as you could get with what they'd got.
Born on the eve of the Chilean coup and recouperating in the backyard,
saying "They got a bloody nail. They got a bloody body.
You want the serpents? They have a bloody house."
We'll have to keep the applause meter turned off otherwise
it'll just get too noisy. I get to sleep next to the night
light. I'm going to CUT myself, so I can go to the office.

The first taco I ever ate was in a graveyard on a date
in Eureka, California. Cut the crap and get on with the subterfuge.
Amsterdam, a good place to be stone. Pathetic Bethesda.
Strike the mojo and give your hand a rest.
My hand became my enemy in 1983. What is brilliant
becomes boring, in the future's perspective, like another
zombette with one uncertainty piled on the other.
Continue the serious action. The note to Harold Fondren.
For sure this is a boisterous barnyard. Very Reverdy.
Give me a bite so I can stop talking too.
Life is a tangle and it's LIVID, because of the chemicals.
I have no checking account, no thyme, no marjoram.
Many times I wondered when they took my daddy down.
The owners can eat pain. A caballero without a horse.
Chairman Mao will never pick up a telephone again.

228   Stephen Rodefer

Begin to think of cruelty as the inability not to be cruel and try
to stay decent. The unearthly crocuses. I wish I were
assured of my condition. Now that we are all here,
will something always continue to stand still, like an agent?
God will hold it against you if you don't believe in anti-matter.
At last, the something of prose. Cello V. My back.
Who is the figure the TEXT of which we are now the event?
You're wrong, master, just and wrong.
Little Joe's. A mural, an aria, the beach. Better than a therapist.
Inscrutable, colossal, and alone, the sands stretch far away enough.
Pretty flashy lighthouse you got here. Cercamon, Marcabru,
and Blackburn too. This certainly is a beautiful "spot."
Entre la campagne, et la ville. I'll call you.
Endymion was obscure too. There follows a wrangle.
See you at La Mamelle or The Stud. Tipica Cienfuegos. Odetta Mo.

Longevity is out of the question. Play by bending.
Van Gogh's pear trees shining like shark paint in the skull-like flowers.
People in bed with themselves do not really sleep with each other,
they're just Buddhists in love. You dream you are the master
of Nottingham and all of a sudden, creditors.
School children are a joy to be held. Peeing in the garden
behind the Preandergestraat, I apologize to the universe
for being alive so long. I was drawing a tree at a RODEO,
and they were throwing down a lot of cowboy boots from the balcony.
Fantastic variations on a nightly theme.
Matthew Smith's nudes. John Martin's apocalypse.
The fairy fellow's master stroke. The Cholmondeley Sisters.
Words in works in Russia. Out the window may be
out to lunch for those who fuck only once, but what about us monks?
Judgment is thistledown. Poetics is job application. Economy was dead in the water.

Stephen Rodefer 229

Dutch has dykes that make the germen palatable with their tongues.
Then there's Bunny at Tassajara. Apply nivea cream and be dumb.
In regards death everybody is a mystic.
Cheeseburgers may be required in Paradise.
House playing geraniums pretending to like tables, windows.
Pure imitation and learning look up to Maxwell Bodenheim in their mistake.
Ted has a knack of using YOU without using you and *that's* a snack.
It's blood that makes us love, at the Galerie Fiolet.
For dinner is a cheap side of poultry; sleep is for the restless.
Buy film! for the emotions to take place at the crack of dawn.
We must give up our tradition and write like ghosts released to their machines.
Whereas in the Blue Room at home Roosevelt invented polio,
picking apart daddylonglegs. Somewhere you'll find an apartment
which is without a Belgian toilet. All the cats of Venice
were brought from Egypt in order to consume the canal mice.

Beautiful Sonia Delaunay. Kerb your tyres. Brooklyn Yoghurt
Chewing Gum—*la gomma del ponto.* Otto Dix, *Portrait*
de la journalist, beside the great Malevitch.
Just in case they had of, I merely thought I wouldn't.
Bill Berkson in an extraordinary pair of wicker sunglasses,
smoking a Kent. Whatever wears you out, you wear out.
Just call the press HARP SEAL, Richard, and forget it.
The nail is unison. I just want to be social and suck, writing
the treatise on suicide *Not To Be,* an incidental Spicerian stanza.
This time *your* water is golden and *I* smell like a bad wing,
recalling the witchcraft of Kathleen. I have played
the horses *Crucible, Nom de Plume, Ecstasy,* and *Werther,*
bleary eyed at the scene of last night's debauchery and drinking
with the dunce's advantage. The moon is for the eye and it is a sin to step on it.
Don't believe except what you imagine. Visit all graves with masses of newly devised beauty.

230   Stephen Rodefer

We must go our own way but remember we are going to have to take *them*
with us. The specter brother who got the pistol but not the STAMINA.
The only problem is choosing which bedroom to get, because there are so many.
Grace Hartigan's post doctoral work leaves one cold, for instance,
while Marsden Hartley is terrific. So much for time and development.
When the student sits down, the teacher appears.
I hold a little Hoolihan in mind. If you will not go with
to see Wendy on her stilts, then you are a piglet.
I have my cadets and I wish they had less power over me this year.
We who find ourselves in these bodies maturing anyway.
I rilke don't trust it. I'd rather have dog shit on my lawn than bottled water.
Instead of what has always been known to be depth, complexity, and pressure
of spiritual thought, you can always make it on hijinks, gloze, and chicanery,
like a COKE machine. Do you not think?
The depression that comes from not being granted is not very impressive.

Most of the fish I have known if they had *had* bicycles wouldn't have been eaten.
By the day what is the record for bank robberies in New York?
Can you believe some English actually made his homage to the BEACH
BOYS by cutting an electronic collage of their seminal work?
No, of course you can't. But a California girl *is* a potential song.
Music becomes gilt. Glom onto some redolent creep and pretend
that you are in love. I'm sick of daylight. I want God.
My name is Gaston and I would like you to make it out to cash.
I don't care an iota to be an atom in the dynamic of ordinary interface.
Remember Toscanini, after all, conducting *La Bohème* in Turin in 1896.
A sure sign of victory, seeing a lot of sable coats and crocodile bags leaving Iran.
This monastic but indulgent plateau series for dissonant and enduring blacksmiths,
moving from laughter to famine in a cycle of determination in which
art does not lament what ears have sung all to themselves.
Still, strange to grow a bush of parts, and exemplary depart.

Stephen Rodefer 231

Here go one. Silent reading! everybody, silent reading!
Meine liebestraum, meine liebesfreund, meine liebestod.
Once upon a time there were four rabbits running along
toward their mischief. This, as in "with this ring I thee wed."
Charles Olson's broad side. We've got bejillions of flowers,
for the Louis the XIVth whose identity has never been established absolutely.
And I was in it at the time when my bed was burnt to the ground.
Not a good prospect from which to become the reigning *Butterfly* of your time.
Strange still to be 28 or 32, and face imminent uterine disaster at any moment.
God may not exist, but he has certainly spoken quite a bit.
You can form a farm, register Democrat, and control more
than ten percent of the county vote, making like *The King
of Marvin Gardens,* a marred but stimulating flic.
Wasn't it Shakespeare who said, "That was not a nice letter"?
And then I started to get this feeling of NAUSEA.

Deaf is lisp for death. Pass me a little of that *petit* pain.
It's supposed to get cloudy and not be so marvellous tomorrow
(rain?). I'm holding out for some black underwear from beyond.
There are two truly effective things women can withdraw
to teach you you have not acted correctly—your children and themselves.
I'm getting out of here and it ain't gonna be on no public transport.
Some people's half lives are longer but that doesn't mean they're lead.
We just want to be a part of NATURE and stay there.
Cornelius Cardew's piano works on proletarian themes. Finadar 6011.
Well I ate breakfast now what? Ursula Oppens plays Frederic Rzewski.
Van. VSD 71248. Dying in a vacuum of endless work
won't work so don't try. Do you have any bottled sweat?
You'll make it hard to sleep alone in the Goetheneum,
even when dead. About as obvious as Dante being a druggist.
Overcome by the percussive element you start up the stairs, and they backfire.

232   *Stephen Rodefer*

The opportunities of this world have become so scarce
that people have stopped applying for them.
The result is that periods of deprivation
have become much longer. People who used to spend
a few weeks or a month seeking a job or a place
to live, or a lover, now are looking for years,
or not bothering to look at all because they know
it's not there, or it's too expensive, or they can't
have it because they haven't already got it.
When breakdowns occur under this kind of UPPED ANTE
(or you could say people are sitting at a table where
there are no longer any cards being dealt),
they are likely to be much more severe—
it is altogether a cruel and unusual turn of events,
but out of it we should not expect a new Constitution.

Let me say this bang out. I wonder what thoughts Hardy was absorbed in when he died.
Every day is a day for a lovely factory worker. I probably like this alot
less than you do. Some people are more like porticoes than patios.
Thereby are they kept from their proper vacation. In love remove your antlers.
Mal Waldron and Charlie Haden take care of all the passion questions.
I am one of the people in the great CHAIN of being.
Now where's the food, where's the money, and where is the love.
You know Hatha Surrender, Dean of JFK's School of Consciousness?
Women and watches have one common power. Byron got his club
foot because his mother wore a corset when she was pregnant.
Sometimes *screams* can give birth to incredible moments,
and eyes depend on you's and a yes for however many sous.
The whales beached in the Bay of California when Charlie Mingus passed.
When we talk of freedom let us have the memory to speak of it
in a Biblical way. Burn the Christmas green at the Pacific.

Stephen Rodefer 233

Feel the original heat of the earth's breast.
The only country with a higher percentage
of its population in prison that the USA
is South Africa. Content and form have always been the same,
only vice versa. Prince Charles owns Dartmoor. The only poetry
which really interests you is your own, but you don't bring this up
since it seems so reactionary and you know it's the same with your friends.
Thank god though that in spite of pretending to be some rock
regardless of what you think you are, you are becoming something else.
Several of your friends are happy at the NEWS too.
Not on your kodachrome. Would you? Nice matin.
Molly is Jane People. Lon Nol is worse than Pol Pot?
Lost one of your glassies? Just ordinary brain damage
due to the difficulty of asking for company.
It's a wonder all the tall trees are not lying down on strike.

In Tehran to show pleasure they throw candy and rose water
on each other in the street, knowing how.
A dry, brown mushroom from Menlo Park with no price.
On his deathbed Brueghel instructed his wife to burn some of his paintings
as they could get her into trouble, lending personality to his oeuvre.
Paranoia is a carful. Step into her bed.
A woman so preserving she wouldn't sleep with you in a bomb shelter.
So do not flush this toilet unthinkingly there is a water shortage.
Take a shit with a friend, picking up on the side Karl
Marx' comic novel *Scorpian and Felix*, the dark little SAVAGE.
Let me answer with red cheeks and white flesh all
such questions of steady income. If you ever need
a rubberband, it's in the front yard.
Marching anciently and out of sight,
the lift is cool and the countess dunked.

   234   Stephen Rodefer

I have an ardor for orgy but it is not an ardor.
Debauchery dies in sedated children, counsellor.
The non-Indian support coalition for indigenous people.
Pawning his coat to buy potatoes, his mother wondered naturally
when he was going to stop writing about it and make some.
Boyfriends were dispensible in the weather in which every other day was capital.
As in Steve Benson's work *Alligators Can't Be Intimidated*.
I am a machine condemned to devour books and then throw.
Smelly recent past. Truly fertile older history.
For carbuncles try port, try arsenic, try opium.
Suffering from syphillis and losing his epiderm,
poor Schubert found solace in composing music he
hardly ever heard AIRED. Plain print, that's what
we long for a century later. Write a long work called *Now Wait a Minute*
or *The Radio Controlled Torpedo George Antheil Patented With Hedy Lamarr.*

How's your suffering zombette, now she's heavy into chicanisma?
There's that grungy cur death, making its first tentative scratch at the door.
Let's have another drink. Another penultimate libation on the grave
of the muse before bed. With HUE like that of some great painter,
who dips his pencil in the gloom of earthquake and eclipse.
Everybody's at some fault. The British Railroad wouldn't hire Marx
because his handwriting was so awful. Remember Irving Flores.
When you are dead to everything, you might as well *be* dead.
The house plants *are* starving for some birth control.
Another quality job by Colleges and Romeo.
Fuck penises! Stand backish. Figone, Provincial, and Maple.
Urine therapy. Berkeley. Journeyperson work.
Napoleon, the inventory of the concealed weapon.
A flying fish high over Twenty Languages. Ruptured Gringos.
Hard Bargain. Johnnie Squeekie. Exuma Cay.

Stephen Rodefer 235

As you expand become all evocative. Upper level
obsession. A green Egyptian by a muddy nail.
Let's just say they enter a room with dubious godsend.
Let me be a Christian to your lion and end this circus
once and for all. The noble look of deep trouble.
Tell him I send him my love and we should be together soon.
After Henry Cowell spent these years I now live
locked in prison as a homosexual, he did not want to be
differentiated from the public and his music understandably
changed direction and became more international.
Dinky Baby. Lisa AKA Chocolate. Lil' Rocky. No
egrets. No LAGOON. The reason the so-called ecology movement
appeals so much to the rich and leisure class is that the country
is the work place of the rich and leisure class. It is the fact
that their environment is being threatened for the first time

on the same level that an industrial worker or someone
in the ghetto has been accustomed to for a life time.
Enter the dope lawyer as a friend of the earth.
The Moment's Pause Hydrotherapy Gallery NEXT
to the MacDonalds in Mill Valley. Though it may not be
smart checkers, I've got my bindle packed and think I'll head on
out, before they blow the goobers off me.
Nothing is true, but everything is real. Bob says "He
sure eats alot!" What did you expect, a hunger artist?
Remember that the sun is big and your mother lives in 11-A.
Remember the triumph over poverty that reaches into jail,
and that you may never touch that creature whom you love.
Vibe means tremulous power, as in *vibrato*.
Of Tanguy I sing. Bivouac. In the guest room of the Apollo Wax Museum.
A man of color, with all of the calluses, who might as well pitch.

236 Stephen Rodefer

Codex

That is the glebe and this is the glissando. The future is nothing
But a flying wing. You must make your case either with names or with an unfolding.
A position or a disclosure, a microbus. The corridor, the cascade, what stuck.
Glacier notes over the tops of hills. To be close again, as it was in the leanto.
Lengthen the line and increase the leading. These are the helloes of progress.
At the kitchen table the books are pored over, much as a neighbor will bum a cigaret.
The bungalow, radioed and occupied, has no other path to follow but the venture,
The undeniable yielding turmoil mapped out for us for life.
Somebody might ought cook someone a square meal. Life in our adulthood
Is mistaken for wanting completion. What it longs to do is continue being.
The BEES are sleeping beneath the pergola. At the end of each lesson is the vocabulary.
If one opening clouds, another will clear, so long as you both will breathe.
Where's a shovel or something, I say, what can dig, or a trowel? Language pointed
To its content. A crowd of people at the beach screaming "Tuna! tuna!" The evening
Breeze, trembling trees, the night, the stars. And there you are, in a manner of speaking.

So at sunset the clouds went nuts. They thought they were a text.
This language of the general o'erflows the measure, but my brother and I liked it alot.
I think I'll just pause long enough here to call God a bitter name.
Ripeness is all right but the lip is a couplet and nobody knows fuck-all about it.
The THREAD has always been bias. There are alternatives to purchasing goods
To recruit admirers. Right, but is it what Verdi would have wanted?
Nor is it enough to be seen by your youngers as having carried the tradition
To a good place. Given disasters everywhere, don't drink from the tap.
And for what reason make anything that is not for flight?
There are treatments to keep your retina from becoming detached but for what—
To see this? Why, there are things about Israel not dreamed of in the Bible.
How could I miss you when my aim is dead. The goal is sea sounds not yet writ.
All right. Enjoy the heads of your beaches. I'm not going in order
To get tied up on spec, but I wanted you to meet your fellow brains. Thank you,
People of destiny, for your brilliant corners. I like your voice. Look where it's come from.

Stephen Rodefer 237

IN THE AMERICAN TREE
IN THE AMERICAN TREE
IN THE AMERICAN TREE

II: East

EAST

A
per
ginning
verted

CLARK COOLIDGE

from THE MAINTAINS

laurel ratio sharp or hard
instrumental triple to or fro
granule in award

one to whom is made

nave
bean
shin
spectacle
as the near wheel

of all subdue
a overhang
or bear over as a knot pass
the spread

that fair
the part
of the part plots
ending in for the most part bolts
as of wholes
golds
come to as risen divides

paper a half surface certain salts
such as full site to the waist
turtle
dative object
flute or the like bonus

soup spindle
cloth ink

pit spring
bones to the axis of the bore to part

holding to do that draft
mar
a pluck comes close to
cones hence or ahead
issue
as or for one dents

humph
that wattled
place over hence
with urchin
which occur in the not true scales
slow green off with blue
more side
also and of those he was suffix

of the clock
note
terminates as an one leaflet
steps
or white person

bid protein
quill in full
lit square flower sulfate
or of another with each other

as a tremor with quoins
game
tape
red bill
also any of several serrate jars
the only place force genus
cause of roll

start from hat
state

or this natural or video
poplar forms meaning coke
envelopes
invert leaves

or more up from middle
blunts
leaves dash by the slip tick
as on

as at which props
a twin
and full agate pass
a jest or the like wad
waff
act in them
as a mote looks on or speeds
whole hence tablets
a double button

coat to send glass
see bill
called a swingle
is so hung as to beat
hence of woolen
lacking and also having
quarts

of flam of extol bean
of using chem
the pea suture inducing insectile
furniture of pole divisions
sending forth with the fold at the top
lens shape back phase
as some one of the nodules

Clark Coolidge 245

woody and rind
prepositon of either
the arboreal mild

a width or the like
most used rapid paste
a small
away or small
between without the mob forms
icing disc-lobed blend
cue tailed
the fried acute

acid
non-czech
also any hours as a chaplain base
after the one to take to not appear against
the painted but having no dim
not one nor one better than none
a state of being the like

intervenes
talc
often noting no milk of the suit lead
to render for sorts as hence
no sort yet left
a disc on the head or the like
one's for a term
repeats cast off spring
sound state in materials
shuns

bleater
the dry hub
to lose or draw
has been like also to be
back or aside

wear or blink
dims and acts

past of blow
blimp one home
blister copper as sap but one
due from ice at tennis
around a cent wind
cynosure
any of a central able carp

dropped
edge of other like
contents that will run out
of several blent
minerals eyelid
to raise in a canon
less flex or more canned hemp
and is much as masses liquidic
canopic
sonorous same kind uranium
dipping which by recipients

row or summons
of being commencement
with a coo or coos
not classed as silk is wound
the coupon
courts in reply to another
habitant
the face of a type

steps also this
as in the mast of a running suit
now only in some set tip running
see court
wholly from the main dormant
broadcast rodent

Clark Coolidge   247

one shoulders
an amount of the day of the dope
used for does not
fend and right reason
dulls or to the doodle plants
fish

a dime
as the one or that which hums
limb in reports of the tube
kept hulldown
gathers in huddles huffs
cards near the resthouse khan
such as cathode meters a cow
cognate realm
or gradual hollow tuft

stances cover
number and neck
as a part in what one is not
subject
matchlock to a masterpiece
or the like things of immaterial scope
lower journal
mongrel moth or mastic solo

called pole
called made or right booms
a mono or diurnal linen
during life
more name
used of a mountain range

from POLAROID

dial around forth enough means that there since
it's still lest closely light dial an around times as yet lots
dial by seen apart than by lots as forth a there that this leave
in case let lest dial really single a matter of one tending may
a lot of match twin seat case will dial leaving places gotten to turn around
aside what's due this to least it's that still may turn lots to tap
head per think dial forth past still going a one some turn let
apart it's and light via but such still and the back but tends times
and is so dial nor even lots around it's come nothing let seem post
                                                                bend nothing
the may during and the come stir by how dialer single around its one
to point to the tend it's then sending open the dials it to part to once then
as get stir as got dials the bend lap of time let be still around
the by now such will onto around say brought tap say bring point
it's everything go because last nothing amid twin along still around
letting least turning cause it and open bend and but for lie stay
which at of yet dial around everything forth to places apart via
the where the one other dial the its one to due closing forth as
a non a single apart lot seldom because very will beneath
upward of all of it on lot dial head matter think lest time case
it dial it stand it just point enough of during forth to around go to see lie
really match what some every singles on all dials most lot of which
it can if it's sending got may to go send to lot last
still dial and just around say forth then often on itself bend
head light turn come upward into near kind stand just
matter let lots past timing casing the dial dials a dial
to or on as in turn in case due around the forth
come may the matter got still its say past why brought to stir
tends loom dial still around on it staying from turn means down forth
the fewer this miss its thing back in a matter due a dial
an it per pass upward forth see from post at bend on
a miss dial a long but close light means those below will like twins
around those then just back away still dial forth
as like tends

twin may what single everything
loom nothing lap lost seat to lap to may twin may what
stand just pointing seldom to matters may act open here a twin
all brought leave and why place it to one past the think bolt
have fewer this what its twin may pass per light per least by all onto tap place
upward
initial it lest it let its due to have that means from a whom forth a those by
nothing miss may it loom twin a match it and seldom let it seem may turn
twins it do time its open clad about one everything by point in standing
tending to initial back by pointing past its least it's light a twin is
act here seat there loom lap by amid such before as a tap may since onto
think see in case due let matter closely least its dip
matching the single twins just kind of near to may around
nothing let missing as acting here under so often of
due to single the twin heads nothing one or and closely
kind into either in a way to cause the why brought clad nothing
pins dip in lots and place much whole under and other yet both
it's a twin and it's since along or a time a senting reach
place open and miss apart its matter its never a reach may aside
lots and nothing brought one along since bolt thing closed left missed
around one
there hence since or may twin let one time upward a stir come to reach this
last the gotten matched tapping a really pin some dip that this
pass one its twin dial along as twin as tending may send
just and still or may and got it's a due lest closely least
it open to tending a never between during a standing
its seem to say twin think on one as seeing things as all itself onto doing it
tho pin cause way place since must over it's a twin one
via heading twin to send close the nothing single to the point truck
seldom lighting has to have to draw everything one match to its loom
twin
may what

clad aside no while light least as it not doing point
because last clad nothing pointing then do leave pin placing truck brought
everything seeming to say clad aside clad
the right deign tap by the pin lots reached appear as appear and
or just or pin go tend as one's clad lapping a time in its case of a matter of
due lapping at act clad here clad in asides the one pointing of everything it's
seat to lap which to what will during a think time a case of
will down a beneath is under an aside by thought never seemed here
a head a clad single everything point out the tho still the stay bend
missing may it clad be gotten a seldom still matter gotten to
matching a post bending a capper to the line appear the clad in its still
ever which some as a dialer any of which twins by the clad aside
bend it's a miss post a timing case via seat lap in its stay seems
the matches really the least seldom loom clad in point in dialing in
of this of aside what's to matter in a light clad each seat
miss having due going because a clad
amid such a clad around the one twins its thus during last gottens
what miss via very besides apart its send and reach causing inch
tap it at back tho all due to still at a same when boths gotten
clads about and matters timing single a cause to why go tending back
in its flinch twin right apart let close a besider the another
come pass pointing the dialing act here a may clad aside upward truck
none and seated back past to its lap open to the stir coming near kind of other
a back it's nothing a cladding light think casing matter
of dip lying will among its case among till due time light
clad standing the place get the truck down means
a clad and seeming light a bent a downing come aside
all singles of everything point till time still open all
its tho its ever on the light things place tending in a clad
this veer lines reaching matter lots on its
go by during nothing
clad least

point seem thing or never one may turn it one to matching
all whole point all seem to a thing a may turning up this it can during
the light of the everything single point to its seem thing
its lap seat head inch truck still least due to close capper light
acting here sending missing matter to a point the thing very once yet may
                                                                            seem
the open of a match send it this bolt to think just standing point
a thing there till within hence all over means to
single till the reach point of everything a heading tend go say
before match around some tho still its emitter seldom the one tho cause
                                                                    about matter
during the let matter the think a point may sending seem can thing
a single match by how long before everything as point to of middle inch
still backing tho all parts may apart by those kind must aside
twinning musts and lighting keep to these say a point to nothing
a whelm keep lap such as the amid on an only often
leaving such place a still tho flap a bolt each thing
of miss nothing looming the lot in match of place the till yet
matching the whom passes the dialing into out of becausing last stay some
                                                                            lost
matters it that the time
trucks turning in stays of lighting a must seeming light
this thus having to may such least a thinking lost the match to a veering twin
one enter tho still a massed line emitter to the stay the since points
to which upward turning gotten aside past the lot it keeps taking
whiles of ago letting the light one may nothing near
see bolt think past the head the lap post a still twinning a bulk along then one
then capper that's what
a capped in that deign twin what's that stilling
to say by seems to staying miss comes its nothing seeing
being or let the point miss one just standing
for or by and of along since the beneath never between very amidst
this nothing one misses tho time and still or light of think loom
                                                place pin bulk dip tap inch

from QUARTZ HEARTS

The mud of the bulk of the back yard.
Itch of wash. The sun through a board
crack a splinter up it. Noise or
rail yards behind white sheets. A nose
turned in window. Lock it up and smell
off the brass shine. Two steps by
a cat. Air and hewn lots. The view
across and the walk back home. Blocks. . .

    .

The some that stands beside it.
Give it a right patch.
Some both will and then one.
More than it can it both will and wane.
The down on the cap of much mount.
Twin latches in the pale of some green
some other nor.

    .

Lights in an ounce. Iron too thin to note.
Quartz axis on a baseless ground.
Higher than the land the handful it seems.
We collect and wave.

    .

Domes behind a head. All the pages
lapsing and locking by. May the twin
not trip. The clock land in its bed.

    .

Soda pounce. Three blocks of tonal
disbelief. A sail. The cigarette

slips through a basement stairs.
An air of cut papers near a fog.
A pocket mailed through the slot.
Crowds beneath ceiling.

．

He walked up and knocked at the front.
His shoe was the same color as the step.

．

The car had an open top that he never
looked out of as he drove straight
ahead. An iron mushroom.

．

Walking up close to the wall, I felt
the heat from above, and heard the
horn below the floor.

．

A black tree on a purple shoulder.
The sock hidden in the stump. Pliers
in a room beneath a wind across a valley.

．

There was a block on the door.
The handle turned out to be square.

．

Little women sending postcards from a
donut factory. They swim toward the

end of the land. An opening gradually
presents itself and arrives.

.

Hello to the hands in the rock.
A placement of bulls in a forest
would not seem so large. Time seemed
to expand into a pin which holds this
picture up.

.

To the stick in its place. Slots for
three lamps. All margins come to resemble
this pie section which I hold.

.

Down in the door the legends have separated out.
Any launch could have been as extremely amiss.
Push the pen, push the pen.

.

High sockets and a sky as blue.
How many tricks have been so held
and then told?

.

Doubtless blame on a machine on sunday.
It was planted in the feldspar section.
A pan of white circuit matter. A last
strew of the peas.

.

I didn't think on that pink ground
of a thing.

.

The grass stands behind a black wall
at the back. The room is covered in
a amber shade. There is no rice at all.
The air is nearly all used up.

.

We have blue water in our toilet.
I pass through the space between
it and the door to my room.

.

A sharp breeze like a lap on the wall.
Three tourniquets stopping a flow as if
on a dime. A blurred crystal slowly
filling with lavender. These windows
do not open.

.

The gum statue of a three car pile-up
revolving in such a state that no one
knows they are. Someone sends for a
flat round white container rather like
an encased watch. The correct length
of wood for a small table is thought of.
At this juncture then all of us leave
this as from a stage.

.

Bright pockets. A collapsible vent
rather like a record album. Three
cheeses in three colors. A man who is
about to let go words of some weight.

.

Somewhat light. Left of the leather.
The tongue on the rod of air instead of
the key axis. Slowly the dusty room.
Anything circular worse than unimaginable.
A stair.

.

I wanted to stand it. To stand it up.
The tack kept falling down behind the
moving picture. The signs were already
partially there. Full moonlight on the
palm for my troubles. The glass through
which.

.

A calming puffin.

.

The Blocks

Starting from some point in a circle these
streets near a tunnel. What of the word
silage. Heads. As if I started it and then
saw he got up on the horse. Closed bottles
you'd have to raise windows to place. Slight
moon on a long game using twigs. I fill a can
with square stones and step back. House going
short. Clang as of kilns or nobody counting.

Clark Coolidge 257

A house closed to the ground opens onto a
square the length of a street to the
next town. Bone.

                            .

Carpet stairs. I stare at the silver circle
flush with my kneecap. The cardboard left
from the books. Long holes I snap over.
Tines. A car can't be near enough to the
hum from a flat. Slots. As if a whistle
could erase marks of the gum beneath.
The stumps lack dolls. But.

                            .

Running through streets he saw a circle.
It was on a house. Closer he saw the cap
come off a bolt sticking from the wall.
Pumice.

                            .

Let's not know what. We're doing the last
thing which came up. Something about charts.
And the pin was at last found in the mine
that started as a thought.

                            .

Black shoes and brown shoes. The cat snaps
her orange tail. Aqua water in the toilet
bowl flushed away. If the disc was certain
one could put it to the man. Lime kiln
avenue in a shower going away.

Blocks. Paper notice. Cement labbage in
a semicircle which appears to be the
drive. A very large meat. Three assorted
caps so which one goes on. The time is
later one inch away. Barley only to be
witnessed. Tame.

.

The hole in the home. Parthenogenesis.
Three litmus leaves fell. Sight of a
snow light across the face. Blame.

.

Frog as part of the bottom of a mug.
A typewriter across town. The light
has stood for a part of itself through
trees on the mountain crest east. Flag
stamps and memos. A battery ration.

.

Standing in back of a building with the
frost on. Large circles painted to the edge.
This is the last week before the books
are returned to the library. The museum
on fire, just a frame house. How could
one push a stick into rock. Too many
papers not enough rock.

.

The blacks are different sizes. The logs
are not careful. Where are the latches.
Count up three frogs of middle rank.
Finish your peas.

The absolutely flat things that I saw
near the corner. The sky isn't so
white anymore. This is the calf muscle
below a board. The brand of my clock
I mean what's the name?

from WEATHERS

XVII

Partly stone only to see beneath the red slips. The fishing particle, on and off, innards of glass. Sun parts hardly, seems to move. The jetty I'm on of tons, afternoon further planks, oil glow dome pending. The salamander owns munch breccia, clots the window in a skid-to piping, glance off sleeving collides. Of a wind and burn scratch reach, the maundering columns. Streaks to score, go on melting button the barks. Do too scooping handle greys form a point off the scarp fist, knuckle crimps eject of pint tone. Lurid, imported word impacts, pans. Storms off packed weight under a whole elk of burlap, and why does that deer to be of stone appear, stemming from lozenges wind and on and off. Do to all but seem to move. Felt it clang to, it fell to a berry.

All so over done so as it is goes down. A might then. Turn by a so filming simple, Shed & Boulders. Old writing oaks hard at a time wringing. Will so meander, bent as brought the winter over? Stencil origin finger. Cones of the plaque to a mint, brand story tugging. A much in space, huddles that erase, mend dwindles? Parrot misting.

Scuffle dander, the ape's missing. Trumpet in a cat through glass to a squirrel and the merging cleave tweets. On a disc mark your paris-green keyboard music to highroad. Dashboard careers. Gone down behind the ape, shuttling trunks, a glass of pining for furs through the port. Divides to crayon box canyon dust fudge organ, of Dashboard Caverns, Action Grosbeak. Daily looks like a job for.

Spirals in the morning too stiff to send ache the cracker back in folded and down for a swallow. The perimeter stickler, violin to a point. Vestibule or caged kitchen arrow, oils to onyx the boil wall. Statue of the bulge. Coiled or sand said to at least stood for. Banner near. Defeat collide. Part a moor.

Blurts up in the morning, a tumbler even with wheat. Thrums at the hatch, later mailed them. Digits after all stems. Off a looped tide, once canned stanches. Up on his overhauls to the bend, encourages tomatos to stope. Glean. Stand frets the depth of heat to stall and read. Carpathians biking. To the frog was not dead but stone. Green as his horn ever empties. Trouser, not pant.

Such cement as was added to my, but could this be. A morning America lapsed so pervading the world in its shell collapses. Perempted bound and all so mild. There are some stones out in the Star Chamber. Oil gloves and the pick snakes. The stick hangs budge. Arbitrary to adjudicate and nevertheless brightness. All the paint burn a hole as it shift goes down. A ton as in spraining a moon. Dole it out tempus rakes collapse. A slide, he mumbled in slots miffed. But what could I, sunk will last the winter all over, space then hardly seemed to move then mild.

A bent oak leaves the afternoon will. He standard political skid-to or lozenge to heft greys withheld goes down. A mice, a going light stick fed up with beams. Legs once spun vested trouncing. He's met, never the, cling, burns. A whole last all over hole as it goes. Then spill to prick dates a desert. The last erase lands a face. Tin powder for a think up. The whole afternoon an ape for mistral more room. Scowls then a moonful, sat out the night of cellar beaks. Freight sticks. More edges the tongue-tapped of porphyry eels. Marble midway threshing. Scum ring.

Comes full from burlap burns ancestor lapses.

XVIII

Cleave shut the canvas crack stems off the grey light. Following blue air glow to the cellars of the sea. Passing and repassing zinc boats in the dark. Copper husband. There very white mass it's moving being said. Template glottis. By tongueless bells the air still. A beamless valley, or rose pocket, one of the starts to glow on. The slightly morning air of an upward progression titled blue.

Rung stalks of a breath bring his work. Has no name but is a still sphere. Bounces wall in. A branch gets turned to the wall. Trees survived without wheels. Metal flickers.

No wheel. He glanced once more at the document, folded it, and locked it away in his desk drawer. A saddled with a pyramid gelid ape, combed and it's fishing. Slammed board to the opens grain in the eye. Limestone ball to afternoon underpinning, eyelash. Clawed horning on bench mark. Flakes unless they strike leaves. Enough so that she's got and what of it gets you. Get waiting for the bending looks to step while furtive, stands. Counts, a many covers. Turned up the one to watch a weed blend with. That ice stand a drink to. Colossal staintite print votes. He's watching I'm saying. And I think watch this note down on the chance. Books lead. To me nothing else but throng.

No wheel that gets stretched so brightens. Falls in leaves. Things up much. To the track an impression full snowing. Tabs being drops, or in an inch, or of temperature. What of it the full of nothing, thunder to lice. How the bent flash reported to the husband. His stones all triangular mounting to stems off the bolas vegetative. Off one branch, the monolog.

Platinum stands for darkness, gold remains of light. Backyard, of which there are none in woods. Enough sticks not to cloud things up much. And in flakes dappling up to pyramid a glow. His munch was to back off the window, reports of depth it fills up with, inches planted deep in carbon growth, a claw balling inward. A pecker of zinc pretends figures at rest.

At most a book the porch. Flames that are at all rails of snow. Flower down winter to vanish. Mite hand stroking flint to a card. Names that it blue. Wheel locked to pyramid through stocking the metal realms. Hit leaves. Participle.

You can't and then a drawer of the wood that spots the sapping rise. The army group fistula a pocketed slump starving of carbon rods. They go and then the lightning moves don't seem up to

Clark Coolidge 263

much. Darkness books on the chance of lead. Nightfall remains, you can't say how, with not a wheel. Spins stones the window covered.

XIX

Lightful overcoat. Must be boning up on tieless affronts the comb ranges. Oversaw his dots backhanding berries while clot erect. Of a strew placed beyond the beakless bark scatter. This is pulp afternoon. Shoes to the grain offhand in spotlit breakfast nook. Places his starts off by lacing rods into coal swarm a cone eye view of the ricket vista. A brewer based on ice. Leafed up the nose in a capsule plot ascent. Nods to cleavage bugs of a scarlet, intermittent tinkle. The chimes of robes on the steeples of the mountains. His trombone marine and numb there. A shrug that would melt a pyramid, flash plasma, trigger its bolts. As with buttons their overcoats, stepped off, the day the earth stood still.

For cloud break measures in eyelash. Needle threads clang, trotting it out. A beam I could away by touchdown, onyx spherical above the bowl. Cheers, that are strands to the pause meter. He rapidly melts one cone per ticket. Lining his ice with lingo, laps socket at the top, tangent to whatever paints clapping. A matter field, slow to close. All reach their hands together at once. One face slipping from the stands. Palms coil to paws. The bowl arose an obsidian sphere, oily to push. Snowfall.

Fabrics away from an overlit world. Razoe boats rowing a herringbone rug. He drank and spoke smiling, dish. Cups in clouds away from the wall. A paper that flowers to winter in gazes. Now they're all on the standing match. You would twist elbows in salt & pepper, caught fallout from spotlight, shampoo of bananas wobble on a bounce dive. This could well send one kempt from shearing. But you wouldn't know do you, a participant plaster? Owl bouillon.

The cat then rattled like a cleaver bounced in case. But through such a tug as though to peep aside I saw him mend. An eye in its jacket resigned. Lemons threshing toward teeth of a stripe, all stop. The signs are: snow plaster, twig marble, radio orange. The cat came in at the tree.

I deposit, these lines in soil feet rock free. Goes up to bark at the tip there are transmitter berries. Every one a grid by longwave nightfall. Contracts his onyx, snores the room to pieces. Index finger partial, fresco perimeter strasse, bunker flat dismal. He's let himself a coil for his own collide. A gimlet stringent as tears. Better dough from its loaf, maple its pails. Now disclosed just how or how often said, the night thread me its eye. To windward bronze sluice pin under apex orders. To understand the substance of a concrete preparation. Slot it. A ha-ha, sunken bounding fence invisible to the idea unbroken, house, space. Or glucose factory for a sandwich lunch. Laid up to some low orange beams, berries roll. Such molds as present to boil gold. Shorn columns in great spite of the guttering dawn.

XX

Moon, you . . . Look, Picasso. Says in a steady light it must be faster. Wherever seedy a barreling scan the bottom holds. In your face all the time on the dream grounds vacancy. A white bright. Of what the sticks were bound to be collapsed in turn. Adhesive light. In which would you whatever turn out from vacancy make it up our road. I'm thinking of, sealed flat. Quick tries to deny the still holding moon. I face.

Cut capsule in luke hand me. How as you and me we are found out walled. Which matters have to get out of bed I pull shades to sleep. Circle that action as a habit back to nearunder. A dream I talk you tell me faster on the one hand its spoon to the wall. We've backed in speech to the work again. Several come single of what do you turn out to being with the moon. The lamp in the cat slung off. Quiet with light patches to send more.

A hand let. Turn over stay little don't change a hair. A wand clangs moon to wall. Wires between to it, in scissored voice. Cough on a bean stays paint. Do you walk from the height creature listing you as attribute. Starling beach. Counter earth edges to fear light. Your stain that goes next point or loose. Doubt work of art then open it to speak are you smart. So what of your moon that it coils springs. Staggers on its stable frames. So calls for ice of a vegetable spin it. Will thorn. End. Piss thrum. A gaggle pressed in delicate. Full as eyeballs the mountains, moons.

I ask you is it faster than to place the fork. You sit a purple blur facing next the moon occular in its almost, there are no, she said, pyramid apex box. All the whole time put one didn't that we sat next. Foolish to stem then pick to discuss, as of ampules. Spell cast argument its twin. You are mostly days you make of it up our road. Stun line under moon.

You speak of a quilt of line one must break matter faster to have. Done lie its rocks stem the moon. But haven't you faced I faced your moon. A stick awake is it? Clangs of snow. Crimson black cracking. Unphotographable facing vacant. Your moon cap of wax thrown under beds, takes there. Stays the night till its stay slips. Off the argument your hands catch what were beams, now shade the moon's threads. Without a diminish in armature beaming. Face that catches on the woods, somehow lit in ovals yours. Those parturient beds.

Moon profile a weather edge. You tell me faster is the work to more slowly talk and stand outside under pennies on a ledge. There be slants on the proper teaching meters. That open beam in metals, sign your hands. Backwards to initial pipe of sentence. Told moon. Paper in hunch. Rings.

A height out in trunks. That I sit it's watching your plate shines, bulk food though keeps coming up, also your head and chest a newel post. Faster than the moon never moves. Than the wall shifts planted geologically. Your hand with fork the pendulum deep beneath art. When do we stop salting, an overcast tattering a

266   *Clark Coolidge*

bit. What with the standard kept a higher tempo than memory caught it. As an avoidance spins its circle in my face. All the what we think the sources reflectors off others elsewhere masked. The what you're speaking I'm recording both reflecting you're absorbing and behind the same wall. This chasm on the spot.

This moon is seen far from an eye unless a blind spot of some light fixes full open the ringing back of thinking room. Doubt to its gaining edges prints you out on. A sight. Blind and moving, no more sides than crannies evince. Now your speech in circular waves of tines coils up a sphere boils a hole in the wall I slide from irons away this recalled so-called moon, gaining edge to spotless light. You haven't changed a hair of, our quickly cut-off road, having made it up.

CHARLES BERNSTEIN

PART QUAKE

The restoration of slighted, by forecast thundering,
faded aggregate sweeps plane in wanton arch
the very lacunas discount. Preclusion of
emphatic instability inflated within cornered
propulsion. Militant valence, or sense of
seen. When fills of, for, former entail
portends an increment, adjourned at what
is loaned, all to sudden screeching. Drop,
instanced bodily (lozenge, prick . . .) by motor
denotes, held in caption, ritual zone
demark.

Learning of the sightless colors with
serpentine grimace, the limp for asking
favor. Favor what polity demands, all
else to regulation.

Alone, unbuttoned, only inbred whisper
of remote inspection. These awnings
bright with happenstance, glance of
idly set elations rounded to deceit.
By glue the stamp of deferential promise—
allure, alas. And ornaments of clouds.

It is for this act alone we wait, this
recompense. A trail followed by a
circumlocution that is homeground. That, as
if by appointment, expresses
the legitimate aspirations of the heart.
Or shows to live in faith,
woe of fact sleek upon,
shower's helpless throw.

A grey eminence there is that
announces its limits in flickering arcades
of slate and implore. Feeling rather
faint and implied in this a remonstrance
that never alone can acquaint, not
that the small ministries embark aboard
a relativized collusion but that they
fend for themselves. Only
noticed once it has passed, irritating
irrespective of promises galvanized
again to the rope's dogma. Here
are two forces, each equally
determined, but neither installing
a claim to degree.

Agitators are heard and then disappear
into the crowd, metering reduplication
forensically around billiard balls.
Still even now you cling to

your habit of music.
They ridicule revolutionary theory
and sneer that having a correct
position is sectarian. For thoughtfulness
recount a tremble for alertness.
This, too, is part of taking hands
into our history. Nothing to
say to structure around an
empty if strategic accomplishment.
On May Day, therefore, the workers'
eyes turn toward socialist Albania,
the shining model of life without
capitalists. And in vain we conceal
our hearts within us, keep out
courage checked. Under fictive
encounters, lament of
overthrown announcement. Of
this no lullaby will now relieve.
Garden that none attain. Are
the working masses, then, to become
broken and wretched slaves
crushed under the iron heel
of police terror and racist
gangs? Near is, and difficult
to grasp. The games are garlands
of detraction.

In the light of, everybody loomed,
a weave of weft (wept) in the

throating dissimulation of occasion.
I rock against these boundaries
to feel them. Make bridges abide.
And the roads ahead demure, a
holiday of retreat. What is
divine, that only can we see—
the dunes amid the rubble.
But strikes only those in
looking, having heard. Cups
of preemptive declension,
rising on tides of neutralizing
disclosure.

So surround a sunken acceptance with the vague
reproach of the already spoken. Sitting there
amused at the habits of the accomplice in
flight, a greater pedantry than last
week's oars, such is the state of
the soil. Or barricaded in, the
sigh of the enclosure, fortified
against oneself, at peace with the other.
Each configuration leads to the same
unfilled potential, a houseguest of
improbable translucency.

Might as well, someone recounts, take the
day into one more foreboding distillate
than has been managed with the Aeolian
jarps of irregular stupor. Famed
condiments of a hereafter believed
in on Tuesday, worldly worthlessness
seriously supposed to unhinge or disband.
These however strike unobtrusive, as if
from behind, and can't really be
adequately counted in the realm of
exclusion. A sudden accord conceals
an unseen presence, as when I say
you don't call you reply the
expectation was all your own.
Erudition become inanimate, the congealed
syntax of forced instrumentation.

With some it's summer, spatializations in
which to pass the day. But the notice
is given and the marks are abridged,
dozens of toothless, topless topologies
regarding their plunder with a weepy
sentimentality sufficient to make
the battery gag. And Bobby Sands
lies dying (dead) in a blanket.

This is the next thought. "I'm going
to cut your face." Disregarding
disgruntlement, akin to principal semi-structure,
the hawking or the having, gears its semiotic
pitch to the blank physiognomies of the
undermasses. A road impossible to ridicule.

Half-inscribed and half-distended, though
such polarities con't hold, X informs
Y of Z, A bedevils B, Q
convinces R to protest to S, M remains
sidelined. How to work that in,
a world that so impinges that
we, an entity it's impossible to
overcredit, push back with a
might that makes only the heavenly
a force with which to contend.

Don't get, replies that, in virtue of, forgetting
actually downtown, pressed insurance, waylay
aboard, which spanning moments engrain. A
pattern easier to remember than disgorge. Or
flicker, pent-up pentagonals, insatiably
barren. Who forecloses on which net? The
burning evidence of the somber frenzy.

Lives mostly unleavened. Arresting torsion
succumbed at lately. There was a sharp
metallic click, the one sound guaranteed
to raise the hair on my neck. The gap
between us, five years at least, was
too great for anything constructive in
the way of action. Turning, rolling,
twirling, tumbling. Cleaving cleverly
till a wrinkle clutches. Nothing
to make of, out of. Hardly or
beforementioned, felled the between.

FOR LOVE HAS SUCH A SPIRIT
THAT IF IT IS PORTRAYED IT DIES

Mass of van contemplation to intercede crush of
plaster. Lots of loom: "smoke out", merely
complicated by the first time something and don't.
Long last, occurrence of bell, altitude, attitude of.
The first, at this moment, aimless, *aims*. To the
point of inordinate asphalt—lecture, entail.
These hoops regard me suspiciously. A ring
for the shoulder (heave, sigh. . .). Broadminded in
declamation, an arduous task of winking
(willing). Weary the way the world wearies,
circa 1962. The more adjoins, sparklet and parquet
reflection, burned out (up). Regard the willing,
whose movement be only remonstration, ails
this blue bound boat. The numberical tears.
Edged out where tunnels reconnect, just below
the track. Aims departing after one another
& you just steps away, listening,
listless. Alright, always—riches
of that uncomplicated promise. Who— what—.
That this reassurance (announcement)
& terribly prompted—almost,
although. Although censorious and even more
careless. Lyrical mysticism—harbor, departing
windows. For love I would—deft equator.
Nonchalant attribution of all the, & filled with

such, meddles with & steals my constancy, sharpening
desire for that, in passing, there, be favorite
in ordinary, but no sooner thought than gone. My
heart seems wax, that like tapers burns at light.
Fabulous ephemera a constant force for giddy flight.
But boxes both in, boated just the same. Mass of fix,
the further theorizing a final surrender, until the next, thins
or becomes transported, nights asleep, day wondering.
Appearance that not so much won't shake but returns, as
the pilot turns his starship into wool. To knit
these phantasmagorias out of white, sheer monument to culture's
merry meal of itself. In eyes that look with mirror's blankness,
remoteness complete—I want but all recedes. Motor
fixation, streetcar trace, the last days of this
water, these fields. To sustain such blows and
undermine the lash is memory's cure. At long
last, image reconciled to friend, chatting
under oaks, rays of a sky no longer our
but all the more possessed. For much that has
no cure. Duplication equal to charm of happier times, those that
disappeared, faster and more fantastic, the loud
despair the softer homily. A shoe entails
its path till, foot on foot, no diversion's
seen. The sky parts, the blinds repair.
A hush that skirts the subtler moment,
the cumbersome charade of weekend and reply.
This darkness, how richer than a moat it lies. And

my love, who takes my hand, now, to watch all this
pass by, has only care, she and I. We deceive
ourselves in this matter because we are in
the habit of thinking the leaves will fall or
that there are few ways of breaking the circuit.
How much the stronger we would have been had
not—but it is something when one is lonely
and miserable to imagine history on your side. On
the stoop, by the door ledge, we stand here, coffee
in hand. Roll top desk, undisguised goodbyes. I
wait but I don't want it. Austerely premature,
scrutinized to the point of a gazeless graph, no past
there, how could it hope to mean to us. These
are the saccharine days, the noiseless
chirps of the sublimated depths. By the train
tracks, halfway down, sitting there, looking at—
a goat knows no better sound. What of colors, what
of characters—anoint with all precision
projection brings, so much sturdier and
valorous than ourselves. Depressed eyes
clutter the morning and we drown in a sea of
helping hands. Better the hermit than the sociopath.
Destruction?—the wind blows anyway, any where,
and the window frame adorns the spectacle. That
person fixes in your head, and all the world
consumed through it.

TO WHICH I NEVER WANTED

to which I never wanted
any other notice.   A
mist intends its
several routines. Abracadabra
chandelabras—all fake
basically—& what, with, all
the,   What follows
another—constructions thrown into
air. A temporary time but
doesn't get punched out. I
say he isn't worth beans.
Rapidly evinced, "advanced upon"
what, drips. No he could
do more with a broom than
any man. But had nothing
to replace it with. Not
'out of the ordinary' either.
Simply, it makes a case for itself
that predates that other claim
"of reason" no more than any other.
Marathon madness, hoola Hopis,
stained windows entreaty—us—
(to) "come forward" (which never
runs into anything else). I
guess eyeglasses. Refracted urges
"a no vote" on proposition nine.

"Thou shalt not" abandons the highway
to, for, by, upon, withheld,
stop that cat. "No, sadly"
incorporates a (bowl), issues
that rely on already learned
itemizations, bad, good, politic,
to amaze with torpid drag.
As if I care. Mellow movements,
no more than a senility of
ambitions, "to be grounded
here" whereby shifts into
that plant that forever needs
water. Headlights I suppose.
Dressing for the soup. A
wan characterization, no
topology, no ingredient
takes from——

THE BLUE DIVIDE

An almost entire, eerie, silence floats above and between the fixtures that separate me from the doorstop. Slight rattle, rolling, scratches the space just behind me, which is helpful, if not necessary, to cast the reflections and echoes in just the way I'm accustomed. A table and window frame sit just ahead, to the side of the walls and corners, slat wood flooring, shelves, the tar-blacked driveway and terraced approach roads. A person waits in a boat about an hour away, floating in totally occasional manner. Stripped of its wood, unparalleled in respect to its riveting and displaced glare, incised by its dimensions, I feel the slight pang of an earlier sensation which rapidly switches in succession to images harder to identify at first, postcard sized shapes, rolling vertices. The sounds are pervasive and only from time to time increase in loudness which looks almost as if it were a tear or rip in the otherwise unbroken intensity. Bits of fabric—plaid, striped, glyphic—hang from fan gliders about 20 feet above and to the side arced formations of smoke languidly drift this way and that. Several hours pass the mood indiscernibly shifting to less substantive pleasures, the hallway rotating airily to the tempo of unforeseen reverberations. A small coterie remains behind to see that the ship departs smoothly, counting their change with an alternating frenzy and tedium. You ask for the lighter but remain seated, seem to recollect what you refused to say, purse your lips and, with a forlorn look, lapse back into thought, then begin to make suggestions for lunch. A fly makes its path spiralling over the campsite, arching toward the partially lit skylight and barraging full throttle into the screen. Men in blue suits and brown hats hurry over to the table and unpack their cases, gesticulating animatedly with their feet and hands. A tall, thin boy with grey callow eyes stares across the walk with forced attention, rubbing his legs and scratching his head, finally sinking into a dull, dejected slump which nonetheless gives the impression of greater ease. Barrels of fruit, uncovered and ageing, fill the area with a distracting odor, the inevitable subject of recurring fantasies for civic improvement. Tendrils, assimilated into the background glare, announce with glum resignation "far better for those with lighter hearts" imminent departure. Blocked, buoyed, incessant, I take for the elevator, dash quickly to the folded bed clothing—you angling loosely toward the courtyard, suffused with contentiousness. After a long walk we return to an almost identical place—the mat on the one side, the hobby horse on another. Paralyzed by the smoke, dazed by the duplicity, an earnest but elderly gentleman hobbles somewhere along the periphery, stooping, circling, tumbling, gliding while making his way to an adjacent watering hole. Not so nimble or quick-witted, the pool attendants make a final resolution to shore up their energies and make a clean break of it. By now the helicopter is annoyingly late and a considerable queue is backed up to the presenting section, obtrusively disrupting the ordinary course of commerce. I get on the megaphone and make these several points but the indifference turning to scorn of the onlookers is too uncomfortable and I turn to a medley of disconnected hits. You look so quiet there it seems a shame to disturb you, eyes lolling about to their own tune of distraction. The icy slope curves beyond reach, careless of index and anticipation.

ST. McC.

graphemic

hinges

discourse

re-ordering

SIGNS

of

few little

whch

speed &

wh.

inter-sentential

connexions

there's

splendid

"here too"

in

not forced

stuff

the rest of

piecemeal

spins off

"ethical"

intrude

wiTh tHaT kiNd oF

schizophallic

categories

enfolding

a proper place

fix(ist)

opting for a

* * * * *

so find

isn't

TURN

face to a

inevitable

picturesque

baulk

DESIRE

token by

topology": the

se e

"OR"

verfrumsdungseffect

autonomous explosions

taste as

blocks, circling

like (star), fl...m...n...g...

aire, leap—

as if we had

not gleaned

in a "possible"

vectorate

these: the

issued

, canopy

as scratch (rune

potential a

s...n...r...ty

the pull

"buckle me"

with a...pAt

      "i leap up"

sights

"iDeaLLy"

being (?)

"happens"

nOt sParTaN

: polish(s) (ed)

11

TO FACE

ou///eg///t///

am (visit, subdue, impulse)

h...l...r...ty

THE KLUPZY GIRL

Poetry is like a swoon, with this difference:
it brings you to your senses. Yet his
parables are not singular. The smoke from
the boat causes the men to joke. Not
gymnastic: pyrotechnic. The continuousness
of a smile—wry, perfume scented. No this
would go fruity with all these changes
around. Sense of variety: panic. Like
my eye takes over from the front
yard, three pace. Idle gaze—years
right down the window. Not clairvoyance,
predictions, deciphering—enacting. Analytically,
i.e., thoughtlessly. Begin to push and cue
together. Or I originate out of this
occurrence, stoop down, bend on. The
Protest-ant's voice within, calling for
this to be shepherded, For moment's
expression's enthroning. Able to be
alibied (continguity of vacuity). Or
telepathetically? Verena read the epistle
with much deliberateness. If we are
not to be phrasemongers, we must
sit down and take the steps that will
give these policies life. I fumbled clumsily
with the others—the evocations, explanations,
glossings of "reality" seemed like stretching
it to cover ground rather than make
or name or push something through.
"But the most beautiful
of all doubts is when the downtrodden
and despairing raise their heads and
stop believing in the strength of their oppressors."
To be slayed by such sighs: a noble figure
in a removed entranceway.

"This is just a little note
to say that it was nice working with
all of you. It has been a rewarding
experience in many ways. Although I
am looking forward to my new position with
great anticipation, I shall never forget
the days I spent here. It was like
a home-away-from-home, everyone was
just so warm and friendly. I shall ever
remember you in my prayers, and I
wish you the best for the future." Preoccupations
immediately launch: to set straight, to glean
from her glance. Terrifically bored
on the bus. Any really you want
go to mixed on me. Sumptuous slump.
As it becomes apparent. Just that I thought.
Contraction that to you perhaps an
idealization. Have I kept. But that
point is—such repair as roads no
joint, what?, these few years must
admit to not expecting, as if the
silent rudeness might separate us out. &
maybe anger would be better than explaining.
When in tents or families in comparative
Which sums digest. Disclaimer
alights what with begin. That's
maybe the first pace, the particular. I mean
I feel I've got to and a few while
I can just look to see unrelenting
amount of canny criticism whatever
occasions overriding for comparison
spin for the sake of intrinsic in that
or that I've already made although
against reaction's consequent proceeding.
But it's to the point that you've
begun to broach like you could almost
fault me on as if you were going to
use could become primarily propulsion

to affinity have itself so. She
gets nutty. Oh she settles in, she
settles the curdles, unhooks the latches,
but I, preferring hatches . . .
When batters, benumbs, the lights
in a basket, portable. Potted & make
believe—you're rudeness amounts to not
noticing, i.e., I'm on a different
scale of jags. To be in replacement
for a number of linings. Tubes of turmoil.
To stroll on the beach is to be in
the company of the wage-earner and
the unemployed on the public way, but
to command a view of it from a vantage
both recessed and elevated is to enter
the bourgeois space; here vantage and view
become consumable. I can't describe
how insulted I felt, it's a ruthlessness
not so much I didn't know you possessed
as that I didn't think you'd turn
on me. When you stop acting in good
faith any residue of the relationship
gets really unpleasant and the gratuitous
discounting severs what I can't necessarily
define the circumferences of. "There are a
number of calls in the June bill
which I have been unable to document. We
believe these calls were made by S————
O———— who is no longer employed by
this project. We presume these calls
to be program related although she
did not keep a log of long distance
calls as requested in the memo
circulated March 11, 1980." It has
more to me than please to note acquits
defiant spawn. But your letter does
not scan its view nor serve our
own resolve. Little noticing sectored

demonstration, or flail with inheld
throng. Content to meet or not to meet
what inlays subsequent flustered
adjustment. "The Good *is*
for the fact that I will it, and apart
from willing it, it has no existence."
"There is no document of civilization
that is not at the same time a
document of barbarism." Blue suede pestilence.
Binds bins. History and civilization
represented as aura—piles
of debris founded on a law and mythology
whose bases are in violence, the release
from which a Messianic moment
in which history itself is vanquished.
That's why I'm perplexed
at your startlement, though obviously
it's startling to see contexts changed on you
to have that done to you and
delivered unbeknownst. The Ideal
swoops, and reascends. "With real
struggle, genuine tax relief
can be won." A manic
state of careless grace. Mylar juggernauts
zig-zag penuriously. Car smashed into;
camera stolen; hat lost; run out of
money, write for money, money doesn't come.
Long interruption as I talk to woman
most of the way back—a runner,
very pleasant. Get off in Boston and everything
seems to go crazy.

       All of gets where
       Round dog-eared head
       The clear to trying
       Forgets issues of trembles
       Address vestiges to remain
       These years after all
       Fog commends in discourse

HANNAH WEINER

from CLAIRVOYANT JOURNAL

Sat May 11
PERFECT COMPASSION   Rhys is doing a 3 day silence 9   if he talks to you *sure*
Monday   you'd like to bang his Virgo head into a wall*not nice*   *He is thurs*
REKA all week because you didn't GO sun night   *nos periods*   to find out why
he's so pissed off at you THURS h*e* isn'*t* *rude yes he is he barely talked to you Mon*
after you took your book in, was cool *ampersand* rude   AND PISSED   *gracious*
OMEN o, men   *have a nice weekend*

discredit him

Sat May 11
Well it's strange you wouldn't fuck with him Sat night   *not the reason* and Sun
cry Mon
was your movie *jealous* was he LIMELIGHT FOOLISH you thought Rhys was
forever
beyond that OH HANNAH   there's been no BATHTUB communication *dont*
talk about it why not you're really unhappy   *walk*   that someone you're in
constant *tooth* with drops out the minute something important happens in your
life, and you can't even talk to him about   *tues night* so you're sorry you called
monday
early *so what* *not a compliment* IT'S NOT EVIL but he didn't call you back
all week *3 weeks* TYPICAL RHYS   Is it? YOu *dont* are really angry   ONE
June
MORE WEEK He acted like a typical male chauvinist *pigstyl*   *You're alright*
SORRY ABOUT THIS PAGE RHYS   *careful*
you read April MAKE NOTES it's pretty funny   you think you're a genius WE
ALL ARE NO GOOD RHYS *Sat night* morning you **NOS GOODS**
BAD MISTAKE you walk through it beer bread butter
YOU HAVE THE FLU YOU HAVE A FEVER you feel awful go home so that's
why you can't go to Nijoles   The Kitchen is having a cocktail party benefit that's
why you can't go to Max *friend* *forget* WATER WHISTLE Wed bed
with Bernadette
Nothing squeaks they copy you you just thought that No mysteries to read *you*
survive You MOTHER see the man at the corner grocery store where they have
the lightest DONNIE rolls he's expensive *cigarettes* why did you buy a pack? 65c
incredible Nothing *come quickly* is in heat *rubs all over us* We A lot of
DONNIE's today   TOO NERVOUS   SEE A DOCTOR   Neither one is in

GET A SHOT   THANKS A LOT   MICHAEL   LUBA $_{necessary}$ You *so*
what realize *think of it Rosemary color* Wed was awful because you were just
getting *sick again*   The interference has a field day but doesn't *government*
explain *neg* why *flu* DRINK NU says the tea YOU HAVE THE FLU   JACK
CONTROL YOURSELF   DUMB You cant believe that the breakfront and
table from *Jerry's apt*   fit perfectly in yours $_{perfec}$ brown wood tall thin cabinet
round holed screened bottom used to be over radiator, put milk cartons ms in it,
in your apt   SHOPPING GUIDE   DOUBLEday and BLOOMingdales *nega*
after you   called Rhys what does it mean   GO THERE   SEE EDITORS
Majorie calls SPEAKING THE SAME VOICES NO POETRY READING$_{bashful}$
why not not conscious yourself take it easy USE SOAP   BIG PROBLEM   NOT
ALL PROBLEMS   You mean there are pleasures IN LIFE GEORGE   OMIT
THE EDITING   you thought you mentioned you read it over and you take out
buts, ands, ifs, etcs. **AND NO PERIODS** and it puts in underlines MORE
EFFORT and a few big words ALSO

Sat May 11 p 3
You got some *donuts*   FROM THE STORE tried twice to throw them out,
you speed on them SUGAR coated rescued them from the hall floor and the
wastebasket, GINGER YOU DONT EAT DESERT YOU NEED POTASSIUM
not alright in almost empty beer *glass*   YOU GET ANOTHER ONE YOUR
VOCABULARY is NOA'S NOT TRUE   You now have 6 glasses   BIG WOW
PHILIP   LAY DOWN   You ^{dopey}dig another donut out from under the dirty
washed floor paper towel and empty tuna fish can NO GOODS   pour some
more beer *Control yourself* you ate less LECITHIN   you didn't get any
DONT MENTION ME ^{TOOTS} says the maple syrup bottle fake you've
taken a swig of it every   night since the doctor told you to give up ^{sweats}sweets com-
pletely   The donuts$_{potassium}$ are awful   NOT GOOD   FOOD   They all taste of

Carbona wall wipe OUCH *You destroyed your chance* COLE SLWA you know
you can't digest that You haven't tried chocolate pudding either   TNAG GOD
DONT LAUGH   The oil in the donuts that dont taste of cleaning fluid is awful
THROW UP   *Begin* IT IS THE LIQUID DRINK A LOT OF BEER DONT
LAUGH NO MORE HOMEWORK   Voice says *dungarees* just to remind you
your *2nd hand* corduroys and the   velvets are both all cotton You do the *count
down* 10 8 8 GODZ NO MORE MILK   you saw *neighborhood*   you had to wash
the dishes to wash the paint brush you knock over the corkscrew into the cat food
spills NOT A PERFECT MASTER printed in beer and dirty yellow sponge it's
PRETTY NO MISTRESS *think*   You almost drink some peppermint tea
poetry   DONT MIX BUSINESS says the cup   You get up to wipe up the cat food
SIT DOWN FOR A SECOND small caps *Dunk every tues* BIG FANTASTIC
hear Rhys's voice as you clean   NO MORE HOUSEWORK big fantastic had
better get his ass over here *negative* monday or call *dont agree with him* THAT'S ALL
BENCH LIGHT   *Light candles* BIG DING A LING   is that Donde's toy
telephone NEGA   YOU LOVE IT HERE   VERY HAPPY YEAR   *not alright
margins ok* SAYS JIM THEY SUPPORT YOU   Where is the word *sensitive
chakra Malcolm you need a typist be confident*   NOT OK   You think you will
stay drunk TIL MONDAY   OR TUES   *wed thurs* GO GIN DONNIE IN
PERSON   says forehead MORE PLEASURE TO COME OBVIOUS RHYSSSSS
MORE SURPRISES MORE INNOCENTS   All those ssssss seem to be negative
NOT COMING   DRINK ONE MORE BEER you can hardly sit up LIGHT
BULB which whose? NO MORE COME   IT DEPRESSES YOU to think NO
MORE *think champagne early in June*   You're getting depressed they're
playing with you you don't like it FUCK YOU   PERRY COMO   *Big enough in*
beer you don't want *see you later*   YOU CRY ALL NIGHT You miss Rhys
children   you want to talk *about Sunday* *it's too late* it's a week *too late   he
feels your anger* DOUBLEDAY
                              I DONST FINISH THIS PAGE

LITTLE BOOK 107   May 13 77

I likes my gray

BOOKS

May is a stupid & silent

13

77

MONTH

MAY IS SILEN

may is popular stupid

AND T SILLY

JUST SHANNAH
CURL YOUR
HAIR IS
GOOD S

May is a silent month repeated

REPEATED

MENTION THE TV

(heard) i n s

P a r e n t h e s i s

STUPID

seen

ONS TV
COMIC
sCREEN

a n y

m a k e

j u s t

TSold

CO M M   E N T S
C O M P L I M E N

sSCREEN
some words
Is Describe

APPEAR
on t h e GRAY
whole
sSCREEN

PAEDII
some across the
M I D   cut
this
short

BOTTEM
I see appears
just across the middle

I SEE W
OR   DS
I SEE OKs
ISEE OK s

                    t comเ
            j u s
        I   LETED
        this hour
        I JUST

        (hear) TOO LATE
        COM   PLETED
        sTHIS
        I am ACROSS

                    s t i l l   s w a i t i n g

        still   waste   paper   stupid
        baby girl
                    STILL
        sWRI I ING

                d
                 o
                  n
                   t
                    c
                     o
                      m
                       p
                        l
                         e
                          t
                           e
        T H I S   BOOK
        FOREHEAD
        CLEARLY
        "shannah I worries
                    MYSELF
                t
                 o
                  s   death"
        the
            OBJECTS
            finish my

294 Hannah Weiner

t
u
s
j
s
I   SLOWLY

            I donst object
            S E N T E N C E
            SENTENCE
            sSLOWLY
            I writes
                  SLOWLY
dont continue with this sentence
S   T   R   U   C   T   U   R
            H
             a
              n
               n
                a
                 h
              d   i
               o   s I SPELLED
                n
                 s
                  t
                      c
                       o
                        n
                         t
                          i
                           n
                            u
                             e
            WITH WORDS
         finish the sentence SEEN

                  e
                  r
                  e
                  h
                  w

         structure
            stupid ONS SCREEN
                    AND SILLY
                       t
                       s
            and   n   forget
                 o   SCREEN
                d
                  it
            I ENCLOSE MY
                SOBVI
                OUS

            SIRUCIURE
         SENIENCE cross my ts
            across the

t h e SIMON
           s
            a i
               n
                t

SEE an n appears
sWHERE
where I write
           N
WRITTEN

completes   my   sentence
                          Bruce
STRUC   laughs
      I FORGOTS MY
         SCREEN
I completes my
                SEN/ENCE
              e
           r   l
        u   N
struct   A   r
     s L   e a
   AND DISAP p
     APPEARS
   just finish the BO
       FOREHEAD
I just
       DISAPPEAR
       sSOMETIME
       I
         j
          u
           s t
              w
               r i
                  t
                   e
                    a
       LITTLE cross my ts

                         e
                      l l
                   i t   f
                 l   o
              a   l l
           r   o w
        u   s
      h   c
    s   r
  o k   o s
t h e   s
          MORE   m y
             OFTEN   t s

296 Hannah Weiner

Hannah this book hurts you a LITTLE

SIL ly

I could save my life myself

I just dont want any more writing in
this book

NOT OKS
just
DONT FINISH
THIS PAGE appears

THIS PAGE
what is the
s   h   a   p   e

1 2 ,,

diagonal
COLOR TV
As LIE
black
AMPERSand
WHIT
I WRIIES
E
cross t
ENDS BOOK

we areWRITING
we pray for our
STAND
RUSSELL MEANS
STAND
I could Russell
Means stand all
day if I didn't
tire so easily
            NOTES
& it didn't
hurt   POCKETS
so much
I have
morning
sickness too
Is cant stand
Another
        we stand
Cut This Hannah Short
who stands with
w r i t i n g
a
   PENALTY
pencil in her hand
dont indent there is a penalty
for writing
            COVER
about cover I said aim subjects
THE COVER STINKS
I stand til
I'm on the cover
of a magazine
I stand like a
writer stupid
HALF I said dont indent ASSED
explain it
              I
book in writing hand
pen in
       each hand

CLOSE THIS BOOK
RUSSELL NAME
this book is closed
same fight
Ali wins
please I cant
stand
please I cant
walk even
Hannah I can
understand it
much better
RUSSELL in the book stupid he doesn't like indented line
Russell was in jail works like an HINT Indian
I SIGNED IT
very unusual
STANDING
book stupid Russell indents paradise Crow Dogs in jail
who takes a chance
only Indians in this century would you believe it
I writes for
Russell Means
alive
        FASTING
60 DAYS
for his life
I lied
for his life stupid
31 days thas enough
I read it the day Ali speaks thats how I write
thats Ali
he knows
he wins it
wro 11th round
he nits hard
please I'm wrong
sometime
call forwarding
SAVES A DAY
IN A LIFE
if its granted alive
that's how my grandmother speaks
please I can't
stand anymore

reverse situations dont joke
understand
please I understand
it Russell leads period
MEANS GURU
SPELL THE NAME BACKWARD
LLESSUR SNAME and it hurts a little published
you're an honest woman stupid
Hannah he sits
SILENT
& we know it
hannah thats all silent means
HANNAHS I WANT
MEANS for his safety Jimmie explains it
        INS JAIL
guess what it means
I just did it
spells awkwardly
Hannah I'm honest about it said Le
BLUE SHIRTS
I am working also
keep yourself
swift
CHANGES
don't apologize
boys I split fast
when I'm ready
I'
  S
   M
     I
      N
       J
        A
         I
          L
I SIT
hannah he was almost murdered in jail
I cant stand all the time
I'M WEAKENED
IS SCARED
I still split fast
RUSSELL MEANS
when ins jail I split
I'sm in jail
one year for my
life

NOV 15
RELEASED I AM SURE
   I PUBLISH IT
on this date released
for work period
continued April
FINAL SOLUTION JULY
BILL MEANS IS ON RECORD IN IT
one day he cheated
and left the jail by it
stabbed stupid
and in the hospital
WHEN HE WAS IN JAIL
by the heart
thats all for the record imm
THATS ALL STUPID
people were afraid
to cheer
for him
HANNAH HE WINS IT NEXT TIME
WHO CHEATS
ONLY STANDING UP
      sign at the end
one September date
they wonder how I know
b
 e
   c
    a
     u   l
      s   l M eans was lying to me all the time all the
       e i
        B

BILL MEANS IS ON RECORD AS A LIAR alway
hannah hes cute
PUTS IT BACK IN TYPE stupid
compromise ins July when he rturns
HANNAH IT WAS A 6 MOS COMPROMISE SOLUTION
STUPID
thats all
publis
book signed
S   L   D
 E   E   O
  N   T   N T
   T   E
    E   C
     N   T   O
      C   H   M
       E   E   P

THAT MEANS HES OUT
that finis publis poem etc means
WHEW
HIS BROTHER IS OUT ALSO TOO omit
I just finish my sentences a little line out to the edge
someone else did
Means DIDNT
AND CANT CHEAT ever again
put it back in and finish the complete sentence
PUT IT BACK IN THE TYPEWRITER AND SIGNED
HANNAH HE THINKS YOUVE COMPLETED YOUR PAGE TYPED and si

BRUCE ANDREWS

from SONNETS (Memento Mori)

a silhouette for its Rousseau
aimlessly

    not just this
    i'm not

foresight in her back
           there's nothing wrong

of my lungs for lint
impressing

the enabling rules for success

lighten a spinning
    hard to pronounce

the linoleum's light hand spirals "those
sex dramas do not terribly   appeal to me"

        ghosted endeavor
        as fast

obedience
not the overall cure for survival

on Ace accelerators
    a gypsum
kneel
a vague runaway
        whatever
cuff hands   tunnel   lightning's gauze

broadcasting from stop mouth

ergo
smokeful
    unanchor
ochre talked

        in all
a fluttery

    sugarin' momentary s.o.s.

Little Johnny Jumpup

thief your   small skivvy luck

pension's choir
la hora
        imagine

inamoratas

    quip trace
of a voice

   "a blind man
      maybe accuses the whole world
      of his darkness"

prankish   then no thanks amened
    waist at supper

plaintiff booms
i did
    as if an easel
    eat ambiguity
        debris feathered

it's . . . in neck . . . several times
and chest . . . and way

yonder ere guess I
lost my head

python in sleeve

silverine wax

FUNNELS IN

"My reasons satisfy me. You seem
unable to understand that."
—Charles Foster Kane

morning and reverent

here is as pleased as they come

are like all said a great deal of

trouble chances with above all pressure

to turmoil with like

ramrod

mistake would

without qualification blink czechoslovakian as
one fetus

all *self* presentations

compass in my man hood

a host will natural eventual carefully gathering it notes

complicates proves be adverbs

lamplight if quenched

you ring

here air

follies all right great who've *lost* that drooping as minxing

that's it

306   Bruce Andrews

a slow pouring over toward destiny you see

my *own* validity   an empire through

you create a thing

                                        sleds

below

suds

                    as your characterization

                    all loosen astride

whose lips bluntly came clumsied coma

are you smiling at

        does to families undifferentiated and *here I*'m

            dynamite the light of the leaves and crooked

                    extol take

    sierra tango hotel

as dress meditation believing each embody such character

        to find whitewashed found utter

        see 'em all

        a texture when virulent sensation knew the names

enthusiasm

talks rose

did not answer motioned

yelling why *silk* that is platened that's

                                        instead

huff puffing began other

was hated by as many more

own talks of colloid reputation end

a passing forth as out of antiqued rhetoric

                              missile into the rehearsal

lint webs

antechamber devotion sky air it a

imagination as watchful manner fallen   listening

                                    paradigm

                        quench queen

fog which decorated the weeping

                              all history as logic

                        unless throughout

pleading now was so clean

                    am nervous

308 Bruce Andrews

publican like shavings are all pled overly quick

                    fog rumbles that resembles bucks

            baseball over tea-cakes

              a succession of caution

       syllabary

      splendid to our turning away about without the eye

                          meth

        an armada

whose pollen will not mate AT ALL

              the animal grace it's everywhere

         always a bridesmaid never a bride

    float   and fade

                 old awful

       are fulfilled

mild-voiced immediately to one over the tube on hook of
the little nations

          on to the ballroom!

              me *own* hook

    accent of any kind another still beside

just as worm-eaten to what was earth that was

                        Bruce Andrews 309

in the past day

       gift grown alone sweet half *that's* lifting

              blue along

        what is was of perfect then again

not as deviant *enough*

                 gimme this

        already weakened their ether

     suggestion

      they would not allow them to be put again out of sight

      either a lot they'd nodded

             weight heat

deep slat

    devils cuspid device

   allure

        the desperations of independence

         the letters that move

      sacred stump their own acting

malign enjoy

          grass beyond her adumbration

310 Bruce Andrews

that my memory forests out alongside

some sang cuisine seventeen button muscling

other instance bump

lingered before ain't you knowledge

stitched the water

before bad gimme this after an hour they'd not

pliers there inscribed

seen since with fearful haste

shorts a clove hitch

of taciturnity that becomes indolence

live *here*?

you say

in any rose

every wicked part of him

that these will be kept crowed the hermit

trying to silence it

better change the concentration of the unexpected

proportion there was nor spoke

and their long *neck* won't tattle

Bruce Andrews 311

made known to itself

with one's what's wrong   o.k.?

box toward anywhere

with alum bottle too in alarm

that is just as devoted to the ladylike lifting of a poker

thin unfasten chinaberry

turned-up rose stop tap-room crooned secrecy suddenly stiff

king's crack put spark

disarranged

trying always to prove something

shrill root

so long as

am older now doughtied

simply lay down patroness shams lofty more of black
than peripatetic

echoes of calvary

seven be all whims right

as lost

in the heart of

wobbled

312 Bruce Andrews

utter lilt
like sewing

                                                      fisticuff

lickerash

        altogether looking for sounds *above* their voice

                                in sheet

            husky whine pump

                wooden girl partner mean *wants* what say

    very few worlds an oar then is favored

        it did not matter and right out

                        truculent cool yes anything

                lie low then

                        him or me

            care worn felt his heart separate

dwindling company

                broke sparing sign

            ladies love *shame*

                        complete

        delicately gingered through the harmless

                the other twin the completed episode

                                    Bruce Andrews   313

as if

enveloped halo as against totem

whoa

bold else

optical decoy

LETTERS

THEIR midst mix power to crystallize which connected the next room hope openings bent her white fragments effusive neck smoked verge of recognition's to hold fast as if unwittingly even to the fissures looming sight shadow surprises stays at home her words for the feeling to an arrow soothed to have who's he put implicit with another origin emergency rusted foliate world abandonment to fold herself together catch exhaustion which different notes some rejoinder necessary to it with unnecessary valor break the vacancy where doesn't threshold depend more slender easel by an inch knew one if anyone had clung hinted about her so what one could give in return blessed impetuosity an arm round an interval of but why ever not space thing thinking what no suggestion of the glance were saying something that in spine without realizing further for the motives was it about being reduced her own body of the sudden exhilaration quaint unaccustomed tasted vibrant almost heedlessly dance vibrato apparently like the figure three law hearts however how had not suspected just suddenly upon them local exquisite suspicion depend her veiled her us much

Bruce Andrews 315

channeled anew and sharing changed added to disorder arms one
to whom toss answered welcome twinings' disturbance easy sup-
posing get over tattered flags so such to assemble outwardly per-
ambulations dwell if it hadn't been pretend indifference weeks
emphasizing alert need the face yet of as unrelated passions dot
in the morning blasts of it doubt doesn't decorated recollection
over faculties were spontaneously results to both of them bodily
cupboard liquid lights indecisive season else consented with which
was dictated to her could hear the speed hypnotized serious giddy
quicken if it you've arranged under similar circumstances and
expected was certainly compared it with that long asked permis-
sion to fabric line monotonous agitation too singing no notice
in the wires animalism lowering atmosphere and answers from
and gave way be an understanding close not yet clear to be pat
pushing aside it scientifically a little out of drawing attempt at
other people's pose disciplines just over the center time elongate
one and row of footlights heaven branches of security emit the way
you look or past flung across day tonight in no way diminished

from R+B

you reisolate tip
envoy prose queer prose bridle
word popcorn at CO-EXCITE
hat incidence lingerie
roll jars divide old lick world
late swirl praline lance CO-EXIST up
something traverse doubt reserve planet
KEEPER poster against showpersonship
secret up on the puts letter faucets
SENSE everyplace woman half
counting blur up dervishes
world show up leg take cover
magnetize flipper FORE yourself
have 've high hit in splint
goat take pretentious excel ear drug
talk CRYPT phone crypt
under head see come dry flea
in you air
here! taffetas cheek are
wein Dutch sweet-talk
once. . . . okay Bambu Patente
pink crisis
happiness plane Mas FINO Y Mas
pay ourself head scene gy
Aromatico manners five bingo penis
practice reunites the posture pedal

structure statements agree with me

just the innate sense of

suspect tin catholic toy

belief jumps lamentable

around classify fish soldier poser

game declaims subjectivity

in eye coup banal jam POLITESSE in place

electric ahead he fashion relentless also-ran

prostituted turf turbine

management bituminous altogether badger sack

skin up pages

end line tap cap letter calm letter point

JAIL serpent slung auto attune

whores is funky stew

moose sewn maxi sap cook little papers

reprimand Texas represents theft

ardent grill STATE lather

ivre zing it's theft rosy want

spectacle bob lament & Fanny's

stick gain vessel tampon

to very else debility doubt

chi chi nothing cadre torch oneself

in fours happily legible

sounds taper CONDUCTRESS zig

shag chinese administratives

critique christ depth lamentation—

a putative Einstein detectives

d-d-d-dialectic steeplechases engulf

318   *Bruce Andrews*

jerrybuilt attention. . . attachment anus

not is not not

four snake bird mud red shut symptom

UP cretin pinch

hook fabricate honey

embroil derail coup solemn

hash gets tampi

jar jet reclaim COMPREHEND

number pussed jocko micro

ratatouille paraquat

ennui an RN tenor bath

not mensch pudding

cancan spent affair acre JUJU

pause main

stipulate bonbons most to home

self-indulgent TALC in aggressive way

in pantry not benign songster

to shoot ACCOMPLICE lady powder underdevelopment

flowery glue out LAVISH snake ain't REPRIMAND

you DROSS up late kind of novel

LITTLE duchamps valet blocks egg

fatten up messing round

from I GUESS WORK THE TIME UP

Apart

meant —licking stick good golly   If

body language

counterfactual   Brittle treble now

pylons afford dignity   She cannot tell where her keep

on husband is when the question because she tried

it said 'Oh no'   Time git up   Second

time be in a water bring it up   that rosicrucianism

nine weeks with body the body hot sake fluster

category by wince spite ozone olive

mama sell Sugar triangulation   We say — Sadie — Boss

I blow that stuff in   & Apex of

these thighs promist install a bathroom   Dowop

forestry butter knife falangist eat you along assassinated

architecture   You got enamel shoes Castro has

position of kitchen on earth the other night   Boom

boom war thee   She first tried to West

Virginia non-Irish people like Pennsylvania

hot pink floss house & farm work weevil billow

billions in milk fracture faster & faster apron

applique to be old troop my   my   my   my   my   my

this years old   Gave each other's hearts

$10.00 that included terms like "platen" "slut"

"queer" and "bed *verb transitive*"   Got ebb

tantamount be healing too extra doggone

too drake gots to get parallax refashion

mean contradiction fire pleasure pain phalanx

up with drops a quarter clarity   Involute

cos' amino acids won't thing to spend self free don't

meant car rims neither   Blue that is u / e

urine   hatband of regret   *TIMES* insufferably ditto

once pretentious again am just a little lamb   Wife had

second hand garments leased her & she would have

had to have had guarantees to have had them

disavowed   Office equip   Boss not mean

mind ramblin fluid   baby's not parable

yakety yak 'deef' automatic-ly so pastoral order was not

no word able quotidien up outer

power influence authority   Telephone hero *STATED BEHAVIOR*

gets what she wants

        Baton Rouge

        Parochial Communitarian Development

        embitter underclass

        competitive sector

        monopoly sector   Cooking eggs

U.S.A.   at night makes us squeamish   Alibis

call you want

her shirtless trickle of sweat under arm uh huh 'deep

study' don't want you   Weren't would facts

be willing wealth is wrong if it wasn't

for   And Chinamen would sing fist-pounding in them bottom

who cauterize imagining for reasons test sentimental

social spoilation   Really tear up glamorous precursors'

buttresuscitation squads   Some one maneuver shake

snake physician person erect belief gang

of women's igloo commandeering limousine   Performative the

noun masturbating the phrase   Presumably is marriage

license by God got heart to vehicle

hell's principality   Refuse to have salt with

outside world on its terms   Do you think that

you or your family would be better off if you died   Do

you think you or your family would be better off if

they died   Afghanistan —— old cadillacs

never die   (and felt so bad)   You got curfew

rope polls like our backs don't bone glimmer angel

dusts to farm parity unexpect the all

night the all frantic one   Disillusioned sighs if

race fixed furniture fears be are so & so

damned crazy plastique dwells sixty minute melancholiac

house mess me in to be righteous   God goons

pop   Babylonian girl specs   CONFINES   cronyism

LOOSELY PREVIOUS LIASON DOROTHY 20 years

who dusts an imbecile   Each idealizes

the amplified beat   Don't want limbs

pediatricians diatribing too borrow it on spool

don't want no thighs noise music   Oh

my mary mary knock-kneed roly-poly sleep-

walkin' pigeon-toed YELLOW YELLOW gimme

mule oiseaux exotiques   Mrs. Garrulous is

apparently such typography so have raybeats

practically no shy in alphabet   Gave $10.00 crossroads of −

workplace waxes carnals to thermometer   Style   Sucker that

spinning President Polk on the rack tracks sly fuss almost thang

as coop much baroque as relevant sumptuousness   Book

-ization   But you can't beat them walkie-talkies   Family

beliefs in foul play   father administers

dead infantilism   Low end behold lah la lah lah

la lah culture sack all turbulent qualify to odds gleam

polyethylene flashlight recruit ocular proof of old sha-la-la

goose musk to mention crystal molybdenum trucking

climax paper   What   leave it on my head

recruit fatuous bedroom   Overindulge in liquor

when she one transplant fool t' another − (*don't call me*

nigger whitey) — lights right broke into closed repeat chorus

car captured by desire at Tremont & Bathgate Avenue   At

any time zephyrous sentence can dislocate

vanishing either arm   Freelance babies makin' babies

babies was close relationship between adjacent axes

at the point them was nostrils that   Well rodan-istic

had dumplings authoritative economy observed faze

passionate people got lots off kiss like passionate

bush lots of killed tetras like that   Blanket not imaginative

same sephardic word turn't muther out   Legs flew christen

develop mussel shell open rib capture twelve device as

nostrum hid

beak off every   Useter linoleums so bad so division

now she fancy party money so that's to semiotic

foodstuffs seem like my vacuum cleaner

she want to put me out   Disco mica

melodica funk   Bring that one woman bottle

to my depedestalization   If drowsiness eager entourage

occur do not operate or be in the way of

machinery   Fuzz a lapse

done all rachet mindless soprano

brain boogie wash on me bewildered   Husband

had tried to enter sexually

his answer and the problem who'd she too

teasing I can't survive which these buffooning

daughters sing Je-sus   You got to

enforce devotion   No flanging

aphex

from CONFIDENCE TRICK

Cherry red kind of washed-out caged & staged quack quack spoke job, pecs & balls juice up, nobody's heroes censor doesn t censor enough; antidote a panic, white eyes — They much jeopardy — They much probability solid pleasure — Moto kitsch, or racial mercantilism?, what about the feds damaging the emissions? — Stereo bust means 'think quicker'; I must eat worms — Flesh with insistence; I insist so it s calculated passion sell-outs? — Andersonville prison

Foo-o-o-l falsetto up me political zip coon shows, especially valuable recitations of commodity authority, madre chingado, cure doing doubt — To torch all Christendom, ready to snap sway pivot chump point use or abuse, get me the sweetener — All power to the prepubescents — Well, you failed as a heterosexual

God is science — First, they have to get more Nazi-like Modern English in their gender qualifiers first indoor life; uncut horse, *right*, almost red, einstein à go-go life elsewhere — Reticence in public was depriving me everything (regimental surgeon stands besides casualties) I want in private, that s it!, rent, the quality of mercy is not so eager; style wars — One pair of tickets, I have got to have the freezer, I d like to sleep to get over you, I am out of two minds — Nor is pacifism a substitute for socialism — Can t follow anthem, puffed up Jack — Garish sentimental sensationalism & rigid conventionality, are these the contrasting vices distort female sexuality? — Rather than disband when polio is at last conquered, the March of Dimes bureaucracy looks for other diseases to fight — Lap acquires a certain difficulty; glitter don t leak; not playing with a full deck, happiness & contempt, doesn t have his oars all the way in the water — Yeah, spandex & parachute, living in your toybox — Somebodies, 85% gender parity is how I get my S.S.I. — I want you to build up my muscle, mono yoyo, positive life — Chief Product spoke having vinyl out vinyl debit, it s economics you know — Can I sleep in the arms of society tonight?

DIANE WARD

PRONOUNCING

I don't know what he looks like. I don't know his name. He trained me twice so I promise resolutions promise again. He trained me so that I could listen and then listen again. Now I make promises over after promising once. I relive first seconds and I relive over many times. I've mastered nothing I've repeated nothing. I've repeated nothing without being aware of repeating. I wore glasses, black and white shoes. I colored over drawing over and over. I've never finished anything but left it all unfinished. I retire early. I retire early. I misinterpret everything he said. I listen carefully and hear I tilted my head but misunderstood. I'm fixed in this spot but not commited. I'm commited but not understanding. He trained me to relax and I can't relax. I stand in this spot to relax. I make myself stand in this spot to relax. I've noticed parts that were touched desire other parts. I've noticed absence. I've noticed repetition. I'm patient and reasonable. I touch something now that desire touches. He's unlike this—his absence. He resembles all other absent people he walks with miserable repetition. He's sincere this time and this time he doesn't remember anything. He's careful to understand. He trained me to relax. He's made up the motion I'm about to make. I'm not commited but without desire. I'm in a place of talk. I don't know what he looks like. I don't know his name. He trained me twice so I promise resolutions promise again. He trained me so that I could listen and then listen desire. I'm in a place of talk. I'm in a place of silence. I'm sending casual time to rest. I'm sorting casual time. I'm resting. I'm furnished all around me. I'm touched. I'm placed upright. I'm finally absent with him. I'm not close not absent. He's not absent not here. He trained me to be tired. He trained me every motion is already tired. He's moving. He's about to leave although he isn't here. I'm sending time a slower way to eat. I'm eating slowly. I'm about to do the thing I'm about to do. He asked me to train him to relax. I showed him how to relax to make himself relax to stand in one spot to make himself stand in this spot and relax. I showed him organization and resistance. I show him organization and how to abandon. He asked me about sorting. I'm around so often. I'm more absent than most. I've never understood. I understand absence. I understand how slowly organization. I understand height and weight. I'm slow to understand. We were him and me. I don't know what he looks like. I'm looking at him. I'm on the side of everything that answers. I'm so quiet I drop. I'm so quiet I drop. He reassures and asks me to show him a slow time. I trained him to relax and measure. I trained him to be in this spot. I'm not really hearing what I listen for. I'm not listening I'm so quiet I drop. I don't remember him. He's a solid mass and vaguely comfortable. He's misunderstanding. He's silence. He's reasonable. He's always asked me to show him and I show him now. He's repeating. I'm organized with wires. I'm in combat with organization. I'm tempted like him. I'm reassured constantly in this spot. I'm always foreign with him. I'm supplying organization. I'm organized in our combat. Combat and him shyly drop. He stops any theater. He desires a theater. He's tricked the silence and it's reasonable. He's remade models of the combat. He motions to drop and I drop. Foreign sound ties my thoughts together. I'm sober with organization. He trained me twice to be sober once in silence once in thought so abstract so foreign to my organization. I was a daddy before him. I was in combat before him. I desired a theater before him. I tied my thoughts together before combat. He's supplied again and mixed with so many thoughts. He's lighter and he drops. He's born and I'm the father before him. He lays around in organization. He's the father before me. He's about to leave although he wasn't here. I'm organized commitment. I'm bent and tied to thoughts. He sits alone and drops. He's surrounded by me and drops. He must leave before. He must arrive. I sit alone and drop. I become the shadow of invisible movements. I'm sending casual time to rest. I'm played. I'm played enough. I don't know his name. His name is surrounded and organized. I don't know what he looks like. He rests as the shadow of my thoughts. He must arrive. He must sit alone when he wasn't there. His is motion falling. His is only combat. His is arrangement of my invisible movements. His is shadows in combat. I show him how to stand in one spot and he asks for organization. I train him to stand in one spot. I'm commited but without desire. I play desire. His is a cathedral. His motion is desire. He trained me twice. Once in my thoughts he trained me once in my thoughts. I relax and I try to relax. I'm tied together by falling. I'm combat in training. He's taught me twice once in my thoughts. I showed him his shadow of invisible movements. I showed him how to relax how to move how in desire everything must move. His desire has motioned to rest. He's casually organized. He's sending desire a start. He's on the top of movement.

* * * * *

Up to the motion I'm about to make caged like the horizon all the time dividing limp from limp territory. Morning plastic bag thought no sounds ears fall to the side of everything that answers. Fast comedies think enemies bubble his shadows around in combat. Attitude loss found on the street desire theater before him. In difference the nerve which is left is left. Not ever in a mirror together. Insight fights desire whose shadow combats the street motion I'm about to make up. Extra words hang around apart. Nearest to harmony clever books and cups. Loose tunes faked to the side of everything that answers tied. Passion tops cautiously. Fastened the final tip called the Fridays after this one. Everyone is making up the motions I'm about to make. Knock down or begin to fall, taking minutes. Speaking like this parallels. Why move yesterday away this quick. Stairways that lead on reversals taped to it and it and its left and its right. Through the window which stumbles over asters and roses and glass unstopped again go on are feelings images dead and naturally life has to move. Move extreme energy in one last move. Move time and the manners written in. Move like all paths leading. Time to mark to direct to me to us. If I had a photograph to analyze. She would like a skinny brown cigar mirrored glasses. She has legs. She doesn't like anything bands playing. She doesn't belong for long. Love: punctuation. Eating is the act. Any word will do like noun silk or soap. Images will soon not last for long and this's the only story. Energy out of the cubicle liking to hanging around but around is a point of absense. I believe she has legs I seem to recall them holding her up as words once rivers once buildings that defined the sky as an interior cube once. By our name her. Curfews are homes from mistakes when obligation calls for why. I don't call you anything beside us. Or like anything past style her. End the curtain our curtain her. How can you speak past. There's still a front two triangles curves. A front is past curves back her. She initiates calling her our name. Hurt significance encourages. One color its own drag its own eyes. Why not reproduce the sensation specialized tracked away before its feeling disciplined as if it were a child and had grown up young. Again it ended no literate version. We'd been caught like history or an *occurrence* whose feet were rotated eyes averted. There was no place but forward now delayed ahead level. This continues to be the medium of a sentence a life or a geographical plot of land. To continue has been distance to stop becomes distance. Recorded back again played. It ended is ethically believable. Nothing has been going to be maniacal. Something has gone to become lore with us a corner with us a door or a symbol of a door. To usually do again. Stay like glass sounds. What year have we laminated ourselves to inward remaining half true and half untrue. Authentic emotions stay up past the hour of square adjustments. That hour is perpetually coming and going that that hour is never here. How a heart blows returns. Think of graphic boredom or a still outline of an organic movement. An emblematical study of an unexperienced event. To be drunk is to know liquor. Total isolation was going to be impossible to be tried forever innocently. Free gorge empty spaces (love). Soon experience turmoil added to an inhuman capacity for love. In fact we're about to become relapsed deviated like fabric that forms the inside of curtain pleats. We're abandoning our survival for rescued juice of the street's light. Truth for something more legitimate. Time ambiguous and romantic. Desire is defined now by what you're left holding/ what you expected to be left. Our conversations want specific pronouns underlined, preoccupations. Seen or ever again since. Words mirror its own action finalized eventual. Later is nonsense with a double meaning. Barrier is a photo fabric too rich assorting. It's ok to take this seriously haunting prejudiced. What's last because of. The only eye is pleasure-impotence. Sense it don't. A downfall's been setting. Want a leg removes chance until the next expressed. The word audio all the times it rained. I want a glass of water I'm going to turn on the faucet. I'm turning on the faucet I'm going to want a glass of water. Out came relations. A void is the remaining complaint. What's wanted is the will to mix up you with what you do. Two pieces of lead are closer together at the bottom than the top. They're exactly parallel. Men are being critical toward the ground, like us. To reason breathe and count. Laying for long recovers the agent reflex. Gone in wanting an arm and out units of difference crowds. Red satin on white skin cloudy water in blue glass. Everyone's pockets are stuffed with everything tomorrow. At home it means light to them. Anonymous played poets revolve nylon into a value system. Moral and evil spin in an independent system same tempo. The forest for the trees and tree-like devices. Nausea masks are worn embarrassed. Hopefuls dream sweeping tender. A risk in the cult of style rib of silence. Zero to put in shoes too mature to walk this way. Little focal in and out. No adjectives and he's not alone. All objects are leveled secured a door closes two feet away a door opens onto no color only service. Now, my spark, the purpose was indifference. Own as harmony let up. Arranged tomorrow a few minutes. Leaving left where its power marries its power. Double tomorrow suited enough of yesterday. Love like productivity normalized routine thoughts break to imitate love. Dream again her and her she was that you again dream. I don't want *not wanting to lose* the object of this which is this: like her over to your side your arm under the camera so out of the picture. Repeating only you let you or below to be you or what you repeated. Do you want to be mangled by punctuation. From away cold trust drops out the front side naked. As if the yellow canary was painted blue to show emotion stark vivid staying roaming working. Lost logic for choice hearing music the room the least the music. In natural evolution silver greatness kept vast as a bird as desired cleanliness honor exits desks. Nothing a painter resists tonight. How to move outside on. On vocabulary a father not a mother. The secretary's first the bricklayer's anytimes first misplacement. Lingering temptations crawl out like monsters. Luck is forced in movement. Stability's chance with reconciliation around freedom. Murky about being freedom and undesired. Facing up to the turbojet. Swaying in visual language white line consternation. Logic choosing the heart as long as morality if morals hurt. The secretary's second of the first conversation. How we placed history thirty. Three taller years get passed have passed lonely. Loneliness a monster unless like a beautiful competition. So linear movement without them. How did to move so now. That's late the thirty places for war. Also a housewife places a mechanic's second shopgirl electrician. Facts pressure to release. Something's passion required. A simple luck how movement how lucky forced its stayed moved. Repeat after me: here how to move. Masters of local brain, local vocabulary: lost or win or lose or win. Even an ape can lay down. Punk fear and foreign kindness lost. A response leaving distance reaches looks. Only by the moon's house the light lost.

* * * * *

The machine non-possessively. Entryways are blocked by one word: combinations enter without sound. My sidekick red brick colored brick. The joys are beautiful. The masterful action produces the masters. It's easy to be one and one and me. Anti-confusion replays the mass falling out. The difference becomes style of exit. Words are said together not chanted but in an unlucky way challenged. The mass falling out, luminous order comforts what he can. He has nothing to do with murmurings seen around him. He collected parts of the mass falling out and hid them away as predicted. Rugs cover part of these. A brilliant light moves somewhere at the edge making the current habits of speech non-sensible. The unlucky part of this is to lose a paragraph. Action doesn't happen. Linear metaphors are distraught or non-existent. The Metaphor is faded or hung up. Only hope is symbolic. It's hard to get around this, the real was an act. Only hope was symbolic. The possible was visual thrown to the center together so speech was speeded to non-communication. With men this way, women this. The absolute end of bondage is pronounced exactly the same way. As a companion as a T.V. Misery approximately enrapture. With long thick hair big white teeth. With blonde hair thin lips. With a passive attitude a passionate pleasure. Then the thighs light up. Bodies

Diane Ward   333

are interchangable 2-dimensional. A room filled with paper thins blended by light. Tight brown bodies are solid thick immersed in a liquid the color of broken boundaries. To feel beautiful surround yourself with color: flowers, lipstick, T-shirts, or jewelry. No numbers announce themselves today. Light creates color also this roomful of 2-dimension, and water that has a sense of humor. To feel beautiful immerse yourself in water block out another sense like sight. Mimic the air or resist it. Hear what you like and ignore the rest. A hotel inside a concrete avenue outside. To feel beautiful don't look down. At the sight the legs are dancing. Music becomes a mood a nuisance intended to confuse. Taste is lazy. Today memory becomes a red and blue indian cotton a rough pine stained a soft red light a thick blue smoke a shiny black. Paranoia can be excessive indulgence or obsessive abstinance. There's no moderation without hope. Memory now is blacked, confused with dreams or pictures of a future without pictures. Does the television look back. With no eyes in the back of the head perception is still confused. Loose light bulbs dangle without electricity or sway with light. Monotony knows how but not what to say. Emotional memory takes on time, an equal match of specific actions and general actors. Define look out. Memory looks out to fit in what's coming. The thoughts at that moment were isolated rationality thrown in. Movements in the third and narrated dense in a self-conscious refrain. Life revolves around one tone, a flower that begins to die as it opens, a whistle blown one pitch higher than the ear can detect. As feelings begin they begin to be controlled. Elongated choices jam up. Laugh, see a painting because context refuses to let up. Images don't move the voice isn't constant. Pretention's a result of fear. Not not alone, explanation gives into itself. More modern, writing her famous couch. Her crouch a mannerism meant to isolate. Attention to the crouch. Ears leveled to the silence of a structural sidewalk movement. Feet leveled to the sidewalk sustained. An enemy massages an enemy. Lower and lower, enter with monotony. All the rage, for effect. Messed up tied up rehearsed over and over a mannerism on the make. Elevators up to the higher floors, more running around. White town connected by blue ink threads on perfumed white envelopes. Close-up and long shot rot in a 2-dimensional room light soothing all illusions eased on by sound which rolls. No more play. This is the perfect look for you after your integrity loss. Pride is a thorn in your side. "It's true I am a woman; it's true I'm employed;" going through the motions like a gun with your favorite pal. Playing around with deep humanity, the bargain was invented. This seems to be lean, deep and corrupted. The word is legs. More like fondling the atmosphere than the object's body. Or ride on top window oddities painted up like paintings. Arrested modesty fades once out on the town. An iced commodity a motion fanning out over every position a body could play. Order replaces disorder. A direction cuddles up to a slice of this magnet world. The chord continues climbing. Total elevators lay down to cherish the thought. Born idle. Ontological sperm. Intermissions tame an ounce of action. A door honestly pretends to control. Bother to aim for a caress out of range. Counting vocabulary as a WHOLE LIFE two hours company. Free secrets left from the bag of absolute truths. This plane of solitude resembles broken vowels limiting the time, space and emotions that will work on a brain trained such as this to release dim golden thoughts.

# # # # #

P. INMAN

from OCKER

debris clud

(sbrim
m,nce

(nome,id

(armb,jor,

(droit,cur.

cocone, emble blems
off diller apiece

       andn'ts,

     bed unes

    meanglence,

   coat qol
    field jah

drune)rupts
v i e w l e t s d o m e b o t t l e d ,   wouldnt be tilt of alphabet
mmence cucumb (out of clock)

cact theme

thru drees, load dickening, keith
all occliffed, plinther, intos thaggle, instance
ilm deodr, mudxeast, paean ximv,'s
another handsome attack, gline leverage, bsidb,
tuned full simple

no drogen

PETER SEATON

from THE SON MASTER

The pro stampede which grows out of our associations of the west completely explodes it.

And here it comes again, father stuff and substitution leaving it to read persons and physiological passages for the sake of you under my own roof. I need my burg tomorrow, wishing us onto a field of appreciation like getting happiness from God or Kings or Congress. It's clear close to the letters leaving everything as a demonstration of alarm, dangers of the test for George for a notion I would like to fix it so. Reading ambition, what the father in English charges streaks as a single line under the thundering thumb.

This is the evening before I ask some questions about you too. I promise to be prepared, no, that's just being tempted. To signal the privilege piece subject to enjoy being temporarily talk like this. The possibility might seem accepting, inviting, obeying and betting to him. And then written followed by words. Copernicus says his wheels okay in Baltimore, his wheels cut a square though in place which is care like an angel and new things line in among the words. Cultivating the emotion sheet field for the time and woman pool some track service near the quarry days, a sample of her physically because she knows what's happening to her, what she says and others could realize it concealing the effect you have to press to wait for saying this pushing it away on hidden hinges. With her arrangement of orbits to read banks of the mind facts, eyes delight, by torchlight cutting or boarding playing it, holding on to it with two sharp taps of a stone. Patience or a monument or a light his father says imagine his face unless the light makes a phrase like figure influence hours at a time. All night you find a statement, the habits of will patterns of bonus will, the position to cheer you up, real or imaginary knees return or stone from the window at the window.

The sun from the sky mounts, and with the sun's help fierce hours on the blooms is leading. Something of images because you have control, you can be somewhere. You can create looks, like it's anywhere, and change its nature. The vision of space with space or one in a particular instance is physical space with the physical set of physical new son space. It could be that physical. Space training in the rescue sphere, in Europe and America it's January in nine cities and two space centers. In Houston, everyone must carry a gun. It's been called the high planning survey and inventory, the study of and investigation into another space day interaction of sun and space effect particles, the space day device space led, space sick, and space is the trace familiar space spell of subject bodies in acceleration causes of space standard space.

Listen to reason. This is the best of all possible worlds. There's nothing to say about it except in exile. Which is where it's such a dirty business being so attractive.

Some people have to return to the face of the Earth, which may be billions of light years away by now. So star drive, the rudimentary notion of light, is having it both ways. Head in the clouds and feet on the ground, the last technician plots a course. He's a man, he's lucky.

But getting back to the march, it's been called a matrix for ambient flesh, movement of the cornering of the heart's desire. This is a problem, frequently worked out as a solution to ethics. Each little child is a female child. Heat is the same as neat in this Heaven on Earth.

For example, instead of internal rhythm, it's axiomatic. There's a plan, it could come from England. There's a pledge and it goes like this. You bet your life reading this.

Some substance, it's got its own life, including others'. You don't even have to spread your arms. You have to look out the window, expecting to be hid. This compulsion, family and friends, family and friends, and these angles and declinations, stored up because a treatise on extra-parental behavior can also be written lickety split.

I used to work for New Hampshire woods. Like any family life, and doses of destructive outposts, designing circuits for Mao, for me to go institutional would be a physical and emotional model sense I see and they are, zone kids get pregnant and get determination local.

The grounds and grooves in large oceans and in the bays of the world, there are species that live on both sides and into both and in the sea in the eastern ocean near the western waves in the waters of the storms at sea. Sometimes they suck up the dark ocean light, penetrating the bottom by the basketfull. The football migration, going from near the mass near the speed of mass near the speed of light into the warm waters of the gulf, catching prey and avoiding obstacles, thought in the long migration sticking up and staying fierce.

Large numbers and warm bodies produced by crushing and prying the ocean period particles of high metabolic rate periods and particle advantage trapped between the air and some other air or skin. A cinnamon species in cold guard bundles through the term thin and too fast to match. But the long migration north leads to north periods of lips. It's the mechanism you can imagine if you open your mouth slightly and swim over the roof of your own mouth and feel grown out to form this apparatus in many places around the world, the world and the film that lived on Earth, a line of sight inflating to become extinct. The lower numbers licked off the tongue and sounds so low in other ways. Some sound speeds and some sound loud. Friendly sounds for migrating, sounds meanings, letting them slide kinds that come from a structure called the case. And the more ordinary air from the finest of air and also not too far and often farther.

Sometimes the champion finds evidence in search of some relatives down in the dark sea. Some think that extends from tip to tip, but no one is really sure. Body distance straight up in the air from a distance and as you are seldom seen you can see straight up and down to stick out like straps and sound in the dark night of the hundred and hundreds. The coming age of quantities was taken from society and towed laboriously out of the village. This was before pits in the frozen ground with the age of plastics. Contemporary numbers plastics, common somewhere and some groups with the patterns on their bodies and kings and queens can move without the magical properties of objects in the dark night.

My hands, hardened to let water in, found that the nails were no longer bleeding; they had rusted causing this operation. The family, and this father, to this same family of the deserts and semi-deserts speaking Americans speaking of the United States east, from Doctor Texas to states of the changed name of the hand at a touch. They might be within the family borders that might be off the land and trouble with practice, either it's calm or there's so much light we could fuse movements on brain pressures to discover any section of The Laws of Storms that close with it. It must be the slam indication of escape, work a property of consideration and the direction a design assumes to go to the ones to the south somehow, staying put and eating in no time because reason got them there but the mirror these two places will join wants books. It's destiny in the mist of an episode going to pieces.

That exposes a flying patch of the sea, a row of the sea in a silence to some extent by a mirage in the sense of certainty. And that it's growing in on either hand to complicate my air. Two ends of the region like this with the light behind one and a warning that all lies in a group like the dark, its dim shape off and on for daylight outside until it did seem in color, under a brilliant sun, a band of purple, green for my point of view, things in detail thousands of feet high and miles away to extend beyond a mountain at least to breed. And which have oceans of the world behind them, their faces are the jagged outlines near the steep hills of light on the French mass fading away. And night vapors dominated by the enterprise discovering them. Your jealous things placed on the real one and spelled with snows of the gray Pacific.

That greatest world has no rivals. It's only a few hours away and plunges down to a great reader: I saw, or rather admitted, a southern ocean. All this may be met anywhere sweeping home every night. I mean that the radius of action would take the jump completing the world. I would add to my memory through that ancient machine, a geographical expression, the chemically objective stuff. It's all the strength in the addition, all of the line in machine around the lower part of a globe. That marks the area in which this vertical existence has geographical snares and where places to most people had lain across it. The name for the rest of the week to the exclusion of a passage, there was a nasty cloud passed over us. The job of the progressive hydro-last idea of west to east, the pioneers introduce ideas for a visible leader in a steam world, chief training, the Chief finishes his pictures, a series of sheets at home, slippery sleep legs, our heads or arms, as I thought, the textbook directions for asking for trouble. If I let food cooks, that's a fright. Dirt from the tropics as its reputation got to hate it, its music which is the great west wind falling into sound. The superlative hand to hand through two split yards up and down, square yards. An imaginary machine provides a proof so that a single sound in principle was a more ambitious mistake for serious alterations for the start.

To which, to take charge, this feature could be any idea of the need for a substitute for an advantage over the sound fracture plate extended rather than dug out, and I could use white line looks to a wall of dark red stone. The shape of one too is so hard that to take charge we had all survived. The elastic remains in the eyes to clear it over. This is a preposition, a possible sight of everyone's appearance without the business people touching. Great logs of the moon used also for legs, light complicated by catastrophe instructions, to move somewhere with a bang and a knock out of us, we know enough. Knocked flat near the conventional center, rest and have dinner and wait all morning so it must have been the rain that fell. The machine cares, but those two can be the same, the moon experience of space of sky throwing out dance and dance invasion.

He used to pitch for the Great Circle Tigers in the Infinite Time and Trouble League. I could lay off a promenade and the safety sweeps, once is a good history for the stone age. It gets the city the finest site to bring her back, the power cubes near the house of houses, but I come back at night to space cities and loose sheets of paper, the right consistency for material ability.

Copying trees out swarms the American pilot. The parts, wealth of detail, washing the light description to see if they were true. See if I understand: one inhabitant, one migration. I got a job to try to get, to get through the flowers of Le Mair, the shortest course for considering any large city, and objects of the conspicuous country amusement thing I could have seen yesterday and next morning. Cause of coast, wall of rock, flat as boards, the most places covered for everybody else, green all over. The green color roar, what we were doing there, seeing heroes watch for possible beauties. Line of sight, start finding the females at home, man interference and run provocation, face to face babies in the world.

To make a proper animal scrub its skull space in the sound range of resting for mothers going or going to knock off scenery, order a paradise dominated by sites free from snow and other grounds among them dodging out of place for walking, a dream form or position, order the rocks and ice and water. Also, talk of intimate islands of smoke written on the opposite page and published to keep a statement English in a mystery.

But it's always possible to be a whisked away subject for a savage. Or a claim to end the impression looking at the light wind and at its strength. I think I know the instrument rate maneuver— an obsession loaded with enterprise—proposition, one's own eyes from lips to observation speed straight in it. A sanctuary takes us in, the last of the legs keep dangling. The first vanishing people will look for it personally. The visible image white feather and diamond twice and secret adventures of levitation and entertainment.

In bed to get a bright red scarf, the pale ghosts of Valparaiso slowly approach. So a stranger wants to see the colossal continent, the tallest thing in the world and mon francais clear in separate actions; but we can see through the frozen surface of the sea.

The eye is hooked on ice. All the place is full of ice. Atmosphere and access in the two summer months. The first moon started with miles of the moon and continues to hit.

The first moon photographs its internal systems to freeze. The sea of the moon's hidden dark side was stopped in July. The path behind the moon was a series of film with miles. The images could blitz the tight end from Earth. Data links landing on the moon. An instrument shaped instrument support powered by images just prior to their impact on the moon. This likely looking moon made with fittings takes us home. One or two days on the moon looking at planets.

Things that make up daily life, meteorites and meteoroids, air, food, housing, the Moon, the Moon's intelligent beings, the circles of space for power or other stars instead of rockets.

Years are stars caught in space at some remote spot on Earth. They could be placed on the Moon to protect the Moon in orbit, or on the Moon and stray extremes of message beings to protect processing. A proposed technique arranged by items, a single image human could be covered, heat for the power forms and appropriate space data duration of space shift periods and film tears loose and left.

The rosy soul ridges of the cities struck into invisibility. It's to isolate a culture till the wind shifts to be active in the evolution of machine intelligence.

The pine peanuts of New Mexico and the orchard memorial to the Indian king.

To every traveler on our western plains the coming of the white man to cure disease for the white man and the residual fluid of the United States in pieces of paint. The desert dried to cultivate smoke and that brings us to an expression applied by another desert preparation families go for. In his monograph, it's the frontier forming and lashed together in the desert. It's consumed as marvels and mass reduced to a syrup. So, pines dipped into their mouths.

The instinct sands colonize the streets of dreams in a country with rain. They have one, and why not? The stands behind the door, and falling from the trees are men, women and children with their own ideas of life so they could not sit all day but they had all night.

My reefs, my trees had fallen. Mention the trees because of their trees and crack the trees to come from the city. And read the page at which the manuscript fell open, there were questions.

Then the reader crowds the page in the rush of his ideas. He surprises himself as a manifestation of precision, the conventions meaning freeze and reread. I know, the production of writing becomes the sense of almost as much as the problem readers do, the readers do one and shift as readers do. They function as poor boys inhibiting structuring. Designed to allow scrambling, Lester Hayes, Lester Hayes, Lester Hayes. The Wausau Cafe and the first lady's name, the natural facts so the names of coming material fits forcing the readers to be conscious, the orient reader route of the seedy reader. Aware that Lewis and Clark stand where we look toward the contract field of needs of reader distribution. What one might call reading and writers.

The idea is that missing the reader more than another father on the path into the woods of policy. The woods seem to be there for writing, what Charles Ives called sound, which has very little to do with writing. It seems mixed up, man father, child boy. And Anthony is something special because he makes me think there must be some special page and word things, maybe to avoid crazy legs to avoid polygamy. He could say the drought in the region of abstract identity reads by children a step and and but put together, so forget it. And books do this to readers planning a shift to other words in lines of writing. They can write clues to the thought is bizarre. Also candy and consequence, the signal break or shift in the present. Writing the full farm of supplying taught in schools, and the syntactic tent, to read bear, to read tests run on a map, and on the original Bonnie Free Fall the objects had read, after a reading delay of pattern attribution, the reader kept hours a day for a week reading reading writing as adults of human actions. The first of global patterns, and especially as readers in this light.

Like preferring to prepare the writer for the room. Reading and read around though in practice, of course, there is it, ritual reading, and testing, to read to write the purpose reading in the conventions of reading to be reading to construct readers. Or should people aim abstract models of the world in physical readers to promote readers in revolt. (Illusory father who can read without writers), images of reading by imagery, switch writing.

In the universe of problem readers and problem writing the reader and reader agree the ideal reader sounds a bit distant. Imaginary writing that the writer is writing at the reader's request: the reader did writing to reader and writer, that-is-as reader and the writer can be writer the reader imagined of the reader easier to write than reader and writer in writing as the situation of written differences concentrating the reader's.

Writing in writing as in sea writing becomes written as written reading. Writers, or reader all that and the writer, in the reader's ideology. In order of writing, a writer's projection, writing to take writing written in written in reading, and writing as writing to the composition reading writing writing goes writing, and writing word to word can be writing the reader between writer and reader and writing.

The origins of stars collapse. Then they become White Clues or Shining stars evolving out of astronomers suggesting the entire universe at tremendous speeds. Distances expand and so do substance hunters and the Jupiter Line from a princess into the sky. In stars forming its face and in this clear star from stars hangs the star of glowing guides to the rare gas of the upper rays and in the particles that come from northern centers like unaided eyes which form into the closest fragments of tidal Earth which takes our years two years in Jupiter space bands, so clear permanent bright spots shine brightly, and when the Earth occasionally appears in them discovered by moons.

Groups are more compact, often moving as distant spots in some fine galaxy. The great objects include the large stars of the largest shadows. The other eight million miles to Earth takes moons close. The western edge diamond details at twelve miles per second in a binary star now seen, now discovered, now seeming to be the position of the region of families when the moon is new. When it's between Earth and moon shadow bodies of the Moon passing over you because the Moon travels rapidly over the Earth and Earth's inverted moon father nights that the frontier stars and skies are seen.

Star light getting used to the dark. Star bright with the stars before your eyes. First star map that contributes to star names in common wish with a sheet of red Greeks, a sheet of thin Roman paper, descendants to the representing stars to one side and star names, the ideas the animal could overcome for centuries, useful and placed in the skies. And planet books on the opposite side of Heaven, star trails including the moon part driven with a clock to the north following points of a landscape on airless Mercury and Venus depending on the west like the Moon's approach to the direction of east on one side and cold on the other to the west.

To compound clouds formed by following the line by name, line grant, chasing away. They like to have fallen by the strength filling up among them and put an end to them. Should the prescription of time by a short speech be caution to his successors, assuming they keep their articles and adverbs first while we are sober.

Peter Seaton   349

The best danger probes to be putting out elements, and one I take to be speech upon pain of death. This was being a commander going to sight fire and suspecting things in order thought to the master business, plunder resistance as he thought to surprise the Chief without a word with the chiefmen ashore in the night.

The master asks who did by the way, assume the desire for an answer, a single being pouring in and grappling with her. The dispute, except one, and only two rose again and get away and drop trinkets at his pursuer. The dwarf is a star from the Pleistocene. It's known from the Pleistocene, stripped white to grey then yellow or blue.

Like a small country beginning to establish its own songs or, quote the empire's rulers, the father had a tendency to fall in love. As he moves he says I belong to this class. Its struggles include the Danube which is happy because it's coming to Hungary. And its logical sequel, spiritual pain, and then one of the heroes is free to write her: "Everyone arrived in New York in October. I was unhappy and depressed by the destruction of Europe.

"America extends towards the east. An inch of the geographical notions of lunar confidence in parts of the world made of tides which cause the sun overhead and movement of the sea of air which expands the movement of the sun and moon until scientists began."

Space was found to be full of the moon causing tides of air, breathing and flying air higher than the sea. To test the theory, make the Earth's gravity measure the air of sun and moon in the form of winds. The weight of the air in rhythm—the velocity of a few inches of sun and moon increases as the speed of the sun's electrons in the tropics reflects parts of the winds of the world fusing the high flying atmospheres with the average Earth curved equator known as calculations of the sun and moon in ripples, in words known as standing or stationary sea on one side and disturbances of the golden sea brown nights of the moon while the moon's famous moon creatures hide in the brains and eyes of the Indies.

So who can keep in tune with the Moon? Columbus, as mysterious night and the theory of mysterious light, sees himself coming from the male bearing females to a hiding place in the laboratory to surface as the lunar moon quantities synchronized with the moon during the full moon in June.

And that's the best time to feast on the sophisticated moon breathing stalks of sand or sand in southern nights of moon sand and new English sand surveys processing for progressive exceptions to control. Speaking precisely when the Moon runs high about the same time for the solid Earth and swarms of hemisphere prophecy that the islands might pull apart where the Earth is under stress in space.

In New York, an influence in the traditional moon pores of planets compresses wood to begin with on the sun, or Jupiter on the same side of the sun. The cause of force named for the arm of the English break from your direction reflected and deflected on the rotating Earth is over. Right back into the ocean, counterclockwise, for the subject of existence toward the west looking spun as a set where lines mean range in English.

There's another midnight system of whole globe behavior requiring the Newton Faith of moon volume and moon power on the Earth view of the universe as global as the moon's movement of a rotating Earth and the Moon's first attention to the moon that completes the moon of the Earth to the sun and the moon with the moon pulling a stone with moon mechanics the same way, the moon revolves around the Earth, the moon is one side of the moon, the side the Earth revolves around or the sense of massive Earth and Moon below the surface, moon to moon between them away from the moon marks of speed in the world of certain parts as it is today.

The muscles have also been to Europe. The muscles keep writing to get reading technique accents. When they are clear they're tightened. And half the secret is Irma, the beauty of the band you played with.

This phrase, according to the pilot, would take people somewhere, and so I had an experience with the position the body deals with live in New York covering the trance prominence signal to lock my ideas through. The verb is always the simple word and the simple word will do.

The old verb lingers on; calling the verb legal, I shall soon present the past today. The finite form of verbs becomes possible like a verb acquiring the verb proper, the verb proper contains questions, the idea of smoke, or a desire to get shook up instead of learning that you intend to desire forms of expression nearer the abstracter verb.

Since the verbs used in here are all words, whenever there is a desire to see the predicate finish your work, suppression of the verb, the verb or some part you tell him where else does a phenomenon of writing go.

This is worth thinking about because your voice feels your mouth emit words in a scene for mastery making good. I felt that merchandise and poetry of a word fact form of you in a way mumbles some words like what I was saying, shall I live as a basis of thin air. The sense of the words alone at home with nothing to do was lined up so it looked like speech. A voice reading them as we had again in what I was to you placed again and we were to answer everyone, answer to us, the imagination of a picture in time touched in a foreign country surrounding our states of mind and heart and sense element rays and receive them during the intimacy of these things.

There is a will, groups of verbs of the present tense. It states words after becoming conceptions. English origin first begins to part by appearing and using the real verb before the real verb with independent elements which the infinitive, i.e., we split the infinitive, forgets in the spirit of our words in the situation as a whole. The name of a person passed in something home for you. We put words into the fusion with the nominative, the nominative of an address. Two classes in the different persons remaining behind or numbers, the numerical simulation of a continuous field requires old forms as logical subjects to take some strong man in some other person or thing, the stronger of the more and the most taller than that.

The superlative kinder man, there never was a man more kind and the person or thing is the highest descriptive, the simple favorite in the world used in an excited language.

He felt these thoughts helped in dreams, like a child, or making decisions, dangerous objects and dangerous forces causing the personality wish that leads to the pages set out and writing right away. And that child is written, his feelings are the feelings of a child. That's a child in the act of a child, the master of the sergeant's life turning to trouble.

All the men were inscribed by then. Then a boy needed some music, I think he was Beethoven, and might have been later couldn't be found. At that moment remember by heart, or, to be more accurate, everything.

An outsider thinks everyone knows eternity is written with discoveries. However, a chemist told me to picture generation after generation living for more thought and things and write women's affairs and cares, women inventing photography for their husbands, making up the children, solving world problems by creating movement to the lovers occupied by monuments, construction for problems in attention to these problems and, to get up and go off to say this is all talk, there's too much talk, too familiar western living creatures, the organism bells of humorous scenes with children.

That makes the henchman think of himself as those dream. Suppose everyone wants to be clean, something under the rule of the given tyrant, the darkest night, the Caucasian Mountains, the people write make the landscape understand contemporary numbers in traditional concepts from memoirs, you can imagine anything about parents. The approach is quite strange, but my tastes keep changing.

Foreign things that I like I like and some I like primarily. For instance, written long ago, he comes as a foreigner. At that time we were born near each other, I, by chance, on the radio. But that's a beginning, and we know favorite words. So people greet us with a vocabulary proving the result of a spoiled master. Said, once said, the writer lives and sleeps like a gambler trading biographies and whispering the joke to the crowds. Power nerves, what could I think a mystery orders? Cast-off dreams?

Is a madhouse exaggerating stronger then and is a madhouse more than living slow movement, the others make poor people grow bored and keep thinking, there were cases, it's still the development, that's how lives and works wrote in energy or tension.

Until the lean years of the revolution it's usually the other way around—a man steals an idea circulating as a plan. Say there was slander, it was worked out in the parallel twenties. All the players left the country suddenly saying so you were hearing the actual sound. To prove dreamily I was a child, I think, the most truthful one. And the war, I don't know, at the same time I like it very much. It's easy to look at. The most popular saying or appropriate interest called the custodial style used to call it a search in an ancient city or a landscape clearing up and a woman walks by and says there's some anniversary movement created by a hope monument made of brick and the bricks broke through and were just put back. And if you don't dig around inside it wears off quickly, take that to the others sleeping at night and falling apart.

Even our distant descendants know how to write. They move their fingers over him in every piece you read.

This was a picture from America. And the spirit snarled, but it was clear. I was going out of my way, my nose and brains were topnotch.

SUSAN HOWE

from PYTHAGOREAN SILENCE

He plodded away through drifts of i

ce

away into inapprehensible Peace

A portable altar strapped on his back

pure and severe

A portable altar strapped on his back

pure and severe

In the forests of Germany he will feed

on aromatic grass and browse in leaves

1.

age of earth and us all chattering

a sentence   or character
suddenly

steps out to seek for truth   fails
falls

into a stream of ink   Sequence
trails off

must go on

waving fables and faces   War
doings of the war

manoeuvering between points
between

any two points   which is
what we want   (issues at stake)

bearings and so

holes in a cloud   are minutes passing
which is

which
view   odds of images swept rag-tag

silver and grey
epitomes

seconds   forgeries engender
(are blue)   or blacker

flocks of words flying together   tense
as an order

cast off to crows

4.

no more a long future   the present
(shelter)   mosses

shade
and violets prim   are torn

from life
by Love   my Oblivion soaring above

tears the theme away

Superstructures of allegory have been

raised
There is a storm at sea

someone seems to die   Blind love
is eyeless

An eyeless king (cloak worn to rags)
moves

backwards and forwards   from reef
to reef   Lost

to grief   How lust
(these were the ghost's words) crawls

between heaven and earth

Dust is birth
of earth we make loam   substance

and strange shadows

But I am reaching the end   Sky
melts away into sand

sand into Sound   (shelter so loved
by its owner)

Lie down and stray no farther (Sweet
evening

quiet thoughts)

blind love and beginning of dark woods

5.

I thought I did not live in night

for the future   I used to say
lighting the light

farewell to star   and star
As if light spreading

from some sounding center   might
measure even how

familiar
in the forest   losing the trees

Shadows   only shadows
mey my gaze   Mediator

I lay down and conceived   Love
(my dear Imaginary) Maze-believer

I remember   you were called
sure-footed

and yet off the path   (Where
are you) warmed and warming   Body

turned and turning   Soul
identical soul   abandoned

to Sleep   (where
are you crying)

crying for a mother's help   (fell

forests or plant forests)   Dreams
wheel their pale course

360 Susan Howe

We write in sand
three thousand proverbs and songs

bottom is there   but depth
conceals it   Dreams wander

through the body of a parent
Rub hands together   stressing how

we are made of earth   inevitable
our death   Wisdom

a sorry thing   dream in a Dream
remembering a dream

mimic presentation stained with mortality

7.

about the historical Arthur
about the passing of Arthur

the wild sea (his lair) War
the throwing away of Excalibur

Through secret parables through
books of dark necessity

along a line of legend winters old
we approach each other   (wordplay

of spell and spell) A listener
on the dreamer's dream depends

dreamers seeming seeing never ends

Two sisters at work under an oak
spinning and weaving   Idea

and Echo wavering so
I wish I could see them (mist)

into clear reason (air)
Music murmurs double discord

(lark and toad change eyes) Figures
metaphysical spectres

cold cold warriors   moving
and mumbling   veiled allegories

deeply veiled

Lips (keepers of thought)
whistle us off   Sound dies away

362   Susan Howe

caught up in clouds to meet the air
A fictive sphere

(hawk and lark soar)
In this wide Quietness   a field

is the world I am a child   Eve
who kisses the bees   enumerates

miracles

8.

Igraine
great with child that shall be

Arthur
lying on the ground   among

sentinels
(wrapped in a military cloak)

in the grey dawn
In the grey dawn

every omen believed   (wolf
in the camp

bees in a tree) dark hyacinth
and errant ivy

Symbols are imaginary   the real
unseen (seems)

clear as far

a theme of empty air   December
harmony

icy transparency   here
we are   (Distance

and Difference   remote in time
death-pale in dream

aboriginal mother and father)

A perfect day
sweet sea-sounds in the pines

all the shores marked

Outside the window fictions are
crumbling

The being of Being is will   was
something—

and to leave without knowing it

City glittering in sunset search after
Eros

LYNNE DREYER

from TAMOKA

Part 1

The little spotted dog licks the adoptees forms.
The fat girl reads the Avon booklet.
The skinny waitress drags a Parliament.

Melancholia—closed visual perspective (pronoun)

Lynne Dreyer—insincere noise (listen)
Cleverly living our interesting lives (dumbstruck)

An old lady in synopsis in a pink bouffant pink hat.

Certain people whom I have known strike a similar pose. I usually can accept by allowing them to read my mind, inserting their own use of free words and poetry, such as a prescribed method, language or device, as in red inducing passion or black and lonely—a picture postcard one that I can really see. I want my poetry understood, as if someone was interested in getting to know me. Then we can be silly and close.

Not one of our favorites, delicately placed.

Baggage identification. I remember the day I started the trip, standing in Alexandria. Your jeans are somewhere floating around in Texas. Can't write anymore, but think it's o.k., a duel book, up-side down, perfect friends. I'm glad you're going now, no more wondering about what could have been, if I had been less judgemental, less like myself. No more watching and denying my own feelings. How you found me in my own corner, deep in the center of my brain, the way you bring lightheartedness to situations, an overall view, practicality.

You've changed now and I'm glad although jealous that I couldn't be a part of it. It had something to do with failure or the ability for you to really try; you said it was upbringing or religion. I disagreed and laughed and cried while watching the sun in Brooklyn.

Money, self-destruction, metabolism, large major things, we always included these in our discussions, the real stuff was felt, your ability to change style, give almost selflessly, explain your life in terms of detail. But when you started to laugh I was out, a different ball game. I couldn't be honest and didn't think you cared if I was or not.

Self contained, artists, family life, and all along me moving different images in my mind, wanting to give you something.

Stooped work.

Don't be shy now. We can read along together on this one. From chicks to women to ladies, the Arbella. "I always think it's more honest and provocative to be genuinely autobiographical, but maybe that's just me." Is Lanier Place named after Sydney Lanier? Wish your father was here.

Pictures-a masterpiece.

Hope you're well and happy.

Hope you're getting on well with the cats and plants.

Hope you're doing well.

Hope to see you at the Big Reading.

Hope you're having luck in your job search.

Hope this finds you well.

Hope all is well with you. Hope you're able to find a better job.

Rob a typewriter.

The chimpanzee throws you a kiss from the condominium in Florida. Years of business from Baltimore to Chicago to Baltimore, selling all the sports equipment and in your outgoing and comical way, the family saddened by the death, not coming to the funeral, only wanting the minks and clothes and perfume, a glamorous pose. Implement the torn black and silken cloth, implement the torn, washing your hands and small chairs and then always again making it light. When you think how great it is to be alive.

But as soon as I say it both of you come back into my mind. Any other relationship seems only partial and fanciful like decorated with what clothes I should wear, the atmosphere, who else is present, looks, detailed, comparisons of the sixties to the seventies, tv, talk of the future, a family.

I try to ignore it, not think about it, become like you, not expect things, don't smoke, become someone else, become helpless, become helpful, be comical, grin, extract memory, get skinny, get fat, be healthy, be only a voice, a vacuole, a moving microplasm on the bus, play a little game of teacher cashier writer and none of these ever becoming games, but like a picture postcard which suggests a certain memory, blue gayne, and illicits memory suggestive to a specific place, "Greetings from the Cozy Motel," Thurmont, Maryland.

I remember you in certain intense situations. The only thing is the players are all wrong. The feeling becomes as contrived as the piece of paper it's written on and placed. I become quiet.

Isn't life grand? Sounds like Irish, sounds like Oh, protection, sounds like someone else will pick me up and I'll go, sounds like this time I'm really not wanting to be alone like in the dream traveling from Baltimore, or dead Presidents captioned on the postcard, the East Potomac Park, describing language.

What I see in him is a seriousness and that seems most important now not funny jokes or making me feel comfortable, topsy turvy, switch, empty apartments, jungle life.

Oh, don't argue with me now. I just need you to look out of the window with me. It's difficult to write about you both separately.

How the timing was wrong, how I never really saw your attempt at making things pleasant for yourself, our beneficial likeness, sight. But none of it matters more than the fact of me denying that I felt anything more than friendship with you. Your one attempt at boldness, telling me I was wrong. Playground days, a doer. Under the tree sexual talks, a suggestion, dead Presidents, replica of arguments, messenger life and resolved pleasantries after convincing you to come back with me. And that is what I despised the most. Picture postcards from the coffee shop. Letters from Yates, wingshaped legs, a cynical cowboy, better than all of that long hair.

Oh, don't argue with me now, how what I really loved was the way you would argue with me, in a way I could accept, so that a certain amount of freedom recalled. Our too critical look at each other. A gain music, a purple people eater, a strong cylinder, a man of your word.

Flash image, people made of cement yaking wildly on the bus image, the ladies in white drinking tea from miniature tea-cups their hair flying off from the tops of their heads, image, the wild cat waiting for me to get some air, image, his pleasant voice only pursued in the machines, the pigs and dogs all herded together in the den, South Euclid, Honey, Ohio, trips, no more black thoughts, Ode to Billy Joe, bugs a sergeant, image, the fish leading the girls by the pool, Haiti, oranged and snow in California, a job of madrigals. Be Bop A Loop Bop, tomorrow at the Boy's Ranch it's where you're going that counts, the black hand tougher in structure but more vulnerable in terms of what it's saying. You're right, I really do have to be in touch with what I'm feeling for the writing to come off.

A testimonial dessert, an acrobatic walk, a physical sunset, an introverted embrace, an accomplished necklace, a stained reaction, an honest V neck, a fractional chance, patient books, directional success, an individual doll, an open carnival, sympathy, crystal methodology, humorous dogs.

Part 2

The locker room aid dances to the radio distraction.
Lost visibility one walking rain.
Sliced vanity serious charm ice.
An economic situation a story.

When she smiles another star is lit saline, floral, ragine shark.
Necessary understanding of sensory input.

When she laughs, she drops the cheese; Little Big Bear Caw Caw Caw, hasting modification of sensory interpretations.

Carrying swollen branches that drip in the wind responsive states, a unique way of working today.

Lynne Dreyer   369

going on stage with a needle in her head biography
reject equivalent of response
overtime the leaves

The digital reflex of the brain becomes classic, wasted directed to
the retina to aggravate the ending.

Exaggerate the ending.

Large non-concrete words form a deep cylindrical well.
Who likes a poetic voice? The Phantom gets tired of Takoma,
socialism and work.

A loose myth, a structured fairytale, an equivalent voice, "A love
spills it".
Helpless as in continued conversation, his mother's voice.
The point of the body of a drowning victim at the point where the
brain stops receiving blood.

"A love spills it."
A raccoon on all fours hanging from a tree, hands in prayer, a
secretary bird, hands clapping a date palm, a blue and yellow
maccaw, a chinese gong, the right hand buttoning a glove on the
left hand, the left hand buttoning the glove on the right hand, a
stone tower lighthouse, a hopscotch, a creel, a beehive hairdo, a
modern windmill, the left hand peeling skin from the right hand,
the right hand peeling skin from the left hand.

from STEP WORK

Line the pictures and think in the distance not unlike the slow thick thrills that ridicule the mind. Now the mind is general with bovine shaped eyes. The tough poems become the fathers on the barrels. Excited by the soft chords, they decide their verdict. He tests the right eye winking. More cynical notes on those who love children and dogs. They look like they'll explode. One thousand whimpers turning into mechanical grins. Sour-hide writing like the country-Danny Boy. The urban ranch becomes puffy edged, glenned, preparing for the uncared adults.

Come you back tiny home. Do you become ancient and tense? The three chords sound dissonant, like how much talking will go on until it becomes smooth and unnecessary. These barrel fathers are ridiculous and their roles are gaudy. Their time is taken, they make the morning seem creeped.

The sun screams on your skin while you feel your slow self become. The couch is the same, the stories are out, and we are clever enough to know them. The religious expression when you thought they were laughing into your voice, you cracked and shattered the image back.

The comic hero's lengthy art disease. "Why Lord! You sound southern!" The visitors are excited. The mother barrels are exclaiming their weight.

How many more plain images can you disguise as a muse? How many more questions can you ask with remarks that cut into the soft body and skin? For rain the picture is tropical, the culture is advertised, the music isn't. Send the tiny adults away, they trust the state religiously. Quiet men who attack the throne gobble food. No urban witticisms here.

He's guessing how many words go down. Women send your free voices through the ship's design! The house will go, she clears herself. They tell you he was afraid of the dogs and you believe he was. They tell you not to love that fear and you do. The pigs come in next to drink the coffee and use the ship.

Was it hidden, lost in a possible life alone? When the barrel fathers come to take the baby away, make it different, easier. Give up casually, make space, work it out, decide. Dog baby, scratching time relieve the wake of the cubicle to make it smooth.

With that brief description, the pen hangs laboriously from the last finger's point. Pain coils into comfort leaving it slick glow. Bobbins in the teeth, the water taking its slow effect, time trapped into a trillion pieces of ice as the memory of the music takes on the meaning of the word do. Dreams are canceled out but there is still more general thought. He names each country as it goes out. A lullaby of shattered makes the thought more individual as huge heads and hands fill the room. Peaceful Indians on the cover counteract.

Are you wearing your tourist outfit to escape the activity? Are you taking a long blocked walk controlled? A fine mist rain falls. The live disciplined house is losing fast. The Greek was where we left him, trying to find the face that was peeling off her kindness while dogs and cats grow by the second, leaving activity to deflate. Then he said, "No expression was worth that much money." The big wing from the car was visible, the rest buried in the sand. Paper scattered drink embodied.

Do you call it a hormonal substitute like fat caring, fat and happy, a fat cat perched with the old fat cigar. Seventh Avenue.

No more meetings, fall years, empathy becomes the general reeling. Crack out the old pictures, we love those. Berkeley, musky office, reading it wrong all of these years. I see the vivid sky, the blood pulsing, the attempts at food. They're happy in their unit where the logs hang laboriously from the sky. The others are thick with respect but don't understand. The impression was that he needed her, was looking at her, when it really was a long time desirous guardian house.

What type of king would you ransom to be? Are the curtains drawn for painting? Swollen words way too pretty. They spend a lot of time by themselves dramatizing the black night.

Devastate yourself as you slink out of the room. Small compact images in rock. The bridge at sunset coming to mean symbols—a future life. Hundreds of clean boxes roll down the mountain setting to dry in the sun. Rest, sleep, dropping names. The tiny men with hats are getting out of town.

Limitless, expansiveness, surfaceless, becoming a lot of small, tiny movements, borrowing houses, an environment, which day it is or how muddled and smooth you want to say. Direct, cut short.

Trapping out tires in the small of the room, boxes filled with more addresses, blocking the air, shimmering in the early maze, cracked out to reveal captures. Seized and reluctant, dramatic and taunting, ridiculous and large and seemingly one. Allow yourself such precision in the dark sky, careless and burning to your private room. You carefully swing over the plants. The wind blows in unseasonal disgust as the war boy becomes the boy on the bus, stealing the scenes from the dawn.

Become turned to the light where sympathy packs in its heavy evidence, scooting fish that make the most of the night. Then things were ideas, not real. Such a lovely time for fall to come. Such a raging time for fall to come. Arlington all strung out in a vertical hue. A long man smiling, raking leaves, equals PKU.

He's beautiful when he notices his hand. The chord relishes the upward swing reminding me of the night where Skeeter cooled it out for all of us. The morning sped with gray becomes lost and oozing in uptown skies and grown men take on a new meaning like nicknames, like seeing them grow. Time it. Throw it away.

Like the characters with the "imitation ears", she takes herself seriously. She made it up as the kicking begins. The sad babies, ditches and gutters; these scenes are flashed, others charred into the fiction future. Sadness buries itself in reluctant poses and comic relief. Hair stands up on head, eyes rolling.

Does the lost brother become the silent guardian? Do they accompany you? The mother guilt games following all the way to the south; so that when he eats alone, he's still trying to gobble it up so quickly and so fast. The cats are pulling apart your body, sucking the skin at different parts. What a tiny way to encounter a loan. The face flaps in the wind.

There were fakirs in the song, the carousel projector, O in the English accent, automatic cassette, interpreter replacement. It laughs just like a friend. It laughs up to me.

He is falling around, more like oozing, flowing, and I think about him being languid, how I've always thought of it as a female trait. But then I think he is, he seems calm until he stands in front of us and declares his hello and that a business is every American's dream come true or did he say back drop to Baltimore to the office moving home—changing his position, trying to decide if they can get machines to do maintenance. Think about the 100 year quarter rest, last reciprocal, needles on the bed, hitting the monkey's head, trying to test their volition, they're crowding them out.

Are the cows home? Are they surviving? Are they complimenting your survival? They're cultivated, luxurious, admitting to be a luxury item. As sentimental as the electric birds, the trip is planned for fall. First on the island, then at the shopping center where everything is smooth, you appear with your yellow silent eyes.

Erskine and Tony are explaining the difference between pat and fat and pat fat. At the end of the process the machine stops. It's not dramatic but it's clear, it's talking about power, about the languid men who pose, the difference between the quiet men and Erskine says, "Aw Lynne, come on, like, don't be bad, don't be serious, Coops his man."—he says, "He knows he will follow him; but not Frank, cause Frank is so clear, he's too concise and too short, and he won't listen to him, he won't take orders from him, from his voice."

It's school, high school, cool groundshirt, reverse to hip and what is allowed and what isn't for artistic lifestyles or P.G. county tough guy shy or joke shy about it.

Or the lifestyle where the women back up their men, they're wanting to be tough like an Antin's airline stewardess touch. "Why honey, look at this new outfit, won't he go wild."

Well Erskine and Tony are moving up, they want to know what other things you can do, such as walk on the outside, hold the door, light the cigarette. It's European, everyone knows you shouldn't advertise, or follow a bike so close where the holiday brings the announcement and are the judges being bought off, colliding? Are these Disneyland ships following the dream where it's too slow and you can't connect, you could possibly find a way to write.

She is holding her ear with her hand, her mouth cast down, wondering if things will go alright with her boyfriend. At the same time, the other guy walks in worrying about her. She glances up, taking everything in. She's trying hard to be light.

Now is the time to be generous and nice. If it gets quiet enough, we will all die. If you don't understand me, I would live. It didn't strike her fancy, it wasn't intelligent, it craved attention and it was ashamed. Does the face feel its soft age?

How blue does the train become? Look around and lose its empty life. Image equaling a duplicate. Naming your child in the Evangelical Church. If they're holding their hands high, they're praying the white man standing in front of the blacks. I need you when I chance to say it, murky eyes lost, two evacuation processes images. Hanging comforting things on the wall and leaving the stationary in a pleasant fashion, making the f as if it was a great whale.

Those who talk for the sake of talking or silence it, take the great black chorus and sing out! Take the sea and describe its ridiculous glory! The mast becomes the lightning cross, personalized to the nth degree, tracking time with heavy steps. Black the time when friends become pods, or appeasing witnesses to your clever deeds. The bridge turns over and over in my mind.

Stop watching proud sow!

While they're waiting for the salute, they show a double take, reminiscent of the "Old South". Then they're off promenading.

What a strange way to play the flute, between two men. Stout illustrated words. Flat about the house. Coy about Boston. A tape to play to Boston. They're acting a certain way. Now they're talking about stinking in a classical, dignified, monstrous, humorous, mod, way. They exquisitely try to pick their noses.

The big white hero has a disease. In a monstrous loud voice he shouts, "The only effect of your death is the lazy side of your mouth." Words become letters in my dream world of poetry, ones I try to understand. I'm not here for all to see, water giggles a common side. You've seen this thing before, when you reached out. Record that into cliches.

Fingers regard the self. I'm not the carousel that reels empathy. Not once on the ship's time were your words with me. Make the time go for a lend when the night turns bright and cold and you're walking white and diligent. The people stand up to chalk

Lynne Dreyer   375

life, to say it's a mere excuse, mere when it's so far from your voice. Why, these big rooms become a sweep and the woman in her long dress becomes the one with her pockets filled with her hands.

When the excellent sounds become a life story, get out, try it out, block the view where it's quiet enough to send you dreaming. The letters had all of that personality, you can't get very far into it with that. You can't think it all by yourself. Extend it, force it out, think and let go, fall back, and let it go. Stop being so cute, no need to be tough, leave that for the movies, calm down, don't try to explode, don't be watching out. The cat comes near you, think it out, don't put it down with the organ and the holiday which become forceful, polished, magnetic, and weak. Write through the lines in the book. There, now you feel better. Do you excuse yourself, exclude yourself? Now, isn't that what all of this is about today? Can I bring myself together thru my words without the image of the grazing cows?

MICHAEL GOTTLIEB

from FOURTEEN POEMS

1.   FOCKE-WULFS
callow
HELLING
screed
HEAD-
      WOUNDS
swab
RAVE-UPS
arboreal
CONVENTICLES
sledges
TUMBLED TO
'narrativist'

2.   DO NOT
CRUISE THE
HELP
fib-
    rillation
RECOMBINANT
doreé
    guessed
BLANCHING
"phrasey"
UTTER DELUSION
the crowds
SHORING
more ink
    for them

9.   c a p t i o u s
            PALIMPSEST
            t o p g r o s s e r
            MONIKER
            b e e r
                 s c h o o n e r
            DISSEMINATION
            b i t e
                s i z e
            JUST SEEMS
                    TO BE
                        EVERYWHERE
            t u r g i d g n a s h i n g
            MOTIVELESS HEIRS
            a n k l e d
                  f r o m . . .

12.   s t a p l e
            USE *ZUD*
            "a n d s u r e
                 e n o u g h "
            SPAM
            l i q u i d a t i n g
            NON(ALLEGEDLY)
                 -AGGRESSIVE
            s t r i c k l a n d h o s p i t a l,
                   p l e a s e
            TRAILING FLAWS
            d r o p s y
            CAMES

II.   from NINETY-SIX TEARS

Then, the big death. Someone's doing. Onto the lap of the Bureau. What does the ham say? Must be kidding if you think I'm going to give you my telephone number. A genius for going pale. See through by dissembling. The look of components which later took on so much of

The foreground therein, then, as only the most hypothetical place to set it all. I have precisely what you need. The half clogged street. "Be a man among men." The problem with sitting home waiting for the agent to call. False morning. Just drop the keys out of the window in a sock.

Fomentive post numerous conjunctive dicatalyptically derived. All the ships at sea. Panglossian optics. Dumb show. Crash course. Where the skin used to be. Red dogging. Bellying up. The sooty grid of the island. A silent E. Unconditional Surrender Frannie. Boulevard to the digs. The

Course of what seems now increasingly as a sort of desert of years, it had become almost routine, to feed, to square off against, to, as it were, steel oneself against, which, now, by the slight virtue of the decrease in ferocity. Alarm, office, luncheonette. Did you have a book or a

Magazine in mind? Racing leathers. Their wives sat back and rolled their eyes. The sole survivor. One went back to law school. One is laying back in the sticks teaching stovemaking. The only one still with a beard. Window envelopes. Unusually rich and aromatic. You *will* like it and come

Back for more. Adjusted gross receipts. Green light. Live freezer. Permanent non cling, 100% banlon, opening can be worn front back or side. Jumping cribs. How their whole day is geared, all 24, to that one hour onstage, all the motel smashing, Corniches in pools. Barney's not

So smart. On me. Erase fodder. Always so tired, at first I thought it was your diet, then, all those drugs, now you eat salads and smoke cigarettes, and still nod out. The semi-distinguishable shambles of trying to point out something that was never really not there. A dent where once

Michael Gottlieb 379

A lobe. Two make arbitrage. One turned out to be NY's top aspirin jingle coiner. Day of purchase to day of redemption. Three months in London in maryjane shoes. Quite an actor after all; certainly not on the strength of his good looks. Frisson of hair trigger Grenoble fain tail im-

Manent hoof maker lanky dalliant noumenon scandales remanding knock blea y gapping droves listing starred. Dashing Dan's unassailable. Now you want to give it all up for another. Raving quart. A petite cinerama. Unstringed dalliance. Another writes MASH episodes in Cen-

Tury City. Just how long do you think you can go on without me? The disused tunnel. Developmental limp wrists. A pension of virtue. If I just wanted to stay high I wouldn't have come downstairs. A glancing cuff. I'm waiting for the letter. The bashful poitrine. Not even if you paid

Me. The waiting, swaying over the barred way, quaking gulfs, a dirtied article of endearment, nonessential, into the twenties, without a stamp, I tried to forget, they did almost everything, a standard diversionary feint, this doesn't matter much anyway, the gem, the chiffon, the sloe,

The league of attaining dissolution. No reason not to tell you. Red Cross and USO installations. Hispano Suizas make me giddy. The quality of entropment. I can't be bothered to respond to those sorts of statements which, if you would be awake enough to realize, are the kinds of things

Which get thrown at us with such a monotonous depressing repetition, albeit not so frequently, or arrogantly, or 'from,' the same, or the same sorts of people that over the years have increasingly found themselves in what we wanted to think of as indefensible predicaments of their own.

Would like to shut him out of it also, if they could. This time I'm not lying to you. Onset of kith. The Ecstasy of Theresa. Starting out near blows, buying for eachother. A Gale Storm impression. The dunnable mapped presentational demonative breaction discanting chinstraps

Disingenous mocked disdain masquerading in the trappings of clear sighted worldliness. Cordite sheets. If it were only, or nearly, a matter of how much time you were to be found in that position. Stasis majeure. I just wanted to make sure I'm not the one who catches it all. But whetted

To an expected sense of affirmation, a scouring assumption, a warping up of the interior correlatives, in the mundane guise still. A hemostatic entrance. Transferance smarts. Fungoes. Dingbats. Sudsheads. Stripes. Rubes. Tunnel folk. Elbows. Boneheads. Sure she'll be your friend. A

Skill you don't drop. Pat internalization. I engineered it for no other reason than to impress you, somehow. On the up and up. Slingback fadeout. Sarajevo zips away. Misbegotten congealation of debasements that has through no one but me, on the odd evening or weekend, the

Slightest utility, or need or sympathy for, as then, unfortunately I found myself with even more thrust upon me of those sorts of unavoidable, unforseeable, moments of *life* that even I, in all my possible pessimism,could have ever predicted or planned. By the by. If gently

Persuasion doesn't succeed. A lanky and amiable attendant. I had it right here a minute ago. Thanks for the kid. Cannibalized from an old Philco. Soon your breathing gets quicker and more shallow. The coin of that realm. The way you really have to sit down, get earnest, and spend

Some time giving strokes, to expect anything, any sort of special pitch or honing of the rarified indicators. Mr. Zildjian. Someone pressed it into my hand downstairs. You think you are so smart. Grizzled credit manager. Sleep or wake? If I had a dollar for every time some joker

Asked me that question. Corset training. It is yours for the asking. I wish just once I could get through to you, make you see, I really don't want to be someone who comes to mind every time your name comes up. Uzi's by the bushel. More like a love rhomboid. A neural possessary.

Michael Gottlieb 381

The funniest thing since the pigs ate their little brother. Maybe someone will invite us out for some lunch. You think I'm paying for any more of this? Soporific pistolero. If this doesn't convince you of the sincerity of my intentions, wait until you see him in the morning. Swarms crouched

Around Union Square. Like two untamed. He won't go for that. A word to the wise. A skill you don't soon forget, either. Working their forms furiously. I wanted to say that by the end of the year I had done more with all this or that time, that I had more to show for it, than this little

Misery. A case of paroled development. A cowlick that effaces itself. A suspension in trading. Soda jukes. Keep going around telling those stories. Spent ink. I forgot about those shirts. How little of the expression of desire truly *emerges* through the dust of a legacy which as a

Stable *soluted* combination whose residing senses lent themselves, by the lights of those who fancied they wanted to know, to the bank of the bearish presumptive, as an outcome of the approaching juncture, such as, or was, as an expectation that having arose between them, was still to

Be searched out, lying undisturbed, where it had been discarded. Some morning you might wake up, east of the Perdanales. Egg on the face. If you are shy, there are various aides to be jogged. Headed for trouble. It's only a flesh wound. Both sides of his mouth at once. When the diaries

Are published, then we can always go to court and, until then, they can shit in their pants. We used to call them Craterface and Tripod Legs. An infectious groan. Debbie abhors it. Please don't touch that one. Two gats. A vast, former street car roundhouse taken over by the telephone

Company; soiled abandoned wedges from the early sixties, musty links to the Berkshires; beds set up everywhere, merchandizing tags removed from the articles, trying not to look out of uniform. A toothy unbegrudging former correction officer. Dismal showing. The Stet im-

Printed on the forehead. "Let's start all over again, this will be year Zero. Everyone get out of town, now." Promises, the limp on the progress, I mean, I wanted to hear everything, not in any way to pass judgement, as if one could remain or could stand aside from things we saw.

We decided we needed to break through the walls and take over the neighbor's as well. The courage to throw it all away. An excuse a doorman might come up with. The kind of monumental or monolithic throw weight bandied about currently. Cantilevered rebuffs. One traffic

Light from here to Kansas City. The kind I knew from childhood. Remove to insert tap. The price of a simple goodbye. The immanatized eschaton. Shirt and pants. I don't want you to think I'm introducing an unwarranted element. That point in an illness when one has been sick

Long enough for the more pleasant ameliorating aspects of incapacitation to have worn off, long enough to find oneself more than a little bored with the routine of it, the worse of the symptoms, though not all of them, having abated, and the monotony of the condition, pre-

Recovery, in bringing a certain blindness to the underlying missing robustness, the essential 'lack' of health, often leading to, as it does here, to that state, that time, the scene when the restless invalid, having decided to summon up some residual or supposed restored, new found,

Reserves of strength, proceeds to roughly cast off the constricting blanket of the sickness, and proceeds to engage in some patently foolish, often excessively public, activity, going out and dancing and drinking, going out for a not so innocent brunch, so that just at the point where he was

About to turn the corner, with complete recovery only a matter of days away, the adventure precipitates, *naturally*, as a matter of course, a return to the condition, in fact less a re-succumbing to the old complaint than an opportunity for it to gain a second wind, or even, better, turn

Michael Gottlieb 383

Into something more virulent, and throw itself, its force, against the decimated susceptible, wreaking, often, more havoc than the original onslaught. Dreamy pursuit. More than ego. It wants to return to the jungle. Barely, like a Delaware corporation. As good a reason as any for

Punching him out. Plutocrat. Imbroglio'd. I had in mind something older, wider, filmier in black less pre-written less formal less tunnel like more attractive of attention. Here I am doing all of your old dishes. "I don't want my hands in any more commercials. No more good *pours*."

The way a family name enters the dictionary. Bringing along a sledge. Tell them "nuts." Does begin counting with naught, 'which odd, which even?' They keep the leaves in the main compartment and the gourd in the ancillary, they're always chewing on something. I

Wondered if you really thought I was as evil as all that. The Coogan law. If I thought this was what I wanted, I would have gone fishing. Coterminal muff. Phlanges. The city line. Cowboy style, as the term is applied, as in, taking several bystanders along with the intended, *cowboy*

Style. Hunkered down. Eminently bored. Junkers. Lignite. Miniscus. Nobodaddies. Overboard. Primogeniture. Quondam. Riddled. Scapula. Quit claim. Timbre. Uranian. Vinegar Joe. Winsome. Xeroxy. Vapid. Walpurgian. Veloute. Younger. The yclept, an underlying anx-

Iety that to engage in any half way explicit revelation of the actual or verbalizable workings of the mind at writing would only serve to expose the paucity, the threadbare quality, an absolute absence of profundity. Latitudary. Accented apparatus. The eyes have it. A total lack of respect.

It could have been coincidence. Why is he sitting home, stalwart mole? The arches of a showgirl. A takeover artist. Closed end leases. Where the fortune really came from. A complete inability to 're-wind' and elongate that sort of contemplative industrialization that was drilled in-

To the thinking around the "stuff" that poems were made of. And, still wanting, finally, to keep up the role and the posture of that, to himself, and others, unsure, he turned to another sort of organization that, at first, in its fixation upon another fancy, what seemed formally as blank a

Superstructure, in roles shifted away the burden from the areas of selfhood he felt he was so unlucky so as to have *wasted his time* pursuing for so long. Eventually, of course, there was another self-unmasking, and he found himself with no other option, he thought, save somehow

Modelling himself after one of his contemporaries, or, even better, he found, several of them, in such a way, hopefully, so, on the one hand not to attract any notice, or at least overt comment, and on the other, perchance, somehow to ensure his place among the company, of this at

Least he was sure, in which he belonged. For, was he not at least as in possession of his faculties, as ready with a carefully turned phrase in the proper circumstance, as generally sensitive to the true pathos all around him, and neither blessed nor cursed with particularly more or less blind

Spots in his reasoning powers as any of his *friends*? It was just that, as he remonstrated with himself over and over again, he was sure that it was so much harder for him than any of the others to simply get the words out and on the page. He *felt* them inside, it was just impossible to get them

Out. He thought, he was sure he saw it in his work and feared others did as well. Beaming caliph. The kind of person, it turns out, who knows a little about a few things. At this point, the soiled hem of the memory. The eye at the top of the thirteenth step, looking toward the East, some

Scrubby vegetation at the base of the pyramid. No matter how carefully, one doesn't see the wall breathing. The impecunity of the strategy. The point was not how frightened we were, but how used we were getting to that state of affairs. The dosed settlement. I've thought I've seen you

Michael Gottlieb   385

Several times since then, improbable as it seems. A bit overboard. The sort of uncritical rage we once directed at closer targets. Paging extirpation. Like feet under the table, some gestures do not call attention to themselves. Had taken in. A real talent for grasping at straws. Bone of

Contention. I'd like a look in your files. New trends in blister packs. Courted, amassing. All I want is for you to get that thing out of my apartment. Never forgetting one's true mission on this earth. Accented on the little people. The way no one says street or road or avenue after

The street name or adds it to addresses on letters. There were precise shadows, fallen between the ribs where, in the time usually associated with the age, they were promptly forgotten. Anamorphic, descending over conversation, enshelling the feelings and glances in a discantation.

The later memoranda. Rowing to the party. A recourse, a featured soloist. The daggered cards. Height famine. I always go to New York to buy. An exhilarating domestication. The cast and crew. Making sure to include one dinner between every two lunches. More than a penchant.

The swimming pool. That you can please yourself sometimes. Well adjourned. "Tlingit Tom." Mortagee's turn. The amiable slab. An internal quotient. Sidestepping how-to. Model remotes. If you could walk a mile in his Lucheses. The page, the flats, the type, the expression on the

Mail face. Something like a Social Security number, in that you could have called me anytime. Rather quiescent regarding the original. Words that you would come across, in your world. If you announce it to enough of them, you'll be shamed into following through. Ritual assumption.

Everything I have learned, on a scale of one to ten. A teleology *where* betters. Shape growing, like a rent in the curtain of security. As it fills you up, wind in your conversation, gliding you up a curiously admixtured swell of certainty, that whatever you hear or may be called on to

Respond to, will, by some incomprehensible 'determination' that may in fact depart as swiftly as it appeared, but, during the tenure of its sway, afford an effortless avenue and inventory or accessibility, of registration—a swiftness posing as a calling up, a summoning, all,

However, tossed in with a sense that all the felicitous conjunctions and freshly raised up synapses, arching over both you and your, in a sense, audience, as well as the *improved* links between your first and outer layers of Presentation, the responding self, and the you that the former

Calls, as it were, upstairs to, leans on, makes liberal use of when possible, that all of the upgraded, newly harmonizing connections, are things progressing forward toward you, somehow a change in the pressure of the atmosphere you swim through, a *trend* that, for some

Reason, is picking you up and bearing you along in its train, not so much with any destination 'in mind,' as in some at the moment largely indeterminable 'direction,' for how long, and yielding what satisfaction or ultimate deficit, likewise, as of this time, remains largely unforeseen.

I didn't want to call them, I wanted them to call me, while I was still awake. Deigned not to recognize. Are you going home in a few years? Duoserve. A tame distance. The judgement of time springing not from any sum of application but out of the weight of all the 'staggering' in-

Volved. Finding the transfigured. Raked with those 88's. The same personality steeples and hurdles. Able to direct any flow of description towards standards and representations of bathos. What pass for fantasies, where we would be now if we'd kept going at that clip. Yammer-

Ing at the vault. As I shook it an ominous drop expelled itself down through a seam at one of the corners. "Literally, it isn't how much you owe, it's how you string out the payments." Roanoke. Flax. Signed landscapes, unroomed, touring the codes, mundanity, the percentages one

Has to be willing to accept. Eventually you'll have to go out and lease one of your own. Racing home from each party and writing it all down. A commital. Mr. Moto Takes A Photo. The dollar standard. Quickstepping. As if it come straight from the smoke all around, sit down, blow

Off some steam. Who devastate their thumbs. Does one, any more anyone, stop in the depth of an evening, and look back, does this kind of reliving, a somehow 'waiting' mode of reduction, an 'aside-I' demonstration, ever find its way through the aging pulls and wraps we

Throw or allow to be drawn across the shoulders of our 'moral effort?' "*Voice*, unrelenting, over and through the wall of standing or propped upright humanity, the entire audience swayed, as one, 'done upon,' recipient wills, an acknowledgement to this Voice; and this room we had

Thrown ourselves into, dark, smokey, seeing no more than a body or two ahead, as one of our number leading us linked armed in a line aimed through the swaying throng, toward that Voice, worming our way to the 'stage,' the far end of the former strip club, I, I confess, found myself

Weary of the bodies I found myself pressed up against and broke my link in the chain and just tried to settle myself in place, keeping in unobtrusive touch with my billfold, with no particular desire to force myself to the front, best, it seemed, to let myself rock with the rest back

And forth there, washed by the Voice and the rest of the music; my eyes let themselves close, the 'refrain' swelled, I thought I was somewhere far away with someone else, a long time ago; time passed; then someone spilt something on my arm, my eyes opened, jolted back, and, thrown

By my sudden start, momentarily leaning against the swell of the rest of the audience's rocking and swaying, out of synch with the crowd, all unawares, I caught sight of her. A mere body length away, all in black, I could reach out and touch her, singing directly into my eyes." Colum-

388   *Michael Gottlieb*

Biana. Mr. Chase's classroom. Paddington. The notorious Five Points. The ability or apparent license, that is, the allowance for an appetite, to be able to return, letting by harboring, generally betokens a lack of pressure, something akin to market forces. Mechanically estruable

Signal. Misty shrubs, fluorescent blocking marks, lingering boom mike. A derailed evening, one breakdown at a time. The kind of posing you suggest. Grazing through the party. It gets soiled from just being looked at. Teaching Boney a lesson. Still and sparkling. This has got to be the

Sulieman expostulating. Like a pitcher with a lot of stuff left, which before I made it to the city, the house before the gates, a conversation in which all the talk is not enrosed, a petulant charm. What seems most regrettable is not the lack of savoir faire but their mystifying inability to

Recognize it as such, your subtle bulldog-like. Kind of traffic we usually don't see around here. Open house, a mask of *let's get on with it*. The basic fear that he would think she hadn't. Verbatim corporation. Ohio-Sealy. The common hydraulic. Lifting call capacity. In the proceedings

Entitled. Hibernia, foils. Closures. Acclamitizing. Travail. Pickup. Hesperidian. Scalloping. Half recumbant. Bootless. Mardi's. Scored. Nattering. Proctorial. Dolmen. Brang. Loping. Stychethemic. Jatted. Gaston. Auguecheek. Reticule. Variegated. Gobelin. Stamens. Cupola.

Fram. Gag. Hops. Condensor. Ribboned. Elemo- lago. Corroborative. Woof. Authoritative. Driller. Tuned. Posting raffine. Crake. Jasper. Testingly. Gleem. Ruminative. Binge. Fain. Lustral. Pons. Descant. Forked. Mind. Duod. Gusto. Carpathian. Nobe. Part-healed.

Redoubtedly. Captivation. Instrumentality. Lissome. Stallworth. Dispatched giantism. 'Flaired.' On-stance. Kalpa. Declassification. Paradism. Remittance. Flocking. Gainsaid. Man-number. Spode. Ex-culpatory. Minions. The Flat Head People. Rumble. Signatories.

Domicile. Gamely. Scarified. Rating-digest. Foment. Vlad. The Glines.
Tolerably. Glassine. Rinky. Morgify. Soft-ship. Adorn. Basted.
Melanomaniac. Laff. Garnets. Just-side. Clasp. Blacked. Smatter.
Gloriful. Raft. Sloane. Particate. Rookies. Mealy. Nabob. Bled. Renter.

"Dwezel." Alum. Walleyed. Nubbing. Trucked. Sharped. Cuff.
Scouted. Anack. Foresook. Goaled. Corruptive. Veil. Clefts. Flume.
Calistoga. Ordure. Stonily. Ward. Slatting. Unchastened. The epitomal
breakfaster. Abreacting. Consumption. Tea y. Ushers. Optioned.

Fraternization. Perm. Haspels. Bowdlerized. Rosters. Knackery. Stax.
Abash. Mantis. Symp. Horology. Pranks. *"Unhappily."* Mortise.
Chasen. Regle. Bibled. Inhaler. Operose. Heeling. "Dukish." Tarred.
Not subway rumble down there. Anchorite. Wreathing. Paced. Ag-

Gregative. Twill. Mans. Kicked. Fingering. Reprobate. Which is your
voice? Mattered. Starker. All of me. Flying squad. *The Inter-Wool
Secretariat.* Confessions are just more trowel work. Roiling. I don't need
to wait for an answer. Alexandria's soup of expressways. I forgot where I.

Something you wouldn't do even with your best friend. Warring
branches. Practical recourse. I always wanted one. Easy tuning. What do
you hide, besides your drafts, that you aren't ashamed of? On the zero
or the one? Get me the founder. Red neap.

TINA DARRAGH

RAYMOND CHANDLER'S SENTENCE

for Susan Howe & her *The Liberties*

Earl Stanley Gardner was one of the mystery writers Raymond Chandler imitated when he first wrote fiction. Chandler would select a Gardner story, rewrite it, compare it with the original and rework it once more. Chandler attributes this practice to his classical training at Dulwich where he would translate Cicero into English then back to Latin again. "I had to learn American just like a foreign language," is the way he himself put it.

But Chandler had spent the first seven years of his life in America, speaking American: a combination of "railroad" American (his father was an engineer for the Union-Pacific) and "respectable old party" American (his mother was Anglo-Irish, daughter of a Waterford solicitor). When his father was away on business, he would hear "small town" American spoken at the home of his aunt and uncle in Plattsmouth, Nebraska. Then there would be the "frontier" American spoken in the transient hotels where Raymond and his mother would meet Mr. Chandler on the road. It was in one of these hotels that Raymond heard the edgy sort of American spoken by his father as he decided never to see them again. Soon thereafter Raymond and his mother sailed to England, where he heard English spoken for the next 16 years.

---

mother tongue SEE
pedestal - at the foot of "to place"
special use of "mother" - dregs, swamp
deserted = away from   a line
                a series
sphere of the father - sign of the future task
"task" - transposition of "tax"

translate SEE "transfer" - to bear, to carry across
solicitor - whole, entire + put into motion
vernacular   literally - slave born in the master's house
fund   as a noun   the bottom
                         a flat piece of land
          as a verb   to make a debt permanent
school   employment of leisure
civil   pertaining to the citizen
                         as distinct from the soldier
math   obsolete use - to mow
                         general use - to learn
country   that which lies opposite one's view
prostitute   to cause to stand, to set up, to place

Raymond Chandler's sentence
"I had to learn American
just like a foreign language"
has had me at loose ends
for over a year
keeping track
of all my associations
with Chandler in particular
& mysteries in general
but as I keep looking
up at his sentence
I continue to wonder
why I've hung myself up
on someone else's feeling
of being out of place
with our native tongue

so I twist myself around
and link up with a memory
of my mother chain reading
mysteries while lying on the couch

392   Tina Darragh

her afternoon "nap" always
our way of finding her
when we'd come home from school
& P. remembering this to be true
for his mother, too
only she would doze sitting up
a paperback face down on her lap
& I wasn't able to know his mother
having met P. after she died
but I think of her
along with my own
when I lie down with a mystery
to read about someone
who knows what to do
when something goes wrong

then one evening *The Big Sleep* is on T.V.
the remake with Robert Mitchum
& snatches of Chandler's prose scattered throughout
in which C has the detective talk to himself
about a father who is owed
the right to remain ignorant
of the bad blood in his line
the underlying reason
why this hardboiled Marlowe
does what he does for no money

which I hadn't expected

because I'd always thought of Marlowe
as outside the story line
of pay up   to protect your reputation   which
is broken   "as an expression"
into its component parts
becomes out as   to cover   (up front)   thinking

& that further confuses me
since in reading C's work
I'm left with the feeling
that I'm facing something
I can't see

so I cut back to C's practice
of learning how to put together a sentence
by taking Latin ones apart
& I recall the various clues
my h.s. classics teacher would give

first — look for the verb
& if the rest of the sentence doesn't fall
into the usual subject/object sequence
the elusive construction
is probably a form of the ablative
something we don't have in our language
— a place case —

place of means or
place of instrument or
place of agent or
place of separation or
perhaps the ablative absolute —
a past participle used to express the future

at which point I cross back over to C's bio
& trying to give the investigation some order
line up information from his life
with my h.s. brand Latin
as in

absence of the father = look for the verb
dependence of the mother = the past participle used to express
       the future
humiliation of a class system = place of separation

   394   Tina Darragh

marriage to an older woman = place of agent
vice-presidential duties at Dabney Oil = place of instrument
drunken binges ending in dismissal = place of means

but in rereading these concocted equations
I realize I needed to create this order
so I could see myself use
the hardboiled genre
to go to my father
perhaps as Chandler did
to go to his
though I need prove it
only for myself

so I'm left with a list
of my favorite Chandler sentences
ones I'd pulled from his texts
to create a final segment
when I'd felt a need
to pull the piece together

but now one stands by itself
as a kind of summation

In "Bay City Blues"
the detective is caught in a frame
& tries to escape by climbing
into the next room and dressing
in someone else's clothes,
even affecting another's voice
but C has the tough cop spot
him anyway & say
"get dressed, sweetheart & don't fuss with your necktie.
Places want us to go to them."

so it's there that I decide to abandon
the project & leave Chandler's sentences
with him & as a parting shot
look up "abandon"
as a way to set off
& following it back far enough
I find it comes from
"to place" under "speak"
just where I've wanted to be
all along

TOM BECKETT

THE PICTURE WINDOW

for Anne

They are curiously interfaced. Their surfaces forming a common boundary. One might say that he thought of her as a person. No one feels composed. She is spectacularly encumbered. They are finding themselves alone. Each of them.

She is surfacing. The extension of a frame can be the limit of a world. Names can be labels of concealment. The picture window is being shattered with a brick. Their thoughts are encumbered. She finds herself thinking. Those sounds of breaking glass might be composed.

They are on hold. Each of them. One might label a window a surface to hide behind. The word *brick* is a noun like the word *glass*. His composure feels encumbered. Some might say that sounds extend thought.

She is not herself when she is with him. Or, rather, this is what he feels given to say. Their thoughts are labels of thinking. Her composure is a surface she can hide behind.

We are a presentable couple. That which has happened can be said to be the case. She has a lovely pair of breasts. I remember meeting. One might feel given to say what one is thinking. She is not herself when she's alone.

He hides behind words like *brick* and *glass*. What constitutes feeling's extension in this world? The picture window is a brick. Labels of person are common boundaries. She found him unfeeling sometimes.

We interface with each other. Sometimes I become depressed about my breasts. Composure constitutes a window no one can see behind. One might pair thinking with shattering one's self.

He sounds the word *glass*. She is not herself today. One hides one's feelings as if beneath a brick. Her breasts extend out from her frame. He finds her thinking.

Your things are out of place. Her thoughts constitute shattered feelings. She finds those labels. One hides my breasts. Sounds of breaking. The window might be made of glass. I become depressed. A frame no one can see behind.

Her composure is an extension of his boundaries. Each of the spoken names is the case. Glass is a brick. Sounds extend breasts. The frame is spectacularly pictured. He sees her interfaced with their selves. One might be alone.

His person forming. The world is common names. That which might feel thinking. One hides beneath meeting so to limit the encumbrances. What constitutes a "pair" of breasts? She finds him sometimes. He sounds her composure. A brick is a given. A surface is a tensive thing.

Our out. Limits each of them. No one feels the word *glass*. A surface *if*. That remembrance when he's alone. Picture sounds. One might pair thinking with breasts. The unfeeling brick.

Your meeting. Curiously composed thought. An interface. A boundary extensive of limits. One might frame her. This is what a surface is. She finds the time. Those sounds are names. Their thoughts might be said to be thinking. She is spectacularly concealed.

His say. The terms of an argument. Out front. Fumbling. One might feel interfaced with a window. Their thoughts are not presentable yet. Her breasts are pressed against the glass. Composure is a thought surface. No one can pair meeting with finding. They are spectacularly curious.

Her world is pictured. Things rubbing or folding. A gap between them. In exhalation. The partition presents a side on the left and on the right. Sometimes one might remember thoughts. A window might be said to be a label or a brick. Depression constitutes this place.

Our outside. She finds herself curiously given to him. Labels compose boundaries. One is so spectacularly right. The surface is a tensive picture. Curious glass. Folding each of the presentable arguments. He sounds her terms she might think to feel could constitute this place.

They are a pair. A window might be said to gap two sides. The partition is a label or depression. A world is commonly spoken. Remember. Sounds are a given. One might fumbling feel breasts. Presents. Sometimes.

Your interface. Extensive meeting. Breasts are exhalations. His person is finding names. Each of them. One hides a brick thinking it is beneath this place. Your unfeeling thing.

Her frame is alone. One might be alone. The word *brick*. One might pair thinking with composure. Meeting to limit her thought. Their thinking might not constitute the terms of an argument.

She is forming. Our out is what? A time. Rubbing a gap in exhalation. She sees him interfaced with glass. Composure is a curious partition. A window might be pressed.

They are constituting a tensive sounding of the partition. The partition is commonly spoken. One might sometimes gap present remembrances. Your meeting of limits is names. One hides an our. Out when he's alone. Each of the frames. They are not one.

Your breasts. He finds her. Interface is spoken. One might fumbling sound two sides of a depression glass. She is not her frame. To limit sometimes that which is out front or rubbing a side on the left or the right.

Her picture. Their thoughts. Curious of those terms. The *glass*. That composure presents. One might encumber shattered thought. The picture window. His presentable case. They are thinking this place.

Our selves. Pressed boundaries. One pair a faced. What constitutes meeting? They are what a surface is. A boundary might name thinking. One might pair thinking with breasts. His bounaries are the names said to be this case. These are the times.

We is an argument. A label is a fumbling interface. Breasts are partitions one is meeting. Sounds are presents. Persons are rubbing a curious window. Each of the encumbrances constitutes a form of thinking. One might limit a faced thought.

Her surface is boundaries said to picture selves. The frame is finding curious exhalation. Thought encumbers place. A world is, remember, unfeeling present window. One might limit each. He might think he sounds right. Our out of the one.

His curious rubbing side. *Brick* is finding partition not frame. Our thoughts are fumbling names. Present window. Nouns shattering glass. Sometimes labels of person constitute forms of concealment. That which has happened can be said to be the frame. They are alone. I become depressed. Her front. The breast. A curious surface.

Our exhalation interfaced with the glass. Rubbing in the terms. This is what is his. Each of them are pressed. He sees her find him sometimes. A gap between them. Sounds surface as givens. The time that is remembered. The encumbered window. Said *glass* to constitute a limit. A side is out. Presents her pictures. Fumbling sound a thinking beneath depression. Pair meetings with remembrances.

We is presents. Constitute a between them. One might be happily encumbered. One might be a limit in finding. Picture exhalation. Out of the gap. Each has happened to be remembered. Breasts are *the* breast. Glass is the window. I become her front.

His curious rubbings are sounds. Surfaces become depressions. Pictures are fumbling interfaces. A world is not frame. This is what is between them. They are givens. One might limit each. He might label her. I become a window. *Brick* is the breast. Glass is faced.

Her herself. The picture window. To limits pressed. This is said. Our out of the argument. A side is a thinking between depression. Partitions are lovely sometimes.

Our place. Their surfaces interfaced outside.

FANNY HOWE

ALSACE-LORRAINE

"Alot of sky litters my view of home—oh
split part, lost."
    Helium balloons spill off the horizon
        & knock her backwards
Jealousy'd be too easy   "I miss
    a better sentiment, ballooning pride
could accomplish." Homesick
for each hand, they miss the fragrance
of their labors in them.

          *

The wind outside is feverish
Rain follows   "Art doesn't imitate
nature anymore" but still he wants
   some bad weather
    Today he smelled horses in the wet meadow
browsing for ice, an onslaught
of neuralgia followed
    Some thought passed through one mind
but couldn't catch it, more like nostalgia.

          *

They need a strap, something to hold onto
    The meadow speeds, they stagger
and not even trees, rooted, can hold them
    Oh do they ever need a strap—It will be time
Now his dream
has changed into her life, they live
inside the
    night meadow, which speeds   A strap, a strap
which will be time, which will hold onto nothing.

                              *

A rainbow
of emotions, shades of purple to blue, the way
    good becomes
        awful so easily   First was the discovery
that everything melts in the sun
Second the discovery that everything does not
melt in the sun   That's where they are today
    Age will change
        the condition, is the condition, a more virulent sun

                          *

The fancy they builded had many,
had their fancy, many mansions once,
but no room in, each one full
        "All in the head" as celestial
mansions be
Now of that collection only an image stays, dazzle
in a travelling surface
Can also hit their hearts by a ballet or Monet
but never build again, outside the house of art.

                          *

She wants to find a really lonely country
        set off, see
in a glade of day lily   this bitter sensation
and early morning dense misting
        White iron where spirits'll meander, the gone
ones she can't believe in
leaving her, the way they hang her heavy head,
        as sculpture, still
saying nothing of the truth's ill tense.

                        *

Stood up by the maple's tap
        no bouquets
or buckets   But across the public's garden
that olive soldier
        cruised in the gradient dusk   "I miss him"
in evening's line along a fountain
        Nowhere was an hour more dour
than where those children wanted
farther to turn into father, nowhere.

                        *

War's end brings some dividends:
        his army
fatigues asleep on a prop of profligate lilacs,
wind chimes   green bottles of Rhine wine
        smoke in silver trees
Great ways all
to numb some primal shocks
as they hitch & gallop round the body's soul.

                        *

"I wish to make others suffer"
& went to a willow and hung his arms over
   grave-colored water,
smell of decay, beds of salmon-sized flowers
   He hung there
for a response   Tore off a branch
and struck it on the trunk
until the willow sighed   Better d--d than dying,
is what he thought, she thinks.

                              *

A war-torn rotunda
& a Maginot's imaginary boundary
is all that remains of
   said sad time
Expressions of goodness all new must be-
come when some didn't do   Oh
Alsace-Lorraine!   Where are the lines, and
in what hemisphere a calm?

JOHN MASON

Red Fred exhumed the orangepeels.

He was very very interested in the designs.

What a fortunate wisdom!

His bicycle sang when the garage was full.

He stood in the doorway when the earth shook.

He excoriated an orange.

Cars, wagons, buses, lunch, all late,
the rain is wearing skates, angry
zebras in the slow umbrella sweaters.
A talk that brushes down the users.
Home is where the house was.
The radio turned to an outsider
a hat   a girl   an ostrich-tree
horseshoeshaped people filled the rooms.
Go for hello the "hi" way
what in the bus is a helping hand.
Saw a bread a cake — a cake a cookie make,
roping in the sweet ways you make fall.
Hurry to line up and get a turn,
you little potato dancer hurt in school,
the trees, the fish, the birds, the king fishers:
no runs to get candy to help?
a blue kite shows us the way.
Fine day for walking into a paper reading
that a yellow yes this way comes.
Old friends, listening in the little doorways.
The light in a room, the wet look, the Eagles,
a mirror, a ring, a bell under the bed,
later we go to lunch, now we talk shoes.
I want to stop and look you over.
I run a good boat here and nose the slow floor.
We can make it to a nurse, am I out of line?
Hurry line, the window is open, you can see through the boats.
For 6 or 7 mornings I wanted to put on a good record to get up to.
A party that swings is a door in a jar, open and turning.
The fish in the pail couldnt get through the mirror.
Bicycle jar shoe, little man in on under.
Trees on the way, songs to get you home.
I stood under a light, not by the old grey man.
My pail in my hand.
An orange, a room, a rope, and jumping.
The big hand is on the eight.

waiters were singing

        the jars were going

as into a room what the falls outside

angry said

    but hungry   and down

   you little tree!   up yours

cats wait you to an orange tree

no bananas, i'll trouble you

little put   to walk in like that & out

     no water can hurt you

lunge or lurch, which one?

scared of wax paper

when idiot is no longer a term of affection

the girl who eats her pusher

i *both* bought em off Enrique! yes i did!

each new vehicle makes up new lanes: skateboard

i thought i'll have a vacation

gargantua showers, and cleans the shower

you don't wanna change just to get a chick, do you?
you want her for yourself!
—two of 'em! i want two of 'em!

doubts & regrets   one leads to the other. i was thinking
i was having d's when i was really having r's

the beehave

human beings? i call them human borings
said the dog, hungry
the police siren
growling in the street
as i moved about the house (empty)
in search of your footprints
the house "bare as your thigh"
(last night you said
"funny you should be ticklish there"
between balls and ass
"the emptiest part of your body")
plants and papers get in my way
want to know everyone but i'm lazy
arranging the pillow spilled
coffee on some dollar bills hung
them up to dry   the police are such
cub scouts   i needed a friend
"has it ever occurred to you that maybe
x doesn't like you?"
the birds tall as grass
some with skunkheads
bathe in the dogdish
the dog whines at the door
now from outside

BERNADETTE MAYER

from STUDYING HUNGER

Listen
I began all this in April, 1972. I wanted to try to record, like a
diary, in writing, states of consciousness, my states of conscious-
ness, as fully as I could, every day, for one month. A month always
seems like a likely time-span, if there is one, for an experiment.
A month gives you enough time to feel free to skip a day, but not
so much time that you wind up fucking off completely.

I had an idea before this that if a human, a writer, could come up
with a workable code, or shorthand, for the transcription of every
event, every motion, every transition of his or her own mind, &
could perform this process of translation on himself, using the
code, for a 24-hour period, he or we or someone could come up
with a great piece of language/information.

Anyway
When I began to attempt the month-long experiment with states
of consciousness, I wrote down a list of intentions. It went like
this: First, to record special states of consciousness. Special:
change, sudden change, high, low, food, levels of attention
And, how intentions change
And, to do this as an emotional science, as though: I have taken a
month-drug, I work as observer of self in process
And, to do the opposite of "accumulate data," oppose MEMO-
RIES, DIARIES, find structures
And, a language should be used that stays on the observation/
notes/leaps side of language border which seems to separate, just
barely, observation & analysis. But if the language must resort to
analysis to "keep going," then let it be closer to that than to
"accumulate data." *Keep going* is a pose; *accumulate data* is a
pose.
Also, to use this to find a structure for MEMORY & you, you will
find out what memory is, you already know what moving is

And, to do this without remembering

Those were the intentions I wrote down, April first. Also, these questions: What's the danger? What states of consciousness & patterns of them are new to language? And what is the language for them? What's the relation of things that stand out, things that seem interesting (like a sentence from a tape I made, the tape was 7 hours long, but this sentence would always stand out: "The food of the mother is better than the food of the fatter father;" like "It could be worse, you could have witnessed a double murder," like poem titles & poem ideas, like the idea "You know everything")— what's the relation of this type of event to the rest & how to develop moments as, "standing out" like language does, like language ideas do. "Some old people try to live on one can of soup a day."

On April second, the first thing I wrote was "You wait." The experiment went badly, real bad. I added to my intentions, this one: to be an enchantress, or, to seduce by design. I thought about sentences that stuck in your mind, like, "How long have you been head of this business?" and "You planned the disappearance of my desire."

At 3:35 a.m. on April 2nd, I recorded that I had eaten too much food.

I was waging a constant battle against traditional language: take this excerpt from the early diaries:
   . . . you think of a word, like *hashish*, like, *group*. The word brings back *one scene*, one scene of a dream (when I'm awake) or one of a fantasy but what predominates is was this: it's Tuesday, the day I get up at ten. What am I hiding? Is was this & is was this morning, it's one o'clock now, this, I'd like to be a basketball player, one of the players, I include no description of their movements. Left out of the group reading, I fantasize (in dream) around the periphery, I control those feelings in dream again, I create a rapid movement in, around, & about that event, event of being left out, I synthesize a dance this is for me alone: I'm active,

I'm looking through windows, I dont speak, I preserve the sheet surface, clean white sheet of my presence in the room. When I get out of bed I move, I dont want to move to the instance where details & foods accumulate later in the day, are the foods I ate later in the day, are the foods I ate late last night digested, are they gone, am I this surface, or does all the work come later like practice. You've seen the other team play, now, so. . . . Outside the performance area I exist. Outside the process the arena the activity, a space for existing: I might float around, or, am I going too far? In this way, from the outside, I put everything in, take in everything, I must spew it all out, what prevents me what seizes me gently when I try to emerge is *that-one* outside the door, she has a purpose, I put her there: let nothing-myself get out of this room, let no judgments be made, let no law & order exist except this: *nothing escapes from here*; . . . . . To refuse a direction, to refuse a guide. . . . a person who has used the word human as a lie without levels, that one might say: you'd rather be in prison where you're different. My responses—I want them to be automatic, my physical movements indifferent, undifferentiated, uncalculated, cool, almost unnoticed, calm. Calm for this activity, what is the activity? Inner motion, emotion, design. Yes it's a surface, you can draw on it, out from it, anything, everything, I know what's going on. . . . It's not the whole story, I've left out the motives, the history & the memory, the parts that have direction, I've left them out because in that way I could be pinned down, possibly tortured.

As I got further into this, language seemed to be demanding its form: lying in bed, head down, muscles arched, colors plotted the outline-sound of a language, an unmarked language, not controlling it. Forget any substance of meaning, forget substantives & their color & get it gradually paler, seeing sound vibrations in sleep-closed eyes. A lamp hanging is a sound. It lowers & disappears.

On April 11 I dreamt the history of all people in the world, good & evil, zooming in on a familiar cat-face. The next part of the dream said to me: this part is about you personally. And this work, said Patti, has something to do with polar ice caps, something to do with seeing polar ice caps.

412   Bernadette Mayer

April 13, cant focus; April 20th, gave up the project.

But I was bound to start again. You see, the whole thing had already had a beginning with a project called MEMORY which turned into a show which turned into a dream or returned to a dream that enabled me to walk. Before this I couldnt walk, I had street fantasies like any normal prostitute. Anyway, MEMORY was 1200 color snapshots, 3 x 5, processed by Kodak plus 7 hours of taped narration. I had shot one roll of 35-mm color film every day for the month of July, 1971. The pictures were mounted side by side in row after row along a long wall, each line to be read from left to right, 36 feet by 4 feet. All the images made each day were included, in sequence, along with a 31-part tape, which took the pictures as points of focus, one by one & as taking-off points for digression, filling in the spaces between. MEMORY was described by A. D. Coleman as an "enormous accumulation of data." I had described it as an "emotional science project." I was right.

So
In June I began again & what started it was that I wrote this:
    You sleep Marie: save them for me, certain moments, I'm resting, I'm restoring, I'm gathering, I'm hunting, I'm starving, I'm you, you say: go on being, peering owl on top of fortress, sounding out, training sound to meet my ear, drive & mark time, I'm a history, her coil, mark time, suffer a moment to let me be like her a history, object, she was determined, defies all laws & rules, is the language I bought from passers-by, sea crate full of junk & language twisting & twisting coil of all morning, I met that guy the guide & cast his bell aside, I'd rather die in sync with just random tones, just war can bury baby brick, your foot's my foot, core, how late you suffer, core, how late, whispers suffer, suffer, whispers into the tape a running water sound at the bell rewinding a vision I got & mystery works at the door, if no one's there, I'll stay right here adding a picket to this to pierce you/me clear through, I saw you, remember, we go through the greatest horrors of the world at last, I love you, you turn over, you dont really wake up, sink a shallows at the oceans deep malaysian sleep, I'll

know new dance the boxes taught today, it's rare code words can sink a ship in the shallows, reform so dry a crease & saw the same crack in the dream before, sink down broad ship at dawn, home plate, they hold it up to their ears, we years, you go on. I'm resting, I saw her once. Her pins prick my skin, she makes me dizzy, she makes me well.

That's what started me off again & that's what opened the question of who is the you. You private person. And now, while you keep in mind my intentions at the beginning & what I've said to try to explain how they got transformed & where they came from, I'll go on

STUDYING HUNGER

STUDYING HUNGER. I had to stop. I had to stop & begin again slowly. A buzz, a confluence of noise around, all correcting & weaving, weaving to call my name. Bernadette. I stopped. Papers & books smoldering, black edges of them too close to the flame, flame easing itself out the cracks, the cracks in the stove, the one in our loft, mine & Ed's, Ed is a man like electric light, a human nature, suffer the flames the fire came from its source, a simple block of wood in the broiler, the source of the flame, the block of wood black at the edges, source of fire, black, & its rectangular shape interfered with, cut off at an edge on one side where it had burned. . .

A burning wedge, an edge burned off, a slice disappeared, it burned, a slice, maybe in the shape of a triangle, that slice, that alchemy slice, that edge off the block of wood, the wood about two by four, Rimbaud slice, the block of wood that was the origin of the flame, the fire in the stove that was threatening everyone, jeopardizing their lives, something was wrong—the fire started. I was used to it. I am the leopard. I am the bear. We found the source of the flame & took it out of the oven. It was a man, laid out. A dead man. It was an image of my father & his father & wood. . .

Gradually then I began again. It was time for my piece, in an auditorium full of friends. No more paper & no flame. I would execute this difficult dance & the secret, the resume, the explication would remain hidden until the end. I had rehearsed. I had driven myself from one moving bar or pole, attached to the wall, hinged there at one end, so that they could swing open & closed like a door. I had driven myself through rehearsals over these posts, outposts, these locations of the histories of individual ghosts.

Ghosts that were not only haunting me but had ceased to be real. They had come alive but were dead. These points of focus were like swinging doors; only the most acrobatic feats could control their random motion. Only a master of equilibrium could navigate the surface of one much less all at once. I had rehearsed. I had worked. Still unsure of myself, I set my performance off to the side like a side show, like a simple element in a complex pattern, a homage to its variety & all living things. The performance was extremely difficult, difficult, she wore black, she had no contact with the ground, she rose. . .

And descended executing the relationships between the horizontal posts which were secured at many levels. To get from one to the next, and its chronology was clear, to get from one to the next, she would make use of a turn in air, an impossibility, her arms must have had the strength, an impossible strength, her feet could never touch the ground, a short performance in tight black clothes, she must make use of every muscle, every muscle is tense, every second has been dreamed of many times before, the performance is over, she is on the ground. And now its crux, its central point, its purpose: her declaration. And she had kept this secret: it was not a real performance, not a process, not a show. The feat, the feats of movement, this exhibition of strength, of study & agility, all this was a lead-in so that I could speak, so that I could say, & I say: Listen: Now that I have done that, now that I have done it, I will never have to do it again.

It's over & I will have to do it over again, and in this recounting I want to be clear, clear about its purpose, about the reason for the existence of this peculiar performance in space, & that reason is this simple statement: I had to do it, really do it, so that I would never have to do it again. And to those who accept a rose from me I add this: I am sorry to cover my feelings with images out of fear, but please believe me there are things you cannot write. And I am writing. I had to stop. I had to stop & begin again slowly.

I want to call you & tell you what color they are, I want to be clear, I want to surface (there's something missing), ocean pile pervert surface oil of current, oil of milk, start a renaissance, at core, at milk, current of generating heart & perfect corn, the food of Indians, my earth's foot touches continent of theirs & feels the heat & eats with them, the food of substance, food of, adore, a saint, a receptacle of all admiration, of all living things, exists a pleasure, exists a pure licentious pleasure, I am free to love you, these are the stones that once made me, & throw them a beautiful woman in the corner in the cast of a, dying of courage in the cast of the man, stones accepted in the current of avalanche, snow, refills me, I said it before that snow falls. I fill me, I enter you now, I am man of before. . .

A start. A stop. I am woman of beginning. You are all at the shore. You are a center, you design a week, the meek, a mile, the shore, endless beginnings of entropy, endless universe of design. New words. What can I speak of, what can I call? Can I call you, all of you, all, call you to me, can I embrace, can embrace all, all parade, all center & all (a picture) never, & ever the bird that speaks, that bird cannot speak, this call to all, eternal rhyme & time, she only knows the simplest words, the smallest prose closed of design. She opens, she is cool, she is call of all that wild, she is unerring, she is fall. She starts. Beginning form & art design, a cell, sublime. She learns from you & you.

Direction of & design, design is all, design is energy & prototype, before proportion, all consumes, she is consumed, enervates what's there, is clear, is empty, is unsure is all. She acts she poses, she meditates, takes foods, she inks the pen & drastically reduces out of time. She moves, kernel of corn, what is line, great design & consuming energy of all to eat love eat & arms wake, ate, slows, real blood arms of veins & full & muscle tendon, solid cells & cell by every cell, none stone, final arms appear, have grown, have custom's design of hair, live in the happy air here, this air will last a moment, air, a reading, full, I miss you all, you who are not here, & still you fill me, I have one, I have one here, a brother then who's full of you enough & simple, scatter now, all brothers & sisters turn to me, understanding, meet as vision, vision sighs, time....

Our energy proposes that we meet, dont disappoint me, I will bear you now, that arms can bleed & bleed more blood than sand & isolated pebbles stones. I know you, you know everything. Come closer, vision closes with a meek & silent look at one who's new, to you the one I'm thinking of, you are two & endless rivers, you know it, find it out, I'll meet you, I'll be waiting, I cannot address you now, now I am formal, formal now, I'm meeting a vision that has been waiting & waiting as I do for you. Accept a blessing in the ancient tradition, layers, structures, deep designs, tradition I am asking to wait up for me, wait for me, wait I'm ready, I'll do what I can, I am a human, I am eyes, it's sweet to speak to you. . .

And what a seduction for my vision, will it take to me & will it hurt, ache, penetrate, execute me in isolation isolate, I am so old from designs, designs of before, humanity language, can I get by, can I get away with it, who are you, who are you who is here, I'm only one. I can see, see fear, see age informing me, my age, years old, & age my century, my design, please help me, so, is sex, is sex is sexual, is why I ask you to embrace me, is why I say lie down with me & pleasures, songs, & far, & far forever forever my eyes, long my dark, my song, the details of my body, it's mine, I start its fear & sweat & eyes, I cant say merge, is it too late, do I emerge, what & ever, dont go away, please wait, I must be drastic energy for you, I will make the drama what you are, I cant say it, dont go, and. . .

Bernadette Mayer   417

Wait, a word, vision, wait. I merge with you it's pain & no illusion as I sway with wind. Wind is yours. I must say it. How is it you got the wind & not me, how did you find it? & how did it, winding painful in these currents, wind up swirled & loved by you, as on a stick of pain, & curling as though dying, dying crying not to lose you, saved by this: there's nowhere else to go, cause you made me, I design, & you're not lost to me now, & never will we swim in the same ocean, ocean of death, of poet death & of my eyes, ancient eyes screw up at you for what you've done through me, & throw it up & start, start over & now i know, you show me the prods & I am large branch in motion, at your prodding.

I hear you whistling & I'm calm & I am whole tree in motion, & I am dawn & doomed by your growing, your growing is my growing, & I cannot walk against you, I had hung you up by design & it's difficult to move against you, you are too strong, I am impostor, you are half, & the damage is elation & the damage is high, & it's cold, & it's rare, I can feel it, I am uprooted, upside-down, I am down, & I am new & I cease to have structure, I am torn, I am divided, my cells apart, there's no resistance, torn & calm calm & blown, & I am scattered in parts so rare, & so minute that I am all & am all, & spread over all & come into you & motion surrenders long ago & extending, screaming, at last, at last it's done, still only once, for once alone. The only reason, as a reason, to be alone.

So there were, and so there are: COLLAPSING STRUCTURES because we (or jonathan & ed) who are danger, let the posts that hold up one end, the lower end, of the barn, fall, or begin to fall, over the waterfall. The building begins to cave: possible escape through the higher third floor windows.

Helen, fear of incest is taboo, worse things could happen, she could have witnessed a double murder—if you are going to panic, dont you know what I mean, you, where there are fears, these fears coming from. . . . if only my stomach didnt hurt so much, dont you remember, I'm scared, doubtful the variety of the men & love some much, the bear came & ate my parents up, I grew with the wolves, he was angry because I didnt come through in the sex show, no, not him, another man, & my grandfather took the bear to Cummington, where there are few bears, there are few bears everywhere, it's safe, we must keep track of where the bear is helen, not lose sight of the bear for a moment, an instant, bear loose is dangerously current among people, & civilization, bear gone crazy, bear gone wild, & what about food, will anyone, is anyone willing to feed the bear, will his big bucktooth, salamanca silence structure, states of consciousness, & sawtooth design, is bear in cage now, & break loose, watch out for bears, & treat bear with care, they may attack you for unknown reasons, bear may have eaten frozen apple, bear may be drunk, you may never hunt bear, few bears are left, only one bear, nothing leaves. Even when bear is not helpless, or caught, you may not hunt bear, only a mad bear, bear gone wild, may be, must be, shot, be killed, be bear, the bear count. Helen is dead. Her stomach grew large & she died.

I ate a long giant fat new potato, with cream & butter, I felt dizzy, I felt sick, dont forget the shapes of the other vegetables, vegetables of only one shape, a father's vegetable, bought & paid for, my head tingles, my muscles ache, my eye is good, a virtuoso or prodigy, I thought I had eaten too much, crazy from the night before, in fear of her life, or his, crazy, forbidden taboo, & outside of this need, which is want, the creation of a new status, a new edge onto the circle of double of the states of varying consciousness, simply aware, free of the fear of freedom, the fear of serious motion, & motion on a tape, cut up, into the system, we have no plan, we have no addiction, we have good eyes, I can predict nothing, I cant predict something, never done, it will be done, I move monstrous shadows onto the wall, monstrous shadows on the wall aside, one by one, a form of pushing, & then, sudden dispersal. She dies & before I know she dies my stomach swells.

So, reread what had been written, write what cannot be thought, a verbal line is interrupted by these spurts from a terrific part of existence emerging. I must tell you about it. . . you make it new. A new state of courage beyond the prediction, a few words from you, you know that, a look, the glance, the eyes, the hands, the wonderful penis, there's no blueprint, there's no plan. For a single moment, we ache. Dont yes, & cut into the lines, & cut into them—reverberate people all over forever, I feel like I've been waiting forever, you are two. You will always be two, a part of you, that part of you, a terrific preserve perverse, continuing, for the animals aware, our country, nowhere, we fight, we spend all our money, we merge & reach, cant go no further, will reach, that's all, stretch a new muscle, integrate, this design, we are original, we are perched, we are white men flying, a white woman flies like a crow, for once, I am not addicted to your power but I am in it, as one, & out, & come, as many dimensions as can fall, I can fall, get up, & edge around the circle again. A constant winning. A message ends, no new words begin. No new words begin. Helen takes me in her arms & says, "If you want I will always tell you where I am."

Impending disaster, impending doom, unending impending, a reorganization of the employment of faculties, a pigeon flies by the window, the subject frames, see, just, so, much, who are you & how did I come by you? I'm anger, my anger is sense, drills into you, I am set in this piece, this, a move, you, little man doll, fall down, little woman doll moves closer, is wounded, you get up again, a miracle, we mate, like two watch faces on the same wrist band, water proof, I hope. Set them. Set them back a few hours to noon. Back a few hours to noon. Inked. Your move, in a certain number of hours-moves-hours. Like you mentioned before, as a reorganization of the one who was mentioned before, to the one my presence here speaks to, I shoot the moon men all at once, & then I've got all this time left to twiddle my thumbs. I've got to get a watch face & start needing it. There's no two ways about it, it's like pissing on the most analytical version of all the stars, it's like breathing, breathe the smoke of your own fucking brand. So I smoke yours. Kools. You renegade, why not admit it & set me free. I hate sets, chess sets. I hate power, except the power I have to show you something. I resign, so you cant move. There are some motherfuckers I would like to show the stars to, stars climbing up in the sky. Not you David. I dont mean you.

Stars climbing up, what a trick, for a trick you get money, see the ones in front of the sun, of course you can, lunatic, for a trick you get money, for a match you gotta win, I want evens, with you. Who am I speaking to? the market place. No deferrals, we do not cash checks, what a lioness she's tempting to be bitter, what a lion is, are you, that is, hungry? Eat meat. Pay at the store. Only thing is, you cant walk out, my legs wont hold you. Better trans-actions go on in the south, at the pole, at random, you wanna know why? The pole at the north, it cant be seen from there, it cant even be dreamed of. Opposites attract a couple hard lines of defense stinks money. Child loves patterns of any kind. Where am I going, I'm going out. I'm mad I'm playing, feinting, fainting mad, I'm always playing, I'm going out to play, I'll play with a few hims & hers, I'll say to one of them, I'll find a chance, & I'll say, you stink, you stink, & then, I'll laugh, you feel so bad, you want me to devour you? Then? Sure, O.K., whatever you say, you say goes, David says goes, what a mess, a great mess, stinking again, I'm no princess to end the day with a start sweetheart, wanna roller skate, I'm faster than you, wanna race, my time is race, I'm sinking ship, noble captains of which are covered with shit. My infection's a rage at the hospital, the doctors are covered with blood. Honor would spit, I just chew naturally, a full count, higher than ever, what a bloody tundra on the pitcher's mound. I curve a fast knuckle spit-one & spew it all round the bend to the monkey-moon, far fucking out, what a gas explosion that was, the crowd's still steaming, all energy is loose, & a little gnu says, new systems can be found on any field or fields. It's unreal, scared shitless who is. Fuck.

What a sport. A few of hers & I will mosey down to Mexico to suck cock, dribble the cream on our blouses, prostrate at the nunnery, invested into the order without oil on our heads, bare heads, new order of the all-of-the-saints cocksuckers, all-stars, south of the border, all the way down, no time for a snooze, it's the rising sun, so pay attention, I forgot to include the fee in this prospectus, coincident with the new day—you dont pay, we levi-tate, like elevators, sentient beings glow with the auras of saints, their very cells, amazing blue light, about two fade away, you'll never see us again, motherfuckers, you, a new race of blacks & us a visitation on your absence of color. We are close, we got this image from the church that made us angels in the red, a vicious lay. Sex slain is sex slayer. Now that we know this, we make the relic institution pay, shell out through its fucking teeth & eyes & nose & asshole, the well-hung robbers of our sex ingest themselves before our eyes, as we get up to go. We go over the preceding was a play. Now let's eat dinner, watch the tube, love design.

I want to leave this place, I want to get out of here, I want to move into an eternal space, the right space, I want to design it, have you freed me to addict myself to take that risk, escape no longer draws me in, just kill the pain, take my wrists in your hands, I cant find anything on the floor, we have no regular game, no drama, in the dark, everything's a mess. There's no end to it in a space as big as this, no walls, & I hate keeping on going, as if the production of something out of nothing, out of here where there is nothing, were worthwhile. Preserve my sainthood. You help to preserve it, perpetrating the finest evil that was ever devised, a false flame on the surface of simple veins bulging, their blood bursts back into the needle & then flows through back through the veins, southeast asia, axis, infusion, injection, replacement, maze, there was a fog all through the city before my eyes, I was sweating, what's the verdict of sleep: I cant find out: Observe me as I trance myself beyond death, Madame Pilau, Mr. Vankirk: write it down, a written record, dead poet, flying crows...

A trace, a stronger texture, impossible to tear, I still imitate, I still review, the fog goes on, there's a name for it: image, the surface of the eyes perverts senses, clouding heavy sky, diffusion in all directions, pose & empty. The idea that I would do anything for him has become a joke. Tomorrow the joke's perverted & I mean it again. What is it? That he would do anything for me is clearer, is accepted, is loved. Sure the love is inherent in murder, & the closeness designs a wish for death, the death of someone is the death of all. Reminded. Can you still see? A small dark & trembling tree is able to reassemble the the qualities of wind within its leaves, by means of them. The tree, its image, is a trick,

come out of nowhere, committed. Committed to an institution—
you must stay there; committed to a man or woman—you must
leave them free; committed a sin, a crime, you must commit
another, & commit another person to crime. You cannot be alone,
escape either. Bulbous images in dark balloons, lustrous growths
of them emerge from under your arms, from your groin from
whatever's beneath your feet, I cant imagine. Insects bite you, bite
your feet, lay eggs on them, hatch & grow even larger than the
haze of your eyes can conceal. You are eating.

Begin again, you leave traces, I dont mean anything, but short,
let go: & merging, complete, unexpected, cells of design, saint a
feint for message hood, & monk's disclosed the edge of the circle,
the mix is as the own body, is as mix with you, as lion is hungry,
as coarse & shooting, confines in cells & caves, mothers & fathers
at their stations, the rest riding four horses, directions, to poles,
we're children, where else can we go, go out to, we eventually
describe all possibilities, as you would describe a circle, tangent
to a point extending indefinitely, you could do it simply, with
your finger, with your finger in the air.

You're happy with that, I wont be satisfied, it cant be seen. Some-
thing funnier is going to happen. I'm committed to it like, fuck
jesus, phrases that ring in your ear, when I'm sleeping you pause.
It's too simple. Insects beyond calculus are at my disposal, magic
isnt subject to elegance, magic's not an art & neither is sleeping—
remembering the past backwards—power without senses—immer-
sion—submersion in the fluids of the own body—how great that is,
the idea of the own, the own body, without motive, the own
body, just a presence & a note—I make this present, in a way, to
you, any way I can.

Sensual power, greatest evil, without design, her rule, the impos-
sible, & pose the finite as a trick. Dont light on me. I'm patient, I
am cruel, I possess your trance. Excess ownership, deacons of the
church, metals drift on the sea. Anything. Pores. Surcharges. Sun-
spots. Masterpieces. Growth peppers edge entrance exit peer.
Like own, his murder tickles the ground, & spills out black ink,

Bernadette Mayer   423

knife drills into you, you are down. Live the night? In dark? And if you move, the movements of branches, cracking, branches speak attack—someone is holding them, bears down on you, threatens, curses, face down, you have no power, flooded, you cant find out, you were warned of secrets, you were told they were necessary, Rosemary, luminous yellow on a field of black, glows.

I sit next to my sister: I am imp of the perverse I have nothing to lose, this is addressed to you rose of the sea, marie & rose-marie, our secrets yellow of a black field on a field, sable, the letter whose imprint is red is black: Theodore-Nathaniel & Bernadette: you've got her name & I've got his eyes: Bernadette sinks ships: Marie, I want sex, I have someone in mind now. Theodore looks in. I change the channel right in front of you, no, I write in front of you now, addressing R: secrets are ours I'm talking to you, rose-marie, keep the order keep the peace—the gun I kill you with & the reverse: you're all there: listen to me, it's blue. Watch my black eyes. . .

Crosses for darkness, parallels for light. What trees are around you, which ones are living, can you move, hold your eyes open, do battle, bend down. This ground is the real ground, ground that circles & stratas to core, it boils, the only ground, crawling, nothing between you. Hanging & crashing. A flame. You are destroyed in the fire, you are black ash, you are stone, charred, fertile, a bed for hundreds of years of black work emerging. Your soul rejuvenates the soil, blood-red flower, an element of the mix, aces your grave. Now I am present, I'm there. When you see my face, white & design, you are fixed to it, repulsed, by its effort to love. We mix. Young & live forever, my blackness seeks the moment of your death, without accumulation. The legs of the flower, bending, screens in rest. Hide us.

ALAN DAVIES

" 101 "

Wind moves the last line.
Shadows cover the wall together.

Light coming in meets the horrible action.
A screwdriver made the smaller letters.

Fish float in light.
There was a problem of silence.

Small patches of sky held the feet.
A dull beat came here this morning.

He did not altogether pass the window.
The sky contains his eagerness.

Only a number obtains it out of doors.
The weak point made possible the new glasses.

Language speaks onto Ontario.
That is above them.

The country stay.
Siamese books comes to the very tiny animal.

The phone number is now the object and the subject.
There is a function of depths.

A highschool bus turns by plane for the hills.
People get speaking of him.

The language is lost by fours.
Sky is loosening.

Nowhere energy is out of the electricity.
Trains are thinking.

Each foil is merely flat.
Miss Betty speaks to a tongue.

The insect walk up somewhere over Ohio.
Smoke is more than yesterday.

Of thought only this communicate.
The pen mounts one.

Tenacious noise smoothes needed.
The landmark is the days.

Boots step from two dimensions to three.
Sleep marks us larger than the room does.

The scale is sound.
A terminal falls from the book to the floor.

There is from the earth to rock.
Morning comes out.

The fish is hidden by her colors.
The magazine is lit with black tonight.

Each sequence is wind.
Fruit rest for something else.

Moons recall attention overnight.
The three tools are to their throats.

A very young woman empties rhythmic sense.
The street is a different color from the coat.

Green candle stands forward through time.
The sounds come out of the air.

A small card breaks together lightly.
Furniture said he could not read the words.

The preening of the words was to let them drop singly.
The fall foliage is all out but one.

Newer days are a flat disc.
White verges the thoughts black.

Whirrings of air are behind three thighs.
Terse announcements come full of light.

The quiet under the table circles the set point.
The urgency is over the stilled audience.

The kneeling posture brings the one lock.
The second whitening is his career.

White separates come and see me.
The fruits are hard here.

The least usual of them is ice.
The three tomes are to the men's talk.

Weather is averse to famous children already.
The paved bricks should telephone Holland.

Light seethes as you say it does.
The curtains are in disagreement.

Duck is lilting.
Arms are increased at the furnace level.

A dancer reads not the way that it is done.
The words cling still researched.

Eventually the movement is colorful for adults.
Stucco is unfounded as yet.

Chairs lose pleasant music.
Wavelengths are to hear with.

The match instantly is a sticker.
Each key came green on the shore.

Going nowhere was the book in seven parts.
The home team loses it to her.

Sentences of verbiage go to her head and feet.
The postage becomes something unknown.

The racks are played too.
Paper is captains.

Lungs then go down light off the ocean.
Chances are his chair.

The transparent part are not simples, either.
Awkward signs will kill them.

Tobacco and logic have power but not here.
The quiet exterior is flat as hard is sharp.

Waves of paint drown a light in the trees there.
The person encounters all cloud.

The cubes are empty.
The glass space is a use for proportion.

A black cylinder thinks of me today too.
Three yellow objects are across time.

The remaining whites are good for cows.
A wanderer is ok.

The graphite is equipped with pavement.
Each line goes to where it came from.

The last one got sick.
Heide never is earliest in the counting.

Water goes in the street to its corner.
Highways are left to itself.

It's been in each pane.
Some serums are early death.

The journey is brown and green.
She contains potential light.

There is two-thirds full of air.
Radio waves add up slowly to the place setting.

The sky is the plate.
There's the gulls.

Cold is largest overnight.
Candles vibrate equally.

A good rain comes through the darkness.
We is inside.

He lost tasteful for the fourth time.
The wind is in smoke to the bedding.

Sergeants salute the presence of tedious waiting.
Chopin's etudes are laid over the fish to dry in heat.

Quince is a dime wasted.
He lay down with the tokens this month.

She could have done to the energies in fact.
He read the way.

The water is a direction for potential travel.
The pansy is lighter.

Alan Davies 429

Ear is the ways of sleep.
Static is their backs on the floor.

Categories of energy are the matrix not here.
Trinkets are before the moving.

The market is to the pace they're laid to.
That's the verbs into spacious fringes.

Pressure is tight in oval fabric.
Radio music overlays the singular.

People don't meet the soft night.
It happens by the umbrella.

We are sour not square.
They have the inner beats.

She listens upright and gone.
In December the waves are black.

The help works united in green and white.
She wrote the two browns.

Donated skills further the dream.
All the keys fit on drought.

The music washes beside the old paste.
The compass holds it up.

All the parallelograms are from the folds.
Three thighs chop up the skies.

Typewriters turn on grey at once.
His singing springs from the old watched ones.

The lamps are a broken time.
Her stated purpose reads them.

He is churlish in the night.
Two letters hang the bent knee.

The glass interrupts the heat.
Five works jerk for small rock.

The coat is alone for two separate hours.
A small grating sound makes the rooms.

The alcohol returns used or sweet.
The page holds their versions.

Ben stands in the largest possible sleep.
Part of the photograph captures its time.

The sky is drying on the rack.
The woman's body angles in mercury.

Part of the smoke that goes in came early and vaporous.
A walkway leads a white light in the blue light.

The cover marks the middling space.
Water in motion is paint or loss.

This sky makes the time from the moment.
The man gazes on wood earnestly.

The shirts keep track of the bit of stone.
Bigger and better books are under snow.

Two pairs of jeans become in the limb of the other man.
Two marks in one space can be said.

Today cost regress.
The letters crossed trepidation.

An ear now sets aura over energies over voice.
Relaxed feeling sets its aluminum.

Alan Davies 431

The people sitting down depart the station to arrive early.
Sound has gone light of feeling.

The moving body arranges for eulogy.
The typewriter keys progress in its sweat.

No one is close.
They leave out.

The size is no break in the text.
They reflect far away as a person.

Death may never be read.
Once the vegetables arrive they approaches.

Arguments to the contrary were how the language gets learned.
Water moved over unknown music.

Deductions opened on water.
The shadow takes attention.

The sight of the man stays the same without changing at all.
A cow came to America with no hair on his head.

The time was out of the bricks.
Sheets of thick rock entered.

The project were no ears worth listening to.
Number two was above the landscape.

The small green machine lay on top of the bush.
A wrist made light going out.

Pictures held the two photographs.
Fragments of work made black clothes on the wall.

77   80

432   Alan Davies

SHARED SENTENCES

Towards the latter days of the evening
a kind restored verbiage, a diligence
came down within, towards us.

You can choose one for life
not exactly misunderstanding obeisance
inherent in subtraction from the crowd.

An agreement is radial in this part, or
a partial and agreed seating
that circumvents the permission to answer.

Swear perseverent patience hales our times
for deconstructing quest, for sense
mixes with this appetite that makes.

Forgetting fail; nor remember to forget the insolence
of destined or desiring force
weakening these knees, our galaxy.

When with evening shuttered space or time
relaxes in our axing excellence, we tread
verbose nerves flattening our layered bed.

Or enter on translucent trust, loom
above the head; ineluctable, irrecoverably
nascent arms wane tainted at our limbs.

Recidivist tendencies in trekking devotions
harden, following elusive cues thoroughly
or dry blood's desiring to be taut.

Or evinces our entrapping sounds
in veinous closure over speech, demands
closure for these fretted hands.

A gentle proving paves us into pleading
these oblate lives; these vectoring, or
the obverse fantasy inflates to die.

The armored motion of engaging persons
seethes with reason; these outside lives
polish the line of sight we return by.

With productions of norm in sanctity, frames
elude all doing with an undone felt
securing feeling, vespers in your arms.

In returning into voices, on
claims, in thought's direct address
initialled pledges trace us to our words.

Inveterate, for reasons, loosen torsion
or pillaried high parts waste out
for losing passion, the bit that starts our heart.

Towards nor past these seen or unseen hands
with moist hierarchy bends this diligence,
starts in seating all that tested stands.

Coming, in parting this passage of time
proposes anklets for verbs, hierarchies
forming proportions, helping us home.

From deep changes with purges ablutions
rise, reach in us a pediment for speech,
this testament, a map prolonging sentiment.

Halving in effusive sentences twill veils
portend this hulled incisive self, abating
twin sails for distancing, in eyes.

Any lessening of feeling's strength,
a durable parameter, duress of being
ever in eventual caress and stasis.

Touring ardor or pacific languor talks
inventing equinox from dream, clearing head for
clarity specific language spots contain.

Never mind; these blousing anecdotes
tend within these trenchant anarchies
a penchant for more bluesy things to find.

Nascent flourishings detail our eyes
with children, nonidentical twins with certain
identical characteristics, a noun and a verb.

Fluctuant quadrants are our heros now,
the eyes discern a median their equal creasing
out of time, habitues the legs forget to fathom.

Alan Davies 435

Propelling arms within these arms at rest
arrest a new dominion; proportions clauses strengthen
in contrasting arrogance, lease aisles of time.

In trancing lives will linger sentience, an
obedient motion over stones that softness bends
to dust, standing vertical what horizontal lies.

Petting in a way with angled vision all occasion,
all tense, two cavalcading lives obey a fiction
in an instant, a desiring motion backing into breath.

ERICA HUNT

Dear Dear

The impact of the pipe wrench banging against copper lines somewhere in the building (the locations change) sets up an irritating vibration that can be heard in all the rooms; the guests have worn out the manager and his assistants with their complaints.

The current group of tourists don't come into the lobby anymore, since it's only their rooms which are air conditioned and the lobby isn't, the humidity there is thick enough to rub between fingers producing a harvest of slugs, too slow to be anything but friendly, but the brochures don't tell the guests that.

The bartender, a scrupulous fellow, boils the water he adds to bottles of liquor he then reseals and sends to their rooms.

Three days after the first pipe burst, the manager sent men to roll up the carpet and put it in storage. None of the guests have noticed, they seldom venture out there anymore.

Thanks to the facsimiles provided by the Visitor's Center the traveller can obtain some idea of what the plaza must have been like. The mausoleums suggest heroic themes. White granite columns, tapered at the ends bestow a timeless dignity to the facades gleaming white like ice cream beneath the fat noonday sun. The northwest edifice shows the scene of the sun fleeing into the west pursued by multiplying pigeons. The brass finishings at the end of the hallway gives the effect of a tree overcome with fruit, or the flourishes that adorn the spines of classical volumes. The lamps, hung directly behind each other, are painted nectarine and small birds etched on them create the illusion of a birdbath in a tent.

Imagine a sequence of murals based on the theme of the seasons. In Spring, rain takes up his hat, as the Sun enters, escorted by women attired in fog. The Sun rides a ram, her escorts wear their veils across powerfully built shoulders. The arms not in service to the Sun, are extended gracefully above their heads, palms up. In the tableau entitled "Summer," the Sun is spread across a blue divan ravished and fanned by her attendants. The canopy above them is the color of weathered copper, along the canopy's hem frolicking infants with the faces of old men play lawn bowl. In "Fall," leaves descend into the coffee cups of a few sidewalk cafe patrons. With the gaze of grateful insomniacs, they sit, interred. In "Winter," the Sun and attendants descend from the dais, picking up their umbrellas by the door. Rain again reenters, holding his hat at some distance from his head, letting forth a deluge.

The hero of the plaza is memorialized in an immense piece of green marble, in the center of the flooded rubble which had once been a tile reproduction of the solar system. His gaze is alert if not friendly. At one time, the hero had been imprisoned and forbidden pen and paper. He cleverly communicated with his colleagues by pouring milk into his rationed bread and taking it with him after meals into his cell, to use the milk to write letters on the blank pages of permitted reading material. Later, when these pages were held over a flame, the words could be read by fellow patriots. Once he was unexpectedly interrupted by a guard and acting quickly he ate the bread; from whence comes an expression, similar to one in English, "to eat one's words," but here it has a different meaning.

Dear

A pinhole of light. Spaces between the words widen them leave rivers on the page I look up. Blurry creases in the lines of trees' reflection standing horizontal in the water. Birds bellies' reflected there too smaller and larger as they veer. you, on your stomach peering into it one hand out as if to touch what's just behind.

I start to dance on the back porch to see shadows ricochet across the planks and railings something flowers umbra do subtly but tree limbs dropping over backyard fence in wind channels do spilling fruit.

Black dog in red bandana moves minimally in backyard all day from shade to shade and resists urge to wag tail at my shadow leaning across.

This is like sending a telegram to heaven "You don't know what you've missed."

Or perhaps knowing too well, you have stepped outside for a smoke.

Dear

I read looks. While passing a store today I noticed sawdust leaking from the dummy in the display. The figure moved abruptly every few moments as part of its musculature seeped out of its burlap skin.

Eventually it flattened out to fit the kind of envelope a box will take. It doesn't improve it but it beats reading the impression left in a round shouldered jacket as you wagging your shoulders in imitation of a serene coastal day on the mesa where August left a pair of shoes on the rocks that complicated the walk back.

If we're not who we were then then who are we now? Characters multiply as the dubbing editor loses interest. Imagination is not a jinn to slight; often we are forced to consent to the supposition that we are as continuous as others imagine us to be. When you change your mind though you make me accessory to a peculiar kind of treason.

Erica Hunt 439

In lighter moments I recall what I liked about you at a safe distance: the way you carry yourself like a Central African ancestor figure, legs bent and parted, stomach relaxed and your back curved in a delicate S comported with no hurry at all.

Secondly you seemed unafraid to call a relic a wreck a belief a symptom a skirmish a fool's errand. What some call domestic others call privileged torpor. What some call security from another angle resembles only the knack of imprisoning oneself with as many objects as can be dreamt of. Similarly I am willing to admit that I often arrange for dramas to be performed with the unwitting assistance of whoever happens to be standing around.

Still I'm struck by the coincidence. I got tired of waking up in a lake. You were eating out of your own hand and not liking it. It's impossible to have a more mutual subject.

JAMES SHERRY

from IN CASE

3.

Crushing idiosyncracies. Puffed up with abstract expressionism, her three year old voice made my skin crawl. Rabbet war : you think it's for smoked salmon? One pail of goods. Bembo. Soda— Lunch. Leon Spinx got great teeth. Exile by transformation. Domestic fortitude. Refocus this to read yourself. Frederick Jackson Turner proven right or wrong. What *we're* doing. Colors how new inflects plus. Slum bunny. They are sisters : We are brothers. Tip toe to mean. I used to be black, but now I'm condescending to my material.

&

Ration felt. Trying to say, appear in flood as let down your hair along the vice. Done dead, then you have me. Mandibles noise it that anonymous knew for sure how sore they let it be until confronting the savagery of their attacks. We left him at food. More weather it out, left there waiting the season in which rain's rain when it rains. Head still on the body, but not as its owner would have liked, not *any* head. The colonel of pocket parks among practically all available precipitation day and night furrowed in files, a combine, as the day comes misspelling assuredly assuredly. Indoors, behind the, out there like a scarecrow lapse. One out of a hundred strikes *something* in Maine. We know what she'd think, so steeped in rational cans, but possibility drives us on as year after year he placed flowers on her grave. Hartford, defamatory, belated name nobody; her smile from the bath worth a whole day like that. . . Then she went on in the next county, some country, on our way to gosh, always in a slow to do, when pines and bush prickle up against the moon. When some Tuesday. As dust off the road swept through the barbed wire, dust from the other field, he had his head on light, field of vision obscured by blood in the corners of his eyes that Bran would not notice from good fellowship. It was blue, grey, green, brown, all the personal colors in nature that supposed so much of our time was, inhibited by attempt to speak, tongue swelled in such people.

&

The Hudson lies building (a). Banks alternate articles and, foreshortened by carp, proud as Tigris masgouf bobbing on the map's waves, nervously look over a fin, rush drops up to Albany semidaily along starch and gum additives. The imperceptibly touching wall, Peter remarks, holds a heart of murder in his hand, a nuts and bolts saga of future self-aggrandizement. I'd like to tell you how it is, but I don't know anymore from Tokyo midget auto models as delivery systems for poisons or bio-rhythms as manipulated suicide means softer. We got over who dies, who sexes, who pines, who walks the spine of the Rockies overlooking sunset and sends no postcards.

&

To let you go means unclenching my fingers. To go means move knees forward. Why? Where? Five p.m. Sunday. Your husband takes a trip *every* two weeks? Imaginary breasts. . baby smell. . rubber nipples fill egg cartons, ambition martinified. We'd lick those Ayrabs in a minute. Unspoken theory, like persons we imagine we'd like to be in love with. Almost easy offer except my books pack ink every line in dear, but I never even say to alleviate that. Two capitulations: Plethora jellies, where the Persian Gulf would empty into proof. Doing it is proof. That it is alongside all of us doing it for want of it. I mean aren't you tired of, climbing ladders to a sill or underline or, clenched in the sandy edge of the stream; Ron or Peter or Peter or Ron up. Bicker because they wear the same shoe size. Program artillery by millennial desperation, they was being chased by the sea until we splash up on the beach in a lucite sphere. (Every sunbather says what (their skin is quite pink)) and we remark what brought us to this point. And here we are being rejected again at the door where only a warrant or gunpoint will go the limit near my hand below the bed in extremis about to white out the future with a phonecall. Let me hear a bell ring and I'll know what to say to you. I know what to say. Say it damn it. Why did you say it?

&

The general feeling of effective in program does justice hardly to going on, about and under my business in this case, followup reports, wound charts and autopsy reports being guidelines to procedure. Anyone, however, could say the same thing. I woke feeling terrible and felt terrible all day. I could hardly. A sedan comes around blasting and I drop to the sidewalk behind a hydrant, squinting to get the plate no., missing, because my eyes fill with tears from knocking the wind out of me on the unscrewed fire plug cap broken off its chain in an effort to trap me. My shoes feel gritting and shower under the trickle while bullets rule the atmosphere. Rather than feeling refreshed and alert, I touch and alienate D.A.'s witnesses, getting nowhere by referring to my feelings and making me out of them, since you don't understand that they mean you. Paragraph, masculinity. The jovial mood of the crowd supports an orange drink stand velvet rope I stand behind as you pass in your perfume. I remembered it just before they hit me with a blunt, bygone spirit of the 60's. Technical problem's been solved in the studio and we continue to be alive.

&

Menopause itself should not discredit a woman, but no one considers supporting it. Can I call you back in . . . three minutes? More wait pays custom about comfortable. This is no time to get finicky. Nothing anyway baroque around. Your bureaucrat's scepticism: I let my say slide through her, then examined the way out, to view remains. We heard this over and over and were waiting for the vestiges to bronze. She told him what she had told us. After we were through, it was late as late could be, and twice I interrupted to say something, but reinforced my silence finally each time a gulp. Jealous visit very elaborate. But finally what he meant came out. Finally, it belongs ahead, to participate in lusty give him a bad time. It's not enough to be just human you gotta, what's more, not a word I could, regardless really what we'd seen and knew was the case, clearly a matter of misspelling held over him five years and what was that compared to how *I* feel about human dignity. He knew she knew he knew him knew her knew he knew him. Every fire custom, lady, don't throw yourself about the truck. My own infraction means nothing to me if I don't feel bad, honest. Why, Ralph, I never knew you cared. Who I know. He posed her pose for her. They had farted around long enough, but habits linger attentively. Just to clear your head about that saying something business, constructed by fluid overdrive, sought and feared with wild-eyed resistance.

&

Meanwhile other bodies, wings darned by ears, sooner call nothing without shape, but it occurs at moments, by bread alone, the time I began to mixture, giving way myself to be returned from the door she sent me to, across deserted areas figure already my hand could not touch. Desire to do it gets me going, then thinking of,

444 *James Sherry*

difficulty that could be encountered by attitude. Let me go, let me be, let me stay, I'll do whatever you say, here you like these I don't, student loans, evidence, besides I like rugs on walls. Or bones last man found in his fish. No way to be only. Less capitalization than possible. End the business, reroute feelings and get impotent. Ha, she said then. Just careful. How usual crowd extremities leaked away into another epoch attitude. Airmen jotted down through cumulus to accumulate data again. The future a thinner present. The airmen jot, mermaid. Deliberately manhood type to let her go her way. She's not interested; she's no trouble. Get out so much taste, but no one's willing to take one. Antiaphorism addict. The little clicks make music to mean. July 10. Hear it. Starting event conducted:

&

Later tiles, an add craven with Sunday's, we b*t*e the the, (I like Listless. We opt out, pickover an alluvial selection, the better to hug with restless plunge. How do I owe a metaphor allowance? Bob envelopes before such. Later Loonies : A broken chicken. Marxist glosses, 45 rpm hem and . . chartreuse. I know her, but she don't know me. Always had strong feeling, smell ambition, muscles, farther from, ersatz, older. Those novels and what slats pose as people detergent the. I always wait to see those large colors. ERE 3) so you're one, too. What baseball that (o yes we do . . Attribute)). Do it go the far. Almonds 1) raw 2) cooked 3) sugar.

&

We have a lot of close animals. The one left really was me. I'll like to so . . . Whatever you say, only say I could not say. Stitched by the bar and allowing firth, or a name at a distance like triangles

James Sherry 445

tension fretter rain by the flush polite. North? Yes. Shouting ex new clothes,—I got a green one and a purple one.—. (Going on morning star vanity.) Breaking in with words, the customer is entitled to recompense of self; some anyway cannot be denied, but by surgery they have in other cities here legislated against superior pressure. To find out the crazy outside feels sorry, too. The murdered man don't feel nothing, so don't get any fancy ideas about writing in your head. I'm protecting property, period. (Sex possessed generations mingle. (You always think so where you're alone.)) What I forget, my weakness, for flies, stroking, divining, Indonesian blasted monkey. When I speak, I make money, it says; doesn't ever shut up. Don't use it to confuse, please. I'll sit and think as long as you want, then I'm. What was wrong with him let him finally see the important clue, which. He sweated in the car, he rubbed in the subway, he became Orion, he fled no further, but stalked the receipt please to sell sleep.

&

Why *didn't* he ask? How to know whether it was pride or that he simply didn't want to? There is something else? There *isn't* anything else? What is claustrophobia? How many eggs chicken? He left? He gave a chance? He vomited and vomited? There is no pattern to moon? Faded lines the stars follow rein? We are getting very old? Collect adipose? "Overgrown conscience?" Matter of fact unreason?

&

The changed point of view relieve me so I almost cried taking the part of that near frantic man whose friend he had divined was dead. The you accidently stumbled through the screen into the read once again where connections the were. But I was not carried off but dropped it in this cup for you to find. His acumen did *not* lesson one. A mirage, an institutional tongue : Basics to back with others.

&

Although the end the detective only solves (materialize from the 25th century with the genetic clue and the murderer writes a letter before his birdseed suicide fails), not even science can bring back the unknown for long, overlapping papery summer. The lizard plays along this faith that if you read it you get yourself back, excitement questioned by conscience, more writing than literature. And we'd let them down the knot of another vivid hustle, the huntsman still at large in the grey and green town, on this large and ancient river that bleeds her. Here we'd let sensibility loose and regret we had when we did and call it it, though that would be a mistake, for detection finds. The summer music shed its scales. See again. Light shells. This crime was cause by . . . Are you along?

SHE'LL BE COMIN' 'ROUND

She'll be comin' 'round the mountain when the shell sometimes is
    empty.
She'll be comin' sometimes and the shell is an evasion,
when she comes around the mountain
to put in an appearance;
and this is the introduction we're all trying' to come 'round to.

She'll be drivin' six white and well-bred young mares.
She'll be tryin' to be comin', when one of the horses slips on a
    curve.
but the traces hold her up
like a beautiful horse about to describe
the great vehicle she'll conduct, when she comes.

And we'll all go out to meet her when the well is dry and cracked
and the water is too neutral to hold
even a chance encounter when we're trying to be comin'
and breathe too much or that's what I
heard when tryin' too hard to meet her, when she comes.

And we'll all have chicken and dumplings in a context
of the human shell, water in the trough,
the gopher holes, how hot leather is in the desert mining town
except to the horses,
when she comes.

448   *James Sherry*

RAY DIPALMA

EXILE

Above the tracks
a slight embank-
ment. Limestone.
Mud. Weeds. A
concrete wall
three feet high
stretches as far
as the eye can
see. Then the
traffic on the
boulevard. Homes.

Below. An iron
meadow. Tar
soaked timber.
Cans. Small
stones. More
weeds at the
back of the
filling sta-
tion near the
track's edge.

To the left
two ware-
houses. Win-
dows broken.
One wall gone.

A staircase
dangles like
the torn wall-
paper above it.
Two women eat
from a paper
bag in its shadow.

To the right
a long ramp
to a viaduct
carries the
traffic over
the boulevard.

GEO

Nothing west beyond
the Canary Islands
along an irregularly
built street turning
to the left
square pocket mathematically
irresistable gold poured
into some hollow
sticks treated as
a piece of
kindness with respect
to the zodiac
and the cycles
of change keys
the profounder the
completer keeping track
of seven planetary
pointers eyes on
months wood glass
silk a depressed
weather color every
now and then
I tell her
a dream I've
had so she
can have something
to analyze Nile
China compelled to
believe the number
ladder If addressed
as If not
mythograph
translators in
the song grotto
a fabric of
charts here is

a piece of
game long since
known to us
as the assumption
when I think
it over however
I am wrong
in treating it
as a greater
imposition at the
bottom it imposes
obligations on me
which I must
be prepared to
make sacrifices to
fulfill anthropos and
sophist a dynamism
in an ordinary
idea mind more
marked satisfaction recognized
dull eyes set
fast tea for
garlic by violence
by great leading
the effects and
properties of ideals
and standards dim
memory only failure
in the face
of privilege can
dislodge common and
direct or what
the horozontal obtains

from PLANH

I

Written granite
outlining two rows
of sultry atmosphere

profile
on the horizon
lofty and obstinate

drew his attention
planted
its initial stages

balancing
continuous
resounding

two principal
ornaments sly
in the middle distance

sleeping with
the action
of his tether

confident
thoughtless
generous

every day
hat stuffed
fossils trembled

imprecise
they asked
for the monotony

authenticity
rolling vision
from staring eyes

into a kind
of stupor seized
by a low voice

that would be
quite sufficient
in this place or that

about their dream
a limited horizon
distrust for balance

movement and novelty
answered
for everything

lay in splinters
smiled at the wheel
the axle broke

and nothing was missing
filled pitch black
like a dream

knees drawn up
mouth open
moonlight

V

A new world
artful as monkeys
without a moment for reflection

bore no expression
follow the procession
poisoned opinion

a single block
he sighed and sighed
he was full of enthusiasm

specks of dust
under the microscope his
voice in the other direction

pompous or subtle
but lyrical disordered
false as fortune

to find disguise
prefer this charming
motionless green velvet

delirium
pick a piece
squatted on a bit of stone

just been raining
bright patches sparrows
through the beeches

with one hand
there another time
pleased he did not confide

Ray Di Palma   455

the prospect
was the subject
bolt the door

light
taking its story
involves mass

dilemma
always agrees
he waited

syntax fantasy
grammar illusion
Voltaire to tell a crow

darkness
conforms to reason
narrow by memory

by intuition
disturbed by doubts
the indignant taste

a bell rang
reconcile delay
chill preliminaries

who had recognized
the most sacred
expression

language fastened
full of nerves
to the talking side

VI

Ceremony
the triumph
planting a drum beat

workmen passed by
alluded to good fortune
the shadow of its branches

had visions
had the advantages
interrupted

files and ranks walked
they became aristocrats
fascinated with glib privilege

gazing up compromise
a contest of delicacy
a plan of action

but politics excited them
the avarice
of neglected ideas

dusty sweaty ragged
weasel-faced inventions
collect stones

clear up the calm jokers
workers murmured and bosses
applauded the moment into conversation

under the clock
in the doorway
the loudest voices dispersed

Ray Di Palma   457

to eat cheese drink cider
nobody wanted
the door kept opening

under the beeches
scratches and bruises
light through the holes

turns the axiom
between phrases when
words lead to crimes and opinion

eyes opened wide
to liberate rights
and frauds out of rabbits

plaster walls share
a rack full of books wing and
torch the democratic stuff

sit them down in a whisper
equalize golden with a plank
catechism of anecdote and shoulders

revenge in a gentle voice
a sort of hallucination
stretched a sack on his back

the dogma of material interests
chinese vases ample armchairs thick curtains
disappear with his face in his hands

the noise of forks
the jaws on the slope
of the abyss

Voltaire the upholstery
sunshine and a damp wind
over dead leaves

back head model
closing his eyes
ceremony movable and immovable

two fluids
phalanx monopoly
thunder and dancing

a chain held high
theories shaken by a laugh
beautiful books and a quiet life

slamming the door
the horizon
an angle of spite

distinction shocked distance
speechless tongues
tapped at the window

blindness art and charm
a rapid gesture
with a long lever

X

One deep in the dark
two sharp like a *k*
vowels shrill

fables to split
memory too much wolf
staring at the ceiling

Ray Di Palma 459

above the ear
the bump of detected
philosophy

where it was quiet
in the shadow
reflected in the mirror

instincts slamming
out of his pocket
justify method and guile

the birdlike faces
of enthusiasts
exchanged observations

opinions
dahlias owe
ringing the bell

Galileo and Newton
gulf the cardinal points
this chair takes bearings

pivots on a long needle
framed behind glass
in the shade of a barrel

marking the far
horizon as if it were
running with the spark from a stone

inventing four wings
and nectar
on the edge of ditches

great bundles
of oak pegs
aligned

with a single shudder
stretched and tangled
in the ears

sanction in a low voice
some notes
irreducible motives

useful exaggeration
the plus sign
removed

ashes
might improve
a delicate instinct

examples are recorded
symptom songs
over a spinning method

shreds tongued
to win the indispensible
mark of origin

mouth wide open
the convenient interval
began with a breath

caught on facts
path talked and seen
read dreaming

sly loop of copper
wire attached
to a silk thread

pen and ink
on a pile of stones
witnesses

out of the wall
stray dogs
done in a pyramid

pushed as a basis
for acts
thought hunted

chatted the system
evidence be
some funny ideas

no more chronicle
turned embellishing
in red buildings

to fix a signal
eyes half closed
with a spasm of pleasure

silence signature
showed the bottom
made deeper

devoid of compromise
the main ideas
following crier

owls which
eat grass
windows are open

Asia runs out of
these oscillations
the convulsions

travel to the stars
make up stories
by the sea

look after bright
pieces in hands
left alone

JANUARY ZERO

I take a glass. I fill the glass. I drink the water. I wash the glass. I dry the glass. I give the glass to you. I take a bottle of milk. I put the bottle on the table. I open the bottle of milk. I take a clean glass. I fill the clean glass with milk. I give a glass of milk to you. I drink a glass of milk.

I go to the door. I stop at the door. I push the door open. I go out of the door. I go into the hall. I pull the door shut. I go to the EXIT. I stop at the EXIT. I push the door open. I go out of the EXIT. I go into the hall. I pull the door shut.

I come to the door. I stop at the door. I push the door open. I come into the room. I pull the door shut. I come to the ENTRANCE. I stop at the ENTRANCE. I push the door open. I come in at the ENTRANCE. I come into the room. I pull the door shut.

I walk to the window. I open the window. I look out. I close the window. I walk to my seat. I sit down. I stand up. I walk to the door. I open the door. I pick up the letter. I close the door. I walk to my seat and sit down.

I pick up the letter. I open the envelope. I take out the letter. I read the letter. I put the letter on the desk. I put the envelope on the desk. I stand up. I walk to the desk. I take a book. I open the book. I look at a picture. I close the book. I put the book on the desk. I walk to my seat and sit down.

This is my book. I open my book. I turn the pages. I look at the pictures. I read the book. I close the book. I put the book on the desk. I walk to my seat and sit down. It is six o'clock. I wake up. I get out of bed. I throw the covers back. I close the windows. I wash my face and hands. I brush my teeth. I put on my clothes. I brush and comb my hair.

It is half past six. I take two rolls and butter. I put the rolls and butter on a plate. I take two eggs. I break the eggs into a cup. I put salt and pepper on the eggs. I eat a roll and butter with the eggs. I take a cup of coffee. I put sugar into the coffee. I put cream into the coffee. I take a spoon. I stir the sugar in the coffee. I stir the sugar with the spoon. I eat a roll and butter with the coffee. I eat eggs and rolls for breakfast. I drink coffee with cream for breakfast.

I take a loaf of bread. I put the bread on the table. I cut six slices of bread. I put butter on each slice of bread. I put chopped onion between two slices of bread. I put chopped meat between two slices of bread. I put jelly between two slices of bread. I make three sandwiches. I wrap the onion sandwich in wax paper. I wrap the meat sandwich in wax paper. I wrap the jelly sandwich in wax paper. I wrap a piece of cake in wax paper. I put the sandwiches and cake into my lunch box. I put two oranges into my lunch box. I fasten my lunch box.

It is seven o'clock. I put on my coat and my hat. I take my lunch box. I say, "Good by." I walk to the streetcar. I wait until the car stops. I get on the streetcar I pay my fare. I ride the street— car to work. The streetcar stops. I get off the car. I walk to the ENTRANCE. I go in at the ENTRANCE. I go into the locker room. I take off my coat and hat. I put my lunch box in my locker. I hang my coat and hat on the hook in my locker.

Ray Di Palma 465

It is half past seven. I go into the work room. I say, "Good morning" to all. I go to my place. I begin to work. I am a worker. I work until twelve o'clock. It is twelve o'clock. I stop my work. I wash my hands. I go to my locker. I take out my lunch box. I go into the lunch room. I sit near a window. I open my lunch box. I eat my lunch. I eat sandwiches, cake, and fruit. I drink coffee for lunch.

It is half past twelve. I put my lunch box into my locker. I go out into the street. I walk around and listen. I come back and go into the work room. I work until five o'clock. It is five o'clock. I stop my work. I wash my face and hands. I brush my hair. I put on my hat and coat. I take my lunch box. I say, "Good by" to all. I walk to the EXIT. I go out at the EXIT. I walk to the streetcar. I ride on the streetcar to my home.

It is a quarter to six. I come home. I say, "Good evening." I put my lunch box on the table. I hang my coat and hat on the hooks. I wash my face and hands. I brush and comb my hair. I go to the dining room. It is a quarter past six. I go to my place at the table. I sit at my place. My plate is on the table. My knife and fork are beside my plate. My spoon is beside my knife. I fill my glass with water. I take my napkin. I unfold my napkin. I eat my dinner.

I take a bowl of vegetable soup. I take bread and butter. I eat the bread and butter with the soup. I take a peach and a pear. I eat the fruit. I drink a cup of coffee. I fold my napkin. I put my napkin at my place. It is a quarter to eight. I go into my room. I look at my good coat. I see the coat is torn. I put on my old coat and my hat. I fold my good coat over my arm. I go to the tailor. I give my good coat to him. I show him my torn coat. I say, "Please mend my coat. I want it Saturday night. How much will it cost?"

It is a quarter to nine. I am tired and sleepy. I say, "Good night" and go into my room. I take off my clothes. I hang my clothes on the hooks. I put on my dressing gown and slippers. I go into the bathroom. I turn on the hot and cold water. I hang my dressing gown on a hook. I get into the bath tub. I get into the warm water. I wash my body with the warm water. I wash my body with the soap. I dry my body with a towel. I put on my night clothes. I brush my teeth. I put on my dressing gown and slippers. I go into my room.

I set the alarm for six o'clock. I put the alarm clock near my bed. I turn down the covers of my bed. I open the windows. I get into bed. I lie down. I pull up the covers. It is a quarter past nine. I go to sleep.

TED GREENWALD

from WORD OF MOUTH

Experience a table of
Contentment   Thumb
Through a continental
Drift index   Break in
The open another case
on skid would converse

Obviously not enough
Place starts to allow de-
Cay to mean a thing to
Anybody   Great cold wea-
There feeling   Whether in-
Side or outside bucket

Straighten out   Follow
For awhile   Bounce ounce
Off nouns   While announc-
Ing for bouncing   Gossip
Sip capsule swallowed
Swollen pull wool over

Temper imply temperment
By taking temperature   A-
Long comes the answer to
Everybody's dreams   No
Fantasy life worth speak
Easy ing about   Sharing

Spit   Shoulders   Live long
Day enough to spend gotten
A job bath   Once-a-mon-
Th-what-a-crowd even-
Ing phobes bot wet sand
Carry streets in litters

But literal dot dot dot
Dat's possible   Woman's
Part in   Suggested may-
Be men   Gravitate via
Gravity to a chair man
Dine on an old agenda

Too much escalates to
The street emotions   Too
Hot to handle to them
Too often wait to the bit-
Ter tears end   Tiny print
Contain all toes it's gonna

Fidget louvers follow
Airflow along a sudden
Diagram   Aggravate an
Injury   Between weeny
Miniature picture of
Translate blemishes senses

Come to   And make wel-
Come   Arms open   Discov-
Er to be true   Twelve
Times twelve in fifteen
Minutes   One city to
Another cylinder capacity

Examples replace im-
Pressions   Pressure al-
Most itself in space
Colon unbearable   Too
Quiet   Rocking as   Point
Of contact suggests

Coronary curtains   Ur-
Bane banish gestures
Vanishing room   Oh, an-
Other concentrate on an-
Other century   Candidate
For the true did-it funny

Alone with a throw-in
Working session into a
White vein in a black
Arm   Gentle person pile
Of crap feel good ev-
Erybody tends to think

A lot of shit, that crap
Scratching a lovely per-
Son personal remark
Land bouquet in mid-
Dle of a bunch   Want
To know why as chin

Fall for   Special
Peculiar skin skill
Unwilling to concede
Proceed with hand
Lotion   Motion to en-
Ter   Quick changes

Total message: a small
Pillow   Beam: barrel
Bed now   Nothing will
Break: doubt it   Un-
Seen waters: gurgled
Whirl around waist

Twtich   Wasted   Astir
With what those fan-
Tasies ask to dream
Face pastry   Dimpled
With haunting melody
Totter off to bed   Die

A gram of sense   In-
Side lounge   Padded
Door walking quietly
Ass behind   Sense
Of where back is after
Reliability afterglow

Bell who's holding   To
Spend all the time
Pending   Patent parent
Injection visions   De-
Cide to make incisive
Remark incision are

Fresh faced   Packed to-
Gether with rest of rest-
Ing body   Ringing look
Recognize lean back
Take rest   Make over
From little muscles out

Sure, call up   City
Leaves refreshed   Why
Rush in   Ladder   In
Addition to   On the
House   Voice coming
Through a sane passage

Cup: Something in
It Hand: pressed
Close to what's seen
As a side Inside
Story: something in
It watch very close

Maybe more Wake
Scallop edge Fig-
Ure in other debris
That's all past now
One chance, that's
It, expect same

Different Greenish woe
Blue shadows Breath
Easy Expect to accom-
Plish Don't think this
Goes with what Listen
To give-a-lift-to white

Requests Standard cun-
Ning Alone in the corner
Ornery slate Pecking or-
Der Levels of intimacy
Deposit Control this not
That way of controlling

Working out Talk out
Side door of mouth Re-
Peat after Flutter
Vacation headiness
Flight out early Fly
Overhead interior

Show an interest   Drive
Nuts   Sit in the middle
Of the middle road car-
Buretor   Last-minute
Invite   Tear open   Read
On the spot   Out damage

Arrive on time   Through
Door good office windows
Of management   Wander
Around friends   Make
Up for it   Stenography
Photograph model gun

Push in door   Structure
Saying   In fact   Fancy
Meeting here   Ligatures
Face expression of   Fill
In the blank blanket
Link with the known

Tracer barge   Move
Slowly on the move
Up the vertical along
The horizontal   Tal-
Ent for fucking up
Talent for beseeching

Throw light on rock
On   Big wind coming
Along without an
Array of characters
Clean out deadend
What's-in-the-air

Too-close-to-closed-
Mouth-statement-of-
Messing-around-with-
Preposition-lead-in-
To-messing-up-by-
Only-missing persons

Witness rust   Prevail-
Ing mode   Punctuate
By chewing out while
Fullest extent of law
Averages verging on
A lawnmower motor

Sure busy   Sure could
Use a cold drink   A
Hot shower   A hand
Sure need a bite to
Eat   An exact defin-
Ition for   An ear

Get easier, no way
To treat to   Reheat
And re-eat   Reenact
Exact order of events
Break off in mid   Len-
Gth of message to   Nth

Big city leave the same
Way slow minded the
Store   Bound by nary
A skinny   Face forward
Thinking back on   Fol-
Low lower instructions

Provide details to the
Letter   Discover a new
Way of doing   Things
Just seem to add up
Again and again   Way
Of keeping score by

Stress energy   Stress
A shitload of values
Stress correct dress
Stress mind over dot
Dot dot   Forgot what
Out of sight out of

Whenever old friends
Get together   Sage
Flash long lashes
Turning inward   Clear
A twin   Blame em-
Blem man-to-man lemma

Corollary capillary
Shorter spans   Pan
Out   To be good val-
Ue never know isn't
Going to keep anybody
From attending tendency

Neat messing around
Kind of day take walk
In cake   Pour intended
Bundle of emotions via
Feelings in a party par-
Ticular direction etching

```
     work between
          spine
Working position
                    whole
       raw face
       told then

Minimize the number
Of removes third per-
Son so-and-so's to be
Found in any one two
Three place external
Secretions shun only

Criticize method noth-
Ing more than   A way
To look back on   A
Weary   Change direction
Uphill give-it-the-gas
Amused by some words

No end in sight   Endless
No's   End to all and sun
Dry modern knowledge
Acknowledge towel a-
Round squarish peg
Head fit in wrong to right

Balance of alliance
Information   Brilliant
Early riser   Lean over
To examine   What an
Important find   What
An important behind
```

Store front in front of
Invented inventory of
Details of invention
Flutes around various
And dry cons   Already
Using new   So why not

Contend with personal
Reason for   Easing along
Other side of the sug-
Gested digest of diges-
Tion   Indent   Dentures
Reaches the listener

Can't quite get it   As
In inanimate object
Together   The pitch   The
Catch   What's the   Or-
Der very imported   Chew
Away shun   Event

Sit hew away from
Sun   Leave over   Cat
Out noticing these
Confuse derrick way
Forever   Go home and
Type up a new type of

IN THE AMERICAN TREE
IN THE AMERICAN TREE
IN THE AMERICAN TREE

III. Second Front

SECOND FRONT

All writing

is a demonstration of method

CARLA HARRYMAN

FOREWORD

The notorious files have ceased to elongate posterity. One might call for an *oeuvre* in reverse.

Alone, two lunettes practice in a port balancing on columns of permanent infinitive visions. Without pressure people go along with drinking and the perpetual movement of cascading eternity. You see her quiddity all the time.

Abstractions, fundamental photographic representations of unembellished objects, swarm onto the bridge. This is not clear in a nihilistic living room with absurd trinkets.

The grandfather fortifies aquariums belonging to a young girl otherwise known as Mom.

Creation not reality.

And so it was with excited fervor that we pressed upon their city a gratis or sublunary sky, the adulatory milk-filled reserved vestments of clouds, abruptly addressing the downbeat of the body, anybody's figure.

There is a seed of truth in the picture.

Human carriage enters the inner topography of the building. The hand walked down the road.

(1980)

RON SILLIMAN, BARRETT WATTEN, STEVE BENSON, LYN HEJINIAN, CHARLES BERNSTEIN, BOB PERELMAN

for *CHANGE*

Begun in the sixties, the writing of the American poets gathered here for *Change* matured into an organized, ongoing literary discourse in the following decade, a period of significant transition for the United States. From the perspective of capital, the war in Indochina was lost, a critical blow to national military prestige. More importantly, 1974 marked the end of capital's longest "boom," the expansionist years following the Second World War (on top of which the essential optimism of every variety of "New American" poetry had been constructed). Simultaneously, the largest generation in U.S. history, the "baby boom" of the 40's and early 50's, passed from college to the daily practices of material life. Tied to that generation and crippled from the beginning by its rejection of historical knowledge, the American New Left rapidly dissolved, although several of its veterans were to re-emerge as leaders of cross-class movements based on forms of personal oppression, as women or as gays of either sex. This moment also saw the first resignation of an American president. For writers, persons constituted as "individual subjects" by their social context, and as subjects of a specific type, previous assumptions were shown to be false. Career expectations, within literature and elsewhere, for example, had been *socially imposed* with no real comprehension of the impact of technological innovation and the resulting recomposition of American class structure. Both the writer and (any potential) audience found themselves displaced, their existence in jeopardy. In such a context, it is no accident that poets such as this *Change* grouping should turn their attention to the origin of this displacement, the constituting mechanism of "private life," language itself.

RS

"New form means new content." The congruence of the writings presented here is evidence of a break with prior meanings. For example, the New York School, an immediate predecessor, aestheticized language "as such." In John Ashbery's *The Tennis Court Oath*, and often in Frank O'Hara, language appears as a material applied to a surface; the analogy is to paint. However, the early work of Clark Coolidge changed the potential of language "as material." Words are the axis, rather than the work of art; Coolidge's disciplined, extensive writings extend art into language rather than narrow language to art. Similarly, the "organic form" of the postmodern Romantics, beginning with Olson and Creeley, which makes writing an act "in process," has been completely rethought. An ethical concern with the "fate of the trace" has returned "process" values to the exterior world in the work of Ron Silliman, Lyn Hejinian, and Steve Benson. Out of this ethical concern, much of the writing presented here addresses direct perception rather than prior literary examples; an early instance of this is in the work of Robert Grenier, where the attack on lyricism in Creeley's *Pieces* is transformed into an attack on the word. This phenomenological basis for writing, implied in the work of the Russian Formalists, connects the work of the American modernist masters of the "word as such," Williams, Zukofsky, and Stein, to the illusionist or constructivist values to be found in Michael Palmer, Bruce Andrews, or Barrett Watten. Exteriorized writing procedures, from sources as different as the cut-up technique of Burroughs and the chance methods of Cage, discover in much of this work both radical psychologies and the insistence on fact. Ethics have been refracted from style; the progress of the work in the last decade reflects this. It has been the writing itself, rather than theory, which has led to further results. Publication in literary magazines and small presses, such as *Tottel's* (edited by Ron Silliman), *This* (Barrett Watten and Robert Grenier), *A Hundred Posters* (Alan Davies), *Tuumba* (Lyn Hejinian), *Roof* (James Sherry), and *Hills* (Bob Perelman), has preceded the articulation of theory in *L=A=N=G=U=A=G=E* (Bruce Andrews and Charles Bernstein) and in the Talks (the San Francisco Talk Series, organized by Bob Perelman). In fact, attempts at a program seem to divide the stylistic congruence into dissimilar intents. But from the point of view of the writing, there has been a recognition at a point in time: style has an ethical rather than aesthetic basis, and the act of writing is set up on a different axis as a result. The writing presented here is clearly a synchronic phenomenon; the important question is the present which it reflects.

BW

The works of these writers challenge and confront one another, criticizing and reconstituting the structure of an unwieldly body of work, aware by a network of personal and professional associations of its function as a resonant chamber as much as as an agent of publicity. Having integrated the impact of the post-World-War-II protest movements both as critiques of authority and as arguments for rights and prizing an awkwardly marginal status in the corporate hegemony, these writers have developed strategies that test more markedly than they indoctrinate, resist rather than seduce or assure; apparent units within their works often function by apparently nonprogrammatic and yet highly intentional juxta-positions such that principles of opposition and analysis are integrated and face off against circumstances including the reader, who is proffered no code to break nor transparently methodical procedure to appreciate. The abrasive assertiveness and lack of agreement among persons of warmly shared interests encourages them to reconsideration of individual custom. The truism that the only people who now read poetry are themselves poets is thus understood rather as potential than as limitation: the reader is presumed not as a consumer of the experience sustained by the poem but as a fellow writer who shares contentiously in the work and can willingly answer the uses of the medium which the writer feels impelled to undertake (and so extend the generation of literary work without indulging the pretentious fireworks of avantgardism for validation, with its tendencies to shortsightedness of enthusiasm and blindness of shock effect). Within this group collaborations on composed texts are numerous and diverse in form and method; the emphatic and critical recognition they bring to magazine anthologies, public readings, talks, performances, and even correspondence as objectified and significantly collaborative works bespeaks a particularly positive valuation for the parameter of interaction between parties engaged in literary acts. The social functions of language are crucially material to the interest in writing; these writers are highly sensitive to the ubiquity of sources and receptors and markedly propose conscious value to what could otherwise be taken as impingements in a literature of autonomous display.

SB

It is useful, here, to consider the writer as the first and immediate reader of his or her own writing. The writer goes more than halfway to meet lines or sentences advancing on their own. The language itself materializes thought; the writing realizes ideas. One discovers what one thinks, sees, says, and as the words unfold the work, the work, directed by form, extends outward. Language in writing such as that collected here is no longer an intermediary between the writer and the world or between the concept of the work and content. Language is not the instrument of expression but the substance. It is inseparable from the world, since it is in the nature of language to be entangled in a system of reference and cross-reference. In a work such as Ron Silliman's one paragraph prose block, SITTING UP, STANDING, TAKING STEPS, the unit is what's contained between the initial capital and the period, that is, the sentence. It is a sentence which lacks a verb yet remains active, even restless, and in the present tense. "Along the coast, on cots, in coats. A warm new storm. Blue ink on a white page between red lines." This is not a diarist's record of observed detail; no eye ("I") could be thus ubiquitous. It is the realism of language, language under pressure, fully present. In works such as those collected here, content is not imposed from without; rather, it emerges from independent initial points in the language itself. This method of composition, for that's what it really is, guarantees the possibility of a proliferation of works whose writers insist on their independence from any fixing program or orthodoxy. Their work avoids the reductive (one notes

Steve Benson & Lyn Hejinian   487

the distaste for closure) and remains full of expectation. In a brief discussion of Bruce Andrews' one line poem (published in the Paris Review in 1972), "Bananas are an example," Nanos Valaoritis writes, "In what way does this sentence differ from the poetic metaphor of the modernist style? It is that it is truncated. An "example" of what? The sentence remains open, available to multiple continuations. It thrusts polysemanticism into a new space. It is no longer a question of allusive obscurities, as in Pound, Eliot, and Olson, nor of the metaphorical system of surrealism. . . . It addresses in the present the ambiguity that language itself possesses and requires collaboration from the reader."

LH

Theory is never more than the extension of practice: the work of these poets has developed primarily in relation to the materials with which they work, informed not only by the synchronic activities of other active writers and the various traditions of literary writing but significantly by far larger frames of writing and art activity current and past. Critical forums for these writers—such as *L=A=N=G=U=A=G=E* or *Hills/Talks*—have been investigations in a manner similar to the work of the "poetry," where writing and the meaning of its modes are actively engaged: no manifestos, no formulation of underlying principles, no "how to write" apart from the writing itself that at any moment has no claim except as another instance. So, implicitly, an interrogation of the meaning of any mode—of "poetry" or "theory"— and an acknowledgement that there is no escape from composition, no logic on which to base the work other than the sense developed ongoing in the actual activity itself. Critical forums have been a way to open up beyond correspondence and conversation the dialogue between the writers themselves—an exchange of "working" information—and to include in this discussion those not primarily involved with poetry, such as other artists, and political and cultural workers, and to suggest possible relationships between the poetry and recent critical and philosophical thought. In this sense, such "critical writing" has often had a different address and a different audience than the "poetry" while at the same time basing itself in the poetic practice and serving to generate interest and insight into that work.

CB

This writing does not concern itself with narrative in the conventional sense. Story, plot, any action outside the syntactic and tonal actions of the words is seen as secondary. Attempts to posit an idealized narrative time would only blur perception of the actual time of writing and reading. Persona, Personism, the poem as trace of the poet-demiurge—these, too, are now extraneous. The functions that narrative had fulfilled, those of creating and resolving tension, introducing material, motivating sequence, are now dealt with more directly by a variety of procedures. A priori forms and lengths may be determined. Specific areas of vocabulary and syntax, or modes of patterning will be investigated.

Narrative-like elements do arise naturally, even from the most steady-state, fractal works. Clark Coolidge's as yet unnamed "long work" moves through areas of vocabulary and subject which are recapitulated in a kind of hyper sonata form. Ron Silliman's prose books reflect, of necessity, the sequence of outer events from which his sentences are often quarried. A deliberately impure narrative occurs in the prose of Lyn Hejinian and Bob Perelman, where memory and writing time interface. There is a similar meeting in some of Charles Bernstein's pieces, where a father's or aunt's self-narrating, self-limiting language is embedded in the poet's less coded syntax. Steve Benson's work often includes bits of autobiographical story as a textural element; many of these writers use language from older narratives similarly.

The most direct investigations of narrative have been Carla Harryman's work, in which a narrative can often be discerned, though it will be refracted and redefined by her language's self-scrutiny. In some works Bob Perelman has presented strings of narrative device without matching narrative content. In some of Peter Seaton's pieces the ghost of a narrative still lingers, not quite effaced by other signal-noise.

This writing has been laying bare the devices of statement and signification, exploring and elaborating new possibilities

Charles Bernstein & Bob Perelman   489

of syntax. Extending this investigation beyond the sentence
approaches and redefines narrative.

BP
(1982)

JACKSON MAC LOW

'LANGUAGE-CENTERED'

The term "language-centered" is ill chosen. The many works thrown under this rubric are no more 'centered in language' than a multitude of other literary works. Many depart from normal syntax. In many, what might be called 'subject matter' shifts rapidly. In some, such as many of my own, principles such as 'objective hazard,' 'indeterminacy,' and 'lessening of the dominance of the ego' may predominate over more usual concerns. But that a writer's efforts are ever 'centered in language' is highly dubious.

That most of these works use language in unusual ways is undeniable. But in what senses are they 'centered in language'? I suppose most users of such terms are impressed by lack of narration or exposition as these literary processes are usually conducted. Admittedly, few of these works tell a connected story or support an explicit thesis. But does this mean they are 'centered in language'?

Certainly, like any other works of literature, their material cause, their means, is language, or elements thereof. —Their *means?* Aristotle would have said 'their means of *imitation,*' but could they be said to imitate *anything?*—actions, movements of thought and/or feeling, the advent of revelatory experiences (Joyce's 'epiphanies'), or anything else? Can these works be seen as imitations in *any* sense of the term?

Seemingly, no. Often one word, phrase, or sentence seems to follow another with little regard for the recognized imports of these signs and strings. Their concatenation seems governed not by their referents, or by relations among them, but by features and relations intrinsic to them as language objects. Indeed, some practitioners and sympathetic critics call such works 'nonreferential,' and one of them has mounted a brilliant, seemingly Marxist, attack on reference as a kind of fetishism contributing to alienation. But this is a dangerous argument, easily turned against its proponents. What could be more of a fetish or more alienated than slices of language stripped of reference?

Of course, as other practitioners and critics have realized and stated, no language use is really 'nonreferential.' If it's language, it consists of signs, and all signs point to what they signify. All signs have significance.

So surely the term 'nonreferential' is also ill chosen.

What I think those who've used this term have meant to point out is the lack of any obvious 'object of imitation' or 'subject matter.' No situation, action, suffering, wave of emotion, or argument seems to be conveyed. (Or where some situations, actions, etc., seem to be conveyed, the work as a whole doesn't seem to have any unifying subject, etc.) The attention seems centered on linguistic details and the relations among *them*, rather than on what they might 'point to.'

But except in extreme lettristic cases, the works in question are made up of elements—morphemes, words, phrases, clauses, sentences—that have at least minimal meanings—intentions. Nouns, verbs, adjectives, and adverbs 'refer' either to particular objects, persons, places, etc., or to any member(s) of (a) certain class(es) of objects, qualities, etc., or to attributes, properties, or characteristics of any of these. They have, as linguists put it, 'lexical meanings.'

Other types of words—prepositions, pronouns, articles, etc.— show relations existing among words that have lexical meanings; they are said to have 'structural meanings.'

But can mentioning these 'referents' be sufficient to do away with the notion of 'nonreferentiality'?

Obviously not. Those who hold this notion are fully aware of all these types of reference. Then perhaps the term 'nonreferential' implies that disjunct 'references' and 'intentions' do not 'add up': if you say 'dog watermelon Racine Wisconsin Jupiter oleaginous to quarter above the of one George Washington Bill threw closeout . . . ,' each of the members of the string has meaning in itself, but the string as a whole does not. The lexical items have their inevitable referents, but most of the structural words do not seem to be showing relations obtaining among the lexical words, and 'worst of all,' the word string as a whole seems to have no referent at all.

Even when verse or prose of the types called 'language-centered' is composed of phrases, clauses, and/or sentences—normally meaningful word strings—the discourse as a whole seems to have no ascertainable referent—no recognizable object of imitation, subject matter, or argument. How is one to deal with this situation without bringing in such notions as 'language-centeredness' or 'nonreferentiality'?

Is there any sense in bringing in such a nonlinguistic and nonliterary term as 'the No-Mind'? This term is used by Zen Buddhists to refer to the deepest 'layer' of mind, below both the conscious ego and the psychoanalytic unconscious. It is impersonal, 'untainted' by ego. Some of us who have used chance operations to produce works of art have seen these works as embodying or expressing the No-Mind. When such works are comprised of words and strings, the attention of the perceiver is indeed centered on such language elements in themselves rather than on anything the authors wish to 'say' or 'imitate.'

I think that I was strongly convinced that this was the case when I began aleatoric verbal composition in the middle 50s. However, the idea is a complex one, and its acceptance depends upon the thorough understanding and acceptance of Buddhist psychological theory. Moreover, many of the authors whose works are in question might resent the introduction of an idea that they may find obscurantist or mystical, and it may not be necessary to bring in this idea from Zen to deal with this field of literary works.

When I began aleatoric verbal composition, I thought of the works as being 'concrete' (I usually resented the application of the term 'abstract' to them): as I saw it then, the attention of the perceiver is directed to each word and/or string in turn, rather than on anything outside themselves. Later, in the early 70s, when John Cage used chance operations to compose a long four-part poem made up of language elements drawn from H. D. Thoreau's *Journals*, he called it *Empty Words*, implying that these words, etc., have no 'content.'

But aside from the fact that most authors whose works are called 'language-centered' or 'nonreferential' do not use chance operations in writing them, I doubt that *any* such works, whether aleatoric or consciously composed through calculation or intuition, are truly 'empty' of all content, even when the authors have none in mind—when they do not intend to say or imitate anything.

The very fact that these works are composed of language elements that have intrinsic references precludes their being completely empty. Even disjunct or collaged phonemes remind us of words in which they may occur. Similarly, words and phrases inevitably lead the perceiver's mind to possible sentences in which they might be occurring, and sentences at least *connote* larger discourses.

The fact that there may be no such sentences in the works themselves or that when sentences occur they do not comprise such discourses does not prevent the perceiver's mind from 'semiconsciously' constructing larger wholes of which the given language elements are parts. The mind moves beyond the language elements themselves, impelled by a complex melange of denotations and connotations and of remembered language experiences and life experiences. That some perceivers are *moved* by some works of this kind is adequate proof of this.

Some writers of the type being discussed may consciously form their works to secure such an effect—some may even have an underlying subject-matter. Others may not. But in almost all cases, in varying degrees, the *perceiver* becomes the center—the *meaning-finder.*

Whatever the intentions of the authors, if the perceivers give serious attention to the works, they will—at some 'level'—be finding meanings. This is what arouses and sustains their interest and sometimes moves them emotionally.

Thus it may be most correct to call such verbal works *'perceiver-centered'* rather than 'language-centered' (and certainly rather than 'nonreferential'). Whatever the degree of guidance given by the authors, all or the larger part of the work of giving or finding meaning devolves upon the perceivers. The works are indeed 'perceiver-centered.'

This should come as no surprise to those of us who were led to this type of verbal work by study and experience of Zen and other types of Buddhism and/or by the aleatoric musical works composed in the early 1950s by Cage and his friends. Nevertheless, I can only put this notion forth tentatively—less so, in all likelihood, than I would have done 20 years ago. I certainly did not start writing this essay with this idea in mind. Yet when I review in my imagination many of the works of the type I've been considering, the fact that the perceiver's mind (at all 'levels') is the meaning-synthesizer seems to be (even when the author offers some cues or is working from an underlying subject-matter or object of imitation) the characteristic common to nearly all of them.

However, whether the perceiver's mind (much less the No-Mind) is the *object of imitation* of such works is not something that I can presently decide. There is certainly a sense in which perceivers are perceiving their own minds at work when they sense meanings in these verbal works. So it might well be proper to call the perceiver's mind the object of imitation. But this may not be the case with many of the nonaleatoric works, so I will refrain from bringing this notion forth at all strongly.

(1980)

ROBERT GRENIER

ON SPEECH

> "My poems exist in my head. They
> need not be spoken or written."
> —Randolph Dud

It isn't the spoken any more than the written, now, that's the progression from Williams, what now I want, at least, is the word way back in the head that is the thought or feeling forming out of the 'vast' silence/noise of consciousness experiencing world *all the time*, as waking/dreaming, words occurring and *these are the words of the poems*, whether they, written or spoken or light the head in vision of the reality language wakes in dreams or anywhere, on the street in armor/clothes. These words of the poem have something to do with the forms of written spoken usage (e.g. Norwegian/American dialect) in which they may be heard/seen, but there is no value in the linguistic vehicle per se, i.e. spoken noises and written letters are signs of the reality of words in the head (of which some few are 'interesting'/get written down, of those few are printed/become widely known/are read aloud to crowds).

In the process of writing what does not then occur in the head is a distraction.

Why imitate 'speech'? Various vehicle that American speech is in the different mouths of any of us, possessed of particular powers of colloquial usage, rhythmic pressure, etc., it is *only* such. *To me, all speeches say the same thing*, or: why not exaggerate, as Williams did, for our time proclaim an abhorrence of 'speech' designed as was his castigation of 'the sonnet' to rid us, as creators of the world, from reiteration of the past dragged on in formal habit. I HATE SPEECH.

There are 'worlds conceived in language/men not dreamed of.' We don't know the restrictions imposed by speech pattern/conventions, though those involving e.g. normal sentence structure thought required to 'make sense' start to show, won't until a writing clears the air.

What can be done. Evidently not more sonnets, and not force 'experiment.'

First question: where are the words most themselves? *Then* (& here Dud's position above seems incomplete): how may they best be spread abroad without distortion, so that the known world can be shared?

I want writing what *is* thought/where *feeling* is/*words are born*.

E.g.:

AZURE

azure
as ever
adz aver

> —Louis Zukofsky
> (from *All: the collected short poems,
> 1956-1965* Norton, 1966)

ROAST POTATOES

Roast potatoes for.

> —Gertrude Stein
> (from *Tender Buttons* in *Selected Writings
> of Gertrude Stein*, ed. Van Vechten, Modern
> Library, 1962)

(1971)

Robert Grenier 497

TED GREENWALD

SPOKEN

The sound in my poems comes from the sounds I hear in my head of almost myself talking to some person. I choose to have as my limitation spoken speech, as you and I are sitting here talking. That's what I test the poem's shape against.

Occasionally, I like to do other things, when I hear a completely peculiar sound or something, see if it works, give it a test run. Eventually, I prefer dealing with items that are still charged with meaning and in fact are open to the change that happens over time in meanings. In other words, if I don't know exactly what a poem means when I write it I'm somehow writing a certain kind of science fiction, because the poem (if I'm right about the direction the language will change in) will eventually make sense on a more than just, say, shape level or form level as time goes by and I'll start to understand it more.

I'm an opportunist: I'll take what I can get. If it works and if it's working when I'm working on it, then I'll use it. I don't care what the source of it is. But I'm saying that the basic motor on my car is spoken (for): What it sounds like in my mind when I read it to myself.

What works has to be grounded in the language, which is the locality of words. Words change in spoken language. "the/form/of/the/words/pump/blood/in/the/form/of/the/heart" That pretty much sums it up.

What I'm interested in and always have been is not what ideas people have in their heads, but what's in the air. The most invisible part of "trends". What is it that two people in the whole world or maybe twenty all of a sudden out of the middle of nowhere start to think about. What's in the air is the shape of things to come—it's palpable—right under your very nose. I hear what's in the air, that's my way of thinking with my ear. You're not working with the idea of something, you're projecting the idea of something. You're not working from models, you're creating models.

It's a romantic notion (where classical means coming from someplace), going someplace, sort of operating more out of imagination and less from received forms. In a specific sense, what it is the interior mind projecting itself into the phenomenological world, telling *you* where it's going. The time we live in is interesting, since there's a tremendous amount of good poetry that's "about" comings and going, this's and that's here and there, not sillyass schools of one thing or another ("in" and "out" I leave to the hosts and hostesses of the world).

Poetry is about a time that hasn't occurred yet, and if it's very good it's about a time you'll never know about. Poems are my pencil and pad for jotting down shapes or ways of embodying imaginary shapes or things that don't exist. But some time will exist on a wider scale. This is even conceptual: They are almost like plans for the future.

I think that the notion that sort of got started with Pound and other modernist artists is that if you were dealing with something you were going to take notes and the notes will usually be in fractional form. What's wrong with writing poetry that uses fragments (or notes) is that there is no everyday language that can be used to test goodness of fit. All there is is some poetic diction or poetic language to go back to that says "This is correct!," but no language in everyday use by people speaking, which changes over time, however imperceptibly.

I personally don't believe in using some form of a poem as a container for a bunch of things ("good lines" for instance). Each poem's form discovers itself as I write the poem. Two poems may not be perceptibly different looking, but there are differences. And, since I write on a day-to-day basis, and try to pay as close attention as possible, by paying close attention can see those differences. And watch the form of the poem, and the meaning

Ted Greenwald   499

and sense of sounds and words, change. And satisfy myself as a good reader with a good read.

(1979)

CLARK COOLIDGE

from A LETTER TO PAUL METCALF (jan 7 1972)

Wellsir, maybe I put you
off a bit talking *SPACE* as "spychedelic" (oops) or whatever—
actually I recall the word Olejonathon used was "electric",
but neither (term) is actually here nor there as opening to
the book. Natch I hope one can read into it without any-
preface, get a feeling of my feeling of words anyway, which
is near the crux. "options open" ain't bad either—it seems
indeed a catch to find *any* new options for words thesedays.
& I really didn't want to dive into a vast aesthetic discus
here in letterform, easir (easier) in person, talky mebbe, if
you're interested. I like Barney Newman's "aesthetics is
for artists as ornithology is for the birds" still in such regard.
As you might figger, I've had many years pleasure & turnon
"at the hands of" the NY 50's painters, & Gertrude Stein,
whose proposals (from back in the teens) still seem untaken-
up by almost all writers in English: just what are words &
what do they do?

Here's a few notes I jotted down reading your letter &
thinking (artists ain't too good at that mode?) it over again
for you. Take 'em or heave 'em over thebackfence—it's all
still a matter of what you can & can't use I guess Ezz??!!!?
- the Necessary Negatives: 'cause the subconscious gets so
   loose.
- Creeley's "you want/the fact/of things/in words,/of
   words."
- DeKooning's "it's very tiny, content"
- to work at the zone of interface tween unconscious &
   frontbrain   (thought / word)
- the Language as Present Fact
- I'd rather the Fudge than the Shine.
- Reversing the Syntactic Polarities arcs new energy across
   the blocks.
- Composition by Unit: read it that way.

Clark Coolidge 501

-I'd rather risk destroying the whole language than bore
   myself.
-Give myself something to read.
-"expressive", "rhetorical", "descriptive", "explicative"
   whatever statement is too abstract to me (by that I
   mean: removed, vague).
-I can't add to all those books.
-Differences, edges, oppositions, polarities, twins,
   offshades, silences, blanks, erasures, shrubbery, echoes,
   strata, repetitions, phasing, plain it.
-If you got something to say you should be a *speaker*
   ("something to say", "whether he tells the truth",
   etc = all part of the Oral Tradition anyway).
-I want a movement of language that stands for me as
   sum of all the axial drives in universe.

A Possible Range

manipulation of language particles	resultant new aggregates of →"meaning" elements	forces of all aspects of language structure → as "metaphor" for (as-yet-unseen?) physical states-of-matter

(1972)

LYN HEJINIAN

VARIATIONS: A RETURN OF WORDS

Think again . . . the twin brother . . . order inscribed . . .

Thought, or, advances. He has, for this aureate making of things, further care.

☆

Lucidities, or, lights (a starry angular). The staring, bright varieties of word and idea. I've always thought so, one who is willing and quite able to make use of everything, or anything. On the nectarine and the clarinet distinction casts a light, in its turn. One has only to look at the thing, and think a little.

Diversions, or, the guitar. It is in rereading one's journals, especially the old ones, that one discovers the repetition of certain concerns, the recurrence of certain issues, certain chronic themes that are one's own. You ask that whatever comes out of the five books on the shelf be new. It is now that I realize that that is impossible. Certain themes are incurable.

(Repeatedly I come upon the thought that everyone thinks, or wishes to think, of himself as unique. Often, one thinks that what one feels, what one experiences, is somehow **more** than what others feel or experience: **my** love, **my** suffering, **my** insight.

To be unusual, original, or new, is thought to be, somehow, important. It is thought, indeed, that to be otherwise is to be repetitive, or banal in thought; to be old and usual. It is implied then that one plagiarizes the past.

Artists often court madness, find insanity romantic, and point out their own eccentricities to prove their special validity.

That is from the notion that the suffering of the madman is especially real—that his madness in fact proves the reality of his suffering and the intensity of his experience. It has 'driven him insane.' But, really, the opposite is true. What characterizes insanity is that it divorces its victims from the actual, producing a state in which a private reality so dominates the attention as to exclude all other general realities. It is simply tht the suffering of the madman is endured in its own non-relational context; it may be no greater than ours. A small bell rung gently in a small box may seem to produce an enormous sound, and, in eclipsing the only peephole, may loom large.

Craziness is more light-hearted.)

The noble, or, the fierce. If a thing seems true, even if only for a short time, then is it true? The truth has a past tense, perhaps. Reality is both temporal and temporary. A cultural reality may make a change, and what was thought to be characteristic be revealed as only apparent. Like the culture of the American Indian, undone in these times.

Combination, or, the metaphor. One refers to 'the courage of his convictions.' The difficulty lies not so much in adhering to one's beliefs as in remembering what they are, in a social confusion. One is constantly exposed to an abundance of valid opinion.

Any thought can be kin to another. The agility of the imagination and its whimsy make this possible.

Nonsense, or, the party. Bursts of talk, this is what is expected of one. Yet one prefers lengths of silence. Neither talk nor silence is by definition charming. Insofar as the charming is aware of itself, it too is not charming. It rattles.

(How rarely one follows a thought through, to its 'conclusions.' How infrequently one comes to the end of a thought. Indeed, in these times, it seems, we back away from thought altogether, we scarcely think at all, given the diversions or the mechanical aids that block thought by making it unattractive or unnecessary.)

Surrealism, or hooves of the clattering trolleys. The figure of action is in motion, yet what moves is not to be seen. I hear the trees, he would say, am a participant in a thin fog rising. Is this confusion, or a spectacle? he asks.

On television the surreal is to be seen in non-revolutionary form. I am thinking, for example, of the show in which the hero's mother returns from the dead in the form of a talking car.

(As I originally conceived of this piece, it was to be a series on varieties of nonsense, but it came thereby to express a cynicism, if not a sarcasm, that I don't really feel, and it was changed accordingly, in conception and in fact. Even in poetry, honesty is more important than felicity.)

Style, or, ink. Occasionally, one must make a choice between a colon and a dash, while verse, in its flounces, sashays about the grounds.

Devastation, or, the wreck. One can't write the words 'wild,' 'cruel,' 'horror,' etc. and by naming it communicate it. Brutality can only result in an extreme and emotional response, and not a written one. In contemporary jazz, the scream, the artistry of high-pitched harmonics, is a primary expression, in response to contemporary brutality.

Further thought, or, further advances. This, or this again, in different terms, may serve to add either complication or clarification. In either case, thinking does in some cases contract but in most cases expand the consciousness. With regard to the former, I am referring to what we call over-thinking, that painful circling which taunts the mind. Yet even then, further thought of a different kind serves finally to propel one out of the morbid circle, toward some insight or conclusion.

(Often what is interesting, when an idea is first related, is not to know the thought alone but to know who is thinking it, who is 'in on' the idea, who is involved in it. This is the flesh and context of the thought.)

☆

As chance must lead you first one way and then another, and as comedy does not always sustain laughter but may provoke tears, so here what is reflected is not always what is visible, and art is seen not to be a mirror.

And here are these other drawings, which perhaps you would want to see. There are elongated letters and numerals, superior, polite, and strange of.

If to think is to dance, it is to fall while dancing, as well; it is to dance among ducks and elephants. Also, of course, it is to dance among the winged horses, the angels, and with the albatross.

(I have read that the albatross is able to stay aloft for long periods of time, often for as much as a year at a time, its wing span being so great, and the winds so strong and constant in the Southern latitudes where the albatross is at home, that the bird can rest in flight. Beneath it are the constantly rising waters and the battered triangles of their troughs.)

And the curving roofs of the old houses in the scattered villages.

Francis Ponge wrote of a comment made by Picasso: "To speak thus is to show as much modesty as courage, as much lucidity as ambition."

To learn a foreign language is somehow akin to working with mathematics. Yet to work with one's own language is very far from mathematics. One is so familiar with one's own language that its rigidities, its laws, pass unnoticed. It is fluid, and in it one is lost, experiencing as often as not the pain and difficulties that such freedom imposes.

There is an artistic technique which could be called a technique of first gestures. One makes a form, sketches it out, looks to see it, and pursues the suggestions it has made. The initial step is a random gesture—the random result of a gesture. In writing, one makes a first word or phrase (less often, a sentence or a paragraph); in music, a first sound or texture of sound.

Relative to this I recall a class I took in college, given by an anthropologist who was also a friend of Robert Motherwell, Grace Hartigan, etc. The course was a study of correspondences between prehistoric cave art (specifically that of the caves at Lascaux),

Australian Aboriginal art, and Abstract Expressionism (the New York School).

What is possibly my earliest recollection is of a brilliantly yellow flower sharp on the grass. From that period also come other purely visual memories. I remember clearly particular wallpapers, the small yellow roses on the yellowing paper in my grandmother's room, the faded green stems and leaves, and the dark green paper of my own bedroom. In still another room was a pink paper, newly hung, which I tore off the wall in long strips as I lay in my crib for an afternoon nap. Because my memory is visual in its nature, that I should have become a painter follows logically. Yet, though my father was a painter, I am not.

Probably all feelings are cliches—which is not to say that they are invalid, or stupid, or even absurd (though like anything else, they may be). Feelings are common to us all, never new, stunning only to the person feeling them at the time, and foolish (or boring) to everyone else. Thoughts, however, can be affective whether one shares them at the moment or not, and they can be original.

Feelings have no potential, they can never be anything but what they are. Ideals and thoughts, however, are full of potential. That is to say, love or melancholy only become more or less as they develop as **feelings**. Yet the **idea** of love or melancholy ramifies indefinitely and can lead off in an infinity of directions.

This is not to belittle feelings—anymore than one would belittle the lungs, or the intestines.

☆

(A characteristic of the morbid intelligence, in its manner of thinking, is to think backwards from a given thought, to search behind even the most trivial and commonplace thought, for its motives (and one's own, in thinking it), and then, to reach again behind that, and again behind that, into the unclear brine of the mind itself. It is a cheerless search.)

Devastation, or, the wreck again. There have been heavy frosts this spring, and the blossoms on the fruit trees have been blackened. The blossoms are black as saints. The ants writhe in the sugar box.

Distortion, or, error. To err is to wander, or to turn, probably in an unanticipated direction, inadvertently. The mistake is not necessarily without advantage, however, nor, if such should be necessary, irrevocable.

Ink, or, the guitar. Returning from the middle distances, to the same points, repeatedly, from whatever direction, one homes, like a migrant bird or fish. Perhaps that is a function of thought, homing. In any case, one doesn't, perhaps can't, escape one's concerns. That is what constitutes a personal style.

Nonsense, or, distinctions. The German is ornate in terms of language, the Frenchman in terms of feeling. One can distinguish between the baroque intellect and the baroque heart.

Explanation, or, explication. In one's journal, one need only write a few words (though, on the contrary, it is there, in one's journal, that one tends to be most verbose, where privacy makes occasion for release rather than restraint. There, too, one may experiment with, and repeat, the shape and sound of old and new ideas.) For oneself, however, one may write, say, Boot, or Inclusion, and summon for oneself the cogent images and their array of meanings. For others, however, explanations are due—if, not forthcoming.

(The connection between thought and nonsense is this, that the double is not divisive. Those things which we term opposite ought, by rights, rather to be termed complementary. That is how we term colors, such as orange and blue, or yellow and purple, which stand opposite each other on the artist's color wheel, and serve to highlight each other, intensify each other, and under certain circumstances can be brought to merge into each other. So it is with love and hate, with light and dark. So it is with thought, which when pretentious is nonsense, and when exercised under certain circumstances is absurd. Thought used as analysis risks absurdity. Also definitions of 'the right way.')

☆

Now, here is the jolly noon. There is a lilt in telling it. The vision climbs, the response is in retreat. The circle becomes careless as one becomes weary. There is a qua ! qua ! of fleeing geese, while thought is a form of lingering.

(1976)

STEVE BENSON

ON REALISM

I always take the norm as some sort of a standard: a standard one can push against, or tack in relation to, in communication, to generate action or a fresh realization or an initiative to response. That is, then, I don't have a sense of myself, my own ways, my own predilections and abilities, as standard or integral; they seem to me rather gratuitous and conditional, while certainly purposive and significant and resistant in circumstances of engagement with some other. The norm, while based on a model of my recognition of the other, I still don't see as being in the other, nor necessarily as an obstacle between us, it's rather the amorphous and uncertain bond, the commonly held language (which we know is always shifting and changing, local and conditional itself, riddled with tendentiousness and misunderstandings of all orders) somehow assumed between the other and me (me: this elastic force that always appears to stem from this body "I" am "in"). The norm in this sense is not to be blamed on the other, since any one of us partakes of it for purposes of society ("Please pass the salt"), except when its terms are falsely imposed by some over others as though necessary or right in themselves ("Don't talk with your hands at the dinner table").

In the sense that I take it, the terms of the normative tend to comprise a language, which itself pretends to the status of a comprehensive mythos of everyday life, a language thus pretending to a stability howsoever conscious of its indispensable contingency, apparently transfixed in a mutability it can hardly comprehend. The assumptions and qualities of understanding and bonding manifest in normative language, however subcultural, I then prefer to take as counters generated to our individual and collective advantage. Inherent within their claims to autonomy are all the functions that could split them, conventionally absorbed on recognition of their ascendancies as terms of themselves, conceived as autonomies in their turn. Because there is no true accuracy in such a language of pretense to categorical authority, earnest efforts at knowledge and communication continue to trouble it and mess it up, though there is no establishing of understanding possible between us that can actually transcend a language. In fact our will to engage the unknown contingencies of the imminent, the immediate, and the inimitable, in spite of their otherness to the language of the norm, keeps the language alive, keeps social circumstances fluent, and affords what we tend to conceive as identities of self and other the potential of active and crucial communication.

(1982)

LYNNE DREYER

I STARTED WRITING . . .

I started writing dialogues. This is how I started to write. I was working as a waitress in "Big Boys" in College Park, Maryland while attending the University of Maryland. Always listening to people and was taking Modern Poetry class with Rudd Fleming who really "opened the door" to all of this for me. I graduated with a degree in Recreation Therapy so the people I spent a lot of time with were frustrated jocks and very social, fun loving, good time party types. At the same time, I was starting to write, I got into yoga. So both of these (writing and yoga) were pulling me into two very opposite poles. By this time, I was writing more internal monologues and stream of consciousness writing.

Last week I went to the library to look up automatic writing. I finally found a definition in an Encyclopedia of Occultism. Automatic writing is as if your arm is possessed and you don't know what you are writing. You may write very very fast and so small that it would seem physically impossible that a human could write it. Much of this type of writing had to do with contacting the dead. When the writing comes easier to me, it seems to be more automatic. Stein was thoroughly insulted when they called her work automatic. She thought it was ridiculous that they thought she was in a trance.

While working for the D. C. Recreation Department, I became involved with Mass Transit, a weekly open reading series. Again here were these two conflicting types. I was teaching a preschool class in the A.M. and coaching sports and other activities (hanging out, ping-pong, the local rec activity). Maybe these conflicts are what kept me writing. I remember buying my first car and how free it felt. Also riding on buses and trains got me writing. The motion and optimism of "new" always set something off. In the beginning (*Lamplights*) the observations and obsessions were much more external—not as heavy. By the next year with *Stampede* (having spent a year in New York studying in Mayer's workshop) everything became much faster, darker and extremely internal, until it came to a dead halt. Climbing out of that with the writing proved to be a slow and thick process which even involved going back to Baltimore where I grew up. Living out the same memories of childhood as an adult was of course painful and necessary.

The next work, "The Letters", was much lighter as if trying to reach out and be witty. By this time I was back in D.C. working various jobs, i.e., security guard, cashier, and receptionist. After being so self-conscious and internal in *Stampede*, I needed to be light, almost comical while writing "The Letters". By this time, a group of us were getting together for a poetry workshop from which *Dog City* has been a result.

To say the life is separate from the writing would be a lie. Not that calming down would slow the work or the other way around. Lifestyle, where living, whether working would all add or detract.

About three years ago, I got a job as a Park Ranger on an old lightship down on Haines Point in D.C. Here was, I thought, the answer to many problems (low pressure job, being outside a lot, on water, pretty isolated in winter and fall), but I found that the amount of time I had to write had nothing to do with my ability to write. I then started writing *Tamoka* which I had intended to be a much longer work. This is the most direct piece I've done (more like a story than anything else). Also I got married about that time, so here was another way "not to hide". I found in *Tamoka* the language was very important and I finally understood what centering the writing on the language could mean. Of course, mine was more of a story but all of the talk about "words" made sense. Certain sections are more language than others.

The pool where I had lifeguarded and taught swimming the summer before I started the Park Service was this huge inner city public pool. There was a lot of slang and while we used to change chairs and clean the deck, I would ask the other guards about the opposite meanings of words (bad meaning good, etc.). This is very common now but I always liked to talk about it.

Now the popular songs that are blasting on the radios are these talky sing-song long tales with a good beat (sort of like Muhammad Ali's poetry). One of the people at the ship would always know the words to them. It fascinated me because he would turn it up and tell me to listen whenever they came on.

In about three weeks. I'll be having a baby. So my whole center is off. The writing has been much slower this summer, will see what the new settled season will bring.

(1980)

STEPHEN RODEFER

PREFACE TO *FOUR LECTURES*

Writing and painting are deeply identical
—Paul Klee

My program is simple: to surrender to the city and survive its inundation. To read it, and in reading order it to read itself. Not a doctrine, but a public notice.

The city, which even before Baudelaire had been a ready-made collage or cut-up of history, constantly remaking itself—a work of art, founded on an anthill. And every art grows out of the same collective desire which informs and compels the idea and reality of a city (Latin *colligere*, to tie together). A district, or a ghetto, is a segmentation, an alternate version which both resists and embodies in a different fashion, that is with an opposing ideology, the original model. Hence, dialect and civil strife are alternating codes of the same phenomenon: the city does not *hold together*. Language, which also binds together and extends, including as it isolates, is a city also.

In such a metropolitan of history, in which the city is literally the mother, the greatest art is painting, if only by the sheer weight of the temporal. Without a city and its structures there would be no painting. The only thing precedent to painting is caves—the Gilgamesh is not as old as Lascaux.

The Greeks had painted sculpture and from the start all cultures have painted their deities. Today we have painted cities, painted conveyances, painted apartments, painted roads, painted people, even painted food. Is it not time for painted poetry as well?

A poetry painted with every jarring color and juxtaposition, every simultaneous order and disorder, every deliberate working, every movement toward one thing, deformed into another. Painted with every erosion and scraping away, every blurring, every showing through, every wiping out and every replacement, with every dismemberment of the figure and assault on creation, every menace and response, every transformation of the color and reforming of the parts, necessary to express the world.

Even the words and way of language itself will suffer the consequent deformity and reformation. The color beneath, which has been covered over, will begin to show through later, when what overcame it is questioned and scraped on, if not *away*.

Political revolution answers the same process. Shapes and lines converging and diverging will formulate new ideas, the true statement of which is not fully disclosed, but fully embodied. There is a continuing direction felt within, but ordered from without. When the oppressed whole is dismantled, the parts will find a new place, more proper to them, or else all fails. In the future it will be said of such a mode, regarding its material and its language, to adapt a phrase Augustus used of Rome, that it found it brick but it left it aggregate. Deliberate decomposition is required in a state of advanced decay.

Marble is no longer the style of course. Our era promises to make the late Roman look small time, if not benign. In a world in which there are more photographs than there are bricks, can there be more pictures than there are places? I'm told that soon there will be more *people* living than have ever died. In innumerable ways we are living in an incomprehensible age. It is entirely unnecessary for this argument (though ultimate) to mention nuclear weapons. The signs are otherwise quite enough.

In art, just as in life, significance tends to emerge tentatively, as figures in an abstraction (or a seascape in Kandinsky), even as the figurative element reveals new structural relations which then re-define the abstraction. For example, say, Rosso Fiorentino, *Nosferatu,* or the latest improvised quartet.

Such a poetry as is suggested here is not a new concept, any more than poetry as music is. In *our* world it's been around at least since Blake, and was revived by Klee, Huidobro, and Picabia. My decision to take up the art again is simply carrying on, which is of course the meaning of tradition. Painted poetry is probably as ancient as the absence of machines, and with good fortune will survive the ends brought on by them.

The old form-content play has always been self-contained, like Hamlet or any good Polish sausage, somewhere between metaphor and metonymy, as the linguists would remind us, or Gertrude and Laertes. The modern world began with the first contiguity disorder, i.e. at birth, when things become wrenched from their similarity. But bent out of shape is also bent *into* shape. New replacements are expected, and they always come. We start to be fed things forcibly. We can throw up, not eat, or fold the spoon in half. Several wars are going on at once, but there is also one big war. The peace that is won with difficulty at times out of this condition will necessarily always be partial. The map will ever be fragmented and changing. The same territory with a different name makes no more sense than a different state with the same name, though we are asked in the so-called post modern world to swallow this kind of malfeasant pitch all the time. The word itself sounds the end.

The events and systems that embody this swarming *state* of affairs have become so mixed, complex, and unconscious at once, that what is required to read it is the ultimate painting. It can be made in any number of ways, but there is no way now that it can be anything but apocalyptic. A vision is intended, rather than an explosion.

For writing is a graphic art, and a word projects either stroke or color. As it is born, a poem is drawn. It can begin with a figure or a line. It can begin to clothe a cartoon or *about* the idea of anything. It begins to paint itself. It can be made with a pencil or with a knife, with a pen or a recorder, or with a keyboard contraption that strikes the paper. It requires patience, approach, observation, technique, impulse, intent, alternation, energy, and obsession. It can be attacked by history, as well as attack history. It can be unknown and done only for itself and nothing other. Its meaning can change in time, and *always* does.

Completed, the art object is nothing but the fantasy of a given artist at a particular time. If fully worked and read totally, it will reveal all there is to know about the life of the artist, the conditions in which it was made, as well as implicate the development of art up to its example. The formation of the work will literally imply the history of the species (*imply*: to fold in, envelope, embrace). Hence it will take its place at the latest point of a tradition that it will then be *carrying on*, no matter what. Tradition as *borne*; not only what speaks to us across time, but that which we *drag along*, what we lift into the picture as well as what by a differential operation we "unload." Footstep, tread, trace, track, path, thoroughfare, method, practise, market, peripatetic *trade*, TRADITION.

I consider the enterprise of poetry therefore to be musical and graphic at once, more than literary. For how much more illuminating and amusing it is (MUSIC/MOSAIC, belonging to the muses) to *compose* language, or to paint poetry, than simply to write it.

As should a book be as deep as a museum and as wide as the world.

SR, March 1981, San Francisco Art Institute

DAVID BROMIGE

BY VISIBLE TRUTH WE MEAN THE APPREHENSION
OF THE ABSOLUTE CONDITION OF PRESENT THINGS

The kind of prose anybody can read. One Saturday night after the poetry-reading we went to a cafe to discuss it. Syntax like a clear window giving onto reality framed anew. Actually we went to a streetcorner near to 3 different cafes & discussed which of them would be best. How I saw it—I stake my life on such assumptions—shows me the way. None of them had room enough to accomodate everyone who needed to be there if no-one was to be left out. One leads instanter to the next, no matter I had those percepts. Driving home, later, we saw a remarkable sight: one car had to stop suddenly because of something we couldn't see that was happening ahead of it; & the car immediately behind the first car, had to jam its brakes to avoid a rear-ender. Painful, this disposition of each necessary element, as if a lawyer wrote it. Now the driver of this second car begins to blare his horn & one of its passengers even squeezes (this car is loaded) out of his door & brandishes his fist at the offender. We are reminded once again that justice is a passion. Even the interruptions give it authenticity. The first car, now able to move ahead, did, the second car with a squeal of tires in hot pursuit. And then it was we noticed that the second car was driving with its lights off. And still we hold there are times when we can bear witness to the present condition of absolute things.

(1980)

BRUCE ANDREWS

MISREPRESENTATION
(A text for The Tennis Court Oath *of John Ashbery)*

> Thus, when the universal sun has set,
> does the moth seek the lamp-light
> of privacy.
> —Karl Marx

* * *

1. "Uh huh." "Huh." "Heh? Eh?" What *had* you been thinking about? Since, from the very start, this outward-looking topic or conjuncture of words is *convulsed*, "the face studiously bloodied" by all that combs the text. "Hush!"

But—the conjunction—registers the tone. "but what testimony buried under colored sorrow". So this is not evidence for some theory but a gloss on loss, regret, confusion, clarity, the net of hope unraveling both night & day. And our reading *registers* this dizzying parade—of eroded representations and wreckage. Are they what we want? "When through the night. . . . Pure sobs denote the presence . . . Of supernatural yearning".

2. One can "smile up at your dark window in the nothing sunlight—". Wait around; "I guess the darkness stubbed its toe". Falters; blanks. "We were growing away from that" —toward desire, with a jeweler's care, ". . . waiting". Always.

It's not just the accuracy of pointing which this work calls into question, or pouts. Rather, we are led to question the efficacy of desire, of *getting through*. Of interpersonal TRANSLATION, a social activity which begins to look like a subcategory of clarity and communicative competence. Are we still dumb with each other; is this "numb hitting"? Am I *getting through* to you (and to you-plural)? "Piercing the monocle . . . because letters". To pierce that, as letters can pierce through: it isn't taking off or opening up shades, but removing historical or social barnacles. Shades are painted shut. The impermeability of the person, the wall-eyed. "It is dumb and night continually seeping in—like a reservoir. . . . Of truth on the bandits".

3. Blabbing causing darkness, & darkness related to the closures, the incommensurability of experiences, the inability to *see*. "I try . . . to describe for you. . . . But you will not listen". But we must agree. "Agreement was possible." Agreement was not readily possible; we weren't ready. Since there isn't some reality out there awaiting our objective operations. Instead, you find a relativism grounded in practices, in the round of language, which demands *responsiveness* from us and not simply *decipherment*. Dialogues, in place of a fugitive 'monologic,' as a means by which reality can be *constituted*. *Paroles*. [The constitutive rules of this game define the second-order ends/means relationship—between the social construction of reality, on one level, and everything that we do & are & say, on the other.] "The facts have hinged on my reply".

4. Communicative competence, and therefore transparency, and social reality itself: all together. What "will teach you about men—what it means"? "Because what does anything mean, . . .?" Yet is anything "wholly meaningless," or if so only by some constricted definition of meaning, one which sanctions only certainties, is transparency or a phoney monologic. So "the things I wish to say"—are they ever without obstructions or emotional overhead? For saying is not just an utterance but a social performative as well. At every step, we perform the dialogue.

5. The borders & barriers & border patrols which it breeds all remind me of those which translation must cross. And translation does or can model all our interactions. Even so, there are problems, familiar problems with this. "All borders between men were closed." The impermeability, again. So that the things we wish to say may even seem motivated by a strong desire (the wish, the personal gesture, the camp), yet in a contextual sense "are needless," or else remain unmotivated or undemanded in a formal sense. Loosed from their context, which gives them 'a formal sense.'

Bruce Andrews 521

"stammered". "But that doesn't explain." ". . . I don't know". "You don't understand . . ." "–I don't know why." The forms *motivate* the human disjunctures, which is their triumph.

   6. Lately, I've heard Ashbery's work mentioned in breaths that include Lowell, Bishop, Sexton, Howard, Merrill, Strand, Rich, Hollander, etc. A community of innocent and therefore more worrisome misrepresentation which poses as representation, as rhetoric. The work at hand is less innocent. It does not content us as established rhetoric. "More than the forms". O.K. Yet this is still like a 'social-work'. It poses for us a radical questioning of established forms, yet at the same time, and so appropriately in its own form, it explores the implications of that questioning–not as an idea, but as an experience and a *reading*.
   I came upon this work early in my writing. Rereading, it seems even less comfortably mentioned in that former breath of names, or even in a breath with the many younger writers who have adopted his tone and manner of discourse. Instead, it still *persuasively* proposes a condition of formal adventure: with elements of Allen's *New American Poetry 1945-1960*, with the work of Roussel, Cage, Zukofsky, with O'Hara, Eigner, Mac Low, Roche, with what recent writing has done (that of Coolidge, Silliman, Mayer, Grenier, DiPalma, Bernstein, others) to help us take a new breath, and with what such writing may do to push us *further* along. Not a conventional dalliance, and not a transcendent avant-gardism. There are other communities, and this work and therefore the possibilities for writing can belong in them. It has opened rooms, even if Ashbery's own work has not walked into them.
   "I am toying with the idea." Yet we read more than "only bare methods", the "sharp edge of the garment", "the . . . . lettering easily visible along the edge". What is here: "A torn page with a passionate oasis". "Back into pulp." The construction itself bends backward, to give us a clearance for the jumps in location and tone and pointedness–a *jump cut*, like the narrative variety in New Wave cinema of that time. Moreover, the construction is not a shawl, enveloping & smoothing the shifts, as in later work,

but is at the heart of our experiencing those shifts at all—the jagged kaleidoscope of melancholia and expiration.

7. "of course the lathes around
    the stars with privilege jerks"

It concerns the undercutting of the image, the visual picture—by juxtaposing the conceivable referents in unexpected ways and also by fragmenting the syntax, that gridiron of outwardness. "The reason ejected" by these 2 strategies—via the constitution of the image and via syntax, both of which are variously shattered. In fact, we could say that only here and in *Three Poems* does the disjunct formal structure fully *double*, or reiterate, the implicit lessons embodied in the discourse: about the fragility of relationships, doubts, breakage, tenuousness more generally, foreclosed dreams & the mortgages of dreamwork, lonesomeness. Not just an ornamentally rhetorical way of talking *about* these issues; here we find them displayed and played out and encoded in the very construction. This is *codic doubling* with a lovely vengeance.

8. Let light shine in? "The bars had been removed from all the windows". But . . . . "What window?" What is at stake— "A signal from the great outside" — is this all?: "against the window." "the observatory"; "specs". These seem. Light and glass, as mirrors, as representation, as lucid rhetoric. He's not wondering if we want this, but is depicting actively what language can deliver. Are we willing to accept the . . . available substitutes? Not our salvation.

Even to the point where language itself takes precedence—is the frontal project. "Inch pageant". And single words are unleashed from a familiarity which their very unleashing helps to undermine. As well, they constitute another reality. Signs & the rules they carry inside them. "Now he cared only about signs." Well, not true, not even here, but he does care very deeply and seems suspicious of their instrumental use, of their *about-ness*, their external determinants. "Panorama."

9. Images, for example— or ornament. "The colored balls were like distant lights on the plaque horizon." Not enough, and

not what it is. "Is not a 'images' . . . . to 'arrange'". No, actually
it kicks the legs out from under that whole project. Here, and
more prominently than in later work, the composition does not
project such an arrangement. It doesn't just juxtapose representa-
tions and accede to their hegemony. No . . . the reading, the lan-
guage, "does not evoke a concrete image". Still, you want to do
more than abandon the possibility: "You have to exact the for-
feit". To do so, you may want to make these illusory or suspect
representations more exact; or question them in one exacting
fashion after the other. "The light goes—it exudes. . . . Your idea—
perched on some utterly crass sign". For isn't it always some
utterly crass sign or image on which it is perched, on which our
hopes are perched? Not what is in front of us. "Photography,
horror of all". As if humans were the miscommunicating mammals,
or those who locate themselves in frames which require so much
more than what we call simple reading, or 'reading off.' Instead,
things are pleased by indirection. "He is not a man . . . Who can
read these signs". Not in this light.

10. Isn't transparency a mark of illusion, and possibly of all
illusions? "misguided": the elysium of signposts, of exact replicas,
clones, control, repetition compulsion. "You cannot illusion;"
this remains as a trace of advice. *Critical Interruptions.* "Lights
stream undeniably away". Their touch eludes. You cannot recap-
ture. And light itself would be an evasion, or a misapprehension,
and even the other-worldly, the distractingly transcendent. If
"escape is over the lighted steps . . . . Misunderstandings arise
cathedral." The radical critique of religion as a source for an Ideo-
logiecritik, and a critique of clarity and transparency and language:
"powerless creating images"; and hierarchy arising historically at
the same time as instrumental literacy (Levi-Strauss) or the incest
taboo. Repent; revolt. In the division of labor, some are left to
dream. Are we left to repeat?
    "We might escape, in the daylight". As if light comes across
here as an escape, "the exit light". Since aren't these the descrip-
tive effects, the lighting, evoked around the edges of an experi-
ence in order to show an unreal way out? This project can be over-
turned: "the undesired stars . . . . needed against the night . . . .

Forbidden categorically". Yet how undesired are they, "the fact the stars", the piercing through of night? Fugitive. Instead, in the dark, we can pledge allegiance to them—to these facts and to their absence.

And not to description. During that pledge of allegiance, these words remain seated. "But a blind man's come poking, however clumsily, into the inmost . . . . corners of the house." Or the book. The reign of description is put on the dock; to place in evidence; to regard as hearsay; to impugn the testimony of. Its effects suggest mere positing: "The apricot and purple clouds were"— while a welter of adjectives has not added up to an external world: cream-colored, lilac, pink, lovely—but to what, a "sullen, careless world . . . . Ignorant of me . . ." Even so, it contains within it such precisely evoked if dislocated pleasures and regrets, as if, in a whisper, to mention the incapacity of language to describe or fix. Badly mortised. "Acting kind of contented in the finishing petal". A fixation, an affixation. What is lost & what is mentioned becomes a parallel division.

11. Description would be choiceless, "unintentional". Personhood might be mere transmission, "am as wire". Behavioral reading, rather than hermeneutic ones. "The persons abolished"—in the horizon. Speech, and therefore action, reduced. "Light sucks up what I did". But a critique in action of the representational capacity of language seems to reaffirm personhood, and choice itself. "For the optician's lenses never told you"; they never told you what you need—to go on—and what can be said. *But.* "Head of shade"—rather than of light, or the evasion of responsibility, or crass signs & illusion. "But having plucked oneself, who could live in the sunlight? . . . . And the truth is cold". With the word "plucked" coming across as harvested, or tended, or having gained in self-consciousness; having done so, it makes sense to be skeptical, to embody in *composition* the doubt that transparency is more than a devious & second-best fraud, fraught with an illusory naturalism, a making into nature what is really our *production.* A tyranny, a myth, an ideology of determinism and reductionism. The work affirms, on the contrary, "The person.... Horror—the morsels of his choice".

12. Some connectives. An order as clarity. Clarity as transparency. Transparency as authority. Formal order, and civil order, & the taboo against transgression, and isn't this a taboo against the person? "Glass . . . . regime". With *regime* in the sense of paradigm, and glass as transparency. A toppling of *this* regime; the delegitimation of *this* authority, and this *order*, this reign, this rein, this *problematique*. "For what is obedience but the air around us": taking as its model a complacent glance upward & not the more strenuous effort to see *through* hierarchy—as a symptom, a veil.

Or to see through the "solidifying disguises"—the image, the representation, the denial of solidity: "Release shadow upon men—in their heaviness". Evanescence: fraud. "It too faded into light". And a horror emerges of fullness, of plenitude, of the body. "Or he hides bodies . . . . stone night."

13. Night & day, light & dark, *chiaroscuro*, present the basic terms of reference. "lighted up the score". "The sky was white as flour—" And light appears as clarity, sense, clear-headedness, as the possibility of both representation and denial: communication. Night—as lack of clarity, or senselessness, on the other hand. "Neutral day-light sitting thing"; sitting things out, setting things up: a declaration of placement, and order, sensible order, and its neutrality. Simple declarative.

14. But so much of this *interrogates* the lighting & our capacity to see, and therefore to interpret, and therefore to speak and be understood. "Murk plectrum," "thistles again closed around voice." Guarded; blocked. "Fatigue and smoke of nights". Blurs; hard of hearing "recording of piano in factory" or chickenshack, or garage. See each other? "Our faces have filled with smoke." "As though too much dew obscured the newspaper". *Film noir*. "bandaged the field glasses." Or: "The sunset stains the water of the lake," staining the otherwise see-through flooring. Consensual truth? Transparency does not yet exist.

15. Faced with the "bilious tide of evening", as an alternative, are we left with "thankless sight"? "The penalty of light forever"—where we may be "Burnt by the powder of that view"

which we desire. Very possibly, this exit leads nowhere. "One can never change the core of things, and light burns you the harder for it." And at that core would be personhood, or character armor, and *therefore* the impossibility of unimpeded communication, of full relation and bonding, of getting through. One "sees . . . . Into the light: . . . . It grieves for what it gives:" or what it reveals. I am naked.

"Lights were brought. The beds, sentenced." Where *sentenced* gives that doubling of penalty and grammatical closure: the end. Or unending but jeopardized from all sides . . . "mirrors—insane" (which is one whole section from the sequence masterwork, *Europe*). Giddyup, references; into the horizon. And light, that seeming mark of transparency, would only be a mark of seeming. A false front, a regret. It actually marks opacity, and . . . our full realization of *absence*. Clarity, in the end, is suffocating. Yet we suffocate for want of it, and still presume it. "My bed of light is a furnace choking me".

16. Memory, too, gives us a system of reference. And opacity gives us a system of amnesia, or a reminder of the mnemonic challenge; "it was fuzz on the passing light . . . . over disgusted heads, far into amnesiac". Eyes closed discover spent youth.

And that amnesia, or character armor, is not a needless intrusion but emotion itself—"or our defences, our intentions"—where "We must be a little more wary". "and that fascinating illumination . . . . that buries my heart". Occlusion springs from the heart as well as from language. Daylight clarity poses the terms of the question again; where *form* is pinned by *sense*—only to be dissembled in its origins, its privacies.

17. "The map . . . Shut up." No speech = privacy = no guides. Where does the public/private dimension enter in? "Darkness invades the tears" & "Tears invade the privacy of private lives". For to invade suggests *embody*—the fear of embodiment, where privacy/opacity and publicity/transparency are poles; they are poles apart. "A strong impression torn from the descending light . . . . But night is guilty." Guilty of what we do, in private, and of the simplest facts of privacy itself, "darkness in the hole".

Guilty of the passionate oases. So: private night, film noir, the disorder—the voluptuous reassuring disorder of night, "carpentered night".

18. And imagination. "They imagine something different from what it is." "My brain concocted" : "and looking around for an opening in the air, was quite as if it . . . . had never refused to exist differently." And those differences are a form of social speech—a source of contradiction, an interaction which lays the ground for our individual longings and imaginings. Heating up the caverns, or "the inconstant universe"—"a beam of intense, white light . . . . —pierce the darkness, skyward".

For otherwise this was "the issue utter blank darkness" : night or darkness or absence; *zero*. "Bringing night brings in also idea of death" : "death preoccupation, beauty." A barely habitable humanism, characterized by opacity, motive, clogging, that which is not understandable; "the darkness will have none of you," and "I don't understand wreckage". Wreckage occludes the orders of the day, the light which is conceivable speech. And . . . "but in the evening in the severe lamplight doubts come".

19. Clarity can thus be regarded in the same way we consider ease of closure, understanding, sight, and translation. The *but* endistances them: "but permanent as the night's infection" and doesn't this remain surrounding us? Something has "rendered speech impossible . . . . There was no sign of light anywhere below— all was a bright black void." All ruses have failed.

As a compensation and yet also as a reminder, the style of this work remains prophetic. The form reemerges from sense by dissemblement, duration, extension of *deadline*, and personal project. Here is subjectivity loose among the bleak structures and attempting to show them up. It goes on—into materiality, refusal, doubt, the artificial, the negation & critique, the less-than-innocuous truths, perfume, and nights with neither warmth nor transcendence. Moving.

* * *

The sense of the words is
With a backward motion, pinning me
To the daylight mode of my declaration

But ah, night may not tell
The source.

* * *

20. "Is perplexed, managing to end the sentence."

(1980)

ROBERT GRENIER

NOTES ON COOLIDGE, OBJECTIVES,
ZUKOFSKY, ROMANTICISM, AND &

. . . .

Words will do it, horses.

> "Horses: who will do it? out of manes? Words
> Will do it, out of manes, out of airs, but"

> "A-7"

. . . .

NO RACE A POSSIBILITY: CC & LZ, ZAZA, 'NECK & NECK'?
. . . .

Language process, body process, one. The words in my mind, hum.
. . . .

But, you come when you're called, some sounds break eardrums, *shutup*. She says, I don't know that it says a great deal, but I hear it. Ears & mouths of animals other than oneself. Strum, strum.

. . . .

Mmmm. Mental muscles flex, sixty-four of these. Ha ha, o *sad*. Spunch n bap bap bap. Fine time, now shift & desire it to push a toot. Set back but articulate a cramp on focus, ordinary reality today. Coffee dear? No no no oh sure oh sure sure flip as deck a half an hour into it, by the clock.

. . . .

Get it out, in the future, of them, out of the head, of the system's romanticism obviously disguised as machine. (Science exactly

530 Robert Grenier

same as poem expressing author's feelings: methodology system-
atically inflicted on things.) Words as objects? However long it
takes, doesn't help to push them around. I did so, yaaaassss, made
that page. Ahab vs. space? I just can't stop, etc., gives me a feeling
of power. I'm in my kitchen.

. . . .

Language process essentially in the world, as a function of common
sentient experience in definition of place. Any time, it makes
room, Kerouac's Cassady's Creeley's *and* Coolidge's *it it*. Get it
out of the fucking workshop, not simply into the performance of
it (vocal performance just another media routine, like 'the book'),
get it off the page, said, out of the mind, through the typewriter,
dig it, unearth or discover, word it into being. This ain't tiddly-
winks.

. . . .

'Animism'?

. . . .

It scares me that Coolidge gets up in the morning & writes (well,
yes, also but differently, envious of his time & can do), like
Hughes Rudd comes on each weekday on the ABC Morning
News, or does he.

Otherwise, a lovely durable craftsmanship ethic, it shines, it's all
right. An 'unspoken pride in the work done.'

. . . .

Difference between Eliot & Zukofsky's use of materials: E.
disappears into linguistic conventions, religious symbols, tradi-
tional view of the world via assumptives of language as statement,
swallowed up by machine he oils, he reenergizes with blood &
verbal capacities, a sacrifice; Z. takes a linguistic structure (e.g.
5-word line in "A-22") or theme (the idea of natural chronology)
as a situation, like a friendship, opening not only his own muscular
display (fast-talking, action painting, wit) but equally chance for

Robert Grenier 531

the realization of another in language & concomitant change in self's nature thereby.

I'm not clear at this point where C stands, on this, whether Williams' reaction to *The Waste Land* could apply to a stunning, repugnant display of man's talent for language bent back upon itself, all verbal system (be it 'non-referential' or 'Christian'), or whether he will or wants to go from Zukofsky, so already *is* revealing the world to us in our time.

. . . .

Mexico isn't the point, i.e. they did & didn't have to go south to Mexico, Neal went right back north north east to NYC to get married in order to go back to California to live with his former wife & Jack was already doing fine back home where *Cody* begins in miserable old gloomy Eastcoast megalopolis Long Island before Sal even sets out for Denver to see Dean (likely story, heading north to Rte. 40 to go west instead of going west directly!), but neither is it 'the blow upon the world,' alone. Clearly the self is in there somewhere, 'sketching' language mediation working upon the world, dwelling on 'crinkly tar' until 'Merrimac' & 'snake' appear as understanding.

. . . .

Writer's attitude toward his work important, places work in a life.

. . . .

CC has a terrific, consistent ability, clearly no equal in his this present generation, for sheer size & quality of facility & in-plant operation maintenance. Reading recent writing, pleasure of participation large & various in mind at work, like touring race car manufactory's factory service center, really goes on & out.

All the lithe sexuality, sense of mind engaging tensile strength of words.

. . . .

532   Robert Grenier

However (or, 'but') or so far, Zukofsky is 'better,' late *A* language process at least as interestingly intensive & variously extensive (point of *another* piece to evidence close reading of C.), *plus* makes more things happen, allows & engenders fervent beings ('manes'?) entering material world of words.

. . . .

Creation is the issue, co-positing not 'meaning,' cohabiting, language as how to live in what world. Who knows what's going to happen, what gets said.

Opposite: be defined out of existence (e.g. 'fired'), by something else.

. . . .

Or analogous instance: by volume (weight, etc.), what % of Stein's language material in *Tender Buttons* truly names something that thereby occupies space, exists as celerity & issues forth.

Symbolism, here, not referential signification, but structural identity, not relation but a circle of correspondence: *x is x*, the word *is* the thing of which it speaks. E.g. "Dining is west." How so.

. . . .

Where are they, before we existed & after words. Meantime or some day, can ask that question in language & write toward that.

What's that 'bush.'

All this emphasis on facts in the present.

. . . .

Anyway, think recent CC & LZ in light of the situation defined by Zukofsky years ago in "A-7" & ponder, as solutions, what each has done.

. . . .

Robert Grenier 533

Hats off & most interested but can't *read* either one, in form in
which it appears, consecutively, though I do, know I'm being
addressed. 'Different techniques' not signs but spans of different
lives. Passages, even, in both appear as mine.

Can't understand the 'enforced' continuity, although altogether
weeks involved in experience of each. Question of how parts make
a whole.

. . . .

To record this, LZ in Franconia, May '74, after initial public
reading of parts of "A-23," response to my question, more or less
can you realize *all* that's happening all the way through in your
mind as you read it. Z. said, "yes" to my amazement (& some-
thing like, take it easy, Bob, I grant your energy, but).

. . . .

Thinking out Olson: Eliot a dummy, not that him not bright
but language there closed system of conventional operations
& assumptions, taken as the world.

What was the wind blew through it,
    . . . .
'It's changed, it's not the same!'
        —from "Diction," from *Pieces*

. . . .

I don't *know*, though *The Maintains* effects fact, that CC doesn't
think the big white wall of language operations all the world the
poem is responsible to & for. Or my stupidity, or why should he.
Feel it, anyway, may well be a common situation of groping by
verbal means (& listening) to find way out of cave under mountain
of language habit (haha, dust to more so) to 'thing in itself,' or
whatever, as words may reveal it takes place. Thus oldtime poetry
& *truth*.

. . . .

534   *Robert Grenier*

Reference vs. non-reference? It's not that simple. Ginsberg sets out (viz. *Indian Journals*) to bring words as close as possible to facts of event perceived & ends up contributing to experience in language. Z. aspires to condition of music & ends up writing nature into existence, clearly telling names & characteristics of things.

. . . .

Pure masturbatory exercise inside no time mind space, with practice possibly virtually all extensive:

> There might be
> an imaginary
> place to be
> there might be.
> —*Pieces*, pp. 58-9

All to oneself vanished in simultaneous extensive word space. Drummers don't drum in time, become time, drum it. We can hear. Clark's as real as anybody.

. . . .

As the State man in the Littleton liquor store said to me today when I asked him for boxes, fella, don't feel bad, we don't give them to anybody. I said, I don't feel bad, I need boxes, I've got to mail a lot of books to California. So he said, did you try around back, take away all the boxes you can carry, if you take all of them, don't leave anything. All right, I said, found *two* good J&B Scotch boxes, yellow with red lettering, & solid. Good luck.

What a romantic. Taxes.

. . . .

ce·ment (sǐ-mĕnt') *n.* **1.** Any of various construction adhesives, consisting essentially of powdered, calcined rock and clay materials, that form a paste with water and can be molded or poured to set as a solid mass. See Portland cement, hydraulic cement. **2.** Any substance that hardens to act as an adhesive; glue. **3.** *Geology.* A chemically precipitated substance that binds particles of clastic rocks. **4.** Variant of cementum. —*v.* cemented, -menting, -ments. —*tr.* **1.** To bind with or as if with cement.

Robert Grenier   535

2. To cover or coat with cement. —*intr.* To become cemented. [Middle English *siment, cyment*, from Old French *ciment*, from Latin *caementum*, rough quarried stone, and its plural *caementa*, marble chips (used to make lime), from *caedere*, to cut, hew. See skhai- in Appendix.*] —**ce·ment′er** *n.*

ce·men·ta·tion (sē′mĕn-tā′shən) *n.* **1.** The process or result of cementing. **2.** A metallurgical coating process in which iron or steel is immersed in a powder of another metal, such as zinc, chromium, or aluminum, and heated to a temperature below the melting point of either.

ce·ment·ite (sĭ-mĕn′tīt′) *n.* A hard brittle iron carbide, Fe_3C, found in steel with more than 0.85 per cent carbon. [From CEMENT.]

cement mixer. A concrete mixer *(see)*.

ce·ment·um (sĭ-mĕn′təm) *n.* Also **ce·ment** (sĭ-mĕnt′). A bony substance covering the root of a tooth. [New Latin, from Latin *caementum*, rough stone, CEMENT.]

cem·e·ter·y (sĕm′ə-tĕr′ē) *n., pl.* **-ies.** A place for burying the dead; graveyard. [Middle English *cimitery*, from Late Latin *coemētērium*, from Greek *koimētērion*, sleeping room, burial place, from *koiman*, to put to sleep. See kei-¹ in Appendix.*]

cen. **1.** central. **2.** century.

cen·a·cle (sĕn′ə-kəl) *n.* A small dining room, usually on an upper floor. [Middle English, from Old French, from Late Latin *cēnāculum*, dining room, the Cenacle of the Last Supper, from Latin *cēna*, dinner. See sker-¹ in Appendix.*]

–cene. Indicates a recent geological period; for example, **Neocene.** [From Greek *kainos*, new, fresh. See ken-³ in Appendix.*]

cen·o·bite (sĕn′ə-bīt′, sē′nə-) *n.* Also **coen·o·bite.** A member of a religious convent or community. [Late Latin *coenobita*, from *coenobium*, convent, from Greek *koinobion*, life in community : *koinos*, common (see kom in Appendix*) + *bios*, life (see gwei- in Appendix*).] —**cen′o·bit′ic** (-bĭt′ĭk), **cen′o·bit′i·cal** *adj.* —**cen′o·bit′ism′** (sĕn′ə-bĭt-ĭz′əm, sē′nə-) *n.*

ce·no·gen·e·sis (sē′nō-jĕn′ə-sĭs, sĕn′ō-) *n.* Also **coe·no·gen·e·sis.** The environmentally determined development of characteristics or structures in an organism. [Greek *kainos*, fresh, new (see ken-³ in Appendix*) + GENESIS.] —**ce′no·ge·net′ic** (-jə-nĕt′ĭk) *adj.* —**ce′no·ge·net′i·cal·ly** *adv.*

cen·o·taph (sĕn′ə-tăf′, -täf′) *n.* A monument erected in honor of a dead person whose remains lie elsewhere. [Old French *cenotaphe*, from Latin *cenotaphium*, from Greek *kenotaphion*, empty tomb : *kenos*, empty (see ken-⁴ in Appendix*) + *taphos*, tomb (see dhembh- in Appendix*).] —**cen′o·taph′ic** *adj.*

Ce·no·zo·ic (sē′nə-zō′ĭk, sĕn′ə-) *adj.* Of, belonging to, or designating the latest era of geologic time, which includes the Tertiary and Quaternary periods and is characterized by the evolution of mammals, birds, plants, modern continents, and glaciation. See geology. —*n. Geology.* The Cenozoic era. Preceded by *the.* [Greek *kainos*, new, fresh (see ken-³ in Appendix*) + -ZOIC.]

American Heritage Dictionary of the English Language, p. 217

· · · · · · · · · ·

My best analogy to what C. is doing is Central African Pygmy music & then I put him way ahead of me, singing, dancing, instrumentalizing, simultaneously, omnipresent activity inside the music all the world.

536   Robert Grenier

He's a one man show. Did all die, or what.

. . . .

HOPEFUL

now you know that's all so

. . . .

Not satisfying to think only in oneself. Too 'romantic,' too
like me.

I go there, inside the work, as often as possible. It's a great place
to be.

. . . .

just alone a lonely stay at home

waking up in the morning

. . . .

"Thou watchest the last oozings hours by hours."
Keats, Oct. 11, 1975

. . . .

How about telepathy, i.e. dispersing of notion of form altogether,
& no person, just pure conversing with it.

. . . .

Loneliness result of self perceiving itself as individual. Empathy
result of self projecting itself on anything. Statement issue of
language conventions taken as fact. *The Maintains* product of
Coolidge's operations. Quincunx translated to lines from fives
in nature. Help.

Ouch. Paint is paint. What a circle.

. . . .

Robert Grenier   537

So anything goes, but "nothing is anything but itself, measured so." (Olson)

Painting paint. Chairing chairs. Words words. Relax into the activity, & in the acceptance of limits, thrive.

. . . .

No, it's a 'lie,' acceptance of only apparently previously given conditions of fact as presently real. It's much more mysterious.

"Form is what happens." It did happen, but it only happened to happen. It couldn't have happened otherwise, we think. *What* happened.

Meanwhile, there's very little knowledge of where it came from. Where is it now. All this time using English, *that* was gone by.

. . . .

Most words just echoes, corpses. Existence is a corpse. You want to stare at it, play with it, assemble it.

It doesn't matter if it's dead. Try alchemy.

. . . .

Awful deadness of metal parts, all heat &light gone out, just reflections off surfaces interesting enough.

What's 'behind' what happens.

. . . .

Language tells, counts & shows, in moments of realization it comes into existence in particular words & dies, as every one does, & is reborn, again & again, in all manner of evanescent phenomena, flashes of light, heat, sound. Words.

Feel C's interest as language process calls things into being again
& again, in *The Maintains*, but does he think these things are
words only.

Existence in part the product of a preposition:
> Roast potatoes for.
>> —*Tender Buttons*

. . . .

AMY

jumprope

dries your hair

while your hair

is drying

. . . .

> Is a door
> for—but
> who enters
>> —*Pieces*

the material spiritual world.

. . . .

Talk like this doesn't often have much to do with it.
Coolidge may be convinced he's dealing exclusively with verbal
relations & by such conviction free himself to think inside
language closely enough to make a place for the gods, or express
himself & his procedures & world the more completely, or even
copy nature. I can blab on about 'material spiritual' etc. & do
nothing with words to effect anything but a troubled idiocy.

Robert Grenier   539

Nevertheless, for purposes of the discussion of writing, the statement that words are as real as anything else & deserve to be treated primarily as facts (not signs) in a physical force field is only beginning to get down to what language is doing.

Coolidge, in his works, has been beyond this blunt idea (it's not conceptual art) for a long time.

. . . .

What's interesting about a word or group of words in time is the same as what's interesting about a person or group of people in a room.

It's not simply that something exists (although that does become a concern, as a question, that that is *that*, a 'mystery'), but who it is, what it is, how did it get there, what's it doing, what can we do together, etc., all age old common place concerns, that involve us or don't: the energy in a fact, how this one conducts itself, & finally (not 'meaning' as meaning something other than itself, toward which it points) what seems to be evidenced in the thing, what's it saying, what's alive there.

. . . .

Last ditch effort of romanticism to establish itself via total control over verbal universe a writer puts there by marking "I" etc. (1000 pages of it), "I" on a page (least interesting as most conventional, traditionally inevitable aspect of CC's work), flips over into wholly new thing, outside the bounds of extant literary criticism.

The poem doesn't exist, as 'poem,' because it doesn't ordinarily say anything—save maybe fuck you to MacLeish by really realizing his 'poem should not mean but be.' The writer is not typically expressing himself in the poem, so work doesn't yield much re information on the writer's condition (understood as how he feels, details of personal circumstance); simply, he did it, or so he says, by signing his name to the work. The world, clearly,

is not normally mirrored. The audience is not apparently
addressed (though involved).

So, what is it, for novice & experienced reader alike, what *are*
these words.

. . . .

What are the relations between language & physical mental process
(not 'will,' not 'personality,' not 'feeling'), such that we perceive
ourselves as existing in language in the head.

What are the relations between words (like 'Fred' or 'Harry') &
the things words seem to call into being, such that we perceive
ourselves as existing through language in the world.

"I" say, "*I* am," "*You* are." These are words. I understand the
structure of experience *in language*.

What does it mean to write, to use these words.

. . . .

CC in his operations provides a massive evidence of mental
process, *how he thinks*, already one of the most extensive &
informative, literal instances of same in literature, which is
not to measure literature by an 'index of personality' (so
convert the poem into statement of the poet's life), but just to
say that his mind exists there in his words, & equally, that the
place of the words, a place, is C's mind.

And we read it—i.e. the work makes room not only for C's
mental activity but that of people at all familiar with English,
all cooperating in the creation of the work by reading it
silently or aloud.

. . . .

Sentences, sentience, words as ways of moving, language process
place for mind & everything so recognizable to exist in the world.

Robert Grenier   541

I see you, says you. All that I can't say or see, being here, & me. Every thing I can.

All this, in such words.

. . . .

The world comes into existence in a tree, this tree in this place & season. An experience of a word involving recognition by a consciousness equally present makes the world (or words don't need us, any more than trees?).

. . . .

What do words know of each other, possibilities of sentience in words as well as dogs, plants.

. . . .

Again, question of *how* words further perception, act in same place same time as mind's experience of objects in situation, like a third party (a sentence) tells & shows you what's happening. Language as operationally interactive definition, or some such, but that's my need.

C. primarily concerned with relationship between language & mental process. I'm more interested in ways words contribute to experience of things. These are different emphases, parts of the whole event.

. . . .

Complacency (?) somewhere in C., a not having to explicitly address connections between language & other real things, or just sort of purposefully simple-minded provisional set that allows writing to go on, a working solution?

Recalls linguistic philosophy not concerned to inquire into questions of origin of language & its function in different human situations, content to accept proposition that it occurs in forms it does & investigate same.

542   Robert Grenier

Rest of the world somehow not a problem, or it *can* be excluded
from the work.

. . . .

Words don't have to say or be anything but what each is & does.
A word space.

Still, each is possessed, by the energy *therein* occurring.

Turn around. What are the creatures standing off the wall.

. . . .

Where words are, we are, so are things. Three things, however
this may come about, simultaneously. Here we are, say any &
each. Now what. As such verbal mental process faculty, sharp
by practice—*whirr-whirring*—CC's ready for anything.

(1975)

Robert Grenier   543

RAE ARMANTROUT

"WHY DON'T WOMEN DO LANGUAGE-ORIENTED WRITING?"

I've been asked this question twice, in slightly differing forms. In conversation I was asked, "Why don't more women do language-oriented writing?" I answered that women need to describe the conditions of their lives. This entails representation. Often they feel too much anger to participate in the analytical tendencies of modernist or "post-modernist" art. This was an obvious answer. The more I thought about it the less it explained anything important. Most male writers aren't language-centered either. Why don't more men do language-oriented writing?

Several months later, by mail, I was asked to write an article explaining why women *don't* produce language-oriented works. The letter suggested I might elaborate on the answer I'd given before. But it wasn't the same question! Some female writers do focus on language. Was I being asked to justify their exclusion from consideration? Lyn Hejinian, Bernadette Mayer, Alice Notley, Susan Howe, Hannah Weiner, Carla Harryman, Lynne Dreyer, Joanne Kyger, Anne Waldman and Maureen Owen seem, to one degree or another, language-oriented. Of course, that's a tricky term. If it's taken to mean total non-reference, these women don't fit. Neither, however, do Ron Silliman, Barrett Watten, Bob Perelman, Ted Greenwald, Charles Bernstein or Bruce Andrews.

To believe non-referentiality is possible is to believe language can be divorced from thought, words from their histories. If the idea of non-reference is discarded, what does language-oriented mean? Does it simply designate writing which is language-conscious (self-aware)? If so, the term could be applied to a very large number of writers. Anyone who sees the way signifier intertwines with signified will pay close heed to the structures of language.

Susan Howe calls our attention to the effect of linguistic structure on belief when she writes

as wise as an (earwig, owl, eel).
as sober as a (knight, minstrel, judge).
as crafty as a (fox, cuckoo, kitten).
as smooth as (sandpaper, velvet, wood).
as slippery as an (accident, eel, engine).
as straight as an (angle, angel, arrow).

(*The Western Borders*, Tuumba Press)

And a minstrel may very well be more clear-headed than a judge. It's important to note this.

Howe's passage amounts to a polemic against the influence of habit. This specific concern is common in language-oriented work. When Carla Harryman writes,

> Although temperature flags on its own, the past dissolves. I wanted to settle down to a nap. The sand settles at the bottom of the ocean. I sink to the top of the water.

("Sites," *Hills* magazine #4)

the word "although" prepares the reader for a contradiction between the clauses in the first sentence. When no contradiction follows, the reader's attention increases. The concept of contradiction is rooted in the laws of logic, cause and effect. Harryman wants to throw these "laws" into question. There is the jar of discontinuity between the clauses, sentences and paragraphs in this work. The lines I quoted do not follow logically, but they are united *linguistically* by the near-synonymous verbs. Harryman puts content at odds with syntactical (or sometimes narrative) structures in order to make these structures stand out, enter our consciousness.

Although Lyn Hejinian uses syntax in a fairly conventional way, her work is less referential than that of most of the writers I've mentioned. Of course, her writing does "say things" about the world, but the significance of these statements is not what interests her. In her book, *A Mask of Motion*, she rings the changes on a number of phrases and words. Each usage of a word becomes a mask for its other uses. Context, placement area of prime importance. When she writes "of the yapping distances, the extended return" one hears the dog she introduced five pages earlier.

Howe, Harryman and Hejinian are very different, yet the term language-oriented might be applied to any of them. I use that term but I'm suspicious of it, finally, because it seems to imply division between language and experience, thought and feeling, inner and outer. The work I like best sees itself and sees the world. It is ambi-centric, if you will. The writers I like are surprising, revelatory. They bring the underlying structures of language/thought into consciousness. They spurn the facile. Though they generally don't believe in the Truth, they are scrupulously honest about the way word relates to word, sentence to sentence. Some of them are men and some are women.

(1978)

TINA DARRAGH

HOWE

When I first read Susan Howe's work, I had no idea of what she was trying to do. She was using the vocabulary of the 'Old World' (terms from the classics, mythology, the Bible, Latin liturgy, and so on) and combining it with experimental techniques such as the fragmentation of words and the isolation of individual letters. With this mix, who would be her readers? I took her work to heart with this puzzle in mind.

From the start, I heard Susan's work against the backdrop of the '70s as the decade of the women's movement 'lit crit' division. Whenever I take up one of her books, I am reminded of the endless discussion groups dealing with the topic of the 'polically correct' woman writer. The sum of these meetings sounded something like this: because the formation of our language came about through commerce controlled by men, our language is structured to serve their needs and is, in essence, 'male-oriented.' The only way to challenge this orientation, then, is through the stream of consciousness technique, since writing coming from the subconscious can bring forth new patterns of information not yet co-opted by commerce. Conversely, to write abstractly was to use the 'language of business', to play Western patriarchy's game and thereby continue the patterns of male oppression.

Of all the assumptions in that line of reasoning, the one that continues to bother me the most is the stereotyping of the 'process' of women's creative power as still the private, intuitive energy that gives birth to something new, another form of 'motherhood'. Analytical thought continued to be man's domain, and a dirty realm at that.

Susan began writing poetry around 1970 (after painting for ten years) and I regret not knowing her work back then. Her first book, *Hinge Picture* (Telephone, 1974) could have brought some needed clarity to our women's group discussions that grew increasingly embroiled in ideological arguments that obscured real feelings and real events, both past and present. *Hinge Picture* begins with Susan stating 'She rises while it is yet dark, to trace a military combination/ in the sand, singing . . .' (p. 5) and trace she does with lists and simple sentences becoming an outline of patriarchial mores incorporating all the characters passed down to us through literature. Technically, she then startles these 'old stories' by fragmenting them and using (for example) isolated 'e' and 's' sounds to screech and hisss at them.

```
                    five princes
                    buried their
                    father divid
                    ed his subjec
                    ts forgot his
                    advice separ
                    ated from eac
                    h other and w
                    andered in qu
                    est of fortun
                    e        (p. 14)
```

&

```
                    a king
                    delight
                    s in war    (p. 15)
```

She concludes *Hinge Picture* by placing her work firmly in the matriarchal tradition: (from 'breaking all the rules', the final poem) 'Deliver us back to the wide world's oldest song/when mother was a fairy woman same root as Finn/pinion on the clean fin clear clear wave'.

All this is not to say that Susan writes as a 'political' poet, but that I read her as one. While other writers were *talking about* getting to the roots of women's literature, Susan had placed herself there and was ready to take on other projects, such as: *The Western Borders* (Tuumba Press, 1976), an elaboration on the nursery rhyme 'oh would I were where I would be!'; an analysis of the word 'mark' and all its definitions (Mark being the name of both her father and her son) that was published as *Secret History of the Dividing Line* (Telephone, 1978); a response to Boswell's quote of Johnson ('. . . The poem might begin with the advantages of civilized society over a rude state, exemplified by the Scotch, who had no cabbages till Oliver Cromwell's soldiers

548   *Tina Darragh*

introduced them . . .') published as *Cabbage Gardens* (Fathom Press, 1979); and her most recent book, *The Liberties* (Loon Books, 1980), a narrative account of the relationship of Jonathan Swift and 'Stella' followed by (among other things) a play documenting in dialogue the fragmented, lonely nature of their lives that is tied to the legacy of literary history by the addition of another player, *Lear's* Cordelia.

I see the final section of *The Liberties*, 'Formation of a Separatist, I,' as a point of departure back into Susan's work as a whole:

> I am composed of nine letters . . .

> solus with a letter

> S

> Here set at liberty . . .

Literally, she is spelling out her reason for writing—experimentation with the patterns of words handed down to her equals freedom. She stands up against the weight of our language's history and, as an intellectual, fights back—an act of liberation that is valid on its own and in many ways compliments the struggle of those bringing up information from the subconscious.

(1982)

Tina Darragh 549

KIT ROBINSON

7 DAYS IN ANOTHER TOWN

Mesopotamian wind
blows the same way twice.

"Forever"

Two bullet holes:
one in the window
one in the arm.

"Something isn't happening
or isn't going to. . ."

Then, sun,
The Wedge

Dear Carla & Benny—

I had a refreshing and wonderful time in LA. Thanks for taking care of me so well.

Carla, I have not written more for your & Stephanie's mag so am sending what I did jot there with this scholarly annotation which you may print too if you want—

Mesopotamian for the UniRoyal plant with its incredible Sargon of Akkhad design. Also for Griffith's depiction of Babylon in Intolerance & the fact that LA, like that metropolitan area, was settled by nomads who had to come across desert.

Wind for that gale that nearly blew us off our feet & made walking to the bank an adventure.

Blows the same way twice (in fact, "forever") in Topanga Canyon where we saw aisles of stone raked up the sides of hills by the air off eons & crouched in curved saucer-shaped caves carved out by same—twice in contrapunction to remark of Heraclitus about not being able to step in same river any more times than one, his point being a universal state of flux, whereas in LA forms tend toward a monolithic eternal Idea, like the movies, or Century City isn't about to budge. "Forever" is what Chris Burden wrote inside the shape traced around his body when he fell off the ladder he'd been sitting on X number of hours.

Like I said the bullet hole in the window was really made by a pebble Larry threw up there to engage the attention of Rene Ricard who was inside talking on the phone. The force of the wind drove it through. The one in the arm is from another of Burden's stunts.

"Something isn't happening—or isn't going to. . ." was said by Rene Ricard on same Topanga drive in reference to sight of a small crowd, several vehicles, unidentified equipment and police milling around on top a bluff. I still don't know what he meant, specifically, but as I'd mistakenly assumed we were witnessing aftermath of an accident, possibly fatal, I took it, morbidly I guess, as a comment on death.

Then, sun, which continues to appear, especially yesterday here, and The Wedge where the surfers go in Newport Beach. Vico claimed the wedge was primal creative form, representing ether,

which carves all creation out of air—hence first Mesopotamian
writing used cuneiform.

Love, Kit

CLARK COOLIDGE

from ARRANGEMENT

    I also want to say that there are no rules. At least not at first there aren't. If you start with rules, you've really got a tough road. What I think is that you start with materials. You start with matter, not with rules. The rules appear, the limitations appear, and those are *your* limitations and the limitations of the material. Stone has a certain cleavage. You can't make it look a certain way if the stone is not constructed to allow you to do that. . . .

                      [*writes on blackboard:*]

        ounce code orange

        a

           the

              ohm

        trilobite trilobites

    This is a poem from a group of poems I wrote in 1966, when I was living in Cambridge in the same house with Aram Saroyan, and he was writing these one-word poems, dividing everything down to the smallest possible thing. . . and I immediately wanted to put them together. I couldn't stand the idea of one word. I don't think there *is* one word. So this is one of those poems. I did maybe twenty or thirty of these. I suppose they're about as unadulterated, pure, if you will, as anything I ever did. I was really trying to work with the words, look at the words, try to use all their qualities. There's no question of meaning, in the sense of explaining and understanding this poem. Hopefully, it's a unique object, not just an object. Language isn't just objects, it moves. I'll try to talk about some of the qualities of these words that I was aware of when I was writing it, as best I can. It was eleven years ago.

"ounce code orange": ways of measuring, in a sense. Weight, a symbol system, a color. "a/the": the indefinite article, the definite article. "ohm" is the unit of electrical resistance, a quality of metal, let's say, that requires a certain amount of juice to go through. In other words, this is a fuzzy, resistant word. It hangs down here, it affects particularly this space. I wanted these things hanging in the middle because they could adhere to words in either the top line or the bottom line. "*the* ounce," "*a/the* code," "*the* orange." You can't say "a ounce" or "a orange," practically. You can say "a code." So there are those vectors going there. "trilobites": you know what a trilobite is, it's an early animal of the Paleozoic Age that was a crustacean divided into three lobes. As a word, to me it's completely irreducible. What are you going to do with it? "A trilobite": it's like a clinker. Angular, uneven, heavy word. So, I made a plural, and I also say, "trilobite trilobites." That second trilobite becomes a verb. And I feel, as Fenollosa pointed out, that every noun is a verb, and vice versa, and there really are a hell of a lot of them in the English language which don't connect except in being the same word, like the word "saw." "I saw the saw.". . .

. . . Well, "trilobite trilobites": it sounds like a rudiment, a paradiddle or something you have to practice. That's what I don't like. It's not [*hums a bop rhythm*]. You know, it's not as shapely, which I've tried to do more of since. . . . I also found out later that "ounce" is the name for a kind of leopard. I don't know if anybody knows that. I think it's Indian, or Tibetan. It's a cat called an ounce. So, you think of "pounce." There are these words that begin to adhere and appear like ghosts around these things. Ounce, pounce, bounce. "code"—I don't know, that's beginning to seem a little neutral to me. "Orange": the color *and* the round thing, the fruit. Now that I've said that, the word "ounce" begins to seem round to me. "A trilobite," "*the* trilobites." That's how that goes. And this is the dead spot of the poem, the resistance: "ohm." And it's also almost like the "Om," the balance. . . .

(1977)

SUSAN HOWE

P. INMAN, *Platin*

Platin is a sequence consisting of eighteen parts. One poem approx-
imately thirteen lines long, faces a blank white page. Except for
the ninth, which has been completely broken apart, each unit
suggests a sonnet. The typewriter (hence the title) is an integral
part of each segment. Even its sound imposes.

#1

leans tain clack. cilk , tasp. blosset

A Sonnet = Three quatrains linked by a couplet. The couplet in
#17 (for Ted Berrigan) 'pill booked of linen'--

ojibing, pense toney ocrurs. (assits. . .)fell(. . .womb)immode.
felds a bring of lyed plane. tile crombie

Typos, space between letters, signs, marks, quatrains, couplets,
commas—all are called into play. *Platin* works on many levels.
Sequentially, acoustically, visually, historically, ly, ly, and ly. Here
words in nowords, names in nonames. There, deftly anticipated
by Messerli's cover (Old Old - New New - Old New New Old).
Inman's work is a pilgrim's progress through Coolidge (*Space*)
Berrigan (*Sonnets*) and Monk (*Sound Modules*), by way of Darragh
(*My Hands to Myself*) and dictionary magic. . . . .
> Let us note in this song the first manifestation of the musical
> symbolism of the alphabet, which Berg believed in all his life
> to the point of superstition. At the point where the text
> speaks of a "white hand in a fairy tale" are heard the notes
> A-B flat-B natural (in German A-B-H), the initials of Berg and
> his wife, Alban-Berg-Helene.
> —Leibowitz on Alban Berg

Inman knows about "the white hand in a fairy tale." Spinets,
harp, quill, veil gilling barn, sim-nickeled willow, some leafgreen
braid, whistled the browns of carbon, gile brilliance - A formal con-
cern remains. Meaning self destructs. Nonsense. The work teeters
at the edge, remains rooted in the shape of time, stops short of
gibberish. Flags go up. Names. Affirmation in disintegration.

Susan Howe 555

aiety builds, yate of ages
bates a life of brings. brattle me
etter gray or her lip

thical of beginning
. . .elair . . .tham one iced

pipple street   pleat glow from like

Like a plainsong fragment, the series can be endlessly interpreted.
Kinship and Contrast: Inman's space is fractured. The action is
interrupted, the situation tense. Construct of equivalencies, ZIP
Brouillons of painters, writers, and musicians, crisscrossed with
erasures and corrections.

"j. lightning franklin",paiuc
close on fram   . . .ckade white ites
                                    . . .fring. . .oply
float went glimmer   . . .glimming giotto paves

No props from an antiquated legend 'termins a Maughm prit'
Barnett Newman to Suzanne Langer
          "Esthetic is for artists
          what Ornithology is for the birds."
Worn words and tattered feathers. Only names remain. Letters.
Can they be saved and how? Forward in a backward direction, a
world of torn words turns to grasp   dimmers knew view
          errit, hist
          well, deafing - smoothing hegel means of a formal
cavett bladened writers braids monitering career beads all torn
plank kerouac paisle achilles   (a sill
                              of crays). . .
fracting to books

Hess said of Newman, "The openness of Newman's work is con-
comitant with chance and one person's knowledge." Inman's too.

(1980)

556 Susan Howe

EXPERIMENTS

Pick any word at random (noun is easy): let mind play freely around it until a few ideas have passed through. Then seize on them, look at them, & record. Try this with a non-connotative word, like "so" etc.

Systematically eliminate the use of certain kinds of words or phrases from a piece of writing, either your own or someone else's, for example, eliminate all adjectives or all words beginning with 's' from Shakespeare's sonnets.

Systematically derange the language, for example, write a work consisting only of prepositional phrases, or, add a gerundive to every line of an already existing piece of prose or poetry, etc.

Rewrite someone else's writing. Maybe someone formidable.

Get a group of words (make a list or select at random); then form these words (only) into a piece of writing — whatever the words allow. Let them demand their own form, and/or: Use certain words in a set way, like, the same word in every line, or in a certain place in every paragraph, etc. Design words.

Never listen to poets or other writers; never explain your work (communication experiment).

Set up multiple choice or fill-in-the-blanks situations & play with them, considering every word an 'object' with no meaning, perhaps just sound, or, a block of meaning, meaning anything.

Eliminate material systematically from a piece of your own writing until it's 'ultimately' reduced, or, read or write it backwards (line by line or word by word). Read a novel backwards.

Using phrases relating to one subject or idea, write about another (this is pushing metaphor & simile as far as you can), for example, steal science terms or philosophical language & write about snow or boredom.

Experiment with theft & plagiarism in any form that occurs to you.

Take an idea, anything that interests you, even an object: then spend a few days looking & noticing (making notes, etc.?) what comes up about that idea, or, try to create a surrounding, an atmosphere, where everything that comes up is "in relation".

Construct a poem as though the words were three-dimensional objects (like bricks) in space. Print them on large cards, if necessary.

Cut-ups, paste-ups, etc. (Intersperse different material in horizontal cut-up strips, paste it together, infinite variations on this).

Write exactly as you think, as close as you can come to this, that is, put pen to paper & dont stop.

Attempt tape recorder work, that is, speaking directly into the tape, perhaps at specific times.

Note what happens for a few days, hours (any space of time that has a limit you set); then look for relationships, connections, synchronicities; make something of it (writing).

Get a friend or two friends to write *for* you, pretending they *are* you.

Use (take, write in) a strict form and/or try to destroy it, e.g., the sestina.

Take or write a story or myth, continue to rewrite it over & over, or, put it aside &, trying to remember, write it five or ten times (from memory); see how it's changed. Or, make a work out of continuously saying, in a column or list, a sentence or line, & saying it over in a different way, ways, until you get it "right". Save the whole thing.

Typing vs. longhand experiments as recording/creating devices/ modes. Do what you do least.

Make a pattern of repetitions.

Take an already written work of your own & insert (somewhere at random, or by choice) a paragraph or section from, for example, a book on information theory or a catalogue of some sort. Then study the possibilities of rearranging this work, or perhaps, rewriting the 'source'.

Experiment with writing in every person & tense every day.

Explore possibilities of lists, puzzles, riddles, dictionaries, almanacs for language use.

Write what cannot be written, for example, compose an index. (Read an index as a poem).

The possibilities of synesthesia in relation to language & words: The word & the letter as sensations, colors evoked by letters, sensations caused by the sound of a word as apart from its meaning, etc. *And*, the effect of this phenomenon on you, for example, write in the water, on a moving vehicle.

Attempt writing in a state of mind that seems least congenial.

Consider word & letter as forms — the concretistic distortion of a text, for example, too many o's or a multiplicity of thin letters (lllftiii, etc).

Consider (do) memory experiments (sensory) in relation to writing: for example, record all sense images that remain from breakfast; study which sense(s) engage you, escape you.

Write, taking off from visual projection, whether mental or mechanical, without thought to the word (in the ordinary sense, no craft). Write in the movies, etc.

Make writing experiments over a long period of time: for example, plan how much you will write on a particular work (one word?) each day, or, at what time of a particular day (noon?) or week, or, add to the work only on holidays, etc.

Write on a piece of paper where something is already printed or written, as, in your favorite book of prose or poetry (over the print, in the white space).

B. Mayer & Members of St. Mark's Church Poetry Workshop   559

Attempt to eliminate all connotation from a piece of writing & vice versa.

Use source material, that is, experiment with other people's writings, sayings, & doings.

Experiment with writing in a group, collaborative work: a group writing individually off of each others work over a long period of time (8 hours say); a group contributing to the same work, sentence by sentence, line by line; one writer being fed 'information' while the other writes; writing, leaving instructions for another writer to fill in what you 'cant' describe; compiling a book or work structured by your own language around the writings of others; a group working & writing off of each other's dream-writing.

Use dictionary constantly, plain & etymological (rhyming, etc.); consult, experiment with thesaurus where categories for the word 'word' include: word as news, word as message, word as information, word as story, word as order or command, word as vocable, unit of speech, word as instruction, promise, vow, contract & so on.

Dream work: record dreams daily, experiment with translation or transcription of dream-thought, attempt to approach the tense & incongruity appropriate to the dream, work with the dream until a poem, song or phrase that is useful can come out of it, consider the dream as problem-solving device (artistic problem, other), consider the dream as a form of consciousness (altered state) & use it (write with it) as an 'alert' form of the mind's activity, change dream characters into fictional characters & accept dream 'language' (words spoken or heard in dream) as gift. Use them.

Work your ass off to change the language & dont ever get famous.

(1978)

RON SILLIMAN

From THE NEW SENTENCE

How do sentences integrate into higher units of meaning? The obvious first step here is toward the paragraph. To quote Voloshinov:

> . . . in certain crucial respects paragraphs are analogues to exchanges in dialogue. The paragraph is something like a vitiated dialogue worked into the body of a monologic utterance. Behind the device of partitioning speech into units, which are termed paragraphs in their written form, lie orientation toward listener or reader and calculation of the latter's possible reactions.

The definition here is not that radically different from partitioning strategies in some current work, such as David Bromige's essay poems. David Antin, in his talk at 80 Langton Street, described his own work in just Voloshinov's terms, as a vitiated dialogue.

Ferrucio Rossi-Landi, the Italian semiotician, focuses on this problem more closely, when he argues that the syllogism is the classic mode of above-sentence integration. For example, the sentences "All women were once girls" and "Some women are lawyers" logically lead to a third sentence or conclusion, a higher level of meaning: "Some lawyers were once girls." Literature proceeds by suppression, most often, of this third term, positing instead chains of the order of the first two. For example:

> He thought they were a family unit. There were seven men and four women, and thirteen children in the house. Which voice was he going to record?
>
> ("Plasma," Barrett Watten)

But this integration is, in fact, a presumption by the reader. In the next paragraph, Watten plays with the reader's recognition of this presumptiveness:

> That's why we talk language. Back in Sofala I'm writing this down wallowing in a soft leather armchair. A dead dog lies in the gutter, his feet in the air.

Whereas two paragraphs before, the separation of the sentences was so large as to suppress integration altogether:

> The burden of classes is the twentieth-century career. He can be incredibly cruel. Events are advancing at a terrifying rate.

Rossi-Landi also gives us a final means of looking at the importance of the sentence. *Linguistics and Economics* argues that language-use arises from the need to divide labor in the community, and that the elaboration of language-systems and of labor production, up to and including all social production, follow identical paths. In this view, the completed tool is a sentence.

A hammer, for example, consists of a face, a handle, and a peen. Without the presence of all three, the hammer will not function. Sentences relate to their subunits in just this way. Only the manufacturer of hammers would have any use for disconnected handles; thus without the whole there can be no exchange value. Likewise, it is at the level of the sentence that the use value and the exchange value of any statement unfold into view.

As such, the sentence is the hinge unit of any literary product.

Larger literary products, such as poems, are like completed machines. Any individual sentence might be a piston. It will not get you down the road by itself, but you cannot move the automobile without it.

I have said that the sentence is a unit of prose writing. Certainly sentences exist in literature before the arrival of prose literature. Grammar, and thus the idea of the sentence, not only extended from models of high discourse, but was and has always been taught and predicated on the idea of such models. As Shklovsky noted, prose enters literature with the rise of printing a little more than 500 years ago. As such, its social role as an index of education became progressively more important as education spread to the bourgeois classes. The more educated the individual, the more likely her utterances would have the characteristics of well-formed sentences. The sentence, well-formed and complete, was and still is an index of class in society.

Now prose fiction to a significant extent derives from the narrative epics of poetry, but moves toward a very different sense of form and organization. Exterior formal devices, such as rhyme and linebreak, diminish and the units of prose become the sentence

562 Ron Silliman

and the paragraph. In the place of external devices, which function to keep the reader's or listener's experience at least partly in the present, consuming the text, fiction foregrounds the syllogistic leap or integration above the level of the sentence to create a fully referential tale.

This does not mean that the prose fiction paragraph is without significant form, even in the most compelling narrative. Consider this paragraph from Conrad's *The Secret Agent*:

> In front of the great doorway a dismal row of newspaper sellers standing clear of the pavement dealt out their wares from the gutter. It was a raw, gloomy day of the early spring; and the grimy sky, the mud of the streets, the rags of the dirty men harmonized excellently with the eruption of the damp, rubbishy sheets of paper soiled with printers' ink. The posters, maculated with filth, garnished like tapestry the sweep of the curbstone. The trade in afternoon papers was brisk, yet, in comparison with the swift, constant march of foot traffic, the effect was of indifference, of disregarded distribution. Ossipon looked hurriedly both ways before stepping out into the cross-currents, but the Professor was already out of sight.

Only the last of these five sentences actually furthers the narrative. The rest serve to set the scene, but do so in the most elegant manner imaginable. Every sentence here is constructed around some kind of opposition. The first takes us from the "great doorway" to a "dismal row" in the "gutter." The second contrasts "spring" with "raw and gloomy," and then has the "grimy sky," "the mud," "the rags of the dirty men" "harmonize excellently" with the "damp rubbishy sheets soiled with ink." And so forth, even to the presence of Ossipon and the absence of the Professor.

This kind of structure might well be foregrounded in a poem, by placing key terms in critical places along the line, by putting certain oppositions in literal rhyme, and by writing the whole perhaps in the present tense. Fiction has a much greater tendency toward the aorist or past tense in general. More importantly, the lack of these foregrounding devices permits the syllogistic or fetishistic capacity of the language to become dominant.

It is this condition of prose that we find also in the work of Russell Edson, the best known English language writer of the prose poem. This is from "The Sardine Can Dormitory":

> A man opens a sardine can and finds a row of tiny cots full of tiny dead people: it is a dormitory flooded with oil.
>
> He lifts out the tiny bodies with a fork and lays them on a slice of bread; put a leaf of lettuce over them, and closes the sandwich with another slice of bread.
>
> He wonders what he should do with the tiny cots: wondering if they are not eatable, too?
>
> He looks into the can and sees a tiny cat floating in the oil. The bottom of the can, under the oil, is full of little shoes and stockings. . .

Other than the hallucinated quality of the tale, derived from surrealism and the short stories of Kafka, there is really nothing here of great difference from the conditions of prose as one finds it in fiction. If anything, it has less of the formal qualities of poetry than the Conrad passage above.

In good part, what makes Edson a prose poet is where he publishes. The poems in *Edson's Mentality*, from which this was taken, were first published in *Poetry Now, Oink!*, and *The Iowa Review*. By publishing among poets, Edson has taken on the public role of a poet, but a poet whose work participates entirely in the tactics and units of fiction.

Edson is a good example of why the prose poem—even that name is awkward—has come to be thought of as a bastard form.

Even today in America the prose poem barely has any legitimacy. There are no prose poems at all in Hayden Carruth's anthology, *The Voice That Is Great Within Us*.

Nor in Donald Allen's *The New American Poetry*.

Nor in the Kelly/Leary anthology *A Controversy of Poets*.

The prose poem came into existence in France. From 1699, the rules of versification set down by the French Academy proved so rigid that some writers simply chose to sidestep them, composing instead in a "poetic" prose style, writing epics and pastorals in this mode in the 18th Century. At the same time, poetry from other languages was being translated into French prose. It was Aloysius Bertrand who, in 1827, first began to compose poems in prose. He published these works in a book called *Gaspard de la Nuit*. By the end of the 19th Century, the prose poem had been incorporated fully into French literature by Baudelaire, Mallarme, and Rimbaud.

The French found the prose poem to be an ideal device for the dematerialization of writing per se. Gone were the external devices of form that naggingly held the reader at least partially in the present. Sentences could be lengthened, stretched even further than the already long sentences which characterized Mallarme's verse, without befuddling the reader or disengaging her from the poem. And longer sentences also suspended for greater periods of time the pulse of closure which enters into prose as the mark of rhythm. It was perfect for hallucinated, fantastic and dreamlike contents, for pieces with multiple locales and times squeezed into a few words. Here is a six sentence poem by Mallarme, translated by Keith Bosley as "The Pipe":

> Yesterday I found my pipe as I was dreaming about a long evening's work, fine winter work. Throwing away cigarettes with all the childish joys of summer into the past lit by sun-blue leaves, the muslin dresses and taking up again my earnest pipe as a serious man who wants a long undisturbed smoke, in order to work better; but I was not expecting the surprise this abandoned creature was preparing, hardly had I taken the first puff when I forgot my great books to be done, amazed, affected, I breathed last winter coming back. I had not touched the faithful friend since my return to France, and all London, London as I lived the whole of it by myself, a year ago appeared; first the dear fogs which snugly wrap our brains and have there, a smell of their own, when they get in under the casement. My tobacco smelt of a dark room with leather furniture seasoned by coaldust on which the lean black cat luxuriated; the big fires! and the maid with red arms tipping out the coals, and the noise of these coals falling from the steel scuttle into the iron grate in the morning—the time of the postman's solemn double knock, which brought me to life! I saw again through the windows those sick trees in the deserted square—I saw the open sea, so often crossed that winter, shivering on the bridge of the steamer wet with drizzle and blackened by smoke—with my poor wandering loved one, in travelling clothes with a long dull dress the color of road dust, a cloak sticking damp to her cold shoulders, one of those straw hats without a feather and almost without ribbons, which rich ladies throw away on arrival, so tattered are they by the sea air and which poor loved ones retrim for a few good seasons more. Round her neck was wound the terrible handkerchief we wave when we say goodbye for ever.

Here we almost have a prefiguring of the new sentence: the absence of external poetic devices, but not their interiorization in the sentence. Mallarme has extended their absence by reducing the text to the minimum number of sentences. The dematerialization of the text in this manner is an example of prose shaping poetic form and beginning to alter sentence structure. But note that there is no attempt whatsoever to prevent the integration of linguistic units into higher levels. These sentences take us not toward language, but away from it.

The prose poem did not take root in England or America. Oscar Wilde and Amy Lowell made stabs at it. The influence of poems in other languages being translated into English prose, such as Tagore's rendering of the Indian songs, *Gitanjali*, was quite visible.

Alfred Kreymbourg's 1930 anthology, *Lyric America*, has four prose poems. One is a long and tedious one by Arturo Giovanni, called "The Walker." the other three are by the black poet Fenton Johnson. I'm going to read the longest of these because Johnson uses a device here which points in the direction of the new sentence. Each sentence is a complete paragraph; run-on sentences are treated as one paragraph each, but two paragraphs begin with conjunctions. Structured thus, Johnson's is the first American prose poem with a clear, if simple, sentence : paragraph relation.

THE MINISTER

I mastered pastoral theology, the Greek of the Apostles, and all the difficult subjects in a minister's curriculum.

I was learned as any in this country when the Bishop ordained me.

And I went to preside over Mount Moriah, largest flock in the Conference.

I preached the Word as I felt it. I visited the sick and dying and comforted the afflicted in spirit.

I loved my work because I loved God.

But I lost my charge to Sam Jenkins, who has not been to school four years in his life.

I most my charge because I could not make my congregation shout.

And my dollar money was small, very small.

Sam Jenkins can tear a Bible to tatters and his congregation destroys the pews with their shouting and stamping.

Sam Jenkins leads in the gift of raising dollar money.
Such is religion.

Johnson is clearly influenced by Edgar Lee Masters, but his sentence:paragraph device brings the reader's attention back time and again to the voice of the narrator in this poem. It is the first instance in English of a prose poem which calls attention to a discursive or poetic effect. Even though the referential content is always evident, the use of the paragraph here limits the reader's ability to get away from the language itself.

But Fenton Johnson may not be the first American prose poet of consequence. Here, from *Kora In Hell: Improvisations*, is the third entry in the twentieth grouping, accompanied by its commentary:

One need not be hopelessly cast down because he cannot cut onyx into a ring to fit a lady's finger. You hang your head. There is neither onyx nor porphyry on these roads—only brown dirt. For all that, one may see his face in a flower along it—even in this light. Eyes only and for a flash only. Oh, keep the neck bent, plod with the back to the spirit dark! Walk in the curled mudcrusts to one side, hands hanging. Ah well . . . Thoughts are trees! Ha, ha, ha, ha! Leaves load the branches and upon them white night sits kicking her heels against the shore.

A poem can be made of anything. This is a portrait of a disreputable farm hand made out of the stuff of his environment.

Certainly we have strategies here which echo the French prose poem, such as the constantly shifting point of view. More important: the sentences allow only the most minimal syllogistic shift to the level of reference, and some, such as the laughter, permit no such shift whatsoever.

But note the word "portrait" in Williams' commentary. His model here is not the French prose poem so much as the so-called cubist prose of Gertrude Stein, who as early as 1911 wrote *Tender Buttons*:

CUSTARD

Custard is this. It has aches, aches when. Not to be. Not to be narrowly. This makes a whole little hill.

Ron Silliman 567

It is better than a little thing that has mellow real mellow. It is better than lakes whole lakes, it is better than seeding.

ROAST POTATOES

Roast potatoes for.

Stein says in "Poetry and Grammar" that she did not intend to make *Tender Buttons* poetry, but it just happened that way. It is sufficiently unlike much that she later called poetry to suggest that it is something other than that. The portraits in *Tender Buttons* are portraits. The syllogistic move above the sentence level to an exterior reference is possible, but the nature of the book reverses the direction of this movement. Rather than making the shift in an automatic and gestalt sort of way, the reader is forced to deduce it from the partial views and associations posited in each sentence. The portrait of custard is marvellously accurate.

The sentences also deserve some examination. They are fragmented here in a way that is without precedent in English. Who but Stein would have written a sentence in 1911 that ends in the middle of a prepositional phrase? Her use of elliptical sentences— "Not to be. Not to be narrowly."—deliberately leaves the subject out of sight. Custard does not want to be a hard fact. And the anaphoric pronoun of "this makes a whole little hill" refers not to custard, but the negated verb phrases of the two previous sentences. Likewise in "Roast Potatoes," Stein uses the preposition "for" to convert "roast" from an adjective into a verb.

Stein has written at great length about sentences and paragraphs. Her essays on them are works in themselves, and in them, she reveals herself to have thought more seriously about the differences here than any other poet in English.

Because of the nature of her arguments, I'm going to simply quote, in order, some passages which shed some light on the issue in the terms in which I have been talking about it. From "Sentences and Paragraphs," a section of *How To Write* (1931):

1) Within itself. A part of a sentence may be sentence without their meaning.
2) Every sentence has a beginning. Will he begin.
   Every sentence which has a beginning makes it be left more to them.

568 Ron Silliman

3) A sentence should be arbitrary it should not please be better.
4) The difference between a short story and a paragraph. There is none.
5) There are three kinds of sentences are there. Do sentences follow the three. There are three kinds of sentences. Are there three kinds of sentences that follow the three.

This of course refers to the simple, compound, complex division of traditional grammars.

From the essay, "Sentences," in the same book:

6) A sentence is an interval in which there is a finally forward and back. A sentence is an interval during which if there is a difficulty they will do away with it. A sentence is a part of the way when they wish to be secure. A sentence is their politeness in asking for a cessation. And when it happens they look up.
7) There are two kinds of sentences. When they go. They are given to me. There are these two kinds of sentences. Whenever they go they are given to me. There are there these two kinds of sentences there. One kind is when they like and the other kind is as often as they please. The two kinds of sentences relate when they manage to be for less with once whenever they are retaken. Two kinds of sentences make it do neither of them dividing in a noun.

Stein is here equating clauses, which divide as indicated into dependent and independent, with sentences. Anything as high up the chain of language as a clause is already partially a kind of sentence. It can move syllogistically as a sentence in itself to a higher order of meaning. That's an important and original perception.

8) Remember a sentence should not have a name. A name is familiar. A sentence should not be familiar. All names are familiar there for there should not be a name in a sentence. If there is a name in a sentence a name which is familiar makes a data and therefor there is no equilibrium.

This explains Stein's distaste for nouns quite adequately. The concern for equilibrium is an example of grammar as meter, which points us clearly toward the new sentence.

In her 1934 American lecture, "Poetry and Grammar," Stein makes a few additional comments which shed light on the relation of sentences to prose, and hence prose poems. The first is, I believe, the best single statement on the problem as it is faced by a writer:

9) What had periods to do with it. Inevitably no matter how completely
I had to have writing go on, physically one had to again and again stop
sometime and if one had to again and again stop some time then peri-
ods had to exist. Besides I had always liked the look of periods and I
liked what they did. Stopping sometime did not really keep one from
going on, it was nothing that interfered, it was only something that
happened, and as it happened as a perfectly natural happening. I did
believe in periods and I used them, I never really stopped using them.
10) Sentences and paragraphs. Sentences are not emotional but para-
graphs are. I can say that as often as I like and it always remains as it is,
something that is.

    I said I found this out in listening to Basket my dog drinking.
And anybody listening to any dog's drinking will see what I mean.

Stein later gives some examples of sentences she has written,
also from *How To Write*, which exist as one sentence paragraphs
and capture the balance between the unemotional sentence and
the emotional paragraph. My favorite is "A dog which you have
never had before has sighed."

11) We do know a little now what prose is. Prose is the balance the
emotional balance that makes the reality of paragraphs and the unemo-
tional balance that makes the reality of sentences and having realized
completely realized that sentences are not emotional while paragraphs
are, prose can be the essential balance that is made inside something
that combines the sentence and the paragraph. . .

What Stein means about paragraphs being emotional and
sentences not is precisely the point made by Emile Beneviste: that
linguistic units integrate only up to the level of the sentence, but
higher orders of meaning—such as emotion—integrate at higher
levels than the sentence and occur only in the presence of either
many sentences or, at least Stein's example suggests this, in the
presence of certain complex sentences in which dependent clauses
integrate with independent ones.
So what is the new sentence?
We are now ready to ask that question. It has to do with
prose poems, but only some prose poems. It does not have to do
with surrealist prose poems, whether of the European or American
variety, or the non-surrealist prose poems of the middle-American
variety, which is poetry by function of social context. The Sur-
realists, on the other hand, manipulate meaning only at the higher
or outer layers well beyond the horizon of the sentence.

570 Ron Silliman

Bob Grenier's *Sentences* directly anticipates the new sentence. By removal of context, Grenier prevents most leaps beyond the level of grammatic integration. This is the extreme case for the new sentence. However, most of Bob's "sentences" are more properly utterances and in that sense follow Olson and Pound and a significant portion of Creeley's work in that area.

Periodically, some sentence and paragraphs in Creeley's *A Day Book* and *Presences* carry the pressurized quality of the new sentence, in that the convolutions of syntax often suggest the internal presence of once exteriorized poetic forms, although here identified much with the forms of speech.

One glimpses it in the work of Charles Bernstein, Clark Coolidge and Bernadette Mayer, East Coast poets with much relevance to many of us in San Francisco. But one doesn't see it consistently there.

A paragraph from the 18th section of "Weathers," by Clark Coolidge:

> At most a book the porch. Flames that are at all rails of snow. Flower down winter to vanish. Mite hand stroking flint to a card. Names that it blue. Wheel locked to pyramid through stocking the metal realms. Hit leaves. Participle.

In other contexts, any one of these could become a new sentence, in the sense that any sentence properly posed and staged could. Each focuses attention at the level of the language in front of one. But seldom at the level of the sentence. Mostly at the level of the phrase or, at most, the clause. "Flower down winter to vanish" can be a grammatical sentence in the traditional sense if flower is taken as a verb and the sentence as a command. But "Names that it blue" resists even that much integrating energy. Coolidge refuses to carve connotative domains from words. They are still largely decontextualized—save for the physical-acoustic elements—readymades.

This is not an example of the new sentence because it works primarily below the level of the sentence. However, there is another important element here as a result of that: the length of sentences and the use of the period are now wholly rhythmic. Grammar has become, to recall Barthes' words, prosody. As we shall see, this is an element whenever the new sentence is present.

Here are two paragraphs of new sentences:

An inspected geography leans in with the landscape's repetitions. He lived here, under the assumptions. The hill suddenly vanished, proving him right. I was left holding the bag. I peered into it.

The ground was approaching fast. It was a side of himself he rarely showed. The car's tracks disappeared in the middle of the road. The dialog with objects is becoming more strained. Both sides gather their forces. Clouds enlarge. The wind picks up. He held onto the side of the barn by his fingertips.

These paragraphs are from *a.k.a.*, by Bob Perelman.

In them we note these qualities: (1) The paragraph organizes the sentences in fundamentally the same way a stanza does lines of verse. There are roughly the same number of sentences in each paragraph and the number is low enough to establish a clear sentence:paragraph ratio. Why is this not simply a matter of the way sentences are normally organized into paragraphs? Because there is no specific referential focus. The paragraph here is a unit of measure—as it was also in "Weathers." (2) The sentences are all sentences. By which I mean that the syntax of each resolves up to the level of the sentence. Not that these sentences make sense in the ordinary way. For example, "He lived here, under the assumptions." This sentence could be rewritten, or have been derived, from a sentence such as "He lived here, under the elm trees," or, "He lived here, under the assumption *that* etc." (3) This continual torquing of sentences is a traditional quality of poetry, but in poetry it is most often accomplished by linebreaks, and earlier on by rhyme as well. Here poetic form has moved into the interiors of prose.

Consider, by way of contrast, this first stanza of Alan Bernheimer's "Carapace":

The face of a stranger
is a privilege to see
each breath a signature
and the same sunset fifty years later
though familiarity is an education

There are shifts and torquings here also, but these occur hinged by external poetic form: linebreaks. In "Carapace," the individual line is so-called ordinary language and is without this torque or pressurization of syntax. Torquing occurs in "Carapace" through the addition of the lines, one to another.

a.k.a., by contrast, has redeployed the linebreak to two levels. As I noted, the length of the sentence is a matter now of quantity, of measure. But the torquing which is normally triggered by linebreaks, the function of which is to enhance ambiguity and polysemy, has now moved directly into the grammar of the sentence. At one level, the completed sentence (i.e., not the completed thought, but the maximum level of grammatic/linguistic integration) has become equivalent to a line, a condition not previously imposed on sentences.

Imagine what the major poems of literary history would look like if each sentence was identical to a line.

That is why an ordinary sentence, such as "I peered into it," can become a new sentence, that is, a sentence with an interior poetic structure in addition to interior ordinary grammatical structure. That is also why and how quoted lines from a Sonoma newspaper in David Bromige's "One Spring" can also become new sentences.

In fact, the increased sensitivity to syllogistic movement enables works of the new sentence a much greater capacity to incorporate ordinary sentences of the material world, because here form moves from the totality downward and the disjunction of a quoted sentence from a newspaper puts its referential content (a) into play with its own diction, as in the sentence "Danny always loved Ireland," (from *Tjanting*, referring to Dan White); (b) into play with the preceding and succeeding sentences, as quantity, syntax, and measure; and (c) into play with the paragraph as a whole, now understood as a unit not of logic or argument, but as quantity, a stanza.

Let's look at this play of syllogistic movement:

I was left holding the bag. I peered into it.
     The ground was approaching fast. It was a side of himself he rarely showed.

This is not the systematic distortion of the maximum or highest order of meaning, as in surrealism. Rather, each sentence plays with the preceding and following sentence. The first sounds figurative, because of the deliberate use of the cliche. The second, by using both a repetition of the word "I" and the anaphor "it," twists that, making it sound (a) literal and (b) narrative, in that the two sentences appear to refer to an identical content.

But the third sentence, which begins the next paragraph, works instead from the direction one might take in looking into a bag and associating from there the sense of gravity one feels looking down, as though falling.

The fourth sentence moves outside the voice of the narrative "I" and presents the sequence of previous sentences as leading to this humorous conclusion.

This double-relation of syllogistic movement, which nonetheless does not build up so far as to move the reader away from the level of language itself, is highly typical of the new sentence.

Further, the interior structure of sentences here reflects also how such issues as balance, normally issues of line organization, recast themselves inside sentences. A sentence like "Clouds enlarge" is no less concerned with such balance than those of Grenier's *Sentences*: the word "enlarged" is an ordinary word *en*larged.

Let's list these qualities of the new sentence, then read a poem, listening for their presence:

1) The paragraph organizes the sentences;
2) The paragraph is a unit of quantity, not logic or argument;
3) Sentence length is a unit of measure;
4) Sentence structure is altered for torque, or increased polysemy/ambiguity;
5) Syllogistic movement is (a) limited (b) controlled;
6) Primary syllogistic movement is between the preceding and following sentences;
7) Secondary syllogistic movement is toward the paragraph as a whole, or the total work;
8) The limiting of syllogistic movement keeps the reader's attention at or very close to the level of language, that is, most often at the sentence level or below.

My example is the poem "For She," by Carla Harryman. It is one paragraph:

The back of the hand resting on the pillow was not wasted. We couldn't hear each other speak. The puddle in the bathroom, the sassy one. There were many years between us. I stared the stranger into facing up to Maxine, who had come out of the forest wet from bad nights. I came from an odd bed, a vermillion riot attracted to loud dogs. Nonetheless I could pay my rent and provide for him. On this occasion she apologized. An arrangement that did not provoke inspection. Outside on the stagnant water was a motto. He was more than I perhaps though younger. I sweat at amphibians, managed to get home. The sunlight from the window played up his golden curls and a fist screwed over one eye. Right to left and left to right until the sides of her body were circuits. While dazed and hidden in the room, he sang to himself, severe songs, from a history he knew nothing of. Or should I say malicious? Some rustic gravure, soppy but delicate at pause. I wavered, held her up. I tremble, jack him up. Matted wallowings. I couldn't organize the memory. Where does he find his friends? Maxine said to me "but it was just you again." In spite of the cars and the smoke and the many languages, the radio and the appliances, the flat broad buzz of the tracks, the anxiety with which the eyes move to meet the phone and all the arbitrary colors, I am just the same. Unplug the glass, face the docks. I might have been in a more simple schoolyard.

I first noticed the new sentence in the poem "Chamber Music" in Barrett Watten's *Decay*. I think that since then it has come forward in the work of not just one or two of us, but through the collective work and inter-influence of the entire local poetic community.

If "language writing" means anything, it means writing which does focus the reader onto the level of the sentence and below, as well as those units above. Heretofore, this has been accomplished by the deliberate exclusion of certain elements of signification, such as reference and syntax. The new sentence is the first mode of "lanugage writing" which has been able to incorporate all the elements of language, from below the sentence level *and* above.

Everywhere there are spontaneous literary discussions. Something structurally new is always being referred to. These topics may be my very own dreams, which everyone takes a friendly interest in. The library extends for miles, under the ground.

("Plasma")

PERIOD

(1979)

Ron Silliman 575

NICK PIOMBINO

WRITING AND CONCEIVING

Natasha: They ordered me not to see you again.
Lemmy: Who? The Alpha 60 engineers?
Natasha: Yes.
Lemmy: What makes you afraid?
Natasha: I'm afraid because I know a word . . . without having
        seen it or read it.

                    from *Alphaville*, a film by Jean-Luc Godard

All experience is conditioned by expectation. The meaning of an interval of experience is defined throughout by the implied or covert meaning of its end. The tension of an interval arises out of the anxiety of evolving a meaning for an event. Debussy confounds this process not by employing an obsessive doubting or repetition of themes, but by allowing a focussed uncertainty to remain. The rhythms are not halting or arbitrary yet they may be felt as not quite intended or distracted but determinedly so, not just tentatively. He gains the continuity ordinarily obtained through a form that tantalized with eventual resolution by arousing different levels of dreaminess and wakefulness. We wake from a dream to enter, clearly, a daydream.

                              *

Writing ordinarily stresses its function of "righting" the meanings of words and word combinations. But the graphic materials of writing also have a mapping and marking function. As records are evidence, the reified word is a token of identity.

The sign distributes the imaged perception as an imprint transferable to the "scratching" of thought against the cave walls of the mind. Signs transmute imaged perception into thought: at the terminus points, always approximate, always tautological.

Each subdivision of an interval is discrete when it is noticed over time, but the remaining subdivisions are more blurred when specific ones are selected for focus. Similarly, a grapheme within a nominal phrase such as a headline or a title would be conditioned by the phrases subsequently selected for emphasis. In present consciousness any subdivision of an intervallic constellation can exist in any combination of the three temporal dimensions or is apperceptively consigned to temporal mutability. The same is true for the relativity between intervals of script and all the hierarchical organizations within the text. The more general inscription (such as a headline, a title or a chapter, or the capital letter at the beginning of a line in a poem) conditions the mode of focussing the related text. The equivalent in remembering is the hierarchical arrangement of significance. The base word of significance is *sign*.

Poetry is a graphic form of unrighting the publicly codified colocation of grapheme with symbolized ordinary writing and speech usage and the imaging function of the mind. The conceptual experience of a poem causes a reconnection with the acausal, atemporal conceiving of meaning by reapportioning the relative values of the scalar organizing function of the perceiving process and the inscriptive, defining level of pre-conscious verbal imaging.

*

It is a certain tone I am after, embellished by persistent varying shades of association. I repeat it as I am hearing it in a kind of suspended listening, paying attention to and allowing to dissolve certain obsessive memories. Deductions, or rather, reductions or vapors like these, afterwards seem immediately familiar, pre-cognitive, felt throughout an extended dejà-vu atmosphere during an imploded time sequence. The puzzle is attempted *only once* in order for the observers to immediately witness its decomposition. It is a simultaneous recording, unwinding and playing, joining and dismantling, similarities momentarily continuing to hold sway throughout or just long enough after an initial and suddenly heightened series of contrasts. Such points of connection are heard in specific invariable tones and intervals. The names of these sounds and feelings may be the objects and words memories attach themselves to. But the feelings that yearned for those names, the ones that offer themselves later as keepsakes are really more memorable. Not the images which are now absent, but the thawing and sketching around that in coming times will be added to the fondness which grows around such replacements for the quality of the actual event. Anonymous, the words and exalted rituals plaintively repeating them.

Lexic qualities of. . . Semantic qualities of. . . Signal qualities of. . . Structuralizing qualities of. . . Quality of constructibility into family systems. . . Geneaology of. . . History of connection with lexic qualities of meaning. . . Graphic qualities of. . . Quality of distribution. . .

Distribution of naming to order spatially. . . Distribution of naming to remind. . . Distribution of naming to induce. . . Distribution of naming to attract. . . Distribution of naming to direct connection to identification. . .

Naming that orders. . . Naming that connotes possession (control, ownership). . . Possession of names. . . Erosion of names. . . Ambiguity of names. . . Plurality of names. . .

Naming, identifying, recording, delimiting, describing, describes, humanness of, clarifies, evokes feeling, vocal qualities of, musical qualities of

*

The activities of the mind associated with the recording and verification of the relationship between identity and physical space are governed by memory and the verbal technology necessary to preserve it. To repeat (chant, sing) the trace, is to elicit a vision of prophecy. The function of poetry is not only to enlighten but also to point us in the direction of the mind for the sources of the enlightenment. Poetic composition is an activity which subtly alters the rules that govern the relationship between the ordering of thought and allowing it to swoon into reverie. Remembering is at its base a connective mode of cognition. From this is expropriated its power to order, to value, to record, to create, to historicize, to catalogue, describe, recreate, make safe, controllable and distant, - to *signify*.

*

As many times as I try to grasp my solitude, I am abruptly thrown into the image of the Other and its absence, mute spectator. Or just as suddenly to stop, trapped in the spectacle of my fear of his or her absence, the patient, responsive, loving Other situated at the side of all that is depriving. To switch so suddenly is to plunge into the mercy of a simple truth: as neutral as the irrational is the subtly perfect, the proposition of all imposters, clown of confusion, enigmatic signature of incomprehension.

*

18. Salvaged Debris.
23. Moisture, remainders, dew, condensation.
24. Reference points on a map, questions of materials, accident

*

To read is to practice a mental resonance between language, thought and memory. As in ordinary thought, to read need not be simply to systematically connect mental processes to their current contexts but to other, related aspects of present or past experience. Such an idiosyncratic variation in reading any text is inevitable, especially in rereading.

Memory becomes history when the impact of events is such that the remembered event is still having its impact when the memory is triggered and is more multiply caused by immediate necessity. History is necessary when memory threatens to fail. Memory is aroused by emotional and physical need. As culture (apparently) changes more rapidly, more attention must be concentrated on the meaning of the shifts. When we are insecure about the memory function we invoke historical (ordering) paradigms.

*

Sometimes I allow somebody else, in some way, to speak through me. I know the somebody else is me, but I also know that some information is coming through that perhaps was picked up peripherally, or has been forgotten and is silently colliding and thus combining with something else. The other voice during the conception of a thought before the wording has taken on specificity. A high altitude photograph and then a zoom-in for details. This permits initially irrelevant details to later enter the framework.

"The scale of the Spiral Jetty tends to fluctuate depending on where the viewer happens to be. Size determines an object, but

Nick Piombino 579

scale determines art. . . When one refuses to release scale from size, one is left with an object that *appears* to be certain. For me scale operates by uncertainty. To be in the scale of the Spiral Jetty is to be out of it." (p. 112, *The Writings of Robert Smithson*, New York University Press, 1979).

*

> The sentence is a prison term
> Why poetry made of fragments
> Irreducible crystal forms
> Lesson. Intermittent continuous connection
> That's why subtract (subtext) poetry
> Instead of abstract
> Seems made of starting
> Hemisphere at images
> Spring-like or spring
>
> Remembrances
> A pause, faces opposites
> Little askew, a tilt
> Framing reflection out of
> Mirror, less a, wanting, unwound
> Each vulnerable, venerable
> Split atom
>
> Cars   Skates
>
> Bikes
>
> Trolleys

*

Writing is reading. I live in a world of signs which acausally direct my consciousness. Thought is writing, just as thinking is protolinguistic. Thought is reading just as listening enforces a transposition of an interval of related sounds into a specific inner focus of attention. Writing silences a babel of voices each of which calls attention to its own point of origin. At the root of all comprehension exists an indeterminate number of possible meanings which are coming into being, into consciousness. All understanding or visual or aural recognition contains within it an underlying chaotically disordered core in flux, moving as a system of connected points toward an entropic state of inertia, a stable pattern.

All systematized language is oppressive insofar as it supports ideologically based repression. Repression serves psychic economy. To "forget"the origin of a meaning, or its specific and unique context, is to suppress energy directed towards associative expansion and purposive expression, that is, the purpose is blurred as is the associative gestalt.

Thinking, reading and writing are forms of preconscious play. Thinking itself, which is imagined to accompany reading, is synchronistically titled, one moment toward, the next, away from, experience. Like speaking, reading and writing, thinking is imagined to be a translation of experience. But this translation does not completely evolve apposite to experience. The sign constantly displays its maddening ability to outwit its supposed "associated" thought, and as its creator seizes on the reminiscence of its genesis, the acausal connecting process of association determines the actual signification. This eventually becomes the "meaning" of the experience. These meanings ordinarily are interpreted in intervallic measures or "beats" of time. Meaning entropically moves towards "familiarization," which is static, rather than "defamiliarization" which is nascent, and closer to the fulcrum of the acausal axis of interval (instance) and pattern (generalization).

*

You lose the actual qualities of the experience when you try to be too precise about the specifics of each interval of the flow. Any exhaustive rendering becomes a compilation of instances. The historical perspective makes instances appear less improvised than they actually are. The decisive moment, the dramatic realization, is itself a heightening of the particular instance from a valued perspective. One examines what one wants to know thoroughly again and again. This is called testing, experimentation.

We wait and try again. We measure and take note. We generalize and enumerate. We *sift through*. This sifting, this remeasurement of experiences, one combined with another leads to connections which are imbued with the feeling of discovery, that are re*mark*able.

Now, as I look out through the porthole of this ferry, even from this distance, I am thinking that one small rectangle of gradu- ated color, yellow white to pink to black, to specks of, pinpoints of, electric white light to blue, brings to light, to mind, the entire dawn.

(1980)

CHARLES BERNSTEIN

WRITING AND METHOD*

1.   The Limits of Style / The Possibilities of Phenomena

An inquiry into the differences between philosophical and literary writing practices is of value insofar as it can shed light on both the nature of philosophy and poetry and, more importantly, on the development and implications of such genre or professional distinctions within writing and thinking. For what makes poetry poetry and philosophy philosophy is largely a tradition of thinking and writing, and a social matrix of publications, professional associations, audience; more, indeed, facts of history and social convention than intrinsic necessities of the "medium" or "idea" of either one. So such an inquiry will end up being into the social meaning of specific modes of discourse, a topic that is both a stylistic resource for the writing of poetry and a content for philosophy.

Philosophy has traditionally been concerned with the nature of the world and the possibilities of human knowledge of it; in a large sense, the nature of perception, phenomenon, objects, mind, person, meaning, and action. Richard Kuhns, in his book about the affinities of philosophy and literature, *Structures of Experience*, writes "Philosophy asks 'What makes experience possible?' and 'What makes *this* kind of experience possible?' Literature establishes the realities for which philosophy must seek explanations." Kuhns bases the distinction between philosophy and literature on the appeal each makes, the address of the text. Philosophy is involved with an appeal to validity and argument (i.e., to impersonal, suprapersonal, "objective" abstractions, to logic) and poetry with an appeal to memory and synaethesia (i.e., to the reader's own experience). Kuhns, then, is suggesting two different,

---

*This essay was written in conjunction with a series on "Poetry & Philosophy" I conducted with Edmund Leites at the St. Mark's Poetry Project in February, 1981.

through interrelated, modes of discourse. "Philosophy" requires "logical" argument and noncontradiction as basic textual modes of discourse: "poetry" seem to reject "argument" as essential, though of course it may "incorporate" argument.—Even were I to accept Kuhns' traditional distinctions, which I do not, I would add that poetry can focus attention on the structure of meaning by the exemplification of structures of discourse—how the *kind* of discourse effects what can be said within it.

Another traditional distinction between philosophy and poetry now sounds anachronistic: that philosophy is involved with system building and consistency and poetry with the beauty of the language and emotion. Apart from the grotesque dualism of this distinction (as if consistency and the quest for certainty were not emotional!), this view imagines poetry and philosophy to be defined by the product of their activity, consistent texts in the one case, beautiful texts in the other. Rather, philosophy and poetry are at least equally definable not as the product of philosophizing and poetic thinking but, indeed, the process (the activity) of philosophizing or poetic thinking.

Jean-Paul Sartre, in his "Interview at 70" (in *Life/Situations*) argues that while literature *should* be ambiguous, "in philosophy, every sentence should have only one meaning"; he even reproaches himself for the "too literary" language of *Being and Nothingness* "whose language should have been strictly technical. It is the accumulation of technical phrases which creates the total meaning, a meaning which," at this overall level, "has more than one level." Literature, on the other hand, is a matter of style, style that requires greater effort in writing and pervasive revision. "Stylistic work does not consist of sculpting a sentence, but of permanently keeping in mind the totality of the scene, the chapter, . . . the entire book" as each sentence is being composed. So, a superimposition of many meanings in each sentence.—Sartre's remarks are interesting in this context because he so clearly exemplifies the poetry / philosophy split, being equally known for his fiction and non-fiction. Yet for me, *Being and Nothingness* is a more poetic work than *The Age of Reason* in the sense that I find it more a structural investigation of perception and experience—"being"—whose call is to "memory and synaethesia", while the novels often seem to exemplify various "problems" using a rationalistic appeal to argument and validity.

Indeed, if one takes it to be a primary philosophical problem—many philosophers of course do not—that the description (ontology) of events, persons, experience, objects, etc., are at issue, and it is not just a question of *axiomitizing* types of these things, then forms of art not only "define the structure of human experience" as Kuhns has it but *investigate* the terms of human experience and their implications. Then poetry and philosophy share *the project of investigating the possibilities (nature) and structures of phenomena.* The motto for this might come from Wittgenstein in *Philosophical Investigations*: "We feel as if we had to penetrate phenomenon: our investigation, however, is directed not toward phenomenon but, as one might say, the 'possibility' of phenomenon."

As a result, the genre or style of a writing practice becomes centrally a question of method, rather than a transparent given of form. It is this understanding of philosophy that lead Heidegger in his later work to reject philosophy and instead call for instruction in "true thinking" (in *What is Called Thinking*), or has lead Stanley Cavell, recently writing on Emerson, to talk of the relation of mood to philosophic inquiry. Or what has lead so many poets to feel the need to reject philosophy outright as a ground for poetry, as Craig Watson recently commented, saying that it sentimentalized a picture of perception. The answer to that is that of course people do get attached to their systems: but this should not subvert seeing the possibilities for method itself, for system, for ways of looking at perception. In *Walden*, Thoreau writes, "There are nowadays professors of philosophy, but not philosophers. Yet it is admirable to profess because it was once admirable to live. To be a philosopher is not merely to have subtle thoughts, nor even to found a school, but so to love wisdom as to live according to its dictates. . . . It is to solve some of the problems of life, not only theoretically, but practically. The success of great scholars and thinkers is commonly a courtier-like success. . . . They make shift to live merely by conformity, practically as their fathers did, and are in no sense the progenitors of a nobler race of men. . . . The philosopher is in advance of his age even in the outward form of his life. He is not fed, sheltered, clothed, warmed, like his contemporaries. How can a man be a philosopher and not maintain his vital heat by better methods than other men?" Which I cite partly for that last sentence—the centrality of method.

If philosophy is to be characterized as a form consisting of clearly exposited arguments whose appeal is to the logic of validity, then it would systematically be limited by the limits of expository practice. I don't think it makes sense to restrict philosophy to this particular mode of discourse, both because it would rule out some of the best work in philosophy and because it suggests that reason's most "clear" expression is exposition. Rather it seems to me that, as a mode, contemporary expository writing edges close to being merely a *style* of decorous thinking, rigidified and formalized to a point severed from its historical relation to method in Descartes and Bacon. It is no longer an enactment of thinking or reasoning but a representation (and simplification) of an 18th century ideal of reasoning. And yet the hegemony of its practice is rarely questioned outside certain poetic and philosophic contexts. On this level, I would characterize as sharing a political project both a philosophical practice and a poetic practice that refuse to adopt expository principles as their basic claim to validity.

For both poetry and philosophy, the order of the elements of a discourse is value constituting and indeed experience engendering, and therefore always at issue, never assumable.

In some sense these are just issues of style; a style is chosen and it is not to the point simply to be evaluative about which is best intrinsically. But to acknowledge that there are philosophical assumptions that underlie given stylistic practices about the nature of reason, objects, the world, persons, morality, justice. At a certain historical moment certain paths were chosen as to the style that would express a quasi-scientific voice of reason and authority—even though, as Thomas Kuhn points out in *The Structures of Scientific Revolution*, this "normal" science language cannot account for paradigm shifts central to scientific progress—a voice that was patriarchal, monologic, authoritative, impersonal. The predominance of this authoritative plain style (taught in such guides as Strunk and White) and its valorization as a picture of clarity and reason is a relatively recent phenomenon and its social meaning will no doubt be clarified by a careful tracing of its origins that would be a central project for the historian of social forms. Morris Croll has elucidated an earlier stage of these developments in his account of the rise of the Anti-Ciceronian prose style in the late 16th century, a development in some ways paralleling such current critiques as this one of contemporary expository forms, in its rejection of a static predetermined formality and its attempt "to portray not a thought, but a mind thinking". Montaigne most clearly exemplifies this movement, especially in terms of his methodological awareness of the implications of style: "I stray from the path, but it is rather by licence than oversight. My ideas follow each other, but sometimes it is at a distance, and they look at each other, but with an oblique gaze. . . . It is the lazy reader who loses track of the subject, not I. . . . I keep changing without constraint or order. My style and mind both go a-vagabonding. . . . I mean my matter should distinguish itself. It shows sufficiently where it changes, where it ends, where begins, where resumes, without interlacing of words, of conjunctions, or connectives introduced for weak or negligent ears, and without glossing myself."

No doubt the history of our contemporary plain styles, with their emphasis on connectives, a tight reign on digression, and a continuing self-glossing, a history that could be traced to the last 100 years, would need to account for the effect of industrialization and mass literacy in order to explain the particular tendency toward greater and greater standardization. But the crucial mechanism to keep in mind is not the rules of current preferred forms versus possible alternatives but *the mechanism of distinction and discrimination itself* that allows for certain language practices to be legitimized (as correct, clear, coherent) and other language practices to be discredited (as wrong, vague, nonsensical, antisocial, ambiguous, irrational, illogical, crude, dumb. . .). This "mechanism of exclusion" is described by Michel Foucault in relation to the designation both of the "criminal" and the "insane", with the comment that it is the mechanism itself and its techniques and procedures which were found useful in creating and preserving the predominating hierarchical power relations of the 19th century bourgeoisie (as well, it should be added, the 20th century Soviet state). It is not, then, the intrinsic meaning of the particular distinction that is crucial, not, that is, the particular standard but standardization itself. "What in fact happened . . . was that the mechanisms of exclusion . . . began from a particular point in time . . . to reveal their political usefulness and to lend themselves to economic profit, and that as a natural consequence, all of a sudden, they came to be colonized and maintained by global mechanisms and the entire state system. It is only if we grasp the techniques of power and demonstrate the economic advantages and political utility that derives from them . . . that we can understand how these mechanisms come to be effectively incorporated into the social whole." Part of the task of a history of social forms would be to bring into visibility as chosen instruments of power what is taken as neutral or given. Part of the task of an active poetry or philosophy is to explore these instruments by a critique of their partiality and to develop alternatives to them that can serve as models of truth and meaning not dependent for their power on the dominating structures.

The contemporary expository mode was adopted because it effectively did the business of the society's vested interests, by its very mode quelling the sound of oppositional language by equating coherence with mannered and refined speaking. In this context, Sartre tells the story of *La Cause du peuple*, a Paris newspaper that the government actively seized, arresting its editors, in the 70's because, unlike the leftist *Les Temps moderne*, Sartre's own paper, it did not speak in the language of bourgeois discourse but had accounts by workers in their own sharper language of rebellions and atrocities throughout France. I think the outrage against accepting black English diction in a school context is a similar instance of a threat to the legitamizing function served by standardization.

The question is always: what is the meaning of this language practice; what values does it propogate; to what degree does it encourage an understanding, a visibility, of its own values or to what degree does it repress that awareness? To what degree is it in dialogue with the reader and to what degree does it command or hypnotize the reader? Is its social function liberating or repressive? Such questions of course open up into much larger issues than ones of aesthetics per se, open the door by which aesthetics and ethics are unified. And so they pertain not only to the art situation but more generally the language of the job, of the state, of the family, and of the street. And my understanding of these issues comes as much from working as a commercial writer as from reading and writing poetry. Indeed, the fact that the overwhelming majority of steady paid employment for writing involves using the authoritative plain styles, if it is not explicitly advertising; involves writing, that is, filled with preclusions, is a measure of why this is not simply a matter of stylistic choice but of social governance: we are not free to choose the language of the workplace or of the family we are born into, though we are free, within limits, to rebel against it. Nor am I therefore advocating that expository writing should not be taught; I can think of few more valuable survival skills. "But if one learns to dress as the white man dresses one does not have to think the white man dresses best." And again the danger is that writing is taught in so formal and objectified a way that most people are forever alienated from it as Other. It needs, to appropriate Alan Davies' terms, to be taught as the presentation of *a* tool, not mystified as value-free product, in which the value-creating process that led to it is repressed into a norm and the mode itself is *imperialized*. Coherence cannot be reduced to the product of any given set of tools. This will not necessarily entail that all writing be revolutionary in respect to style or even formally self-conscious about it—though that is a valuable course—but rather that styles and modes have social meaning that cannot be escaped and that can and should be understood.

This understanding should lead to a very acute sense of the depletion of styles and tones in the public realm of factual discourse, including in professional philosophy and the academy in general, but also newspapers, magazines, radio, and TV. Indeed, even within the predominant styles of contemporary philosophy, few of the tones and moods that potentially exist within the chosen style are utilized to any great extent. Indeed, the only significant alternative to the neutral-toned plain style of most philosophical writing of the present time is the weightier tone of judiciousness; but rarely whimsical tones or angry, or befuddled or lethargic or ironic, as if these tones were moods that have been banished, realms of human experience thus systematically untouchable. Not only is the question of method suppressed, but even the possibilities of tone within the style are reduced!

All writing is a demonstration of method; it can assume a method or investigate it. In this sense, style and mode are always at issue, for all styles are socially mediated conventions open to reconvening at any time.

Yet, along with the depletion of styles and tones of writing is a repression of these categories as chosen elements. Appropriating a similar division by Barrett Watten, one might speak of concentric circles of technique, style, mode or genre, and method; each of these terms encompassing a sequentially larger circle that informs the possibilities for the categories within it. That is, a technique exists within the context of a style toward which it is employed, a style can be seen as an instance of a more general genre or mode, and a mode is informed by a still more general method that gives rise to it. Different works will show vastly different indications of these domains. A row of suburban houses, for example, may mask the uniformity of their style by slight alterations (personalizations) made by the individual owners. Art or movie reviewing, for instance, will usually focus on the style or technique and leave unexamined the prevailing assumptions of mode and method, either out of blindness to these aspects or out of a conviction that such issues are contentless or imponderable. Indeed much "normal" philosophy and poetry simply adopts a style and works on techniques within it, without considering either the implications of the larger modality or its methodological assumptions. On the other hand, a "constructive" mode would suggest that the mode itself is explored as content, its possibilities of meaning are investigated and presented, and that this process is itself recognized as a method.

One vision of a "constructive" writing practice I have, and it can be approached in both poetry and philosophy, is of a multi-discourse text, a work that would involve many different types and styles and modes of language in the same "hyperspace". Such a textual practice would have a dialogic or polylogic rather than monologic method. The loss of dialogue in philosophy has been a central problem since Plato; Cavell, applying this to his own work, and that of Thoreau, talks about the dialogue of a "text answerable to itself". Certainly, *Philosophical Investigations* is the primary instance of such a text in this century, and also a primary instance of taking this practice as method. I can easily imagine more extreme forms of this: where contrasting moods and modes of argument, shifting styles and perspectives, would surface the individual modes and their meaning in illuminating ways and perhaps further Heidegger's call for an investigation into "true thinking". (Thinking is also a construction.) Indeed, I can imagine a writing that would provoke philosophic insight but keep essentially a fabric of dance—logopoeia—whose appeal would not be to the validity of argument but to the ontological truthfulness of its meanings.

Another alternative type of discursive work is suggested by the later writing of Laura (Riding) Jackson. Riding's work has consistently investigated the limits of meaning and the limits of our forms of trying to mean. After 20 years of active poetic practice, she renounced poetry in 1938 as "blocking truth's ultimate verbal harmonies". Had she been a philosopher she might have made a similar renunciation, as, in a sense, Wittgenstein did toward the kind of discourse he and Russell had done in the early part of the century, or as Heidegger did make in his later writing where he characterized philosophy as at odds with "true thinking". Riding's renunciation cuts through distinctions of philosophy and poetry, suggesting that it is the professionalization of—the craft of—each that is the mistake. I've suggested here that if philosophy is reduced simply to a mode of employing argument then the attention shifts from what Riding might call "telling the truth of us all" to the technical perfecting of the mode itself, the kind of tinkering with the mechanics of given arguments, refining their formal elegance, that is apparent on any page of *Mind*. Yet this professionalization, Riding points out, is a danger in poetry itself, as the craft of fine expressiveness she feels necessarily supplants "the telling" that was poetry's initial motivation for the poet. A view that is useful to consider if overly scriptural in its imagination of what this telling is. Riding's appeal in *The Telling* is not to the internal validity of her argument, or to the beauty or virtuosity of her performance or expression, but to the truthfulness of what she is saying in respect to our own, as readers, experiences and memories. We refer back to "ourselves", in that sense are made aware, conscious, of ourselves as readers; by addressing the reader, this work refuses to let its words disappear.

In his "Preface" to the *Lyrical Ballads*, Wordsworth writes: "Aristotle, I have been told, has said that Poetry is the most philosophic of all writing: it is so: its object is truth, not individual and local, but general and operative; not standing upon external testimony, but carried alive into the heart by passion; truth which is its own testimony, which gives competence and confidence to the tribunal to which it appeals, and receives them from the same tribunal. Poetry in the image of [humanity] and nature."

2.   Self as the Problem of Other Minds

Poetry, like philosophy, may be involved with the investigation of phenomena (events, objects, selves) and human knowledge of them; not just in giving examples but in developing methodological approaches. This implies not that the two traditions are indistinct but that aspects of each tradition, especially in respect to the basicness of method, may have more in common with aspects of the other tradition than with aspects of its own tradition; that the distinction between these two practices may be less a matter of intrinsic usefulness than of professionalization and segmentation of audience and so of the address of texts.

Twentieth-century writing has had as one of its most philosophically interesting projects the mapping of consciousness, an investigation implicitly involved with the nature of "mind" and "self" and indeed with the interrelation of these two conceptual constructions. The banners of this work are numerous—stream-of-consciousness, psychic automatism, surrealism, memory, free-association, impressionism, expressionism—and represent much of the most interesting writing of the first half of this century, continuing, indeed, into the present in various forms including chronicling of the life in persona, confessional, and autobiographical modes. A value of this writing for epistemological inquiry was the alternative model of mind it provided to the rationalistic constructions of neo-classical and quasi-scientific discursiveness, since the organization of words and phrases, and so picture of the mind, is based on the perceiving and experiencing and remembering subject rather than on the more expositorily developmental lines of the "objective" and impersonal styles that picture the mind (and self) as a neutral observer of a given world. More importantly, this writing encouraged a different kind of reading, a reading that could be extended much beyond the specific writing practice itself. Indeed, all writing becomes open for interpretation as the trace of a self.

Yet, while certainly offering a different picture of mind by foregrounding the role of the self, this conception of reading/writing shares with more impersonal forms a projection of the text as sealed-off from the reader. Conventional reading/writing styles project this by the monologic character of their presentation. Both events and characters are assumed as being pre-constituted and the discourse is presumed to be restricted to naming instances of these, of commenting on them (the writing becoming the so-called "transparent window on the world"). Just this picture of reality is what, traditionally, has allowed the skeptical argument its strongest foothold. (How do I know that these things I see are not just an hallucination I am having, that the external world, that other minds, exist independently of me?) For this picture—"holding us captive", a "bewitchment" of language itself, in Wittgenstein's phrases—cedes from the first my role in the world as a partner in constituting its meanings, picturing instead my passive consumption of meanings already determined. Which becomes a paradigm for both reading a text and reading the world, and for a style of exposition—the neutral observer looking out—that itself projects this subject/object subject/subject split. What we are presented with is a picture of a person as tourist in a world he or she does not fundamentally affect; but we cannot see the world without at the same time touching it, changing it.

The mapping of consciousness in writing does undercut one sense of the sealed-offness from other minds by charting the role of the self in mediating human knowledge of the world. The peculiarities that form the trace of consciousness and make it specific or individual demonstrate the *partialness* of any construction of mind or reality, in sharp contrast to the universality of claim in the tone of many conventional writing modes. This acknowledging and charting of partialness does in fact break the monologic spell of writing seen as a transparent medium to the world beyond it, but it does so only by making a projection of self central to its methodology. In the end, this practice leaves the reader as sealed-off from the self enacted within it as conventional writing does from the world pictured within it; while the trace may frame the reader, it also exteriorizes him/her while it critiques the suprapersonal transcendental projection, it creates its own metaphysical fiction of the person. The experience is of a self bound off from me in its autonomy, enclosed in its self-sufficiency. The power of this besideness is that it (re)creates the conditions of nature itself, and so is a model of the human experience of it, human relations to it. But I feel not only simultaneously outside nature and constituted by nature, but also that I am constituting it! "Self" writing demonstrates this last condition in terms of its own construction of reality within the text, but the *reading* of this construction *as* the trace of consciousness structurally neutralizes this demonstration by presenting the reader with the self itself assumed. While reading/writing in an objective mode grotesques and theatricalizes my separation from the world, as if presenting only the hollow fronts of buildings as in a de Chirico painting, reading/writing in a subjective mode reinforces that separateness with its uncanny mimicry of my own experience of otherness. To be beside, to be next to (para/noid) is at least a significant break from a practice which places me outside, out of (ec/noid—out-of-one's-mind); it is the position of being in history, conditioned by time and place and body; and it is true that my relation to "things-in-themselves" is more accurately described by this account of experience of a self than one that simply presumes such experience as impartial.

There is another conceptualization for writing and reading that presents a rather different idea of a map than that of mapping consciousness. The text is again seen as a map, but in the sense of model, or outline, or legend and not trace. Rather than work which is the product of the "author's" projection / memory / associative process, it is work for the reader's (viewer's) projection / construction. The text calls upon the reader to be actively involved in the process of constituting its meaning, the reader becoming neither a neutral observer to a described exteriority or to an enacted interiority. The text formally involves the process of response / interpretation and in so doing makes the reader aware of herself or himself as producer as well as consumer of meaning. It calls the reader to action, questioning, self-examination: to a reconsideration and a remaking of the habits, automatisms, conventions, beliefs through which, and only through which, we see and interpret the world. It insists that there is, in any case, no seeing without interpretation and chooses to incorporate this interpretive process actively by bringing it into view rather than to exploit it passively by deleting its tracks.

The skeptical argument founders on its assumption that knowledge is a thing that can be possessed rather than a relation that can only be enacted; its argument holds sway only in a discourse that seeks one univocal definition of knowledge for all situations rather than one that has the capacity to acknowledge specific situations in which things get known. A writing that incorporates the issue of interpretation and interaction—use—insists on knowing as a response rather than a neutralized perception. By banishing the stasis of the monologic picture of a world sealed off in its preconstitution, the "picture" that "holds us captive" is dissolved and we are given in its place a world with which we must interact to understand: in which I know you not by a passive consumption of your persona, or by gazing intently at the trace of your body or mind, but by my response to you in a specific situation, my call of your name.

The individual is the product of a discourse, and so of a power relation in society, not an entity acted upon by all discourse. Writing (or reading) that uses the self as its organizing principle, either through a persona or through the more open field of consciousness mapping, appeals to as artificial, as socially constructed, an entity as expository writing's appeal to logic. As such, "self" writing or "self" reading has no intrinsic claim to universality, or to the primacy of its picture of partiality; its methodological assumptions both invest it with a domain of descriptive and explanatory power and also set its limits. While this reading/writing practice may have strategic significance as oppositional to the hegemony of scientistic modes of discourse, those of us who support this opposition need not maintain that any mode, per se, is the most direct path to truth; rather, the struggle is to bring to conscious scrutiny the social function different modes of reading/writing play and how they function in legitimizing or constituting or undermining the hierarchial power relations within the socious.

Writing as a map for the reader to read into, to interpolate from the space of the page out onto a projected field of "thinking" ("thinking" as a sixth sense, to borrow Richard Foreman's concept, a perceiving/interpreting dimension or function more like tasting and smelling than seeing, or more like the kind of seeing that goes on if you imagine seeing as a kind of thinking, as Arakawa suggests, in his work where "verbal language becomes a proposition of the visual world", or in the sense John Berger discusses in *Ways of Seeing*). So that the meaning of the text is constituted only in collaboration with the reader's active construction of this hypertext. This construction by the reader transforms the text in a way analogous to a stereopticon's transformation of two photo-slides, except that the final construction is not uniform with each reader / viewer. Indeed, this conceptualization could allow for indeterminate possibilities for the final construction of meaning, as theorized by Robert Morris in respect to his minimal sculpture of the late 60's, or to a more contained degree, as allowed for in the chance-derived compositions of Cage and Mac Low, in which the possibilities are narrowed by the greater specificity of content. By map or model, however, I mean a much greater degree of design, detail and intention in which variations of final constructed meaning would have close "family resemblances" to each other and where, in fact, the kind of differences within this would be part of the intentional (instructive?) strategy of the text.

(I am not suggesting, of course, a work which is more coercive than ever of the reader, which, by its scale and indeterminacy sub-liminally induces the viewer's projections and so effects an invest-ment of authority in the work or what stands behind it. This type of coercion and control is predicated on a very specific kind of projection controlled by the context in which it is viewed, by minimalizing what is projected onto, and by a suppression of the fact that projection is being induced. In antithesis, what I am dis-cussing brings to consciousness the fact of projection as part of the content. Indeed, all forms, all modes, all methods are coercive in that they have a relation to power. What is being suggested is that this be brought into view, a critiquing which has potentially liberating effect.)

The conception of a text as a map or model whose final constitu-tion requires the reader's active response is a theory of reading. This concept of reading extends beyond the text into the world, into the realm of reading human culture, furthering the activity of critique in Marx and interpretation in Freud. In such writing, the autonomy of a text is not broached, nor is the relation between reader and writer gesturalized or theatricalized. In contrast to the predetermined interpretations of a text based on the primacy of the self or of logic, it is the formal autonomy of the text as model that elicits a response, an interpolation. Its presence demands that I measure my relation to it, compute its scale. It is neither incomplete or sealed off. Its completeness consists of its inclusiveness not exclusiveness. Its autonomy is not of the self or logic but of nature, the world. Its truth is not assumed but made.

(1981)

BARRETT WATTEN

METHOD AND *L=A=N=G=U=A=G=E*

(This is the second half of a talk originally given at 80 Langton Street, San Francisco. The first half is published as "Method and Surrealism: The Politics of Poetry" in *L=A=N=G=U=A=G=E*, volume 4, and is a discussion of Surrealist methods (and motives for them). The second half of the talk begins with a discussion of the continuation of Surrealist values in postwar American art and then jumps to the immediate issue of method as it was represented in *L=A=N=G=U=A=G=E*.)

Method in American art after the war incorporated numbers of Surrealist concepts. Traces of automatism and objective chance fuse in the renegotiated value for "the self." That recognition and the self are equivalent terms is coded into a wide range of art work. Logically, "the method that is no method," which so many artists have claimed, is consistent with the dominant ideology, aesthetic and otherwise, of the time. The method of no objects, the method of many objects, and the method of the reconstituted object all have their postwar forms, as critiques. The dialectical frame is absent; the predictive potential of method degenerates into the condition one is in. The only place for discipline to go has been technique. Where Breton argued for "the self" as an historical inevitability, that point of reference has become a static absolute. And it is difficult to call into question—it rhymes with common sense. Bill Berkson describes the 50s art environment in this quote from "Talk" (in *Talks, Hills* 6/7, ed. Bob Perelman [Spring 1980], pp. 14-15):

> O'Hara's reference to art, any art . . . is: Who does it. It's not granite critical terminology. What strikes me reading any of his criticism or poems, is that his terminology for art is a terminology of social life. And his terminology for social life could also borrow from the stockpile of art criticism. That seems to make living in the total language more possible, make it total, rather than have specialized languages

for special experiences. . . . A curiosity of art production is that it's done by people. You name the name and call up a body of work.

Looking for a way out of this "real-time" self has led to a minor reaction in the name of Surrealist method. Philip Lamantia's glossary entry on "Poetry" in the Rosemont edition of Breton's *What Is Surrealism?* (London: Pluto, 1978) makes this claim:

> Surrealism's fifty years of poetic evidence demonstrate the initial steps taken toward this supreme *disalienation* of humanity with its language, an emancipatory leap in opposition to the civilised debasement and fragmentation of language by reason, that is, language conditioned to serve as aesthetic object, submission-to-reality, mirror-trickery, every-day speech, pseudo-revolutionary mystification, personal confession, conscious self-expression and other idiocies—all of which, I insist, can be summed up in the self-condemned monstrosity that was Ezra Pound, his emulators and what generally passes for poetry and good writing in this country.

Here the American takes on the European mentality whole, and the violence of the rejection is equal to the pathos of the position without any access to its specific time and place. Williams saw a similar dynamic in Poe, and he went on optimistically about the proletarian writer H. H. Lewis in an article in *The New Masses* (1937): "When he speaks of Russia, most solidly in the tradition, not out of it, not borrowing a 'foreign' solution. It is the same cry that sent Europeans to a 'foreign' America and there set them madly free" (in *New Masses* [New York: International Publishers, 1969], pp. 257-63). It is a matter of record that Surrealist energies were transferred to New York during and after the war. But Lamantia's attack, twenty or fifty years late, is an image of stasis; the work of the Surrealists has already been coded into many of the aesthetic options he rejects. The beginning for further exten-tion of method is in the reflexiveness of "the self."

A reading of a number of the early articles in *L=A=N=-G=U=A=G=E* yields a series of reflexive positions. That "the distancing device is the staff of life" (Hugo Ball, 1919) is again true of a number of writers here. But the distance, in addition to being cultural, is a part of the method itself; the differentiation of

600 Barrett Watten

meanings produced calls into question the person at the center. The mediator ultimately is directed to a larger scale.

It is significant that $L=A=N=G=U=A=G=E$ opens its discussion (vol. 1, no. 1) with a statement by Larry Eigner. In "Approaching things / Some Calculus / Of Everyday Life . . ." the point of departure for writing is the position of the writer *in situ*. There is an absolute identification with day-to-day life; experience is the language medium for Eigner:

> No really perfect optimum mix, anyway among some thousands or many of distinctive or distinguishable things (while according to your capacity some minutes, days or hours 2, 4 or 6 people, say, are company rather than crowds), and for instance you can try too hard or too little. But beyond the beginning or other times and situations of scarcity, with material (things, words) more and more dense around you, closer at hand, easier and easier becomes invention, combustions, increasingly spontaneous.

Writing is a structure of response or evaluation ("to find the weights of things") within the context of a present language:

> Well, how does (some of) the forest go together with the trees. How might it, maybe. Forest of possibilities (in language anyway) - ways in and ways out. Near and far - wide and narrow (circles). Your neighborhood and how much of the world otherwise. Beginning, ending and continuing. As they come, what can things mean? Why expect a permanent meaning? What weights, imports?

In Eigner the implication of structure is in the way words appear on the page. The poem "is a made thing," but there is insight into the structure of experience in the way that it is made. Beginning with "care to find as it may be perceived," the poem extends beyond this—"so a method is glimpsed, by the way."

In Clark Coolidge's "Larry Eigner Notes," immediately following, the homage to another writer appears as notetaking for a re-entry into Coolidge's own work. Here, as in much of his criticism, Coolidge is looking for points of recognition or congruence. In so doing he transposes the reflexiveness of language and experience in Eigner into values seen in language "as such." "I do not think of Eigner." Coolidge's approach in general preserves a romance of language taken as a whole; there is a useful exclusion of any interpretation in this stance. An operator in a language medium looks at others doing similar work; finally the operators disappear and one language looks at another. The terms Coolidge uses in talking about Eigner are the terms language would use in talking about itself:

> an invisible & steadying "is" behind everything . . . all particles in the pile soon to reach / *nounal state* . . . the word "air" & its immediate prepositioning . . . these "scenes" don't exist, never have . . . the poem is built // each line / equals / its own completion // and every next line / its consequence . . . wholes are made only by motion . . . Each poem sights into a distance of all the others following . . . word-activation of the imagination in the act of seeing . . . a synthesis of presence.

Here "the self" has become generalized as "language," or, put another way, "the self" has exploded and disappeared. According to Coolidge, "Writers will now have to focus from a greater distance still subject to everything." The mediating persona has been abandoned.

The opposite tack, though in fact connected, locates writing as a specified mediator in relation to an organic continuity. Nick Piombino's articles, as "Writing and Free Association" (vol. 1, no. 1), look for a reflexiveness that would have therapeutic value:

> The method of self-disclosure called "free association" wherein one writes or speaks all one's thoughts in consecutive order (also sometimes called "automatic writing" in literary criticism) is comparable to serious attempts to read, write and understand poetry that directs attention to the *totality* of the thinking process. Memories and awareness of the present collapse into an experiential field composed of verbal presences which can be re-sounded for various interpretations and alternative directions.

Writing here has a literalness of purpose. Value, rather than inhering in a made thing, is given by personal use. This is possibly the most radical statement of "process" poetics to date. In the work of Robert Kelly, Theodore Enslin, and others, writing imitates a highly literary, derived notion of process. For Piombino, the poem is a process of the use of language in a practical sense. Rather than an exemplary, exalted self, as in Breton, Piombino proposes a quotidian, commonsense self, where the methods of writing or psychoanalysis are applied not as exercises in collective myth-making but as procedures that will "get results."

In "A Short Word on My Work" (vol. 1, no. 1), David Melnick writes, "I doubt that any statement will mediate *Pcoet* and its audience." *Pcoet* is written in a style close to what the Russian Futurists called *zaum*, "transrational language." Language is broken down below the morphemic level to letters of the alphabet, bits of debris. According to the Formalists, this kind of writing is motivated by an overplus of meaning on conventional planes; the need for pure expression is at odds with the available means. By randomizing phonemes or disrupting word forms, Melnick presents a sound texture of qualitative absoluteness not threatened by "meaning":

> What can such poems do for you? You are a spider strangling in your own web, suffocated by meaning. You ask to be freed by these poems from the intolerable burden of trying to understand. The world of meaning: is it too large for you? too small? It doesn't fit. Too bad. It's no contest. You keep on trying. So do I.

In a simple dialectic of sense and non-sense, "trans-sense" language proposes an organic meaning or wholeness apart from either. Melnick separates sound from reference in language to produce an acoustic spectacle in the reading of the text. This strategy is elucidated in a remark by Robert Smithson on the nature of abstraction, which for him is "a representation of nature devoid of 'realism' based on mental or conceptual reduction . . . [that] brings one closer to physical structures within nature itself." Melnick not only avoids the reduction of "realism" but that of "abstraction" as well, in order to render both the world and his work into physical wholes. An uninterrupted "nature" is the end product of Melnick's text—a return to things as they are by means of a language without false literary mediation.

In Zeno's paradox, the commuter never gets home because of the parcellization of the distance. In the "Zeno's paradox of biomorphism (or organic form)," fallen language never arrives at either the self (in Piombino) or the world (in Melnick), in spite of its endless refractions. Steve McCaffery operates a kind of synthesis of these two problematics. His "solution" can be exemplified by a performance (as one of the Four Horsemen) in which he poured Alpha-Bits (a cereal in the form of letters) on the ground from a ladder and then physically read them by rolling around on them while making noise. This was intended as a kind of "deconstruction" of the text (the complete text being *in* the cereal box, perhaps). Here the physicality of language (stated by means of creative vocalization in the style of Schwitters or by destruction of its "object status," the letters) is argued against the false reification of the commodity. McCaffery's aesthetics are consistent with this analysis; in "Repossessing the Word" (vol. 1, no. 2) he is quoted:

> Marx's notion of commodity fetishism, which is to say the occultation of the human relations embedded in the labour process, has been central to my own considerations of reference in language - of, in fact, a referentially based language, in general - and to certain "fetishistic" notions within the relationship of audience and performer.

The identification of reference, and of normative grammar behind that, with the commodification of language might be true in a given time and place. For example, the French bourgeois education received probably approached this kind of social coding. But writers in the present would be lucky to have had the lids on that tight. While toying with the idea of an essential absolute (reference = alienation), McCaffery's values are perhaps better seen as a part of a performance dynamic, of the flow of energy between performer and audience:

> To demystify this fetish and reveal the human relationships involved within the labour process of language will involve the humanization of the linguistic Sign by means of a centering of language within itself; a structural reappraisal of the functional roles of author and reader, performer and performance; the general diminishment of reference in communication and the promotion of forms based on the object-presence: the pleasure of the graphic or phonic imprint, for instance, their value as sheer linguistic stimuli.

"A whole person in a whole world" is here a kind of fictional premise for an acting out, one in which energy is released within specified formal bounds. The question of whether this energy in fact transforms is mediated by the irony of the dramatic presentation. Here the artist is taking himself apart for his art; still there is the danger that dissociative methods repeat themselves, continually giving the same results.

Beyond such absoluteness, the strategy of *L=A=N=-G=U=A=G=E* has often been to "provide information." Simple lists are juxtaposed with extreme convolutions. For example, there have been various bibliographies: literary magazines, current journal articles, featured writers, "recent readings," and so on. The overall editorial procedure might be seen to parallel these—there are a panoply of views, a multi-axial reference system, a system of poetic relations. Many articles in *L=A=N=G=U=A=G=E* give evidence of being one of "an endless number of points of view"; method is rarely given a full space for development but is, rather, represented. The various possibilities are located on their appropriate file cards, ready for quick recall. From "Articles" (vol. 1, no.3):

> *Ideology & Consciousness.* No. 1, Easter 1977: "Marxism and Linguistics," "Theories of Discourse," "Ideology and the Human Subject."
>
> *International Journal of Man-Machine Studies.* March 1977: "Machine understanding of natural language."
>
> *Journal of the Acoustical Society of America.* January 1978: "Hearing 'words' without words: Prosodic cues for word perception."
>
> *Journal of Aesthetics and Art Criticism.* Fall 1977: D. Kuspit, "Authoritarian Abstraction."

There is a kind of professional librarianship (special collections) operating here. Meanings, rather than being developed, are referred to—at the reference desk. So the radical poetics of *L=A=N=-G=U=A=G=E* are mediated by the commonsense functionalism of a professional role. Perhaps this is symptomatic of a cultural fact—that the intellectual is himself commoditized, by the university system.

If professionalism has atrophied, the avant-garde has exploded. Peter Schjeldahl has commented, roughly: "Not in the Surrealists' wildest dreams could they have imagined the life we live now," in regard to the New York art scene in the 70s. In fact, not in the wildest dreams of the New York art scene could the methodological rigor of the Surrealists be imagined. As an example, Bernadette Mayer's St. Mark's writing workshop has produced another kind of list, of "Experiments" (vol. 1, no. 3):

> Construct a poem as though the words were three-dimensional objects (like bricks) in space. Print them on large cards, if necessary.
>
> Cut-ups, paste-ups, etc. (Intersperse different material in horizontal cut-up strips, paste it together, infinite variations on this).

> Write exactly as you think, as close as you can come to this, that is, put pen to paper & dont stop.

> Attempt tape recorder work, that is, speaking directly into the tape, perhaps at specific times.

Here there is a proliferation of techniques. The overall equivalence of activity leads to a "state" in (real) time in which particular motives are effaced. Inspiration might be constant. Technique for Breton, on the other hand, was dialectic—automatism was a paradigm for method rather than an end in itself. The logic of inspiration, itself to a degree "objectified," was in its timely approach to a larger scale. While the advantage of Mayer's techniques is their adherence to the quotidian, there is no further integration. The "permanent avant-garde" vaporizes, leading to more conventional roles. As actually happened—in the course of Mayer's later editing of *United Artists*, the stylistic opening-up returns all these techniques to "the self."

The specter of "too much possibility/not enough necessity" appears likewise to Bruce Andrews in his review of John Wieners's *Beyond the State Capitol/Cincinnati Pike* (vol. 1, no. 1):

> AND how (and where) is consternation in the realm of reason a confrontation of the unknown, and do we know it?
> Or just, "You think I'm normal, they do a lot of things to my mind"? : a senseless indecipherable deluge, where nothing contextualizes an other thing?
> Not a frame outside, and not a kernel inside? Are we all collage, all dense, tensed, & unlocatable?
> The soundless permeation of madness upon sanity : would this be the quandary gotten by viewing the language as the cure for artistry?
> As a rebuff to social order, to emotional and perceptual order?

As in Coolidge's "Eigner Notes," one language is looking at another. But while language and writing in Eigner are stable, in Wieners the forms of writing are breaking down. Andrews eyes this breakdown in the form of a perpetual question: "Is this my reading?" "What have we got here?" Here the psyche is fending off an incursion by an "other"; Dali's "paranoia-criticism" comes to mind. The skepticism or questioning is both consciousness and its projection, a blank wall that words (both exterior and interior) bounce against. "CONFUSION? Decor? Meaning? Memory? Body?

Space? Rhetoric? Reality?" The poet mediates by insistence on such a *mode* of questioning; by taking himself apart he places his judgment in the world. Thus it is appropriate that Andrews is dealing with Wieners, who is likewise taking himself apart. But the identification is complex; where Coolidge locates another artist in Eigner, Andrews admits to "phenomena" in Wieners as much as "art."

The "exploded self" entering the world carries with it a critique based on its own organization. The inner argument is reciprocal, obviously; poetic reference is not only a question of "the world in the work" but "the work in the world." In a crude sense the negotiation with data taken in at the outset conditions the means for answering back. If in Andrews the response is skepticism, in Ron Silliman it is a passion for explanation. In an early article, Silliman wrote: "What happens when language moves toward and passes into a capitalist stage of development . . . " as the first term in an argument concerning alienation and reference. This causality is most possible in a subjective perspective—the only place where "language" and "capitalist stage of development" can both be given equivalent ontological status. It is only the extention of the writer's language into the world that can accomplish the desired equivalence of terms; so the underlying motive of the explanation is the elaboration of a new poetics. In his piece on Walter Benjamin, "Benjamin Obscura" (vol. 1, no. 6), Silliman writes:

> The obliteration of the gestural through the elaboration of technology occurs across the entire range of cultural phenomena in the capitalist period. It is the principle affective transformation of the new material basis of production. Guttenberg's moveable type erased gesturality from the graphemic dimension of books. That this in turn functions to alienate the producer from his or her product is tangible even to authors who compose on the typewriter: to see one's text in a new typeface (inevitably asserting different spatio-visual values) is almost as radical a shock as first seeing oneself on film or videotape, or initially hearing one's voice remarkably *other* on a tape recorder.

Locating "affect" in the literal writing process is not gratuitous here. Rather than arguing "between texts" (as in the case of numerous Marxist critiques), Silliman extends himself through the medium of alienated texts by means of his own literary "production."

Where Andrews identified with a text breaking down into languge (in Wieners), Silliman places broken down, peripheral, alienated language from any number of sources at the heart of his writing procedure. There is a proliferation of facts in Silliman's work ("Revolving door. A sequence of objects . . ."), but these alienated *things* are not only given as paradigms of content. Their use is in their identification by the writer as the essential problems of "the self." The mind that thinks its way into the world of things is the same mind that perceives things as having argued their way into existence. Exterior causality becomes the same as the writer's interior romance. Finally, what can be written is no different than what can be thought or perceived.

The "explanatory fiction" of Silliman's criticism is motivated as an extention outward; in the case of the reading of Benjamin, the desire is to reconcile newspaper typography or tape recording (the self objectified) with the pen in hand (the writer at work). At the heart of this method is the belief that the word, even as it is taken in by the subject, is an *other*. The passion for explanation in Silliman is an act of compensation for the autonomous word; in the act of writing the word is returned to the world, though this time the writer too is in it. Here the gradual movement of the skeptical self toward identification with its objects begins to take on its truly constructive potential, despite the difficulties of the method.

In the development of method in *L=A=N=G=U=A=G=E*, the increasing reflexiveness of the writer occurs parallel to a new value given to exterior fact. The dialectic that Breton saw as somehow taking the poet away into the clouds of a final realization (as in the state of mind achieved by Nietzsche) arrived at a stasis of method at the exact point where exterior reality itself underwent a change. *The* dialectic kept the upper hand, but one wonders what the world would have been like "after" Breton's revolution had been accomplished, anyway. The failure of Surrealist method was prefigured, and this perception from the outset was part and parcel of the absoluteness. That foreknowledge does not appear in the positions taken in $L=A=N=G=U=A=G=E$, possibly because the scale of foreknowledge at this point is simply beyond that of the individual. Rather, there is a day-to-day reality in which the extremes of identification partake, and on which method builds, through the means, either referential or purely linguistic, of writing itself. In this sense the answer is yes, a language corrector can be a generator of more language and of future possible acts. The idea of revolutionary suicide has been abandoned by means of a consideration of the power of words.

But what does this reflexiveness *sound* like when placed next to the Surrealist "purity of tone"? It would be interesting to juxtapose the writing itself of Surrealism next to examples of work being done now. This is from section 9 of "Soluble Fish," the automatic text that Breton included with the first *Manifesto* (*Manifestoes of Surrealism* [Ann Arbor: University of Michigan, 1972], pp. 65-66):

> Foul night, night of flowers, night of death rattles, heady night, deaf night whose hand is a contemptible kite held back by threads on all sides, black threads, shameful threads! Countryside of red and white bones, what have you done with your unspeakably filthy trees, your arborescent candor, your fidelity that was a purse with dense rows of pearls, flowers, so-so inscriptions, and when all is said and done, meanings? And you, you bandit, you bandit, ah, you are killing me, water bandit that sharpens your knives in my eyes, you have no pity then, radiant water, lustral water that I cherish! My imprecations will long follow you like a frighteningly pretty child who shakes her gorse broom in your direction. At the end of each branch there is a star and this is not enough, no, chicory of the Virgin. I don't want to see you any more, I want to riddle your birds that aren't even leaves any more with little lead pellets, I want to chase you from my doorway, hearts with seeds, brains of love.

This is a highly structured work, even though it involves a considerable dislocation of image. But there is a consistent voice, and a consistent address to an other; one can imagine the narrative voice in *Maldoror*, although in this case the voice is turned inside out—a kind of Klein-bottle effect of a continuous surface is achieved. Compare the continuity of statement in this prose poem to that of "Cult Music," by Carla Harryman (*Under the Bridge* [San Francisco: This, 1980], p. 31):

Got worn out screaming in the theater as if words could be a substitute for hard work; furthermore, the soft line of the jaw by pampering leans into steaming table: mutton, fish, greens and potatoes. Fed period music in a boxcar. Something infantilism—roams around, captures monsters, wants a lot. A great mind to waste. Surrounded by fleshy hulks and rocks that move toward voids and purple swamps. It's pink. Bird maps secured. The sky is turquoise. We always find the thing we do not seek. Eyes to intersections, the artifice's mercurial stuckness on the wall. A converted mausoleum. Fish heaps moving under feet. Dread of serene continent, webs, mites inland, an intoxicated community, rides into glory of sun, cars simmer into destination (or an arena) (the freeway is disguised). Entwined in the stone limbs the statues preen to the waves instead of cotton and synthetics or the organdy effusiveness of the sailor at port. The spine curved in right above the ass which was strong and perfect.

Here the writing is concerned with the evaluation of each sentence. The thought procedes up to the moment of the next thought; unlike Breton's high rhetoric, it's also capable of stopping. There is a tension between this mindfulness and a good deal of "automatic" content. The image content, though extremely interior, is still given a distance and particularity; there is also much more distance to the "you." Compare to this excerpt from a poem of Breton's, "Vigilence" (*Selected Poems*, trans. Kenneth White [London: Cape, 1969], p. 63):

At the hour of love and blue eyelids
I see myself burning in turn I see that solemn
        hidingplace of nothings
That was my body
Probed by the patient beaks of the fire-ibis
When it is finished I enter the invisible into
        the ark
Paying no attention to the passers-by of life
        whose dragging footsteps echo in the distance
I see the ridges of the sun
Across the may-blossom of the rain
I hear human linen being torn like a great leaf
Under the nails of absence and presence in con-
        nivance

The subject of this poem is transformation, though the image given is to some extent impeded, evoking rather the desire for transformation. The syntax is accretive; each line could be another of a sequence of events; the poem appears to be always coming out of itself. The transformation is in the creation, by linear means, of an imagistic tableau. A contemporary counterexample is "In the American Tree," by Kit Robinson (*Down and Back* [Berkeley: The Figures, 1978], pp. 9-10):

A bitter wind taxes the will
causing dry syllables
to rise from the throat.

Flipping out wd be one alternative
simply rip the cards to pieces
amid a dense growth of raised eyebrows

But such tempest (storm) doors
once opened, resistance fades away
and having fired all the guns you find you are
      left with a ton of butter,

Which, if it isn't eaten by some lurking rat
hiding out under the gate, may well be picked
up by the wind and spread all over

The face you're by now too chicken to admit is
      yours.
Wheat grows between bare toes
of a cripple barely able to hold his or her breath

And at the crack of dawn
we howl for more
beer. One of us produces

A penny from his pocket
and flips it at the startled thief
who has been spying on her from behind the flames

That crackle up from the wreck.
The freeway is empty now, moonlight
reflecting brightly off the belly of a blimp,

And as you wipe the red from your eyes
and suck on the lemon someone has given you,
you notice a curious warp in the sequence

Of events suggesting a time loop
in which bitter details repeat
themselves like the hands of a clock

Repeat their circular travels in a dream-
like medium you find impossible to pierce:
it simply spreads out before you, a field.

Now you are able to see a face
in the slope of a hill,
tall green trees

Are its hard features,
a feather floats down
not quite within grasp

And it is Spring.
The goddess herself
is really

Feeling great.
Space assumes the form of a bubble
whose limits are entirely plastic.

What is transformation in this poem? It would not seem to be a specially valued state or a state to be inferred from the images. There is a definite arbitrariness in the work; certainly there are levels of diction the Surrealists would never have used. But although the landscape is mutating, the driver is always in control of the car. The attention is directed to the progression in the poem, and the image content is undercut and distanced by that fact. Illusion comes with a tag. The transformation in Robinson's poem is not the coming into being of the image but of something even deeper— the perception of mind in control of its language. Distance, rather than absorption, is the intended effect.

CONTRIBUTORS

BRUCE ANDREWS Books: *Give Em Enough Rope* (Sun & Moon, 1985); *Love Songs* (Pod, 1982); *Wobbling* (Roof, 1980); *Sonnets –– memento mori* (This, 1980); *Legend* (5 person collaboration, 1980). Booklets: *Excommunicate* (Potes & Poets, 1982); *R + B* (Segue, 1981); *Jeopardy* (Awede, 1980); *Getting Ready To Have Been Frightened* (Roof, 1978); *Praxis* (Tuumba, 1978); *Film Noir* (Burning Deck, 1978); *Vowels* (O Press, 1976); *Corona* (Burning Deck, 1974); *Appalachia* (1973); *A Cappella* (1973); *Edge* (1973). Editing: *L=A=N=G=U=A=G=E* (co-editor with Charles Bernstein, 1978-1981); *The L=A=N=G=U=A=G=E Book* (co-editor; Southern Illinois University Press, 1984); *New Political Science* (1978-1980). Essays: on poetics, language and politics, Left social theory (late '70s on).

Born Chicago 4-1-48; living in New York City since 1975 (41 W. 96th St, NYC 10025). Teaching politics at Fordham University, Bronx, N.Y., 1975 to present. Scholarly articles on the domestic roots of U.S. imperialism, the political economy of world capitalism. Book in progress: *Surplus Security: Interpreting America's War with Vietnam*.

Also: live improvised music performances with audiotapes, 1983 on. Co-director (with Sally Silvers) of *Barking* (multi-media performance group): *I Can't Hear You, Make A Mistake* (1983), *Eagles Ate My Estrogen –– Gender Damage Kabuki* (1985).

RAE ARMANTROUT: I have published two books of poems: *Extremities* (The Figures, 1978), and *The Invention of Hunger* (Tuumba, 1979). A third book, *Precedence*, is forthcoming from Burning Deck. Recently, my work has appeared in *Conjunctions, Credences, Hills, How(ever), Ironwood, Partisan Review, Poetics Journal* and *This*. I'm living in San Diego where I teach at UCSD and SDSU from time to time.

TOM BECKETT edits *The Difficulties*. His writing has appeared in *Acts, Chicago Review, L=A=N=G=U=A=G=E, Interstate, Gallery Works* and other journals. Work is forthcoming in *O.ars, boundary*

2, and *"exposures'* (U.K., Lobby Press). *Moving Letters* (Paris, France) will publish an excerpt from his work-in-progress, *Economies of Pure Expenditure*, in early 1985. *Soluble ~~Senses~~ Census*, his first collection of verse, was published by Tonsure Press in 1984. He lives in Kent, Ohio, with his wife and two daughters.

STEVE BENSON: Books—*As Is* (The Figures, 1978); *Blindspots* (Whale Cloth, 1981); *The Busses* (Tuumba, 1981); *Dominance* (The Coincidences, 1984); *Briarcombe Paragraphs* (Moving Letters, 1984).

Work in periodicals, as yet uncollected in books, includes dialogues in *QU* 6, 1982, *Channel*, 1983, and *Contact II*, 1984, 'quartets' in *This* 12, 1983, "Talking Leaves Reading" in *Hills* 9, 1983, 'blue books' in *Little Ceasar* 11, 1981, *Tottel's* 18, 1981, and *Gnome Baker* 7/8, 1982, "at all" in *This* 8, 1979, "Views of Communist China" in *Hills* 6/7 Talks Issue, 1980, "(substituted for)" in *Sun & Moon* 8, 1979, "Beethoven's Sixth Symphony" in *Moving Letters* 1, 1983.

Criticism—in *L=A=N=G=U=A=G=E, Poetics Journal, 80 Langton Artists and Writers in Residence 1980, Poetry Project Newsletter, American Book Review*, etc.

Original project for tape cassette distribution—"On His Own," Wide Mouth, 1980.

Public Readings have often involved improvisatory and other performance- and process-oriented composition in situ.

Videotape of reading with improvisational work and props, and of collaboration with Jackson Mac Low, 1983, distributed by Poetry Archive, San Francisco State University.

Talks—"Views of Communist China," 1977, "Careers in the Arts," 1978, and "Close Reading," 1980, in series curated by Bob Perelman (the last revised for Poetry Project, N.Y.C., 1981).

Acting—Drama voice (male parts) in *"A"-24* by Louis Zukofsky, 1978, "Loop" in *Third Man* by Carla Harryman, 1980, and "Bunker" in *Particle Arms* by Alan Bernheimer, 1982.

Directing—*La Quotidienne* by Carla Harryman, 1983.

ALAN BERNHEIMER is the author of two books of poetry, *Cafe Isotope* (The Figures, 1980), and *State Lounge* (Tuumba, 1981).

His play, *Particle Arms*, was produced by Poets Theater in San Francisco in 1982. He is the translator of Valery Larbaud's *The Hamlet of the Bees* (Whale Cloth, 1981).

CHARLES BERNSTEIN's books include *The Sophist* (forthcoming, Sun & Moon); *Resistance* (Awede, 1983); *Islets/Irritations* (Jordan Davies, 1983); *Stigma* (Station Hill Press, 1981); *The Occurrence of Tune*, with Susan Bee Laufer (Segue, 1981); *Disfrutes* (Potes & Poets, 1981); *Controlling Interests* (Roof, 1980); *Legend* with Andrews, Silliman, McCaffery and DiPalma (L=A=N=-G=U=A=G=E/Segue, 1980); *Senses of Responsibility* (Tuumba, 1979); *Poetic Justice* (Pod, 1979); *Shade* (Sun & Moon, 1978); *Parsing* (Asylum's, 1976) and *Content's Dream: Essays 1975-1984* (Sun & Moon, 1986). He is co-editor, with Bruce Andrews, of *L=A=N=G=U=A=G=E* and *The L=A=N=G=U=A=G=E Book* (Southern Illinois University Press, 1984), an editor of two anthology collections of poetry for *Paris Review* (1982) and *boundary 2* (1986). He co-founded the Ear Inn reading series in New York, and co-ordinated New York Talk and St. Mark's Talks. Bernstein earns a living doing freelance editorial work.

DAVID BROMIGE: Books: *Please, Like Me* ('68), *The Ends of the Earth* ('68), *Threads* ('70), *3 Stories* ('73), *Tight Corners & What's Around Them* ('74), *Out of My Hands* ('74), *Credences of Winter* ('76), all from Black Sparrow; also *The Gathering* (Sumbooks, 1965), *The Quivering Roadway* (Archangel, 1969), *10 Years in the Making* (New Star, 1973), *Birds of the West* (Coach House, 1974), *Spells & Blessings* (Talonbooks, 1975), *Living in Advance* (Open Reading, 1976), *My Poetry* (The Figures, 1980), *P-E-A-C-E* (Tuumba, 1981), *In the Uneven Steps of Hung-Chow* (Little Dinosaur, 1982), *It's the Same Only Different/The Melancholy Owed Categories* (Last Straw, 1984), *Red Hats I-IV* (Tonsure, 1986). Also a number of works on audio- and video-tape, one-shot items (performances), critical articles and reviews. In '73, half an issue of *Vort* (#3) was dedicated to consideration of my work; the upcoming issue of *The Difficulties* will explore it further.
Other useful reviews include Davidson's "The Poet As Language" in *Credences* II ('75), Silliman's *Modes of Autobiography* in *Soup*

2 ('81), & Fredman's final chapter in *Poets' Prose* (Cambridge, '83). Michael Anderson in an upcoming article deals with my Residency—"How to Talk About Important Matters"—at New Langton Arts in SF, July '84. In '79, I won an NEA grant; in '80, a Pushcart prize. Served as editor for *Northwest Review, R*C*Lion, Open Reading*, etc.

CLARK COOLIDGE was born in Providence, R.I. in 1939 and now lives in the Berkshire Hills of Western Massachusetts. His more recent books include: *Own Face, American Ones, A Geology, Research, Mine: the one that enters the stories* and *Solution Passage (Poems 1978-1981)*.

TINA DARRAGH: I was born in Pittsburgh, PA, in 1950 and was raised nearby in McDonald, where I began writing in 1968. From 1970-1972, I studied poetry with Michael Lally at Trinity College (DC) and worked from 1974-1976 with Some of Us Press and the Mass Transit community bookstore/writing workshop group after spending a year in Ireland and England on a Watson Fellowship. Since then I have lived in Mt. Rainer, MD, with Peter and Jack Inman (with the exception of a year we spent living in Champaign, IL). My work has been published in *Abacus, NRG, Washington Review of the Arts, Personal Injury, La Bas, Roof, Dog City, Pessimistic Labor, Paris Review, Ironwood, L=A=N=G=U=A=G=E, PJ*, and *The L=A=N=G=U=A=G=E Book*. I have three published books: *my hands to myself* (Dry Imager, 1976), *Pi in the Skye* (Ferguson/Franzino, 1980) and *on the corner to off the corner* (Sun & Moon, 1981) for which I received an NEA Creative Writing Fellowship.

MICHAEL DAVIDSON teaches at the University of California, San Diego. He is the author of *The Mutabilities* (Sand Dollar, 1976), *The Prose of Fact* (The Figures, 1981) and *The Landing of Rochambeau* (Burning Deck, 1985).

ALAN DAVIES is a critic and a poet. He is the author of *split thighs, ACTIVE 24 HOURS, Mnemonotechnics, NAME*, and other books. His critical work has been widely published. He lives and works in New York City. He has recently said that "Poetry is a small pile of papers on the upper left hand corner of the desk."

JEAN DAY is the author of *Linear C* (Tuumba, 1983), *A Bronzino* (Jimmy's House, 1984) and *Flat Birds* (Gaz, 1984). Her work has appeared in *This, Vanishing Cab, Sun & Moon, Ironwood, Telephone, Low Company, Hills, The Washington Review* and *The Antioch Review* among other journals.

RAY DIPALMA was born in Pennsylvania in 1943. He attended Duquesne University (B.A., 1966) and the University of Iowa (M.F.A., 1968). Before moving to New York City in 1975 he traveled in Europe, and taught college in the mid-West. In the late 1970's he was an adjunct professor with the Union Graduate School at Antioch College. Among his books are *Max* (Body Press, 1969), *All Bowed Down* (Burning Deck, 1972), *Works in a Drawer* (Blue Chair Press, 1972), *Soli* (Ithaca House, 1974), *Max/A Sequel* (Burning Deck, 1974), *Accidental Interludes* (Turkey Press, 1975), *Cuiva Sails* (Sun & Moon, 1978), *Two Poems* (Awede Press, 1982), and others. In addition to these collections are publications which in part extend the notions of textual image. They include: *The Sargasso Transcries* ('X' Editions, 1974), *Marquee* (Asylum's Press, 1977), *Genesis* (Underwhich Editions, 1980), and *Startle Luna* (Sleight of Hand, 1985). His visual works, which include one-of-a-kind artist's books, collages and prints have been exhibited in numerous group shows in the U.S., Europe, and South America, and in a one-man show at the Stempelplatt's Gallery in Amsterdam. Edition Vogelsang in Berlin published *13 Works* and *23 Works* in 1982. Ray DiPalma still lives in New York City & homesteads a small farm in the Hudson Valley.

LYNNE DREYER was born in Baltimore, Maryland in 1950. She began writing in the early 70's after moving to Washington, D.C. and has published three chapbooks including *Lamplights Used to Feed the Deer* (S.O.U.P. Press), *Stampede* (E.E.L. Press), and *Stepwork* (Tuumba). Work has appeared in various magazines including *Tottel's, Mass Transit, Dog City, Washington Review of the Arts, Delirium, Black Box, Vanishing Cab* and *Roof*, and two anthologies, *None of the Above* (Crossing Press) and *The Big House* (Ailanthus Press). "Writing has been a way to explain and personalize the world to myself." She lives in Falls Church, Virginia with her husband, David, and two sons.

MICHAEL GOTTLIEB: Born and currently residing in New York City. Author of *Local Color/Eidetic Deniers* (Other Publications), *Ninety-six Tears* (Roof), and several chapbooks. Work has appeared in a wide variety of magazines, in the U.S. and internationally, from *This, L=A=N=G=U=A=G=E* to the *Paris Review*. Publisher of Case Books and Casement Books. Co-editor *Roof* magazine. Producer of Last Tuesday poetry and performance series. Favorite TV shows: Lifestyles of the Rich and Famous, People's Court.

TED GREENWALD was born, in 1942, in Brooklyn, raised in Queens, and has lived for years in Manhattan. He coedited *Ear* with Lorenzo Thomas and was the editor of the St. Mark's *Poetry Project Newsletter*. He was the organizer of several reading series, including 98 Greene Street Loft, the Clocktower, P.S. 1 and Ear Inn. Among numerous books are *Common Sense, Licorice Chronicles, Use No Hooks, Word of Mouth, Smile* and *You Bet!* He is the director of Ted Greenwald Gallery.

ROBERT GRENIER: Born Minneapolis, Minnesota, August 4, 1941 of Norwegian & French-Scots stock. Father, Judson Achille Grenier; mother, Beatrice Olivia Bjeldanes. Birch & pine, berry-picking/fishing trips to Northern Minnesota, March car rides to Texas & California, basketball in high school. Space for life. Harvard College scholarships (A.B., 1965, with thesis on Williams' prosody), translated Trakl, studied with Robert Lowell three years (Harvard Monthly Prizes, 1964, 1965). Fellowship to Iowa Writers Workshop (M.F.A. 1968). Amy Lowell Traveling Scholarship, 1966-67. N.E.A. Poetry Fellowships, 1979, 1985. Eleven years' teaching literature & writing at Iowa, U.C. Berkeley, Tufts, Franconia College, New College of California (subsequent, apparent spiral 'out'/away from lit. establishment's recognition coordinates, *non grata*/gratis *exactly* when writing becomes something/*other*– 'can't get published'/'can't find work' teaching–despite having 'paid dues' in college/graduate school & 'excellent employment record,' scholarly work done: sobeit!). Presently legal proofreader/ editorial assistant to poet Larry Eigner. Kathleen's 'husband' & Amy's father.

Primary sources: Keats, Emily Dickinson, Gertrude Stein, William Carlos Williams, Ezra Pound, Charles Olson, Louis Zukofsky, Jack Kerouac, Robert Creeley, Larry Eigner. Responsibility for/attention to sources I think evidenced in teaching, first; and see editions of Creeley's *Selected Poems* (order of poems 'doctored' by publisher), Eigner's *Waters/Places/A Time*, notes on Stein & Keats in *L=A=N=G=U=A=G=E* (ed. Bernstein, Andrews) & forthcoming statement on narrative as "Attention" in Olson series, *A Curriculum of the Soul* (ed. Clarke). For 'task of writing" (in part), see extract from four presentations given as "LANGUAGE/SITE/WORLD" at Intersection in San Francisco in *Writing/Talks* (ed. Perelman).

Generation compatriots: Kenneth Irby, Anselm Hollo, Joanne Kyger, David Bromige, Alice Notely, Lyn Hejinian, John Batki, Charles Bernstein.

Publications: *Dusk Road Games* (poems, 1960-66). Cambridge, Ma.: Pym-Randall Press, 1967.

Selected Poems: Georg Trakl (co-translator). Ed. Christopher Middleton. London: Jonathan Cape, 1968.

Sentences Toward Birds (41 poems from *Sentences*). Kensington, Ca.: L Press, 1975.

Selected Poems (editor). By Robert Creeley. New York: Charles Scribner's Son, 1976.

Series (poems, 1967-71). San Francisco: This Press, 1978.

Sentences (500 poems on 5" x 8" index cards, boxed, 1972-77). Cambridge, Ma.: Whale Cloth Press, 1978.

CAMBRIDGE M'ASS (265 poems on 40" x 48" poster). Berkeley: Tuumba Press, 1979

Oakland (poems). Berkeley: Tuumba Press, 1980.

Waters/Places/A Time (editor). By Larry Eigner. Los Angeles: Black Sparrow Press, 1983.
A Day At The Beach (poems). New York: Roof Books, 1984.
Twenty-Six Poems (author's ms., photocopied). Berkeley: 1984.

CARLA HARRYMAN: Books: *The Middle* (Gaz, 1983) – San Francisco
Property (Tuumba, 1982) – Berkeley
Under The Bridge (This, 1980) – Berkeley
Percentage (Tuumba, 1979) – Berkeley

Editor: *QU*
Playwright: plays include "Third Man," performed by Poets Theatre in San Francisco, 1980, and published in *Hills* #8; "La Quotidienne" performed at 80 Langton St. in San Francisco, 1983; and "There Is Nothing Better Than A Theory" to be published in *Moving Letters*, Paris.
Writer In Residence: 80 Langton St., San Francisco, April, 1983.

LYN HEJINIAN was born in 1941 in San Francisco. She is the editor and publisher of Tuumba Press and the co-editor (with Barrett Watten) of *Poetics Journal*. Her work hs appeared in various literary magazines since 1964, including *Hills, Roof, This, Tottel's* and *L=A=N=G=U=A=G=E*, in the U.S., *Change* and *Action Poetique* in France, *Grossteste Review, Figs,* and *Alembic* in the U.K., and work in translation is scheduled to appear at an unspecified date in *Innostranaya Literatura* in Moscow. Her books include *A Thought is the Bride of What Thinking* (1976), *A Mask of Motion* (1977), *Gesualdo* (1978), *Writing is an Aid to Memory* (1978), *My Life* (1980), *The Guard* (1984), and *Redo* (1984). She is married to the musician Larry Ochs and has two children.

FANNY HOWE has published several novels and collections of poems. Her most recent work of fiction was *In the Middle of Nowhere* (The Fiction Collective). Tuumba Press recently published *For Erato: The Meaning of Life*. Books are forthcoming from Sun and Moon Press and from Avon Books which has published her books for teenagers. This one will be the fourth. Her last book of poems was *Alsace Lorraine* (Telephone Books).

SUSAN HOWE: I have written six books of poems that have been published by small presses since 1974. The three most recent are *Secret History of the Dividing Line* (Telephone Books), *Pythagorean Silence* (Montemora), and *Defenestration of Prague* (Kulchur). I have just finished a book length study of Emily Dickinson's poetry, called *My Emily Dickinson*, that will be published sometime by North Atlantic Books. At present I am working on a new manuscript of poems.

ERICA HUNT reads more than she publishes. Her individual prose works include "Reach Extended," "Evidence," "The Rest of Esther," "Dr. No Backs Out," "Exchange Rates," "Speech Acts," "Prefaces" and "Getting Even." Her published prose has appeared in *Vanishing Cab, QU 2, Poetics Journal, Idiolects* and one of the "Prefaces" will appear in *boundary 2* in spring of 1986.

P. INMAN: Books include: *Platin* (Sun & Moon, 1979); *Ocker* (Tuumba, 1982); *Uneven Development* (Jimmy's House of Knowledge, 1984); *None of the Above* (ed. Michael Lally) (Crossing Press, 1976); *The L=A=N=G=U=A=G=E Book* (ed. Andrews & Bernstein) (Southern Illinois University Press, 1984).
Magazines: *Abacus, Brilliant Corners, Ironwood, Paris Review, Roof, Sun & Moon, World War 4*.
Grew up in Long Island, school in Georgetown, live in Maryland w/ Tina Darragh & our son Jack. Work at Library of Congress where I'm also an AFSCME shop steward.

JACKSON MAC LOW, born in 1922, has been composing poetry, stories and other prose pieces, and music since the 1930s, and (beginning somewhat later) plays, criticism, radioworks, and performance works involving language, vocalism, and/or musical instruments (pieces called "simultaneities" when performed by two or more people). From 1954 much of his composition and performance has involved chance operations, indeterminacy, and/or improvisation, though most recent works were composed nonaleatorically. He has read, performed, and been published throughout North America and Western Europe, and has had works performed also in Japan, Australia, and South America. He has appeared in many anthologies and magazines. In the 1980s three commissioned radioworks have been produced in Cologne and one in New York, and the following books have been published: *Asymmetries 1-260* (New York: Printed Editions, 1980), *"Is That Wool Hat My Hat?"* (Milwaukee: Membrane Press, 1982), *From Pearl Harbor Day to FDR's Birthday* (College Park, Md.: Sun & Moon, 1982), *Bloomsday* (Barrytown, N.Y.: Station Hill, 1984), and *French Sonnets* (Tucson: Black Mesa Press, 1984). Scheduled for 1985 are *Representative Works* (New York: Roof Books) and *The Virginia Woolf Poems* (Providence: Burning Deck), and for 1986, *Pieces o' Six* (Los Angeles: Sun & Moon).

TOM MANDEL: I was born in Chicago in 1942. I have taught college and worked in publishing. I have been a short order book in a donut shop and a cultural worker. I have worked in politics and been a salesman. I have been a software entrepreneur, and I am a businessman.

I have published three books (*EncY*, *Erat*, and *Ready to Go*). A book called *Some Appearances* will appear later this year. Another, *Central Europe*, is scheduled for early 1986 if I can finish it in time (think so). I have recently completed a book called *Realism*.

For a little while in the 1970's I edited a magazine called *Miam*, and for an even briefer interval I was director of the Poetry Center at San Francisco State University. I have two children, and I am married to a woman named Gaelyn Godwin. Besides Chicago, I have lived in New York and Paris and now reside in San Francisco.

JOHN MASON is the author of *Fade to Prompt* (Tuumba, 1981). His poems have also appeared in magazines such as *Hills, Famous, Nadir, Nadine, Truck* and *Loon Attack*. He and Susan Davies have two children and live at present in Saratoga Springs, New York.

BERNADETTE MAYER is the author of *Story, Moving, Memory, Ceremony Latin (1964), Studying Hunger, Poetry, Eruditio ex Memoria, The Golden Book of Words, The Incidents Report Sonnets, Mutual Aid* and *Utopia.*

DAVID MELNICK was born in Illinois in 1938 and was raised in Los Angeles. By the age of 7 he had invented a private language, and at 13 he constructed a semi-private one with a friend. He was educated at the University of Chicago and the University of California at Berkeley, and now lives in San Francisco. His first book, *Eclogs*, containing poems written in the 1960s, was published in 1972 (Ithaca House). *PCOET*, written in 1972, was published in 1975 (G.A.W.K.). *Men in Aida, Book One* (Tuumba, 1983) is the first book of a projected poem based on Homer's *Iliad.*

This poet's politics are left, his sexual orientation gay, his family Jewish. He has wandered much, e.g., to France, Greece and Spain (whence his mother's ancestors emigrated in 1492). As of this writing, he has never held a job longer than a year-and-a-half at a stretch. He is short, fat, and resembles Modeste Moussorgsky in face and Gertrude Stein in body type and posture.

MICHAEL PALMER was born in New York City in 1943. Education includes a B.A. from Harvard College in History and Literature and an M.A. from Harvard University in Comparative Literature. Since 1969 he has lived in San Francisco where he has frequently worked with contemporary composers and has collaborated on a number of dance compositions with Margaret Jenkins and her company. He is currently a member of the faculty of the Poetics Program at New College of California.
BOOKS AND CHAPBOOKS
Plan of the City of O, 1971
Blake's Newton, 1972
C's Songs, 1973

The Circular Gates, 1974
Without Music, 1977
Transparency of the Mirror, 1980
Alogon, 1980
Notes for Echo Lake, 1981
First Figure, 1984
EDITOR
Joglars (magazine, with Clark Coolidge), 1964-65
Code of Signals: Recent Writings in Poetics, 1983
TRANSLATIONS
Voyelles, Arthur Rimbaud, 1980
in *The Selected Poetry of Vicente Huidobro*, ed., David Guss, 1981
in *The Random House Book of Twentieth-Century French Poetry*,
    ed. Paul Auster, 1982
Jonah Who Will Be 25 in the Year 2000, John Berger and Alain
    Tanner, 1983

BOB PERELMAN
books: *To the Reader*, Tuumba Press, 1984
        a.k.a., The Figures Press, 1984
        Primer, This Press, 1981
        7 Works, The Figures, 1979
        Braille, Ithaca House Press, 1975
        Forthcoming, new work from The Figures, 1986
editing: *Writing/Talks* (16 talks by writers), Southern Illinois Uni-
        versity Press, 1985
        Nine issues of *Hills* magazine, including *Talks, Hills* 6/7
        (11 talks) and *Plays and Other Writing, Hills* 9 (fea-
        turing plays from the San Francisco Poets Theater)
articles and talks: "Exchangeable Frames," *Poetics Journal* 5.
        "Words Detached from the Old Song and Dance," *Code
        of Signals*
        "Sense," *Writing/Talks*
        "Plotless Prose," *Poetics Journal* 1
        "The First Person," *Talks, Hills* 6/7
        "*1-10*," *L=A=N=G=U=A=G=E, Volume 4*
I initiated and curated the San Francisco Talk Series, 1977-81.

I have had two plays performed by Poets Theater, "The Alps" (in *Hills* 9) and "The Dark Ages."

NICK PIOMBINO: My work in poetics, in such articles as the one published here, and "Writing and Imaging," "Writing as Reverie" and "Writing and Experiencing" (all originally published in the journal *L=A=N=G=U=A=G=E* and republished in *The L=A=N=-G=U=A=G=E Book*, Southern Illinois University Press, 1984) focusses on forging connective links between modes of comprehending, expressing and denoting the thought process in poetry, psychoanalysis and in other areas of art and science. My most recent essay, "Towards An Experiential Syntax" (*Poetics Journal* 5) explores the omnipresence of visual/verbal tracking models in the authentification of human experience. My work as a psychoanalyst and poet living in New York City continuously alerts me to the value and necessity of appreciating resonances between all communicative phenomena—in all languages.

My first published poems appeared in *American Weave* (1965). In the 1970's my poems were published in such journals as *The World, Telephone, Roof* and *100 Posters*. More recently, works of mine were published in *Lobby Newsletter 18* (a tape cassette magazine published in Cambridge, England) and in *boundary 2*.

LARRY PRICE lives in San Francisco and works at The Poetry Center at San Francisco State University. He is the editor of *GAZ*. He has published one book, *Proof* (Tuumba, 1982).

KIT ROBINSON's books include *Riddle Road, Tribute to Nervous, Down and Back, The Dolch Stanzas,* and *Chinatown of Cheyenne*. His play, *Collateral*, was produced by Poets Theater in San Francisco in 1982. He is a former director of the Tenderloin Writers Workshop and has been active since 1976 in California Poets in the Schools. He won a creative writing fellowship from the National Endowment for the Arts in 1979. With Lyn Hejinian, he founded and produced "In the American Tree: New Writing by Poets," a weekly radio program of live readings and interviews for KPFA fm in Berkeley, California. Articles by K.R. on Tom

Raworth and Anselm Hollo will appear in *The Dictionary of Literary Biography*, forthcoming from Bruccoli-Clark.

Born May 17, 1949, in Evanston, Illinois, Kit Robinson spent his early years near the shores of Lake Michigan. A graduate of Walnut Hills High School in Cincinnati, Ohio, he received a bachelor's degree in philosophy and English from Yale College in 1971. He has worked as a writer, teacher, editor, photographer, and actor. His recently completed book *Windows* will be published by Whale Cloth Press. State One will publish *A Day Off.*

STEPHEN RODEFER's *Four Lectures* was the co-winner of the 1982 Annual Book Award given by the San Francisco Poetry Center. His other books include *Plane Debris* (Tuumba, 1981), *The Bell Clerk's Tears Keep Flowing* (The Figures, 1978), *One or Two Love Poems from the White World* (Duende, 1976), *VILLON* by Jean Callais (Pick Pocket Series, 1981), and *Oriflamme Day*, with Benjamin Friedlander (House of K, 1984). He has also published translations of Rilke and sections of the Greek anthology.

In the mid-sixties Rodefer was part of the group that formed *The Magazine of Further Studies* out of Charles Olson's classes at Buffalo, and in New Mexico in the early seventies he edited, with Larry Goodell, *Fervent Valley: a Magazine of the Arts.* He has written on art and culture for such varied places as *downbeat* and *WET* magazine and has been an active member of Poets Theater in San Francisco since its inception. In 1983 two of his dramatic works, *Tennyson* and *A & C*, were produced at Eighty Langton Street in San Francisco.

Rodefer has taught at SUNY-Buffalo, the University of New Mexico, UC-La Jolla, and now lives in Oakland and teaches at San Francisco State University. His recent writing can be found in *Sulfur, Grosseteste, Conjunctions* and *boundary 2.*

PETER SEATON: With entropic escapes from alienated labor, desperation for determination and others' steadfast extrusions into the creation of sheer contemporaneity, there was always reading for dear life.

Still, pen didn't pass through paper in the agreement of *Agreement* (Asylum's Press, 1978). *The Son Master's* (Roof Books,

1982) thinkable scansion pursued frontiers of the vertical west with Oedipal use-value. And the writing of *Crisis Intervention* (Tuumba Press, 1983) occupied a pace in which the trappings of the past would redeploy through current activity in the throes of a literacy which remains agent of and subject to the present cornucopia of verbal resources.

More than ever, the struggle is to generate and maintain an aggressive responsibility for the visceral proportions of a challenge incorporating the contradictions in the conscious exploitation of a dynamically open linear point of view.

Critical rigor, spiritual consanguinity and perceptions of the diverse integrities of heretofore chimerical properties associated with the obsolescence of public, elitist languages continue to be sought and brought to bear on this effort.

JAMES SHERRY is the author of *Part Songs* (1978, poetry), *Integers* (1980, collaboration with dancer Nina Wiener), *In Case* (1981, prose), *Converses* (1983, poetry) and *Popular Fiction* (1985, prose). He is the editor of ROOF Books, ROOF magazine, and director of the Segue Foundation in New York City.

RON SILLIMAN was born in Pasco, Washington, in 1946. He was raised in the Berkeley area and has lived most of his adult life in San Francisco. Variously a political organizer, newspaper editor, teacher, college administrator, lobbyist and radio commentator, Silliman is presently poet-in-residence at the California Institute of Integral Studies. Among 10 volumes of poetry are *Ketjak, Tjanting, Bart, ABC* and *Paradise*, these last two containing portions of *The Alphabet*. Roof will publish a selection of his talks and essays, *The New Sentence*. In 1985, an issue of *The Difficulties* was devoted to his work.

DIANE WARD was born in Washington, D.C. and lives in New York City. Her work has appeared in *United Artists, The Washington Review of the Arts, So & So, This, Code of Signals* (an anthology edited by Michael Palmer), *Ironwood*, and *The Paris Review*. Her latest book, *Never Without One*, was published in 1984 by Roof Books and is available from the Segue Foundation in New York City. Her previous books are *On Duke Ellington's Birthday, The Light American*, and *Theory of Emotion*, all out of print but available in facsimile form from Segue Foundation.

"Reading Ward and other 'logo-scientists' is to become a participant in a dynamic building up and tearing down of language and idea. . . ."—Kenneth Funston *Los Angeles Times.*

BARRETT WATTEN founded *This* magazine with Robert Grenier in 1971; in 1974 he began publishing books under the imprint of This Press. He is the author of *Opera —— Works* (Big Sky, 1975), *Decay* (This, 1977), *Plasma/Paralleles/"X"* (Tuumba, 1979), *Complete Thought* (Tuumba, 1982) and *1 — 10* (This, 1980). A book of critical essays, *Total Syntax*, was published by Southern Illinois University Press in 1984. Roof will publish *Progress*, a book-length poem. Since 1982, Watten has been co-editor, with Lyn Hejinian, of *Poetics Journal.* He is a Board member at New Langton Arts (formerly 80 Langton Street), San Francsico, and teaches at San Francisco State University.

HANNAH WEINER was born in Providence, R.I., and attended Radcliffe College, graduating in 1950. She began to write in the 60's, producing *The Code Poems*, and engaged in many performances: Code Poem Events, Theater Works, The Fashion Show Poetry Event which she co-ordinated with John Perreault and Eduardo Costa, and Street Works and World Works, which she co-ordinated with John Perreault and Marjorie Strider. In 1970 she became psychic and began to see energy fields and pictures in the air, and in 1972 she began to see words in the air, on other people, and on her forehead. Her clairvoyant books are *Sun, June 9, Clairvoyant Journal, Little Books/Indians, Nijole's House, Sixteen* and *Spoke.* Her non-clairvoyant works are *The Magritte Poems, Code Poems* and a new poem, *The Zero One*, part of which is forthcoming in *Eye* magazine. *The Fast*, a journal of her early clairvoyant experiences before words appeared is forthcoming from Prospect Books. Two journals, covering the years of early words 1972 and 1973 remain unpublished.